D0438570

Crazymaker

Crazymaker

THOMAS J. O'DONNELL

Harper Collins *Publishers*

If you purchased this book without a cover, you should be aware that this book is stolen property. It was reported as "unsold and destroyed" to the publisher and neither the author nor the publisher has received any payment for this "stripped book."

HarperPaperbacks *A Division of* HarperCollins*Publishers*
10 East 53rd Street, New York, N.Y. 10022

Copyright © 1992 by Thomas J. O'Donnell
All rights reserved. No part of this book may be used or reproduced in any manner whatsoever without written permission of the publisher, except in the case of brief quotations embodied in critical articles and reviews. For information address HarperCollins*Publishers*,
10 East 53rd Street, New York, N.Y. 10022.

Cover photo by Bob Harrington

Printed in the United States of America

HarperPaperbacks and colophon are trademarks of HarperCollins*Publishers*

ISBN 0-06-100425-1

To
Margaret Guilfoyle O'Donnell

ACKNOWLEDGMENTS

Portions of the research for *Crazymaker* were supported by grants from the English department and from the General Research Fund, University of Kansas. I am greatly appreciative of this support. Throughout, Michael Johnson, chair of the department, gave me time to develop the book.

In the initial stages two people were especially helpful to me. Jean Valk read endless drafts of chapter summaries and enthusiastically edited some early chapters. Subsequently, Mrs. Constance Scheerer provided a house for me to write in. Almost daily I would walk across her brick courtyard to discuss her poetry and her reading and I would share my writing.

My young daughter Erin endured my years of writing with tolerance and humor. My involvement in her life has enabled me to understand what it would be like to lose a child.

In the last year of writing this book, I was elated to find my agent, Hy Cohen. Immediately he understood what I was doing and praised what I had hoped readers would praise. I especially admired his honesty and toughness.

Jessica Kovar, my editor at HarperCollins, skillfully guided me and the book through the Scylla and Charybidis of publishing. At times when I feared, her optimism triumphed. Always direct, she understood well my intention and hers. Above all she was patient with me, but not too patient.

There are others who helped with "nameless, unremembered acts of kindness." Among them are Roy Gridley, James Gunn, Roger Martin, and Charles G. Masinton.

I also laud the voices of the participants who spoke so eloquently of these tragic events.

Throughout the last years of researching and writing Mary Klayder has been unrelenting in discussing, revising, editing, and encouraging, as if she were my second self. Her sophisticated understanding of language and literature was invaluable. Without her dedication *Crazymaker* would not be written or published.

". . . what one has done in the secret chamber one has some day to cry aloud on the house-tops."

—Oscar Wilde, *De Profundis*

"Any woman is innocent who denies having sinned, and only a confession of guilt makes her guilty."

—Ovid, *Amores*, III, xiv, translated by Geoffrey Hill

Crazymaker

THE VICTIM'S FAMILY

1

When Ed Hobson first saw Sueanne Sallee Crumm selling tickets at Skateland South that November in 1977, he said to himself, "I want that!" Sueanne was standing high up and warm behind the glass, Ed below in the thin light of the cold, empty entryway. He bent over awkwardly to speak to her through the half circle cut low in the glass. She had dark red hair tightly curled around a small face; her nose, strikingly beautiful, curved up just below the bridge, breaking the perfection of her face, then came down gracefully to tight, thin nostrils. Even in that dim light her lips closed precisely and the fine line of her face was clear. Everything about her seemed to be drawn with the cleanness and tight elegance seen in sketches of perfected women modeling fitted dresses or shorts in newspaper advertisements.

Quite unlike Ed Hobson. Ed was blond and blue-eyed with a short, thick body, a thick nose, and an eagerness to please. Now thirty-five, Ed wanted a family, something he had little enough of to this point in his life. He had come for the first time to Skateland South in Overland Park, Kansas, with his only child, his eleven-year-old son, Chris. More than a year before, Shirley, Chris's mother, had died painfully and slowly of liver cancer. Since then, Ed and Chris had lived alone.

Sueanne, divorced for seven years and living with her twelve-year-old daughter, Suzanne, also needed a family. Sueanne was aware that Ed was coming. Mary Jacobs, Sueanne's psychic for ten years, an innocent black-haired grandmother, the daughter of an Arkansas judge, lived north of the Missouri River twenty miles away on a hilly street in a small red house cluttered with knick-knacks. Two years earlier she had told Sueanne during a reading that she would "meet a blond man at work, that he would be supporting a child, that he would be alone."

Sueanne had lived in Prairie Village and Overland Park, adjoining affluent western and southern suburbs of Kansas City, virtually all her life, first with her well-to-do parents, then with her first husband, now with her daughter. Johnson County, Kansas, where she lived, was one of a half dozen of the richest counties in the country and she had never wanted to live anywhere else.

Ed Hobson had rented an apartment in Overland Park three months earlier. He still worked in the mills of Ralston Purina in the wastes of the river bottoms and flats curving around the north side of the city where the Kansas River runs into the Missouri; now he drove south to Overland Park at night.

Ed was told his son, Chris, needed special education classes, and for his boy's sake he moved south into the best school district in Kansas. Though Ed had lived in the Kansas City metropolitan area most of his adult life, he had no friends in Johnson County; the suburbs were as strange and new to him as they were to Chris. Ed had always been a loner and had few friends anywhere, yet he would fasten tight to a woman and, for better or ill, wouldn't let go until she became the whole world to him.

The drive from the gray mill in the Kansas river bottoms to Overland Park was no more than a quarter hour on the Interstate and, now, Ed wondered why he had lived so long in the worn-out sections of Kansas City, Missouri. Interstate 35 was built over portions of the Santa Fe Trail that, in the middle of the nineteenth century, came out from Westport, cut south through what was later named Johnson County, and skirted the edge of Miami County, where the trail turned sharply to the west.

Just beyond the edge of the Kansas City metropolitan area,

sections of the Santa Fe Trail abandoned a hundred years earlier were still visible, as if created by some small natural catastrophe. The settlers' wagons had scored muddy ruts so deeply into the earth that ever-wider arcs were cut until one couldn't find the original narrow trail except on a map. The great ruts were still there, a quarter of a mile wide, wider than the great slash of the Interstate.

Driving into it in any season except the dead of winter, Overland Park feels like a Southern California city. The buildings in the office parks on the city's edges stand back from the Interstate and the newest are like mirrors reflecting other office buildings. Two enclosed shopping malls, Oak Park and Metcalf, are the main public points of orientation and smaller shopping centers radiate out from them. On most days there is a perpetual twilight caught in the malls and they feel sealed and empty like great refrigerators.

Off the Interstate the streets are wide and the public buildings are new and clean, as if part of some business park or campus. Even the large police station on Santa Fe Drive has expansive treeless green spaces around it that no one ever walks in. The station itself could be mistaken for the administration building of a junior college with its curving, low, corrugated-cement exterior.

Skateland is at one end of a low, small, L-shaped shopping center that opens off 103rd Street at the southwest edge of Overland Park. In 1977 it was at the limit of Johnson County's intensely built-up area. Open fields stretched out on two sides of Skateland and the land rolled down to the south. In the daytime one could see, several miles away, office parks spaced at wide intervals along Interstate 435 as it circled the entire metropolitan area.

Skateland itself is a squat, windowless building. A set of orange steel doors penetrates the building's flat, brown, concrete-block surface. No natural light comes into Skateland. Except for the intense alternating red and blue lights shining down on the edges of the wooden skating floor and the great chandelier reaching far out from the center toward the edges, the rest of the building is left in virtual darkness.

When all the children had passed through the entryway,

Sueanne came out from behind the booth to rent skates to them. She would stand behind a high counter totally covered with an orange rug, as if the counter were a vertical extension of the orange rug on the floor of the broad concession area, as if the rug were devouring the counter.

His first meeting with Sueanne was enough for him, and Ed was suddenly filled with purpose. He and Chris began to come night after night. Ed courted Sueanne as best he could while she worked. Though she had little to do with him at first and took an immediate dislike to him, he was patient. Once he was in love, nothing would change his mind. The managers of Skateland, Jim and Norma Hooker, both heavyset, both working-class, both religious, befriended him. The Hookers were amused as Ed drank up all the free coffee at the concession stand and stood patiently and respectfully before the orange counter. He always waited for the children to stop coming so that Sueanne would come out from behind the ticket booth and he could speak with her while she passed out the skates. Jim Hooker secretly gave Ed Sueanne's work schedule and Ed would always manage to be there when she was.

"Sueanne was a lady," Norma said. "Whatever else she was, she was a lady. She had a lot of reservations about Ed. Of course Sueanne knew he wanted her. He was always there drinking a bucket of coffee."

To Jim, Ed would whisper, "Love that small butt! Love that butt!"

2

Sueanne at first was irritated by Ed's persistence, then embarrassed by it. Despite Sueanne's attempts to discourage Ed he was driven by an energy and an optimism that would not let him fail with her. Ed had known little happiness in his life. He had been reared on a small, hilly farm near King City, Missouri, sixty miles north of Kansas City. He bluntly told Jim Hooker, or whoever would listen, about his childhood. "My parents told me I was a mistake. I don't know whether they loved me or didn't love me. They didn't give a damn about me."

"On the farm I did the work," Ed said angrily. "My father sat in the house playing with a ham radio—night and day, all the time." His face would redden, yet he spoke easily of his father and his mother in the language of a child without embarrassment or disguise.

"They had no photograph of me in the house," he said as if it had all happened yesterday and he was still puzzled about it. "There were no little fuzzies in life from them."

Though he seemed to be the sort of man who cared little about personal safety and who would fight easily, Ed's face was smooth and unmarked, his teeth even. He was only five-foot-eight, but his broad shoulders and thick chest and arms made him appear larger.

In the small high school in King City he had become an honorable-mention all-conference football player. His other achievements in school were minimal; he learned to write no better than a sixth or seventh grader, and even as an adult he wrote in a great hand on small lined sheets of paper with many errors in spelling and grammar.

After graduation from high school Ed enlisted in the army. "When I enlisted," he said, "junk and clothes were all over my parents' house and three years later the same stuff was lying in the same places exactly." After he got out of the army he returned to the farm for only a day or two. He had little love for it or his family. Summing up his early life, he said, "In my opinion my dad was too lazy to work and my mother didn't keep house well. I was reared in King City, Missouri, in a pigpen."

When Ed's mother died, Ed was working as a mechanic for an automobile dealer in Kansas City an hour's drive away, but he didn't know about her death for two months. Ed blamed his father for not telling him. "When I heard," he said, "I told my father I'd never see him alive again." Ed kept his word.

At twenty-two he drove five hours south to Miami, Oklahoma, the nearest place you could get a license and blood tests done in a day, to marry a beautiful, red-haired woman fifteen years older than he, a woman named Shirley Teed, who had two half-grown daughters. Although Shirley's appearance was diminished later by liver cancer, Ed always spoke warmly of her beauty when he first met her and remembered vividly his first days of winning her.

Shirley Teed Hobson gave Ed more than enough to do for the rest of her life. Shirley had divorced Frank Teed, a career army man, who, Ed would say dramatically, was in the CIA. Fifteen years before her marriage to Ed, Shirley was Kansas City's Miss Mona Lisa and one autumn, when the new cars were coming out, she was Miss Ford. Her show-business name was Marlena Mason, and when Ed married her she was an exotic dancer at King Arthur's Lounge in downtown Kansas City. Sometimes when Ed would come home from the garage, there would be several men sitting with her in his parlor, men whom he saw regularly when he would come down to King Arthur's.

Once Ed beat up Shirley and a few nights later some men he thought were sent by the men who sat in his parlor set upon him in the street and beat him so badly that he never hit her again. Marlena Mason had friends who protected her, he had learned that. Ed always respected that kind of authority. Years later he saw photographs of the men who beat him and he read their names in newspaper accounts of a Mafia trial in Kansas City.

"Shirley made my life hell on earth," Ed said. Yet he was loyal to her. In 1966, at forty, Shirley told him she was pregnant. Ed thought she did it to keep him because she knew he wouldn't leave the boy, knew he always saw things through to the end.

From birth Chris was a sickly child. He was operated on at five weeks for an obstruction in the duct between the stomach and the small intestine. He lived for years, Ed remembers, on skimmed milk and 7UP. Yet even then Chris was, Ed said, "a blond, smiley faced child." When Chris began to get well at the age of five, Shirley began to die of cancer, though she was to live nearly four years longer.

Jerry Wilson, Shirley's sister, said that Shirley could be "the nicest, sweetest, most loving person, or the most vicious person you'd ever want to be around." Ed remembered most the pain she gave him, not the love. Sometimes Shirley would throw hot coffee on him in the midst of an argument or threaten him with a loaded pistol. Excited relatives would come over in the middle of the night to pull them apart, to calm them down. Their children, dragged out of bed half-dressed, remembered those battles with fear and pleasure all their lives; grown, they narrated them eagerly, carrying themselves back to that violent life.

Tani Teed, Shirley and Frank Teed's youngest child, was twelve when Ed married Shirley in 1964; her eldest, Lailoneh, was sixteen. Ed, only ten years older than Tani and closer to her age than his wife's, became greatly attached to her.

Shirley loved Tani, too, though once, a few years after her marriage to Ed, neighbors called Shirley's sister because Shirley was out in the yard screaming and burning Tani's clothes, throwing them in a rusty steel barrel, the flames coming right out over the top. In a rage, Shirley had threatened to put Tani in an institution, had driven her daughter away; she shoved the girl out of the house with only the clothes on her back. "I was yelling at her," Shirley said. "I was pretty upset, but she knows the way I am."

"I'm going to find Tani and bring her back," Ed shouted. "God damn you! God damn you! If something happens to her, you'll be responsible." It was the first time Shirley's relatives had seen Ed stand up to his wife.

Years later Shirley's sister would say, "What's the matter with Ed? The matter with Ed is that he stayed with Shirley. I don't know why he stayed with Shirley and put up with all the stuff she did."

Yet Tani loved Shirley and disliked Ed, her stepfather. Nobody understood that because Ed always defended Tani.

3

Something did happen to Tani. At fourteen Tani claimed she was raped, but police declined to press charges against the teenage relative she accused, and she had an abortion.

Tani grew up to be a bright, small-boned girl, pretty despite the thick glasses she always wore. After graduation from high school, she attended Central Missouri State in Warrensburg and made the dean's list. After a couple of years at Warrensburg she enrolled at the University of Missouri in Columbia, where she majored in sociology and taught a course in the department during her senior year.

Ed, now thirty, seemed to shine when Tani was present and his broad face, as expressive as a puppet's, would open to her. On weekends he would drive her back to the University of Missouri, more than two hours from Kansas City. Tani, in the backseat with her friends, would sing, and he would sing along with her, and laugh like a lover at her jokes.

Something else happened to Tani, too. In 1973, at the age of twenty, she fell in love with Gary Hollandsworth, a twenty-five-year-old navy man enrolled at Missouri in the school of engineering. On Sunday, February 18, about ten at night, she was in her apartment studying when she got a call from the Dixie Club; the hostess told Tani that Gary had been drinking heavily and needed a ride home.

Tani lived almost directly across Interstate 70 from the Dixie, though one could only cross the expressway by a circuitous route. Gary's friends picked up Tani and drove her to the Dixie. She coaxed Gary out of the bar and into the passenger seat of his pickup truck.

Out on Interstate 70 going east, driving back toward Gary's house by the fastest route, they argued; Gary ordered Tani to stop the truck and he got out—or she stopped and ordered him out of the truck, nobody knows. He got out on the south side of the Interstate near its junction with Route 63. Tani turned off the Interstate, crossed over it to the north side, and looped back west on the access road paralleling I-70 on the north. She drove at an angry speed back toward her own apartment. Gary must have crossed both lanes of I-70 also, climbing over the steel rails and coming heavily through the ditch and up the incline to the access road, coming with remarkable alacrity for a man so drunk. Tani hit him straight on and he was thrown up on the hood.

"Mama, it was like 'Twilight Zone,'" Tani told Shirley the next day. "All of a sudden Gary's face was up in front of my windshield. He was looking at me with the strangest look—like 'Why are you doing this to me?'" Gary was as heavy as a deer, suspended there by the force of the truck. As the truck swerved to a stop he rolled off like a sack.

"Tani jumped out," Shirley said. "She went back, saw that

Gary was still breathing, felt his legs, saw him bleeding a little from the head, ran back to the truck, and went and got her landlady a little way up the road." Tani's landlady called an ambulance and the two drove back to where Gary was lying. He was dead before the ambulance got there.

The police arrested Tani for drunk driving and charged her Monday morning. Shirley and Ed drove two hours to Columbia to post her two-hundred-dollar bond. They spent the next two days with Tani, first in Columbia and then in Kansas City. They returned to Columbia Wednesday afternoon and left Tani at her apartment. As they got into their car they begged her to come back to Kansas City for another day or two, but Tani told Shirley that she would miss too much school.

The Hobsons tried to phone Tani Wednesday evening, and when they didn't get an answer, they asked the Columbia police to check her apartment. The police called back to report that the door was locked and nobody was home. Ed, Shirley, and Chris, now six years old, drove back to Columbia that night.

"We got down there about fifteen minutes before midnight," Shirley said. "Tani had a glass door; the screen door was open, but the door was locked. We ran upstairs and got the key from the landlady. We opened the door, and as you open the living-room door you can see into the the bedroom. As we walked in Ed said, 'Oh, my God! Get an ambulance!' But we had all seen, just as you walked in the door, each one of us seen, she was dead.

"Chris got to her first. She was sitting up, the top of her head two and a half inches above the headboard, and was as neat as a pin. Her skirt was down. Everything was perfect about her. And she had a horrible look on her face. There was no blood anywhere, except from the living room coming into the bedroom, there was four drops of blood. Ed lifted her up around the shoulders and laid her down with her head on the pillow. The window was open; the curtains were drawn open. There was some kind of old jacket or coat over the chair. The rugs were all pushed back under the bed. Her teddy bear, which don't have any eyes anymore, usually set in this chair and she didn't let anybody sit in this chair. Instead, the teddy bear was lying on the typewriter with its back toward her, facing the wall.

"There were cards of Gary's sitting on the bed and there were

Gary's keys on the bed. Her hair was a mess. Her shoes were on; if Tani was going to do this, she'd have to take her shoes off. Her glasses were in the living room on the desk. I squatted down by the blood. It was very red and it looked like diamonds. It was so brilliant, and the lights shined. It just glittered, but it quivered a little bit."

Tani was shot in the stomach with a 20-gauge Magnum with long barrels. Shirley could not believe her daughter had killed herself, even though she found a note written on purple paper: "She had drawers full of paper," Shirley said. "Tani would never have written anything to me on purple or lavender paper, because she knows this is something I've had a terrible shock from—and the color alone—Tani was trying to tell me something by writing this."

As Shirley remembered it, the note read:

Dear Mother,
    Forgive me for what I am about to do, and I know you will because you love me. I could never appease my guilt. I've known what I can and cannot do, and I could never appease the guilt I have for not only the wreck, but also for what I did to Gary. By Gary's death, I've known what it was to lose someone, and by my death I will never have to feel the pain and torture of grieving for you. Let there be no guilt around my grave, for I take it all with me. Would you rather it be I that feels the pain and sorrow you do now? I think not. I want to wear my black skirt and white blouse. I love you, Shirley, more than anything else in the world.
    Forgive me.

Tani

On the desk there was a photograph of Tani and Gary together; in the photograph Tani was wearing her black skirt and white blouse.

4

Tani's body was taken back to Kansas City and lay in state in an open casket at a Roman Catholic funeral home on Sunday after-noon and evening. Ed and Shirley left the chapel at nine-thirty.

The Hobsons were shocked when they returned to the funeral parlor the next day for the two o'clock service. The first to arrive, they saw that the flowers and the chairs were meticulously ordered, but the casket had been tampered with.

"Tani was a mess," Ed said. "Her blouse was loose and pulled out; her rosary was clear out of her hand; her rose was gone that we had put in her hand; her hair was all messed up. She was lying over the back of the casket and her skirt was all loose and wrinkled."

"They'd broken her belt," Shirley said. "Her blouse had been split in the back. Her legs were spread apart; her mouth and eyes were open."

Shirley and Ed hired Lance Welch, the most flamboyant lawyer in Kansas City, to sue the funeral home for negligence. They argued that Tani had been murdered and that the death of Tani and her defilement were connected.

Shirley and Ed repeatedly drove to Columbia to discuss the case with the police. They insisted that Tani, a petite five-footer, legally blind without her glasses, could not have reached the trigger of a shotgun to shoot herself in the stomach. They pointed out that Tani's wallet was missing. They even argued that Tani was forced to write her suicide note. Months later Ed and Shirley asked to have the body exhumed, but their request was denied.

To pay for Lance Welch and the private investigators, Ed Hobson had to sell some of the land in northern Missouri that his father had left him upon his death the year before. "I will keep at it," Shirley had said. "It's not the money, it's justice we're after."

The police in Columbia had the suicide note and that was enough for them; They thought the case was routine, but the Hobsons got a reporter in Columbia interested in Tani's death and kept the case alive in the local newspaper for six months.

For a time the police patiently answered the questions of the reporter and the Hobsons. "There's a point beyond which it's unrea-sonable to go," the county prosecutor finally said. Welch and the Hobsons got nowhere in the suit against the funeral home, and until the day she died of cancer Shirley believed Tani was murdered.

Her relatives wondered if Shirley was just angry enough and crazy enough to defile Tani's body herself. Ed always referred to his stepdaughter's death as a murder.

Shirley's cancer had spread to her liver and grew increasingly painful, yet she lived for three years after Tani's death. The drugs she took in those years made her even more unstable than usual.

In the last year before her death Chris, blond, with his mother's face and persistence, would come into her darkened room to ask her to read to him; he had been diagnosed as dyslexic and sought what help he could get. She would scream at the boy, curse him, and drive him away; he was puzzled and frightened. Sometimes Shirley would even put a gun to Chris's head, then to her own, and she threatened to kill him and herself because, she said, she didn't want him to grow up in this miserable world of suffering. At the end, Ed had to put her in a hospital. After several months he got the doctors to remove Shirley's life-support systems.

Ed had been married to Shirley for ten years, most of his adult life. When he met Sueanne at Skateland, Ed knew he needed a wife and he knew Chris needed a mother, and he had been looking for a woman for more than a year now.

5

At first Ed didn't tell Sueanne much about his life, and what he did tell her made her afraid. Her life was nothing like that, she thought. Though Ed and Chris found Johnson County unfamiliar, Sueanne had lived there virtually all her life, coming from the prosperous Sallee family, and she refused to live in any other part of the metropolitan area. She found everything she wanted out there.

Sueanne and her daughter now lived across the street from Skateland in the Wycliffe West Apartments. The apartments closed a third side of the L formed by the small shopping center, and extended uniformly for an eighth of a mile alongside it. Ten or twenty of the apartments were attached together in large blocks. The apartments were all two stories with great, crude, wooden mansard roofs coming down a story and a half, crushing the squat buildings.

Sueanne had been working for years as an executive secretary at one or another of the great international grain-trading companies located just off the Plaza in Kansas City. At night she sometimes sold tickets at Skateland. She had long been friends with Jim and Norma Hooker, the managers, and selling tickets at the rink enabled her to keep an eye on Suzanne, who skated there in the evening in every season.

Sueanne was the only child of Don and Ruth Sallee, who had lived in Prairie Village, an older suburb adjacent to Overland Park, since Sueanne's birth. Ruth Sallee had been a legal secretary for many years. Don Sallee was a draftsman, one of a dozen people who founded and spent their lives working for Marley, an international construction company that specialized in building industrial cooling towers for great corporations. He himself had supervised some international projects.

Yet, despite Don's success, he and his wife lived quietly and frugally, almost reclusively, in a two-story corner house with deep green shingles. White shades always filled the windows and were drawn down tightly to the sill. Their home was on a street of small houses and the tops of the trees grew together thickly in the center of the street. Somerset Elementary School was at the opposite end of the block and Sueanne could walk to school in late spring and early fall and never get out of the shade. Her parents had great hopes and plans for her; when she was just beginning school, they even took out an insurance policy to provide income to support her college education.

Sueanne had been reared in what she described as "a very protective, genteel home. My father was soft-spoken. My parents raised me never to be associated with anything that even gave the appearance of scandal. When I was growing up, we didn't have any trouble. There was no yelling and screaming and fighting. There was always a peaceful, calm, loving atmosphere." She learned there, she said, "that people were basically good, honest, and would help you when you needed it."

There was something of the rearing of a beautiful only child about her, a child who had been protected, for all who spoke of her—those who came to love her and those who came to fear her—said how naive she was, how gullible. She sometimes said so herself. "I'm a very naive, too-trusting person. My daughter, Suzanne, has always summed it up by saying I'm just too nice."

She came out of that comfortable, protected world of the Sallees anxious and timid. "I was fearful of the real world," she said. "People are cruel and don't care when they are. And they're petty and jealous too."

Her parents raised her, Sueanne said, so that "you do not show your dirty linen in public, but maintain a very reserved, respectable image."

Yet she sometimes told her daughter Suzanne and her friends and her first husband, Jim Crumm, other things about her parents. When she met Ed at Skateland in November 1977, she hadn't spoken to her parents in five years.

No one knew what had gone on inside the house on the shaded street with the deep green shingles and the white shades drawn down tightly to the sill. Norma Hooker said that Sueanne constantly complained about conflicts with her mother.

Not every day was difficult. "Sometimes Sueanne would come home to find her bed laid out with new things that her mother had bought her to make up for the day before," Norma recalled. "Even long before she absolutely refused to see her parents, when she dropped off Suzanne at the Sallee's, she'd stay outside in the car and explain, 'Mother and I aren't speaking today.'"

When deeply afraid of someone, Sueanne would compare the person to her mother. Ruth Sallee was barely five feet tall, thin, and even slighter than her daughter. Her hair was twisted tightly into a topknot.

Don Sallee was hard at work developing Marley into a Fortune 500 company, sometimes going right around the world to do it. At home he would withdraw to his extensive library or to his workshop in the basement. He never interrupted his wife's incessant speech; she never seemed to require even a comment from him. Years later when asked about his grown daughter, he remembered almost nothing about her; he could scarcely think of anything to say.

If there was a problem in the green house on the corner, it was not brought to the attention of neighbors and counselors.

The family observed the proprieties. Whatever happened must have been on an intimate scale, must have been going on deep inside the house, behind the green shutters and white shades.

In high school Sueanne said she liked "history and reading and sewing, and anything that really wasn't athletic, because I wasn't any good. I was a good student most of the time." She was in the future-nurses club, the interior-decoration club and the drama club. In her senior year she was featured in the yearbook on the page titled "Shawnee Mission's Wall Street"; under her photo was printed, "Sue Sallee had that 'calculating eye' needed for work with business machines." She was self-effacing to most of her peers and few of those in her class remembered her at all; "mousy," one who did remember said.

The fall after graduation she enrolled at the University of Kansas in Lawrence, thirty-five miles west of Overland Park. The first semester at Kansas she failed biology, math, English—all the courses she took that semester. Later she often told people she had a year of college, sometimes two. She didn't study—"goofed off," a friend said—then fell ill and returned home.

Back home in Johnson County, a year after her high-school graduation and a month after her nineteenth birthday, Sueanne bolted from her mother's tight control. She suddenly married Jim Crumm. She left home at the same age Ed Hobson fled from his family to enlist in the army.

6

Sueanne had little to say to Ed Hobson or anyone else about her ten-year marriage to Jim and its difficulties. She spoke of Jim years after the marriage as if she had loved him at first, as if the marriage were a love match. When Sueanne did discuss her marriage, she spoke almost abstractly of Jim's problems with money, of his drinking, of his abuse of her, and of her growing fear of him.

"He beat me and drank heavily," she would say concisely. For Sueanne the details faded after the divorce, first swallowed up in anger, then indifference.

Jim Crumm had not let Sueanne go quite so fully or easily.

She remained vivid to him and he held elaborate memories of her, memories of ten years of marriage, memories of her leaving and of her return. To him Sueanne was still the central force in his life, even seven years after the divorce, a force changing each year, but still there affecting him, an enveloping force, like gravity, that determined and exposed his limitations. A direct man lacking Sueanne's intensity and intelligence, Jim was full of guilt and he was still puzzled by her complexity.

Sueanne saw no complexity in Jim. Though afraid of him during the marriage, and afraid of many things besides him, by the time she met Ed she seemed to have a confidence in her judgment, a certainty, a sense of direction and of purpose that Jim would always lack.

When they first met, Jim Crumm was strong, broad, and stout; he was built solidly, like the high-school fullback he had been three years earlier. He was a man's man. He had good humor and openness and thick, hard flesh that seemed to be lit from the inside in summer. He was already letting his tight body relax and open a little, but his large, square, florid face and crewcut reinforced his appearance of physical strength.

To Jim, meeting Sueanne was a turning point in his life. "We met in the last part of 1959, or the first of 1960, through Donna Storm, Sue's friend," Jim said. "My attraction to Sue at first was physical and we sort of hit it off. How in the world we did, I don't know. There were six kids in my family. We were poor. She had money. We ran off and got married."

As Ed and Shirley were to do three years later, Jim and Sueanne got married in Miami, Oklahoma, in September 1961. Jim described the marriage as a whim: "We just decided one day at the last minute to get married. We went down to Oklahoma. Just once on the way down I pulled my '56 Pontiac over to the side of the road, stopped for a minute or two, and thought, 'Is this what I want to do?' We left early in the morning and went right down to Miami, got married, and got back late that evening."

The Sallees were not to know. "We were going to keep the marriage a secret," he said. "I got her home that evening, dropped her off, then I went home; I was living with my mother. I'd been home probably forty minutes and Sueanne called me.

She said that her mom and dad wanted me to come over the next day, and they knew about it. She had taken some clothes with her, a nightgown, and her mom discovered that some clothes were missing while we were gone that day. So I guess her mom, maybe, always checked her personal belongings."

"I went over the next day and faced the firing squad," Jim said. "Mrs. Sallee was very, very, very upset about the whole thing. And Sue's father sure in hell wasn't happy. Nobody ran out and threw their arms around me, I remember that very much."

Though he was saddened by their anger, Jim knew well enough why they were upset. "I came from the other side of the tracks," he said. "I couldn't offer their daughter what their daughter was used to having in life—the best clothes that money could buy, plenty of spending money, a nice home. When we got married, I was working construction. In bad weather you worked two or three days a week. They wanted her to marry somebody from Johnson County, where the money lived. It sure in hell wasn't in the part of town I lived in."

Mr. Sallee had already made a decision. "Her dad said, well, being that we were married, we needed to be living under the same roof. So we went down the next day and rented an apartment near the Plaza across the state line in Kansas City. We were married in September; the first two weeks the management was remodeling the apartment, so we had to stay in a motel room."

The two spent only a few weeks together in the apartment. "I had already enlisted in the marine corps reserves and had to do six months," Jim said. "That was one of the reasons we were going to keep the marriage a secret. During the last of October 1961, I left for boot camp at Paris Island. She was pregnant. She told me just before I left. I didn't know it when we married, and I'm not sure she did, either."

At boot camp Jim felt lonely and abandoned. "When I was at Paris Island, I went for quite a bit of time and never heard from her," Jim said. "I had to get permission to make an emergency phone call home and I explained to my drill instructor what the situation was and I finally got her on the phone. In fact, at the time I called she was at the apartment with her dad, preparing to move, since she was going to be staying with the Sallees for a while."

Later Jim found out why she hadn't written. "Sue had talked

to her dad about having an abortion and getting the marriage annulled. I sure didn't want her to have an abortion. It was Sue's idea to get the abortion and the annulment. Her dad wouldn't let her do it. When I got out of boot camp, she even told me she tried to have a miscarriage. She'd run up and down steps, whatever—all she did I don't know. She didn't want the baby."

Jim Crumm and Don Sallee were allies in opposing the abortion, maybe the only time they were allied. Jim did not forget that and he always spoke well of Mr. Sallee. "Mr. Sallee was upset about the marriage, all right. He was a very soft-spoken man. I never heard him raise his voice. I liked him; he was very firm in his beliefs, and once he made up his mind, that's the way it was and it never changed. He was very meticulous and very, very smart, a very intelligent person."

What Jim saw in Sueanne at first was sexual, though he also realized that he had carried away a prize from the class above him. What Sueanne saw in him initially, except an escape from her parents, was less clear to him. Jim thought her attraction to him, at least at first, was also physical.

Long after the marriage ended, Jim said angrily, "In me she found somebody who would put up with her. I tolerated a lot of her bullshit, her tantrums. I'd just kind of ignore them and go on, say to myself, 'She ranted and raved again last night.' Back then I was very wishy-washy. If there was any way to avoid an argument, boy, I'd do it. Over the years that we were married I did everything I could to give her everything she ever wanted. I went into debt so damn far trying to give her everything she ever wanted! From the day I met her it was all downhill."

Jim had a large extended family, all living in Kansas City— brother, sisters, mother—all relatively close physically and emotionally, tied together by Grandmother Crumm, its strong matriarch. After his marriage, Jim's family soon stopped visiting his house. His sister Dorothy said, "We really weren't comfortable at my bother's house, so we didn't go there a lot. My brother Jim came over quite a bit and saw us."

During much of his marriage Jim worked as a lineman for Kansas City Power and Light in the day and had two filling-station jobs at night. "When Sueanne would buy something, it wasn't cheap stuff," Jim said almost proudly. "It was the best. Once Dorothy said to me, 'Every time I come over to your house you have new furniture and new drapes.' The problem was that on what we were making we couldn't afford the best, so we borrowed money and borrowed money. Money, status, and materialistic things were most important to her. Sue even lied about where I worked and what I did."

Jim, firmly of the working class, saw her aspirations as destructive, but he yielded to them, perhaps because he shared them. "After I came back from the marine corps," he said, "Sue and I lived in a real nice little house in south Kansas City, a real nice little house. We had the whole inside remodeled. Boy, it was real nice. All of a sudden we had to move to Johnson County because Johnson County was a status thing. If you lived in Johnson County you were uptown. So my idea was, okay, I can go along with this, but I didn't want to sell the house. I wanted to rent it out; we would be paying the house off and socking a little bit back. And Sue's statement was, 'People who live in Johnson County don't own rental property.' It was embarrassing to her to tell people you owned rental property. How in the hell did she think all these people got all their money over there?

"She got me to sell the house and we moved into a rental house in Johnson County," Jim said. "We were renting a house on Colonial Drive, which we couldn't afford; the payments were just out of sight, but we were in Johnson County."

Jimmy Crumm was born in May 1962. He weighed five pounds, eight ounces, and Sueanne said his birth had been a few weeks premature; in part this explained his arrival eight months after the marriage, in part the slight deformity he had. Jimmy had a problem with his feet and wore corrective shoes until he was ten or eleven years old. According to Jim, Sueanne felt there was an imperfection in their son's body and she was ashamed of him. When she first took him over to show him to his grandmother Sallee, she wouldn't unwrap him fully.

Their daughter, Suzanne, was born four years after Jimmy almost to the day. Sueanne's medical care of Jimmy and her daughter was always meticulous. She saw that they were taken to dentists and doctors and that Jimmy saw counselors and psychologists. "I was determined my kids were going to be well, whole people who could go out into the world and be self-confident, self-assured, and be able to handle themselves in any situation," she said.

Suzanne seemed to have no developmental problems, Jimmy many. By three, Sueanne had Jimmy tested at a clinic for a delay in his language development. He had poor articulation and she wondered if he were retarded. The doctor found the language delay negligible and said the boy was bright, his IQ well above average. Yet Sueanne never felt quite comfortable with Jimmy, and before he was eight years old, she had the family doctor prescribe Ritalin to control what a specialist diagnosed as hyperactivity.

Jim admitted that he had behaved badly in the marriage. "I saw a lot of screaming," he said. "The screaming got to the point where I couldn't handle it anymore. At that time I had a bad temper. It took a little bit to get it there, but once it got there I'd get mad, do dumb things. I never hurt anybody. One time I slapped her. That was all. I thought about doing other things, but I never did them. I'd get angry at Sue or at the whole situation. When you get mad, you lose all reason; you're not really responsible for things that you say or do within a split second. I once opened a fortune cookie and it said, 'A man that loses his temper closes his eyes.' I'd never hurt anybody, I'd do things that are too embarrassing to tell; I'd punch a hole in the wall, punch a hole through the door. Don't get me wrong, there weren't holes all over the house.

"One night I was even guilty of having her pinned up against the wall," Jim admitted. "She had me so mad I could have hit her and killed her right on the spot. I often thought of how somebody could keep needling you, egging you on to the point where you lose control. Sue had an ability to manipulate people. She controlled you. It's worse than a big bully coming in and picking on you. But it's a woman—small, fragile—and you know that you've been taught all your life that you can't hit women. So you become frustrated. What in the hell do I do? She wouldn't shut up, she wouldn't listen to me."

Despite Jim's repeated assertions of her control, her manipulation of him, Sueanne was deeply afraid of this violent man who punched holes in doors, who pinned her against the wall, who slapped her. "When Jim said something, I was afraid," she said years after the marriage. Speaking slowly and emphasizing each word, she insisted that "Jim intimidated me then; he would not intimidate me today. Jim is a bully."

Before the divorce, the family moved again. Jim said, "We moved from Colonial Drive to High Drive in Prairie Village, which wasn't too far from her folks, but it was an area that had been built back there in the Second World War and they were older, cheaper homes, and we moved in there for a lot less money than renting. That's where we split up. I moved out first; I moved out for three or four months, then I moved back to try it again. We tried it again and it didn't work, so the next time she moved out for good, her and Suzanne.

"At the end we fought all the time," he said. "There was no sex anymore. It boiled down real simple: we didn't love each other. Period. That's making it as simple as I can. I was tired of fighting all the time, of all the bills. We'd fight about money, sex, you name it."

In 1969, more than a year before the divorce, Sueanne had taken a job at Bartlett Grain, her first since Jimmy was born, and had soon taken on a lover. Sueanne had an affair that spanned the end of the marriage. Jim seldom spoke about the affair, though once he started on it, he couldn't let it go. He spoke not so much with anger as with a kind of nostalgia for a time when a wrong turn was taken, when coincidences secretly and slowly conspired against his happiness. "There was a guy I went to junior college with, and I'll be damned if I can think of his name. I had met the guy over there at Kansas City Junior College and then I dropped out and went on back to my regular job and life. He went to work at the same place Sue was, Bartlett Grain Company, and she came home one night and said, 'Do you remember . . . ?' God, I can't think of his name, but anyway, she says, 'Oh, he just started to work with us.' So we started going out with him and his wife. His name is on the tip of my tongue, but I can't get it to come out. I can even see the guy's face now.

"Well, we used to come over to a bar on Main Street, me and Sue, and the guy and his wife. They used to have a fashion show every Friday night. They would have models come in and model different swimsuits, and slacks, and different dresses and stuff like that, and you could sit there and have drinks, and it was a lot of fun and we'd dance. Even at that time, I found out later, Sue and the guy were messing around. So it went on for quite a while, I'd say a year at least before Sue left.

"I didn't find out all at once. After this guy went to work at Bartlett, Sue would have to work overtime. And I called up Bartlett Grain one night for some particular reason. I wasn't even thinking about checking on her, that wasn't the purpose. I let the phone ring and nobody ever answered, so I asked her about it the next day and she said, 'The switchboard's closed at night.' That made sense. I never thought about it, so it went on a little longer. Then one night something fairly important came up. I think I had a chance to go to work that night for Kansas City Power and Light; it was on storm damage—that's on overtime when you make good money. I let the phone ring. I was just getting ready to hang up the phone when the janitor answered and I asked him if Mrs. Crumm was there. The janitor was a colored guy and I'll never forget his voice. He said, 'Shit, man, there ain't nobody working up here tonight. They're all across the street partying!' Then things started coming to click a little bit. When I confronted her, she didn't admit anything. 'We were there working,' she said, 'but we just didn't hear the phones.' The guy left his wife, and Sue and I split. That was the second time we split up; that was when it was over with.

"Sue and this guy dated for quite a while after we separated. He left his beautiful wife—I just cracked up thinking he left that for Sue. I even helped her move into an apartment; I wasn't a villain all the time," he said, laughing.

Yet even years later Jim was angry, not so much at Sueanne as at her lover, for his friend had broken a bond among males. "I confronted him once," he said. "I was in a little cocktail lounge called the Streetcar, and it's a little streetcar. I was in there with some friends of mine and he came walking in. He didn't see me until he was already in the place too far to leave. When you're half-drunk, it's not the time to talk to somebody. You're not too realistic about it. And I was still mad and upset. You know, this was the guy I'd gone to junior college with and I considered him a friend at one time. So I confronted him up at the bar. Back then I was young and dumb. I told the bartender, 'You give this son of a bitch a drink because I'm getting ready to whip his ass.' It was dumb and I knew it. And I've sat back and laughed at myself a thousand times for even saying that. I had no doubt that I could have whipped him at that time, being as mad as I was, but what in the hell would be proved?

"Sueanne moved into an apartment a few months before the actual divorce. I stayed in the house in Prairie Village. Suzanne went with her mother and Jimmy stayed with me. She told me before the divorce that she did not want Jimmy, that he was to stay with me, but she wanted legal custody of him. When she left, she ripped out all the pictures of her and Suzanne and left the pictures of me and Jimmy in the album. She definitely was easier on Suzanne and favored her, because Jimmy was too much like me. When she looked at Jimmy, she saw me. She even said once, 'Jimmy reminds me of you too much.' The woman hated me with a passion. She also said that Jimmy reminded her of her mother, though I don't know why."

7

Sueanne described the divorce and the choices she and the children made calmly. "We were divorced several months prior to what would have been our tenth wedding anniversary. Our divorce was final in June and we would have been married ten years in September. Legally, I received custody of both children. Suzanne lived with me and Jimmy lived with his daddy. His father gave him a choice and Jimmy's choice was to live with his father and Suzanne's to live with me. Jim decided he wanted to take Jimmy sometime before I moved out of the house."

Though all lived in metropolitan Kansas City, from the day Sueanne left with Suzanne and Jim stayed with Jimmy, neither parent saw the other child more than a couple of times in the next seven years. When Sueanne left, Jimmy was nine, Suzanne five.

"I saw Jimmy for a short period of time after the divorce," Sueanne said. "Sometimes I went over to Jim's house."

A year after the divorce she lost touch. "Later, when I found out that Jimmy was with his aunt Dorothy, my father and I went over there to get him a couple of times and Jimmy wasn't there. When I finally saw Jimmy six years later, he asked me about that. He said, 'I always knew when you were coming, Mom, because it was the only time Dad ever came to see me. You were stupid enough to call Aunt Dorothy and say that you and Grandpa were coming over to get me and Aunt Dorothy would call Dad.' I looked for him all those years. And when Jim says I ran out on Jimmy, he is a damn liar. May he rot in hell!

"My parents hired detectives to try to find Jimmy and they couldn't find him. It is always the big if. If Daddy and I tried one more time, if they had tried one more time with the detective. . . ."

Jim had similar problems. "I spent a lot of time looking for Suzanne," he said. "Once Suzanne walked down the street and saw some Kansas Power and Light workers and she said to them, 'My daddy works for you.' They came back and told me. I tore out to the place and looked for her, but never did find her. We didn't hear from Suzanne for seven years. Disappeared."

Yet Sueanne had Jim put in jail three times for failure to pay back child support in the months right after the divorce. "The funny thing is that I was paying child support in cash," he claimed. "That's how dumb I was when we got divorced. I inherited all the bills; I'd give her money in cash. No receipts."

"Once when I had him thrown in jail for nonsupport," Sueanne said, "Jimmy met me outside my job one evening and told me he'd put me in St. Mary's if I did it again. There's a cemetery and a hospital called St. Mary's out there, and I didn't know which one, so I backed off."

Jim soon stopped paying, if he ever had paid. In those seven years when both claimed they couldn't find a child they dearly sought, Jim continued to work at Kansas Power or at construction jobs in the metropolitan area and saw the same circle of friends and relatives and Jimmy stayed frequently at his aunt Dorothy's. Sueanne still worked as a secretary at one or the other offices of the great grain companies located near the Plaza, first Bartlett, then Continental, then Louis Dreyfus, and she still saw most of the friends she had seen before her divorce.

"I wish to hell I'd tried harder to get Jimmy back," Sueanne said. "I felt guilt, anger, frustration, hurt."

After the divorce Jim began to have increasing difficulty controlling his drinking. Despite his anger about Sueanne's infidelity, about her manipulation of him, about her extravagance that had him working two jobs, he fell down on his knees before the three bags she set out in the middle of the living room when she left for the last time, and in tears he begged her to stay.

"Yeah, I was upset when she left," he admitted. "I got to the point where I was having a hard time handling the divorce and was drinking too much. I went to the bottom of the barrel. I got fired because of my drinking."

Within a year Jimmy was being passed around from one aunt to another. Yet he still saw his grandparents, Don and Ruth Sallee. They provided clothes and other things he needed that his father could not provide in the years after the divorce.

Sueanne and Suzanne fared much better on their own than Jim and Jimmy during those years. Sueanne seemed to thrive on the independent life she set up for herself; she was always employed and successful at her work. Like her mother, Ruth Sallee, Sueanne became an executive secretary. The orderliness she had demanded in the Crumm house and, for the most part, got—that drinking glasses, for instance, be lined up in the cupboard and each toy have a labeled place on the shelf—served her well as a secretary.

"Sueanne and I shared similar troubles," Beth Clarkson, her close friend at work, said. "We were both divorced with children, comrades in arms. She befriended me when I started at Louis Dreyfus." Beth was a rougher version of Sueanne. Lean, dark, intelligent, Beth couldn't harness her overabundance of energy at work, and her harsh judgments of others drove her from job to job. "I take no shit from anybody," she'd say, laughing.

"Sueanne was very neat, very fastidious," Beth noted. "Her hair always looked perfect; her makeup always looked perfect. More important, that was Sueanne. She was meticulous in everything she did. She could be extremely hard on someone who didn't do a job right. Sueanne used to say, 'If you want a job done right, do it yourself.'

"Sueanne especially had a view of an ideal family, almost a

fantasy of one. Most women were raised to believe that you married, had two kids, lived in the house with the white picket fence, the dog, and the station wagon. When you know you must go out and support kids, it's extremely hard to make that transition to becoming a working woman. Emotionally we weren't set to handle that transition. Sueanne did it, and she did it very well."

Of course Suzanne was named as precisely after her mother as Jimmy was after his father. Suzanne was the image of Sueanne; in the years from five to twelve that they lived together as a couple, they grew more and more like each other. Suzanne had the Sallee nose, and her mother's fine features and intensity. She was not so much like her mother as a child but like her mother as an adult, the way the face of the child Christ in a Renaissance painting comes to have the same knowing look as the crucified Christ.

Sueanne always kept her daughter with her and provided for her. She insisted on and got a good academic performance. Yet the child protected the mother as much as the mother protected the child. "Suzanne is my baby," Sueanne said. "She is very protective and loving. She is also much less naive than I am."

Though the Sallees helped Sueanne set up a household right after the divorce, she broke with her parents two years later and the separation was to last for more than five years. "We had a disagreement over family problems," Sueanne said. "My grandmother Sallee was one of the problems. Also a misunderstanding over a heating problem, and over Jim."

Mrs. Sallee described the break as "a slight disagreement, a piddling little disagreement." It was not, she said, "Sueanne's fault; it was my fault. I have very Scotch blood; I have stiff-necked Scotch pride and I would not give in. Sueanne gave in."

Sueanne's grandmother Sallee became the one member of her extended family she could depend on. Nearly ninety, five feet tall and two hundred pounds, she had begun to use a walker. Sueanne would go to her when the bills piled up, and they did pile up, for she never bought anything that wasn't the best, even in those years of independence. Grandmother Sallee was the last remnant of her family Sueanne could still hold on to and she loved her. She alone had given Sueanne an unconditional love that her parents could not give.

In those seven years after her marriage ended Sueanne had two lovers who helped her out. For a time she considered marrying Tim, the man who worked at Bartlett Grain, Jim's former friend. Gradually, her interest in the affair waned.

In September 1972, a little more than a year after her divorce, she took a job at Dreyfus. Soon, she became the lover of a young Dreyfus executive. Sueanne never actually lived with him; rather, he set her up in an expensive town house at the Essex Apartments across from the Brookridge Country Club just off 103rd Street in Overland Park. She once told Norma that he bought her a beautiful bedroom set, among other things, though what arrangement they had over the years was unclear. Certainly Sueanne wanted to marry him, Norma thought, and she was faithful to him.

Later Sueanne discovered that her lover was having an affair with another woman. Unfortunately, the woman wrote to him at Dreyfus and Sueanne opened the letter. Suddenly his mail was directed mysteriously to the Dreyfus office in New York, even his personal correspondence. He was never sure what had happened to his mail, but he had his suspicions. Sueanne soon moved a half mile west on 103rd Street to the Wycliffe Apartments. Though she still saw him occasionally for several years, she never trusted him again.

In those years immediately after her divorce she began counseling sessions with Dr. Robert Craft, a minister who had begun a lucrative practice in psychology. He had been Beth Clarkson's therapist for several years and Beth put Sueanne in touch with him.

Sueanne would go down once or twice a week to see Craft in his office on the Country Club Plaza. The Plaza was the most expensive shopping district in Kansas City, a shopping center founded seventy years ago and held together loosely by Moorish architectural references to Seville, Spain.

Dr. Craft was a broad, fat man. He was quite genial and confident; he seemed to Sueanne like an overgrown child and she affectionately called him "Baby Bob" to her friends. She started therapy, with him in 1973 and ended it in 1975. Until she began therapy, she seemed to her friends cowed, afraid. After a year of therapy she was much more confident, more assertive. Dr. Craft, in a series of sessions, got Sueanne to accept her feelings about her mother, to let her mother go without the guilt that had weighed on her since early childhood. She said that Dr. Craft taught her, in one long night of group therapy, that it was okay to hate her mother.

Yet during her therapy she still sought psychic readings, sometimes sending away to have elaborate, expensive horoscopes done. She would send in the minute of her birth and its precise location. What came back was a thick file about her sun's shadow and her lunation cycles. Frequently she would talk to Mary Jacobs, but there were other local astrologers she also sought out. "She didn't move without consulting an astrologer," Jim Hooker said.

Sueanne always dressed in white or black, though more in black than white. The way she lived reflected similar radical opposites; she seemed to keep people in separate compartments. According to Norma Hooker, she always had two sets of women friends, those who were interested in family and those who were party friends from work whose families were in various stages of disintegration.

Norma considered herself one of those who saw primarily Sueanne's family side. She had known Sueanne and Jim Crumm in their marriage, had baby-sat Jimmy and Suzanne.

After her own children were half-grown, Norma kept foster children around her. She adopted one of them at a year old, Jennifer, a slim, blond girl. In the Hooker home, among torn curtains hanging over doorways, among broken chairs and empty fast-food boxes, Sueanne would sit rocking Jennifer, holding her for hours.

Norma never met Sueanne's other friends, though she heard about them from her. They were women like Kandy Sams, whom Sueanne knew from Dreyfus. When they first met, Kandy had just graduated from Kansas State University in home economics and was learning to work the switchboard at Dreyfus. She was a blond, open, fresh-faced girl with optimism and confidence. She had taught home economics for a time at Benedictine, a small Roman Catholic college near Kansas City. She and Sueanne would play tennis together in the early morning at the Essex apartment complex; they both played so poorly they dared not play when observed by others. And when Kandy, newly married, moved to Buffalo, New York, and found herself in a painful marriage, Sueanne would call her every day in the late afternoon on a

Dreyfus WATTS line and talk to her for hours. When Kandy divorced her husband and returned to Kansas City, she quickly resumed her friendship with Sueanne. Soon she became a successful real-estate agent.

Margie Hunt-Fugate also met Sueanne when she started to work at Dreyfus. After Margie quit, she worked mainly as a bartender at the Brookridge Country Club to support her two young boys. She lived across the state line in Missouri and she would bicycle to her work at Brookridge in Overland Park. Often, after the bar closed, she would bicycle a little further west on 103rd Street to the Wycliffe Apartments where Sueanne lived.

Margie was blond, with hair dyed a shade too light for her skin, broad-hipped, and with a beautiful, bursting, fleshy feel to her. She had a clear, honest stare and an intense, handsome face. It was with Margie that Sueanne would go out to drink in the evening.

With the exception of Kandy Sams, the women Sueanne knew when she was single were all working class, or on the lower margin of the middle class. Yet they were all strong women, independent women, all divorced at one time or another. Norma Hooker had been divorced years before, but remarried, and was the only one who remained married in the years she knew Sueanne. All were intelligent women, if not well educated, who had learned to fend for themselves.

Surprisingly, when Sueanne was with Norma Hooker, she would attack Beth Clarkson's interest in men, and run down Margie's life-style, too. "Trashy" was Beth's impression of Margie based on Sueanne's version of her. Norma herself was described as an incredible slob to both Beth and Margie.

Except for the savagery and precision of her attacks, Sueanne was, perhaps, no different from others in her duplicity. She did not ever choose to bring her friends together, yet she maintained friendships for years with all of them.

8

After Sueanne moved to Wycliffe, her relationship with the Hookers became a working one as well as a friendship and they observed with constant amusement Ed's courtship of their friend. Sueanne quickly knew what Ed wanted. "She knew what Ed was after," Norma said. "You'd have to be deaf and dumb and blind not to know!"

When Ed first came to Skateland, he was drinking heavily. Ed did what he could to hide his drinking from Sueanne, but Jim Hooker knew a drinker when he saw one. He himself had been one before he found religion.

After weeks of talking with Sueanne at Skateland, weeks of her refusing his invitations, Ed finally convinced her to go out with him. "At Skateland I either worked taking tickets or behind the snack bar and Ed used to hang around the snack bar," Sueanne said. "After I had talked to him for about a month or so, he asked me to go to a play at a college."

From Sueanne's point of view the two seemed to get along together fairly well on the first date, but the second date was disastrous. Ed drank heavily that night and his drinking reminded her of Jim Crumm's. "Ed and I went with another couple to a bar and then to their home, and I didn't see him after that for quite a while," she said. "I was mad at Ed the last night I saw him because it was two o'clock in the morning and I wanted to go home and he wouldn't take me home." Ed's size, his build, and his bravado must also have called to mind Jim, though Ed's energy and single-mindedness were much beyond her first husband's.

Ed remembered their first dates with dismay and humor. "One date and it was all downhill from there," he said, laughing. "I drank too much and drove too fast. She was a lady, very proper. She let me know right off she wouldn't put up with that stuff."

It was summer by the time Sueanne dated Ed again. "Several months later I was dating somebody else and Ed called and his voice, unfortunately, sounded like this other man's voice," Sueanne said. "It was a luncheon date. I asked him what he was doing home and he said he took the day off. The fellow that I was dating was a salesman and could do things like that. Not until I saw Ed in the waiting area at Dreyfus did I realize that I had been mistaken. I thought I was making a date with another person and it turned out to be Ed. We went out for lunch two or three times before I'd go out at night with him. That's how it started up again."

Soon they were dating regularly. "Ed took us anyplace we wanted to go," she said. "We took the kids to dinner. We also went to dinner ourselves. We took them to the show, to skating, we played miniature golf. Ed owned a powerboat and he took us out in it. My daughter and I had never waterskied; Chris taught Suzanne how to waterski, but I was afraid and wouldn't do it. I like water, but I don't like it that well."

Ed was proud of the restaurants he took her to during their courtship that summer—Jasper's, the Savoy, the Buttonwood Tree Lounge—expensive restaurants recommended to tourists and conventioneers. After dinner he would sometimes take her to the Starlight, a huge, outdoor theater in the middle of Swope Park.

As the summer neared its end he began to plan carefully for the night he was going to propose to her. For weeks he tried to anticipate her reaction to his proposal; his life seemed to hang on her answer. He had never fallen in love with a lady before. It was a chance to better himself and he saw that he might now win her.

Ed arranged to have Chris spend the weekend he proposed at a neighbor's home. He filled the house with red and yellow roses and bought nearly fifty dollars' worth of premixed margaritas. That day Ed drove Sueanne up to King City to show her the farm his father had left him. It was evening by the time they got back. When he asked her to marry him in a formal, stiff voice, she would not give him an answer.

The following evening Sueanne and Ed went out for a long walk. He had wanted her from the first sight of her dark red hair, her graceful nose, her small buttocks, her leanness, and he wanted her for her intensity that somehow complemented his. Sueanne was a little like his first wife, Shirley, red-haired, small-boned, clean, with a kind of energy, a force that, close up, almost approached anger.

Yet even on the second night Sueanne was still reluctant and they walked a long time through the dark suburbs. Ed remembered in detail her answer to his proposal and he was exultant in telling it, laughing proudly.

"She said, 'I have some demands I'm going to make of you.'

"'That's okay,' I said.

"'My charge accounts are too high and I can't afford to pay them off.'

"'No problem,' I said.

"'Some expensive demands,' she said.

"'That's okay.'

"'I want to pick out my own engagement ring.'

"'No problem,' I said.

"'It's going to be expensive.'

"'That's okay.'

"'It's going to cost at least four thousand dollars,' she said.

"'That's okay,' I said.

"We went to Kriegels in the Oak Park Mall," he boasted, "and I bought a ring costing forty-seven hundred dollars—and that was after a forty-percent discount."

The ring itself was one Sueanne had Mr. Brown at Kriegel's design for her, more of a cocktail ring than an engagement ring. "Do I remember it?" Norma Hooker said. "How could I not? It was a blood-red oval ruby with three stairsteps of diamonds coming up around the oval and setting it off. Women would kill for a ring like that."

9

Ed wanted to get married immediately. "I said we've got to set a date for the wedding," Ed recalled. "I insisted. She flat ran out of excuses, but she still kept putting me off. Finally, I gave her three days to think it over—this was early October—and she chose the second of December."

"I wanted to wait for a few months more," Sueanne said. "Ed wanted to get married earlier. He wanted to get married the next week and I wanted to get married in June and we got married in December. We compromised on December."

Elated, Ed immediately began looking for a new place to live. "I leased a condo in Overland Park because we were going to get these two families together and we had to have more space," he said. "Sue had November to get the place furnished and redecorated and set up. I paid for it all. I didn't begrudge her anything. Sue had spent too many years trying to make ends meet. Dressing and status were important to her."

Chris and Ed began to stay at Wycliffe much of the time during the next few months until the condominium was redecorated. Suzanne was dismayed. "Here was this man I didn't even know and suddenly I'm supposed to see him as a father figure," she said.

Chris, eleven, and Suzanne, twelve, were thrown together now. Sueanne knew conflict between the children was inevitable and she immediately arranged for family counseling. Again she chose Dr. Robert Craft; he had helped her a great deal when she underwent therapy three years before. She considered Bob and his wife, Delisha, friends and she planned to ask him to marry Ed and her. "He was a minister of Leawood Baptist Church and he was also a doctor of psychology. I wanted to meld the family together. I think four distinct personalities need to have some kind of basis to start a good family, and we were all four very different people, and we were all four very strong-willed people, and we all liked different things. I wanted harmony and unity. And the kids were so close in age and there was petty jealousy at times."

"Family counseling sessions started sometime in August or early September," Sueanne said. "We all went once a week. We were trying to put four people into one place at the same time and trying to get everybody happy. We all had different likes and dislikes and it was a give-and-take situation. At various times Bob talked to each one of us individually."

Dr. Craft helped bring the family together slowly. Sueanne had had an ideal vision of a family, one that she had not achieved in her first marriage. With Dr. Craft's support, with Ed's cooperation and generosity, she intended to succeed and she bent her great energy toward that end.

10

Sueanne had another surprise that fall, one that changed her life almost as much as Ed's proposal. Suzanne hadn't seen her brother, Jimmy, for eight years, hadn't seen him since she left the

Crumm house with her mother at the age of four. During her frequent visits to her great-grandmother Sallee's house, Suzanne always studied an old photo of Jimmy on her dresser. In the midst of the turmoil that the preparations for the wedding caused, she asked her how she could get in touch with Jimmy. The old woman had not been able to see Jimmy herself since Sueanne's divorce and she encouraged her great-granddaughter's interest in seeing the boy. Suzanne had to ask her to spell Crumm, for she and her mother had been living under the name of Sallee for years. Mrs. Sallee told her there was a double "m" at the end of "Crumm."

That evening Suzanne looked up "Crumm" in the telephone directory. Though she knew her mother would be angry if she found out, she tried to call Jimmy from her great-grandmother's house. Her father answered the phone. Jim Crumm had not seen or spoken to his daughter in seven years and she had to tell him who she was.

Jim remembered the call well. "One evening Suzanne, Jimmy's sister, my daughter, called the house. Jimmy was not at home. I talked to her for a few minutes, and she identified herself. She told me that she went to her great-grandmother to find out how to spell my last name so she could look it up in the phone directory. She wanted to see her brother. She told me then that she would have to call back and talk to Jimmy and she would get in trouble if her mother knew she had called. The next evening Suzanne called and talked to Jimmy and then Sue called back and talked to me. A week later Jimmy and myself went over to see Sue and Suzanne in their apartment there in Overland Park."

On Saturday Jim drove his son over to meet his sister and his mother. Sueanne and her daughter still lived in Wycliffe, right across the street from Skateland, where she had first met Ed eight or nine months earlier.

"It was like four strangers meeting," Jim said. "Nobody knew anybody really. It was very strained for everybody. Sueanne and Jimmy didn't even touch. I didn't even know how to greet my own daughter. Do you hug her? Do you shake hands? I never did hug her. I put my arm around her, I think, and I talked to her a little bit. Sue and I took Jimmy and Suzanne up to the roller-skating rink. The people that were running the roller rink—at the time I didn't realize who it was—were old friends of Sue and me when we were married, Jim and Norma Hooker. Sue and I sat and talked for a while at the rink, just a few minutes. The only compliment I threw her way was that she had a nice-looking apartment, which it was. It was almost like a museum, like she always kept her house, just spotless and everything just perfect. Then I took Sue back to her apartment, dropped her off, and went home.

"The visit was very cold. I mean it was worse than four strangers meeting, because when you meet a stranger, you always kind of meet him with a little bit of anticipation. You know, 'What are they going to be like? Who do they look like?' You go into *this* knowing what one person for sure looks like. But I wouldn't have recognized Suzanne if she passed me on the street. I mean that's pretty bad, if you don't even recognize your own daughter."

Two years earlier Jim had married a woman fifteen years younger than he and had adopted her daughter. He had begun to settle into a new life and had brought his son back to his home after years of leaving him, first at Jim's mother's house, then his sister's, then his brother's.

"In the back of my mind," Jim said, "I had always dreaded that Sueanne was going to reappear somewhere along the line before Jimmy got old enough to be able to accept or reject her. I don't know if he ever would have been old enough. I was always worried that she was going to reappear and, boy, damned if she didn't. I don't like to use the word 'hate,' but that would be about the closest feeling I would have toward the woman. It was like a nightmare come true."

Sueanne's version of the meeting differed considerably from Jim's. "Jimmy said, 'Hi, Mom,' and we hugged and kissed. The kids went to the Dairy Queen on my money; as usual, Jim didn't have any.

"By the time I saw Jim again, I was no longer afraid of him and he didn't bully me and he didn't scare me," Sueanne said, "He walked in saying, 'This is the way it is going to be,' and 'You know I always wanted to get back together and marry you again.' I said, 'You're married,' and he said, 'It doesn't make any difference.' I said, 'You have ceased to exist. I don't hate you; I don't fear you; you have just become a nonexistent person. And, no, we're not going to be married.'"

Seeing Jim again after more than six years, suddenly Sueanne remembered their marriage with pain and horror, remembered Jim's penury, his beatings, his drinking. In particular, she was angry about his abandonment of his daughter. "Suzanne thinks of Jim as a biological accident, not as her father," she said.

Jimmy knew little about his mother, except for the perceptions of her that he had when she left him to his father at the age of nine. "Nobody talked about her after she left," Jimmy said. "My father never said anything about her." Jimmy learned little about his mother that day directly from her. Suzanne, not his mother, had called him back to the family and it was with Suzanne that he spent his time that afternoon.

Jimmy was now sixteen, Suzanne twelve, yet he looked younger than his age, she older. It was as if he were from a poor family, she from a rich one, or so he thought. The two seemed to know each other immediately, magically, and they went outside in the thin August sunlight to talk freely and wander about the apartment complex. Jimmy had never lived in a place where there was a pool and tennis courts and where everything seemed new and well kept. He recalled nothing about going to Skateland or to the Dairy Queen with his father and mother.

At once they felt like brother and sister and he was grateful for her call and the new possibilities it suggested. It was Suzanne he thought of now, not his mother and their awkward meeting. Jimmy told her of the houses and families he had lived in and the schools he had attended. He told her stories of his undisciplined life and of the grades he got in school. Suzanne was astonished. "If I had those grades," she said, "my mother would kill me. She'd ground me for life."

Jimmy recalled how the two laughed together, fascinated by the differences in their lives. He had been passed on from grade to grade, though he had received mostly D's, F's, and an occasional C. Jimmy was struck most by the high expectations his mother had for Suzanne, Suzanne by her older brother's daring life of drink and drugs and his freedom from parental demands. He seemed to represent a world of irresponsibility she had never seen, never imagined.

Yet Suzanne's world held freedom and promise for Jimmy. That world seemed almost within his grasp. He saw, or thought he saw, that Sueanne, already his mother again, had money, order, status, and discipline—all the things that were lacking in his own father's life. Jimmy looked toward her to help him in some way he could not yet imagine, but which, he hoped, would soon be made clear. He knew that day that he had won over Suzanne, that he was already her big brother, her protector.

A week or two later Jimmy was invited back to the apartment. At Suzanne's insistence he soon began to spend weekends there. Jimmy found a ready audience in Suzanne and Ed and he began to tell and embroider stories of the deprivation he experienced in his father's care. He told of his father's drinking, of beatings he had endured, and of his father's refusal to let him use the Crumm car. The abuse and deprivation, fantasied or real, especially enlisted Ed's sympathy, for Jimmy's stories paralleled those of the family Ed was born into.

Jimmy soon learned of Ed and Sueanne's wedding plans. In the early fall he began going on family outings with his sister. Once he went with Ed and Chris, Sueanne and Suzanne, to Worlds of Fun, a theme park just north of Kansas City. Jimmy first began to notice Chris; he was eleven now, nine months younger than the sedate Suzanne. Fair-skinned, but big for his age, Chris would drift away from the group and vault benches or duck into penny arcades, leaving the rest of the family to hunt for him. Sometimes Chris sought the family's praise, sometimes he pretended that he didn't belong with them. Always he sought their attention like a child hiding in order to be noticed.

11

Less than two weeks before the wedding, Norma and Jim Hooker invited the bride and groom and their children over to their house for Thanksgiving dinner. The Hookers now considered Ed and Sueanne their closest friends and already saw the three children as part of the Hobson family.

"Ed and Sueanne were deeply in love," Norma said. "The largest part of Thanksgiving Day Sueanne sat on Ed's lap. That was not unusual for them. That same day Sueanne said to me that she thought she would like to have Ed's child.

"She was very taken with Nicki, the black girl we had just adopted and brought home at three days old. I sat while she held the baby on her lap. She sometimes sat and rocked her legs back and forth watching Nicki sleep.

"At first at the rink Sueanne didn't want anything to do with Ed. He didn't represent dollars. She came to know and realize that he would offer her the love and security and warmth that she never had. There is no doubt in my mind that Ed was absolutely crazy in love with Sueanne and I very honestly feel that there was a point in time that she was very much in love with him.

"I knew a very warm, a very loving, a very giving Sueanne. Sueanne is somebody I've laughed with, cried with, played with, spent New Year's Eve with. While Jim was at the rink one New Year's Eve, Sueanne and I were at her apartment drinking tequila and peppermint schnapps and laughing half the night."

All the Hooker children had known Sueanne since childhood and had come to call her Aunt Sueanne. Thanksgiving evening they began to call her fiancé Uncle Ed.

Both Ed and Sueanne got pleasure out of pleasing Jenny and Tammy Hooker. That fall Sueanne learned that the two girls had not been able to find a particular style of headband to wear to school, the only style that the in-group wore, and she and Ed looked all over town for them. After hours of searching, they brought the headbands back triumphantly to the delighted girls. "This was loving, giving—it was not a pretense," Norma said.

Norma had not seen Jimmy for seven years. Her first impression of him was of how childlike he seemed compared with his sister. " Jimmy was a lost child looking for the little love that he could get from just anybody," she said. When Norma first saw him again, she thought of Kimmy, an abandoned Vietnamese child that she tried to adopt; Kimmy would raise her arms to be picked up and she would sit quietly and soberly on the lap of any stranger who would hold her.

Chris was also, Norma thought, "a sweet little boy looking for love." Yet Chris had a father who loved him and Chris was stronger, more independent than Jimmy, and he had enough trust to be kind. "He'd do anything for you," she said. "Though he wasn't above lying and manipulating, he was loyal."

Nearly two weeks after Thanksgiving, on Saturday, the second of December, Sue and Ed were to be married. The entire family, with the exception of Jimmy, was already living in the condominium Ed had leased.

Sueanne, during the week before the wedding, seemed to be under a strain. "Of course Sueanne is a highly nervous person and just getting everything together put a lot of pressure on her, because she is very, very highly organized," Norma said.

On Friday night the wedding party rehearsed in the chapel of the Country Club Christian Church, Dr. Craft's church, where small society weddings are held. Afterward a few friends who had come in from out of town drove back to the condominium for a party.

Chris wasn't at the rehearsal or the party. Norma missed him and asked about him. "Christen is grounded; he doesn't know how to behave in public," Sueanne told her curtly. "If I had my way, he'd stay home from the wedding, too."

Sueanne and Ed were married on a cold, sunlit December afternoon. Ernestine Bean, one of Sueanne's friends at Dreyfus, had sewn forest-green dresses for the attendants. "Sueanne's gown was more like a cocktail dress," Norma said. "It wasn't a frilly wedding-dress thing. Like she said, they'd both been married before and white gowns were not her taste. It was a very soft fabric, a very lovely dress, and had a little bit of a jacket effect. It had a rose tone to it." Suzanne was a junior bridesmaid, Ernestine the matron of honor; Norma herself was "a bridesmaid, too, or whatever you call it." Margie Hunt-Fugate kept the guest book.

Jimmy gave the bride away. As he came down the aisle with his mother on his arm, it was as if she truly depended on him, as if he were being wedded to the family also.

Dr. Craft married Ed and Sueanne, Baby Bob's height and weight dwarfing and enfolding the couple as they stood before him. "Sueanne was a vibrant, beautiful bride," Beth Clarkson said. "Ed was extremely nervous, almost to the extent of its being a first marriage. It was a small wedding, perhaps thirty people were there, but a very tasteful, very beautiful wedding. They made an attractive couple."

Beth was optimistic about the marriage, despite her own divorces. "Ed was stable, a widower, not fly-by-night," she noted. "His child added to his stability. Ed could offer her security, love, something she had not had before. There is an awful lot to Ed Hobson—a quieter, stronger man than the kind I liked. I liked a very outgoing, very domineering, weak man, who had to be domineering because he was so weak."

After the wedding the guests walked over to an adjoining basement of one of the buildings at the church. "Most of the people there were Sueanne's friends, friends that I had never met," Norma said. "Margie, Beth, Ernestine—these were party friends. Jim and I were not the go, go, party, party, drink, drink type. We've always been very family oriented."

No more than one or two of Ed's friends attended the wedding. Ed seemed to have no ties to the past, no lifelong friends, no relatives except Chris.

Jim Hooker was surprised when Ed asked him to serve as his best man. Jim had known Sueanne much longer than Ed; ten years earlier she and her first husband had come to get a loan from him at a finance company he worked for. Jim had seen Sueanne blossom after the end of her first marriage and her therapy with Craft.

Ed paid dearly and happily for the wedding; he liked to boast about the cost. He hired the official photographer of the Kansas City Chiefs to make a record of it. Also, he had, at Sue's request, special white lilies flown in from California to match her dress. "Those few flowers just for her and her matron of honor cost four hundred dollars," Ed said, laughing.

Despite Sueanne's threat to ground him, Ed's son, Chris, was there, his light hair, his innocent, open face identifying him clearly as a Hobson. Yet Chris's eyes belied the simple black-and-white emotions of his father, belied his father's desire for submission rather than control. Chris's face was narrower and more pointed than Ed's; he looked in many ways like his mother, Shirley. Unlike Jimmy, Chris would come forward comfortably into the groups the photographer was paid to find, for he had known the family long enough to feel relaxed and confident among them.

Jimmy had a brand-new brown suit, the first suit he remembered wearing, and it was a little too tight, a little too flashy for the occasion. His hair was long, hanging to his shoulders; it blurred sexual differences and rounded his face, making him look even younger than his sixteen years.

Jimmy's face clearly resembled his mother's, with that beautiful, precise, unmistakable Sallee nose. He was as slightly built as she was. Like her, he seemed to evince a delicacy, a fragility, an edge subject to breaking. And, like Sueanne, he kept a part of himself withheld a little so that a hand on his shoulder or an arm on a back would touch something cool and flat, like a stone wall inside a building.

"I've never been much for intimate family involvement," Jimmy said. And in truth, he felt acutely self-conscious coming forward into the boisterous wedding party, none of whom he knew well, not even the bride, especially the bride, though he was treated as if he had long been one of the family, as if the years of his exile had never happened, and he alone was left awkward and uncertain.

Margie Hunt-Fugate, bored by her duty to stand behind the guest book, tried to make Jimmy feel comfortable. She had two half-grown boys of her own and knew how unfinished and self-conscious they were. In many ways, Jimmy seemed no older than her own boys, who were nine and ten. Margie, unlike frail Sueanne, was blond and fleshy in her tight, forest-green dress, and she paid more attention to Jimmy than anyone else did. She seemed to like boys and men. She told him how handsome he looked, how graceful he was as he escorted his mother down the aisle, how gently and carefully he took the arm of his beautiful mother dressed all in rose.

Jimmy felt embarrassed by Margie's interest in him. He would spend much of his time in the bathroom, chain-smoking or looking at himself in the mirror, studying the slight acne he had sought to cover. As soon as he came back into the reception hall, he began looking for another way to slide quietly out of the room.

Yet Jimmy did have an important role to play in the ritual. And the manners, the clothes, the love, the money or the appearance of money, were what he wanted, what pressed into him all the while he was there, like a change coming that December day.

He had almost been at the center of the wedding. There was a momentum drawing him away rapidly from his father, drawing him closer to his mother. Yet he knew that when he saw his grandparents again, he would have to apologize to them for giving the bride away. The Sallees had been generous to him and were the only stable points in his life after his mother left. He would have to apologize, even though her parents no longer lived to please her, and his grandfather had washed his hands of her.

2
STRANGERS

1

Saturday, after the wedding reception, Sueanne and Ed drove two hundred miles south to honeymoon for a few days in Shangri-La at the Grand Lake of the Cherokees. Shangri-La was a resort just south of Miami, Oklahoma, in the foothills of the Ozarks and only twenty or thirty miles beyond the state lines of Kansas and Missouri.

Once back from the army, Ed had traveled little; Sueanne had not traveled at all. They chose to honeymoon near the town where each had been married before a justice of the peace nearly twenty years earlier. Like a miniature Las Vegas, marriage was still the main business in Miami and little white clapboard chapels appeared on all sides of the courthouse square.

Though Sueanne did not like to be around water, she and Ed took boating excursions out on the lake in the mild, late-fall weather. Just before the wedding Sueanne had sent away to have Ed's horoscope done and the chart had come back predicting his death by water. Sueanne had told Norma Hooker about the fear she had. "She said Ed was going to die in an accident having to do with water, and she made him get rid of his powerboat. Sueanne didn't breathe without first consulting her horoscope."

Jim Hooker found Sueanne's dependence on astrology and the occult an assault on his Christian beliefs; he feared the devil worship at the heart of it. But Jim laughed when he heard Ed's fortune and he told Norma, "Yes, when we first met Ed, I thought he'd drink himself to death the way I nearly did."

2

After the wedding reception, Jim drove Suzanne, Chris, and Jimmy back to the Hookers' rented town house in the Rigg Apartments so they could change their clothes and go roller skating. Jim had to open the rink for a school party he had scheduled months earlier and he took the children over to Skateland three or four blocks away. The three children skated together until well after dark. When he closed the rink, he dropped off Suzanne and Chris at the Hookers' apartment and drove Jimmy back to his father's house in Raytown, Missouri.

During the Hobsons' honeymoon Suzanne and Chris stayed with the Hookers. Right away Norma had her hands full with Chris and Suzanne and soon found herself mediating between them. "The kids were doing homework downstairs," Norma said, "and I was upstairs and there was a ruckus between Suzanne and Chris. Suzanne got all upset and I couldn't understand exactly why. It was over some little piddling thing that Chris had done. Suzanne admitted that she would lie and get Chris into trouble and her mother would believe her over him. Suzanne was a manipulative, spoiled-rotten little wretch. I didn't like the child. I liked her when she was a tiny baby."

The dislike was mutual. Aunt Norma, as Suzanne called her, wanted to put the girl to work taking care of Nicki, the mulatto baby the Hookers had adopted nearly a year before. "I didn't like changing diapers and baby-sitting and serving people just because Aunt Norma said so," Suzanne said.

Suzanne especially didn't like being separated from her mother for even a few days, and she wouldn't yield to Norma. "When Ed first came to live with us before he married Mom, I was supposed to call Ed 'Daddy,'" Suzanne said. "Well, I liked being the only child. My mother was two mothers; I liked the mother I had before she married Ed."

Chris, too, was made anxious by his father's absence during the honeymoon trip. Before the marriage neither dared to speak out in the presence of their parents. With their parents gone, each child blamed the other for the plight they shared. Neither could imagine the life ahead. Both felt trapped and transmuted their sadness and fear and frustration into anger against each other.

Norma, who had been divorced and had children from two marriages, knew the difficulty of bringing two families together. "Teenagers can be vile and vicious," she said. "Christen was a sweet kid; he was a very typical teenager. Yet, given the chance, I think he could be just as vicious as anybody else's teenager. Children are master manipulators. Certainly Suzanne had manipulated her mother. And when Chris was not getting what he thought was his fair share of attention from his father, he manipulated Ed until he got it."

Norma didn't envy Sueanne's job. "She was integrating all those backgrounds. My God, that would be difficult under normal conditions. If you count Jimmy, five human beings from five totally different backgrounds. My God, that's like putting nitroglycerine in a paper sack and running across the street with it!"

3

On Thursday Ed and Sueanne returned home. The home was a condominium, one side of a duplex really, in a large complex of condominiums designed exactly alike on the southeast edge of Overland Park, a half block south of 103rd Street and three miles east of the Wycliffe Apartments. More expensive homes began just north of 103rd. Yet the street circling the complex was broad and the white duplexes seemed protected and private. No windows faced the street, just double garages and short flights of steps going up toward doors that were not visible except at an angle.

No sidewalks paralleled the street. It was a neighborhood where children could play or bike in the street itself. Just beyond the driveway to the Hobson condominium, a blue-and-white sign in bold letters read, NEIGHBORHOOD WATCH: WE CALL THE POLICE!

A couple of hundred yards south of the complex, Nall Park

began. Built in the floodplain of Indian Creek, the park extended for miles along it. Its irregularity and the placing of fields and paths among its great trees made Nall seem like a meandering English park. Indian Creek, sixty feet across from bank to bank, had cut fifteen feet below the level of the fields along it. Except in the first hours after a great rain, the creek usually had a small stream running through its bottom with a few wild ducks in it.

The distances between the sides of the duplexes were small, the backyards deep and ill defined. A half block away there was a common clubhouse and a swimming pool.

Though there were only a few small trees around most of the condominiums, the Hobsons had a corner lot and their entryway was shaded by a large pin oak. Even in December, the oak still hung on to its dark orange, deeply cut leaves, and they rattled dryly in the winter wind until the surge of spring.

This was the first house that Sueanne had lived in since she had left her husband and child in the Crumm house in Prairie Village eight years before. Sueanne had worked hard to clean the house in the weeks before the marriage and she had plans to redecorate it totally, taking it room by room. "I was always proud of the houses I lived in," she said, "and I wanted to make Ed proud of his possessions, too."

"Sueanne had been a long time without," Ed said, "and she wanted things and I wanted to give them to her." As both soon realized, his salary as a millwright wasn't enough to pay for the things he wanted to give her.

Sueanne immediately quit Dreyfus and got away from her lover. She began to work part-time at the Pine Tree Condominiums near her home, working enough to help her pay for some of the debts she had accumulated in the years of living alone with her daughter. Ed didn't want her to work at all; he wanted her to devote herself to the family and the life they were building together.

Sueanne quickly began to understand that Ed meant what he said about giving her things, that he meant literally everything he had said during the courtship. She had been uncertain about the change marriage would bring to their relationship. A couple of months before the marriage she had asked Ed to sign a premarital agreement that she would draw up subject to his approval. Ed was angry that she trusted him so little; he refused vehemently and she withdrew the proposal. For a day or two she thought their plans to marry might fall apart, but she calmed him, and he quickly forgot about it.

A month after the marriage Sueanne and Ed drove up to tiny King City in Gentry County, Missouri, and put the land he owned in both their names. Less than four months after the marriage, Ed sold one hundred sixty acres of farmland, and both went up to sign the bill of sale.

Sueanne kept the family's accounts. Ed gave little or no attention to them because, for the first time in his life, all his bills were paid on time. He didn't care where the money went, and he was proud of her, almost as if she herself were the bouquet of lilies flown in from California or the oval, blood-red ruby ring she wore. She was in a class beyond him and he felt lifted up by her to that class.

When she bought something expensive, she would come over to him, dressed in white, and sit like a child in his lap caressing his broad face with her long, thin hands, saying, "Why is it you don't complain when I buy things? My friends' husbands always check up on them; they'd go into a rage if they came back with that old wooden Victrola I bought today. Why aren't you like that?"

Ed would smile broadly saying, "That's okay, honey, that's okay."

The sale of the land made possible the dark blue Lincoln Continental Mark V, the redecoration of the condominium, the antiques, and the jewelry. Soon Ed himself was wearing a Krugerrand on a gold chain around his neck. Sueanne was ordering rings and jewelry from Mr. Brown at Kriegel's in the Oak Park Mall as if Brown were a stock salesman. Ed was proud that the land he had inherited from the father he despised could be turned so easily into jewels and cars and antiques.

Ed got up every weekday morning at five-thirty to go to the mill. Sueanne would be dead asleep as he left their bedroom gently and quietly. The night before she would carefully pack his black lunch box with soup and sandwiches and the pie she knew he liked. At eleven-thirty, when he ate his lunch, he would call her and she would always answer the phone immediately. Unlike any other woman he had known, he could depend on her to be there, to do what she said she would do. And when he came home in the evening, the house would be neat and orderly, unlike the pigpen near King City, Missouri, that his mother kept.

Ed had great energy and he liked the work he did; he liked the order of machinery and the male world it gave to him. As the first spring of their marriage came on, he would work in the evening on the Model T he owned, which now bore the personalized Kansas license plate SUEANNE. Chris would help him or play beside him. Frequently Ed would fix a coworker's car or his minister's, usually for nothing but the cost of the parts.

Ed spent a lot of time at work, sometimes six days a week during the summer and fall when the grain was harvested. The machines he tended would break under the strain of constant use and he would work late to repair them. Ed was also an elected union official and he had to spend some evenings negotiating contracts and grievances. The other workers wanted him at these meetings because they saw how persistent and uncompromising he could be in the face of a challenge from the company, and they knew he would be honest.

Every morning when Ed left for work, he would look in on Chris, whose room was across the upstairs hall from the master bedroom. Ed remembered how different it was just two years before with Shirley dying and no hope anywhere in the house or outside it. Now Chris had a mother again and he had a wife he loved; together they were building a family, building a relationship. He drank less now than at any time he could recall in his adult life. This was the best time of his life and it gave him pain to remember that earlier time with no hope and Shirley dying.

For Chris it was otherwise. He was in a new school, a new house, a new family, and there seemed no stable point in his life. At eleven, almost twelve, even his body had begun to betray him, to change rapidly. He was already at least as big as his stepbrother, Jimmy, who was almost five years older than he. Yet Chris was very dependent, emotionally much younger than eleven.

Chris had had his father all to himself for more than two years. He still grieved for his mother, Shirley, who terrified him when she came to him in dreams.

"When we first got married, Chris was jealous," Ed recalled. "He was jealous of my relationship with Sueanne. Chris and I had almost three years that we were by ourselves. Now he was having to share me with someone else."

Chris was also jealous of Sueanne's attention to Suzanne, her preference for her daughter in everything. He didn't remember ever having a mother who wasn't threatening or ill or dying, and he wanted a mother who could love him without judging or comparing him. He thought he knew how to win that love, though he had never before won it from any woman.

Sueanne herself was jealous, Ed thought, jealous of his relationship to Chris, "but not too much. There was some adjustment problems, but nothing that I could see wouldn't work out in time."

Sueanne required order in her life; she needed an orderly house, needed control of her circumstances. "Sueanne is not the most patient woman in the world," Ed said. "When she wants something done, she wants it done right now." As a child Sueanne had felt helpless and fearful before her mother's depredations; grown up, she felt helpless before Jim's drinking and his threats. She could not bear messes. In the eight years she was unmarried, she began to achieve, for the first time, order and discipline in her life, especially after her break with her mother. Her therapy with Dr. Craft enabled her to accept her hateful feelings toward her mother. Like Chris, she, too, was looking for love and security, for tenderness and warmth. Until she fell in love with Ed, she had been unable to trust anyone enough to receive love, unable really to give love herself.

She felt deprived of love as a child; instead of love, her mother gave her things. Money and things became substitutes for love, signs of love; in the Sallee family things were the only tangible expressions of love. And money was a way Sueanne could control her circumstances, clean up messes.

Dr. Craft had helped her get control of her life before. As soon as she had accepted Ed's proposal, she had insisted that she and Suzanne and Ed and Chris meet with him for family counseling. The counseling continued for eight months after the wedding. She felt the problems of bringing the two families together might best be resolved in group therapy. Sueanne, who had talked to Dr. Craft so much over the years, now let the others speak. Chris spoke the most; he had a captive audience to whom he could tell the troubles of his past life. He felt secure from retaliation, for Dr. Craft was in control, an authority who would listen and change things.

Chris already knew that Ed, who appeared so strong, who spoke so boldly, would do what Sueanne wanted. If Ed hesitated, Sueanne would come over and sit patiently on his lap like a child. Besides, Ed was working most of the time and Chris was left in Sueanne's control, left with a stranger about whom he knew little.

Unlike the others in the family, who seemed to understand that Sueanne's long years of individual therapy with Dr. Craft gave her an advantage, Chris spoke plainly in the counseling sessions. He spoke of his violent mother who pointed a gun at him and threatened to kill him; of his mother's scream when he found Tani propped up in bed with her eyes open; of his father, whom he had clung to during the last two years and who seemed to be leaving him for another; of Ed's drinking.

And he spoke of Sueanne herself. Sueanne would sit crocheting or studying her nails, not looking at Chris as he spoke. When Chris stopped speaking, she would begin to correct him patiently and carefully, distinctly emphasizing each word, gaining control of herself in the heavy rhythm of her speech and seeking control of those to whom she spoke.

As Dr. Craft's weekly sessions went on Chris brought up the problems he had with his stepsister, Suzanne. They were rivals in the family for the love of Sueanne, whom both called "Mom."

Yet they were unevenly matched. Nine months younger than his stepsister, Chris behaved as if he were a child of eight or nine, Suzanne as if she were a young adult. Suzanne, with a wide network of friends, would run Chris down before them, mock him within his hearing. Struggling to make a few new friends, he would retaliate as best he could by spreading rumors about his stepsister. When the children quarreled, Ed would act as peacemaker, seeking to moderate their disputes and to deter or ameliorate the punishments that Sueanne sought to inflict.

"They were no worse than my sister and myself," Ed said. "What do you expect? They were both nearly the same age, both twelve in those early months; I knew they would work it out. They'd fight one minute and the next minute they'd be outside kicking a ball around."

In the spring of 1979, four or five months after the wedding, Sueanne began to be impatient. Ed realized that the whole family, not just the children, was having an adjustment problem. "Chris and Suzanne," he said, "got along, on the average, pretty good. There was a little bickering back and forth. The natural disaster was using someone else's tennis racquet. I would just say to Sueanne, 'Give it a little time, things are working out, it just takes time.' She says, 'Well, this is why we went to counseling.' And I says, 'Well, we take all these steps, but you can't solve all the problems in counseling prior to or right after you get married; you're going to have to have a few adjustment problems like everybody else.'"

Ed rose early and worked late. "During 1979 the company also started sending me to night school," he explained. "I'd be gone two nights a week to a technical institution downtown. I went to school all through the summer and fall of that year, and the class ended up in December of '79, just before Christmas."

In Ed's absence Sueanne assumed most of the responsibility for solving family problems. In her first marriage she had great trouble getting control of her own boy, Jimmy; she never really felt she succeeded. Chris was older and even more difficult.

Sueanne herself was easily angered by Chris. She was irritated by her failure to get control of small things. He needed discipline, he needed it now, and she told Ed that. Chris wouldn't do the housework she gave him to do; he wouldn't study properly; he lied about Suzanne. She tried to take up the issues with Ed one at a time. Chris ate like a glutton, she told Ed, and he had no manners. Ed understood; he and Chris had lived together like bachelors and ate what came to hand and didn't bother about niceties, about napkins or place mats or elbows on the table. They had eaten the way most people eat when they eat alone, the way men with crusted hands eat during the noon break. Yet he married a lady to gain the polish he had always admired and felt himself capable of achieving; he married to refine him and his boy, Chris.

The mastery Sueanne sought in little things veiled from both her and Chris their greater struggle for control. The most important battle was for control of Ed. Sueanne's mother had kept her father from her, won him over. Chris, she felt, was taking her mother's role; he was taking away Ed's love the way her mother had taken her father's love from her. In her own home Sueanne would not accept the position she had endured in her childhood. And Chris knew that if his stepmother controlled Ed, he himself would be left at her mercy. At first neither quite understood that; later both thought of little else.

Chris had ways of getting under her skin. Sueanne's minimum requirement for a decent life was a clean, orderly house; she had definite rules and she sought to enforce them as absolutely as Ruth Sallee had done. No violation of a rule was insignificant. She had a rule that any dirty glass had to be put in the dishwasher immediately after use and any clean glass removed from the dishwasher had to be placed in a line in the white cupboard, as if the glasses were soldiers awaiting an order. Chris would never place a dirty glass in the dishwasher voluntarily. When Sueanne ordered him to do it, he would move so mechanically, so slowly, so painstakingly, that she would be yelling before he was halfway to the dishwasher. When Suzanne was younger, Sueanne would slap her in the face for such violations, but she dared not touch Chris; Ed did not hit him and she dared not hit him.

To Sueanne, Chris was a Teed and she knew the Teed family only through Ed and Chris's descriptions of them. Shirley Teed made life hell for Ed and now there was a Teed in her family. Sueanne could not bear to have anything that belonged to Shirley around and she gave Norma Hooker Shirley's long, dark mink stole, the stole that Ed had given to her. Shirley was crazy, Sueanne thought, and she had made her daughters, Tani and Lailoneh, crazy, and perhaps Chris, too. Though Chris regularly visited his aunts and uncles in Kansas City, Sueanne would never invite his relatives to her home. They were, she thought, people beneath her, even lower than the Crumm family. Fortunately for her, Ed's entire family was dead and she did not have to deal with them.

Sueanne wanted to make allowances for Chris. She understood that Shirley's threats to kill Chris, and Tani's suicide, or murder, were enough to disturb any child. Still, in the boy's presence, she could not be tolerant. Chris's obsession with the violent Teed family even came to dominate the counseling sessions she had arranged for her own family. The life Chris led with Shirley, Sueanne thought, was a thing of the past, an excuse really. Chris needed discipline and Ed would not administer it so that it would tell on the boy. Ed grew tiresome to her in his apologies for Chris and his arguments for patience.

Despite Ed's short temper and impulsiveness he was the one who negotiated disputes among the children on evenings when he was home. Sometimes he shouted and threatened, but he never hit either child.

A month or two after the wedding, Sueanne and Ed filed papers to cross-adopt Chris and Suzanne. Both parents had a strong ideal of family. They held the ideal all the more firmly because the only families they had experienced were those that came together in conflict and suffering. In April, five months into the marriage, Sueanne and Ed signed the legal papers for the cross adoptions.

Sueanne thought formal adoption might give her a respect and authority she never had been able to win from Chris, give him and her a lifetime commitment to the relationship. She soon realized that she had gained little from the adoption of Chris—some legal, formal advantages perhaps, since the property left to Chris by his mother might someday become part of the property of her family—but little else. Chris remained as intractable as ever.

Jim Crumm, still living in Kansas City, did not contest Ed's adoption of Suzanne; he thought she was going to a better life than he could offer her. When he met her at Sueanne's house the previous fall, she was a stranger to him and he felt little for her. He was more embarrassed than anything else, as if he was meeting an old lover he had jilted. Besides, he had already adopted Mary Crumm's daughter, Anna.

Jim let Suzanne go more easily than Sueanne had expected. There was the issue of Jim's failure to pay the back child support he owed Suzanne. His financial responsibility had never been resolved by the courts. If he were to oppose the adoption, Jim imagined that Sueanne would bring him to court for what he owed, ten thousand dollars or so by now. If he did not oppose her, he thought he would be quit of her.

Chris and Suzanne were quiet about the adoption. The marriage was now five months old, yet each still preferred to live alone with his or her own parent. Suzanne told her mother that "Ed was the first real father I ever had," but she told her friends she could not bear him and avoided him whenever possible. Suzanne had little idea of what it was to love a father and Chris had loved only a frightening, arbitrary mother. Living again with a single parent now seemed impossible to both children, yet each had plans.

4

Jimmy and Suzanne came to love each other and to depend on that love. They were both attractive, intelligent children with thin, sensitive faces like the face of their mother, children who had suffered and who now could share their suffering and their pleasure in a new dispensation.

"Suzanne worshiped Jimmy," Sueanne said. And Jimmy, separated from Suzanne for so long, felt very protective of her; he needed someone he could love without qualification. "I would do anything for Suzanne," he said. Their bond was the only part of his original family that he could remember fondly.

Suzanne thought she could rescue Jimmy from the drunken father who had abandoned her and who, she believed, was abusing her brother. Jimmy had concocted tales of beatings, of moving from place to place, tales of his father's drunkenness, of his painful life during the years Sueanne had sought to find him. He also told Ed and Sueanne stories of how he was a service manager at a gas station at night, struggling to make grades in school despite all the work, how he had to earn money to pay for his clothes and his school supplies, how his stepmother, Mary, treated him like a child, gave him no more freedom than she gave her own little daughter, Anna.

"We had talked about him living with us before Christmas," Sueanne said, "but Ed and I were only engaged at the time. Jimmy had told us some of the conditions under which he had been living, and he was very unhappy, and we felt that it would be good for us, and good for him to have him with us. I brought the subject up to Ed, and it was a joint decision. The invitation was extended and it was up to Jimmy."

"We would go over to his house in Raytown, where he was living with his dad, and pick him up and we would bring him back and he would stay with us on weekends," Ed said. "I won't say every weekend, but almost every weekend he was around here someplace. We'd go to Worlds of Fun and other places together. Well, one Saturday afternoon we went over and got Jimmy and he was having a problem with his stereo. I went down into their basement where his two-by-four room was, and I looked at the house and I looked at what Jimmy had and I was got. Walls made of blankets hanging up! Everybody deserves a good start and I just felt sorry for him. He had nothing compared to what our children had. He told me that he had to work and couldn't go to school. He didn't have any clothing."

Ed identified with Jimmy and with the abuse and deprivation Jimmy claimed he had suffered. Jimmy understood that quickly and he exaggerated his grievances against his father. He liked Ed and saw how easily he could be manipulated by any strong emotion.

And Ed remembered how he had been forced to work long hours on the farm from the time he was nine or ten until he left to join the army, how he was beaten in the barn with a strap, how lazy his father had been. He understood that he himself was deprived of the love of his own parents, that Jimmy, too, had been deprived of love, kept from his loving mother by his father. Ed had money now, and what he wanted, and what he thought Sueanne wanted, was the whole family under one roof. He told Jimmy bluntly what he could offer. He would see that Jimmy did not have to work to support his schooling; he would give him an allowance and the use of a car.

In his unfinished basement Ed would build a room for Jimmy. He took Jimmy down past the family room looking out on the large backyards separating the condominiums, then down a narrow wooden stairway. At the bottom of the stairs they had to walk around a brown cardboard wardrobe closet in which Ed had temporarily stored his gun collection. In a corner just beyond the furnace he and Jimmy would build a room together. They would panel the walls with rough, dark brown wood; the low ceiling would be divided evenly by a furnace pipe wrapped thickly with silver insulation. The room would be basic, Ed said, but he pointed out to Jimmy that, at the top of the low ceiling, there was a little window just at ground level looking out the front of the house. They would build the room together.

Jimmy thanked Ed quietly as they made their way back up the stairs. Things to be done in the future were not to be depended on, Jimmy knew. Still, Ed said he would help in any way he could.

Sueanne also offered him things. She was appalled and angered by her son's deprivation; her anger toward Jim's treatment of their son seemed to absolve her of her own responsibility for his situation. "He had very little clothing—it was old and ratty looking—and not a lot of possessions," she said. "The first thing that Ed and I discussed was the fact that he didn't have any clothing, and we went out right away and started buying things. He didn't even have enough underwear."

She did for Jimmy what her mother had done for her. On afternoons after she had fought with her mother, Sueanne would come home to a bed full of new clothes. Now Sueanne would go out and buy Jimmy jewelry and dozens of pairs of slacks, more slacks than he could manage to wear in the season he was given them.

Jimmy had felt bereft, not just of love, but of any emotion he could call his own, any attachment to people or places, bereft even of anger. Yet he understood that if these things he was given were not love, they were signs of love. Certainly they were signs that Sueanne herself required. Sueanne must have felt, he thought, that the money and things Ed gave to her unstintingly were tangible expressions of love. Her possessions seemed always to be signs of something else, for they were given away as easily as they were acquired.

When the invitation to move in came, Jimmy was, his mother

said, "thrilled." The invitation was what he had sought since the wedding. He would be seventeen in May of 1979 and in the fall he would be a senior in high school. He could move out of the small house in Raytown, move out to Overland Park, move into a condominium with a swimming pool, join a family with a dark blue Lincoln Continental, a family that seemed to have unlimited money and resources. He could enroll in a new school, make a new start, perhaps the last new start. Ed had even discussed his going on to college the following year.

Magically his mother had returned, offering him money, a comfortable house in a pleasant neighborhood, and possibilities he could not have imagined a year before. On the day the Hobsons invited him in, he felt as if he had won something against long odds, like a lottery, something that would lift him up, transmute his life of failure lived among failures—the only life he knew since his parents had divorced.

Yet there was his father, who had never told him anything about Sueanne, his father with whom he had slept for months in the double bed in the back bedroom in his uncle Stacy Crumm's house four years before. The only human beings he had never lost touch with were the Sallees and his father.

Jimmy had painful memories of the first nine years he spent with his mother and these memories gave him pause. What he remembered most about his childhood was his desire to please his mother, his failure to do so, and his fear of her. He remembered how well she kept house, how even the toys were to be taken from the shelf one at a time, played with, then placed on the precise shelf from which they were removed. There was to be no rough playing, no wrestling, or running in the house, and, as he grew, finally no playing inside at all. If he would stumble, knock a bowl or glass off a table, nick a wall with a toy, she would scream at him, slap him in the face, and he would cower before her.

In the second grade, when Jimmy was seven, he remembered that his mother became angry for some reason he had long ago forgotten and chased him through the house until she caught him, knocked him down, and kicked him, breaking his arm. There was always tension in the house; that tension was what he feared, but also what he came to desire, or thought he desired.

His father seemed ordinary when compared to the passion his mother displayed in even the minutest things.

"I never knew when Mother left the room whether she would come back in the same way she left it," he recalled.

He was, he thought, denied a childhood where he could fall and err. "She expected me to have the grace of a forty-six-year-old," he thought, "and I never met anyone who could live up to my mother's expectations." He felt unwanted as a child and at times she told him he was unwanted.

He knew she never trusted him. Even when his mother was in the house, she wouldn't let him care for Suzanne. "According to her, I could never be relied on, even for something that little," he said.

Yet she could be spontaneous, unlike his grandfather, Don Sallee; she could be warm and funny and witty. She could give things to him and Suzanne, even give her love and approval, hug them, let them sit on her lap. But for Jimmy there was always the sense that the gift would be taken away. The intensity with which the love was given, the intensity with which it was taken away, wore him down, emptied him.

Jimmy had a similar choice before, almost eight years before. "She said to me, 'Do you want to live with me or your father?' I said, 'I'd rather live with my father.'" Sueanne didn't try to argue with him; she began to gather her things together. She set her bags and Suzanne's bags out in the middle of the living room near the front entrance. His father was crying, pleading with her to stay, down on his knees finally.

"I didn't stay downstairs where she could kiss me," he said. "When she got her things together, I went upstairs to her bedroom to watch her go. I watched her through the window as she left that night. I didn't cry. I heard her go out. I knew she was leaving; I knew I wouldn't see her again; I felt she was gone for good. I saw her go back and forth to the car carrying things and I saw Suzanne and her get in. My father was still downstairs crying. I didn't cry. I just said to myself, ''Bye, Mom. 'Bye, Mom.'"

Jimmy spoke in an orderly way, as if he had narrated the scene to himself many times before, and he repeated twice almost all his short phrases. His life had been irrevocably changed at that moment, determined by his choice. In all those years he still hadn't quite let her go; he was linked to her forever by her leaving, more powerfully drawn to her because she had left so suddenly and so completely. No matter how many times he told himself about her leaving, he still felt guilt for letting her go and helpless to stop her going.

He felt he was always without the emotion he imagined others had. "I grew up lacking emotion and I get tired of it," he said. "I never get angry." He tried to explain his lack of anger by something he had read: "Anger is a secondary emotion."

Despite his clear narrative of her leaving, Jimmy was confused about the event, as if the original confusion and pain had never lifted. He would say, "I never thought of going back to her. I wondered where she was. I didn't want to take the chance of being abandoned again. She left me." He did miss her, he said, but he thought that she did not miss him. Yet still he insisted, "When mother left, a weight was taken off me." Jimmy could never determine what he really felt about her, even seven years later. He was as confused as if he had been abandoned by a cruel lover who returned unaccountably warm and generous.

Sueanne did see Jimmy infrequently for at least a year or so after she left the house. "I guess I saw her a few times when I was still living with my father in the house in Prairie Village. I saw her at her apartment, I think, a year or two after the divorce. Yet seeing her then seemed dreamlike to me."

"We were divorced in 1971," Sueanne said. "I saw him up through '72 at my apartment and at the house in Prairie Village. I saw him at someone else's house, but I can't think of her name. Jim brought him over; sometimes I went over to Jim's house. The only time I can remember now is Suzanne's birthday and Jimmy's birthday, which are three days apart." This was in late May 1972, the first birthdays of Jimmy and Suzanne after the divorce, and it was probably her last meeting with Jimmy for several years.

From 1972 to 1978, Sueanne was not discussed by anyone in the Crumm family. "Nobody talked about her after she left," Jimmy said. "My father never said anything about her. It was like she was thrown down a hole."

5

"I never once said anything bad to Jimmy about his mother," Jim Crumm said. "I felt that this was important, that a kid should not think bad things about any one of his parents. I think I was wrong there. I think he should have been told the truth about a lot of things. The truth should be laid out in front of a kid for him to accept or reject."

Jim felt guilty over what he had not told his son and even more guilty over what he had not seen in his own house, or what he had seen and ignored. "Jimmy has the same delicate build, the same basic features as Sue, but he was very active like me. He was not allowed to go out and play in the dirt like other kids, unless I took him out there myself. Jimmy enjoyed sports. We went through the Boy Scouts; we went through Little League—through basketball, football, soccer. He loved them."

Sueanne had sought to make Jimmy passive, like a girl, Jim said. "Most mothers spend a little bit of time playing with their kids. Sue didn't do this. 'You don't play in the front room,' she'd yell. Jimmy was sent to his room to play by himself. He was active, he wanted to do something. Sue finally badgered the family doctor into agreeing that Jimmy was hyperactive and they put him on medication to slow him down, which I, to this day, think that's a crock of it. Jimmy was no different from the kids that lived down the street."

A few months after Sueanne had divorced Jim and Jimmy was visiting his aunt Dorothy, Dorothy said that Jimmy dropped a glass one day and she came in to make sure nobody had gotten hurt. According to Jim, "Dorothy came walking in there pretty quick, but definitely not mad, and when Jimmy saw her coming in, he cowered down into a corner thinking she was getting ready to hit him. That was a pretty good indication of a hell of a lot of things that were going on when I wasn't there." Yet Jim admitted he never saw Sueanne abuse Jimmy in any way beyond "a reasonable childhood spanking. If she did it, she didn't do it in front of me."

When Jimmy broke his arm in second grade, Sueanne told Jim, "We were going to race from the front room to the bedroom." According to Jim, "She never played with the kids. She wouldn't even allow running in the house. How in the hell is she going to be racing him through the house? 'He tripped and fell into the wall,' she said. Of course I could never prove anything but I don't think that's what happened. Granted, the wall was caved in, but I've got my own feelings on how that wall got caved in."

Sueanne divorced Jim, yet as much as he professed to detest her at the time of the divorce, as much as he did detest her, he still wanted her back and wanted her with him. She left him for dead.

Jim's life disintegrated quickly. "Most of my friends then were bartenders," Jim remembered, "and one of them said that the way he saw it was that I was so happy to be away from her that I had a hard time handling the freedom. After I got fired from being a lineman at Kansas Power and Light, my friends went the whole nine yards. I was broke. The company kept my tools because the credit union had sent them a list of my bad checks and they were holding my property. The foreman just took the tools out of my locker and put them in my trunk. Then I went over to the bar and the owner slipped me fifty bucks. I learned I couldn't survive without friends. And my brother Stacy helped a lot; he was my best friend through all this."

Jim and his son lived in the house in Prairie Village for six months or so after the divorce, but Jim couldn't handle the divorce and the drinking. He decided to move out of the house and into a small apartment. "One evening before I moved out, I had a talk with Jimmy. I told him that he was going to live with his aunt for a while, that there were some financial problems, and I was going to be doing a lot of traveling. I wasn't doing that much traveling, but it was something to tell him. I knew my sister Dorothy could take care of him. He had known my sister for a long time. They had always been close and she had a strong affection toward him, and he had a strong affection toward her, and I knew she would take real good care of him."

Jim had brought two suitcases to Dorothy's filled with what clothes and possessions Jimmy had. "When I got over there that night, Jimmy was upset, clinging to me," he said. "He was nine, you know. He didn't want me to leave; I mean he was upset that I was going to leave him there. I stayed there late that evening until he was asleep. I virtually dumped him."

"Jimmy lived with Dorothy approximately two years. I would go over to see him on weekends and have him over to the little apartment that I had at the time. I tried to see him every weekend, but there were a few weekends that I missed. Occasionally I did get by during the week, but I couldn't always get over there—or I didn't always get over there—like I should have."

Dorothy Reffitt accepted the responsibility for Jimmy easily; she liked him and she liked her brother. A blocky, square-faced, quiet woman, she saw herself as an ordinary housewife. "My brother had a really rough time after the divorce from Sue," she said. "Jim did some heavy drinking and Jimmy needed someone, and we all loved him, and he came, and I have four children, and we shipped him right in. He shared a room with my boy David, who's a couple of years older than he is, and he went to school with my kids. He was just like a son to us."

Sueanne never came to her home in the two years Jimmy was there. Dorothy said Sueanne never saw Jimmy at all, "Not birthdays, Christmas, nothing. We didn't get a phone call, a birthday card, or anything, except one time after Jimmy had been with us probably six months, she called me. I don't remember why."

In the summer of 1974, after Jimmy had spent two years at Dorothy's, Jim's brother Stacy took Jim aside and told him he should think hard about the irresponsible way he was living. "I had a long talk with my brother Stacy," Jim said. "He told me that it was time that I got my head back on straight and that they had an extra bedroom there that Jimmy and I could move into until we got back on our feet. I kind of decided that I should be raising Jimmy, take him back with me. We moved in with my mother for the summer and then, when school got ready to start, we moved in with Stacy and his wife, Jackie, and their two girls." Jim and his son had the whole basement and shared a bedroom in it for a year.

"In the fall of 1975 I remarried, and then we moved into a duplex in Raytown," he said. "Mary, her daughter Anna, Jimmy, and I moved into a house in 1976. Jimmy got along all right with his stepmother at first, then I took a job that required a lot of traveling and this caused them some problems, so at the last they didn't get along very good."

Jimmy's stepmother, Mary, was fifteen years younger than his father. In her early twenties when they married, she had a six-year-old girl, Anna, whom Jim soon adopted as his own. Mary was brought up around girls and knew little about boys, Jimmy said. Mary's supervision was much stricter than Jimmy had been accustomed to in the years he had moved from house to house after the divorce.

The boy was an extremely poor student. His grades in Raytown South Junior High and Raytown High were generally "failure" or "inferior" and, if anything, they got a little worse as he grew older. Yet even in the eleventh grade, his final year at Raytown, his performance on standardized national tests was above average.

Certainly motivation was a problem. No one had taken any consistent interest in Jimmy from the age of nine until seventeen and he felt unloved and unwanted and unattached. There were other reasons. Some of his difficulties in school were caused by his use of alcohol and other drugs. Jimmy was drinking hard liquor at nine or ten years of age and he started to use drugs at ten or eleven. He mainly used marijuana at first, though by sixteen, when he met his mother and sister again, he was regularly taking "hallucinogens, downers, and speed."

Despite drugs, throughout his early teenage years he played soccer and baseball on the school teams. He also became a good photographer and he was working toward becoming an Eagle Scout.

The Sallees, Jimmy said, "stepped in to fill the void when I was living with my aunts and uncles. They gave me a lot of things, saw that I had clothes, new shoes, new equipment. I saw them once every other week or so and on Christmas and birthdays through the whole time I was separated from my mother." The only place Jimmy could get in touch with his mother's side of the family was at the Sallee home. Ruth Sallee became his main confidante. Sometimes when his grandfather was in the basement in his woodworking shop, he and his grandmother would talk about his early life with his mother.

Jimmy's only experience with middle-class life was with his grandparents. At the Sallees' home it was possible to have aspirations. Jimmy admired Don Sallee and the successful life he had made for himself as a draftsman at Marley, and he wanted to become a draftsman like his grandfather.

6

In April Jimmy told his father of Ed and Sueanne's invitation to move into the condominium. He didn't mention that Ed was already considering adopting him because he didn't want to hurt his father. Still, despite his desire to live with his mother, Jimmy was saddened by how easily his father let him go to her.

Jim had reasons for letting him go. Jimmy was a disruptive force in the household, a constant source of tension between him and his wife, Mary. The new life he was setting up with Mary and his newly adopted daughter might not survive if Jimmy remained. He was now a traveling salesman selling tree-trimming equipment to industrial users and utility companies. In the weeks he was gone Mary had trouble handling Jimmy. "Besides, the Hobsons offered the moon to him," he said. The boy would get a better school, get a pool, a car, his sister, his mother. Jim had nothing comparable to offer.

"Jimmy and I had a talk one evening down in the recreation room, I guess the day before he was to move out," Jim said. "He was nervous and excited. There were things that had been promised to him, you know. I think anybody would have been excited about moving to Overland Park and the idea of reestablishing contact with his mother." It was the third of May and spring was at its height. Jim spoke quietly and gravely to his son that night, but he did not have a clear purpose in speaking.

Jimmy was dejected after the conversation. Yet he had really decided at the wedding six months before what he was going to do if the chance came. "Dad wasn't real happy," Jimmy recalled, "but he said it was my decision."

He was abandoning his father as his father had abandoned him seven years before on the night Jim had left him at Aunt

Dorothy's. He was evening out an old score.

"Once Jimmy was out the door, it was probably two or three months before he came back by. We lost touch for a while there," Jim said casually.

Sometimes that summer Jimmy would drive his mother's Lincoln Continental slowly past his father's house, always planning to stop and go in, but he did not go in and he did not stop. "I walked out on him, betrayed him," Jimmy said. But without consulting anyone, he immediately and silently took the surname Hobson; he would be known as Jimmy Hobson from this day forward, in his new life across the state line in Johnson County, Kansas.

Even on the night before Jimmy's departure when he spoke to his son, Jim had withheld a passionate attack on Sueanne. The attack would have been an embarrassing admission of his own weakness and he didn't have the courage to expose himself before his son. Sueanne had gotten a power over Jim that nearly destroyed him. "Sue had an ability to manipulate people," he said. "She controlled you. You've got good examples with me and with Jimmy and with Suzanne and Ed Hobson. You've got four good examples right there that she pulled the strings on. She played the tune and you danced.

"I can't put my finger on it really," Jim said in frustration. "The last thing in the world it would be is sexual control. It wasn't as simple as saying, 'Well, if you do this, then you don't get any.' It wasn't that simple. That was not the way she controlled you.

"She had a purpose for everybody—even if she would meet you at a party or wherever," Jim said. "And it's something about her, it's a gift. Maybe that's hard to swallow, but she had the ability to place you into a role, and once she got what she wanted from you, whether it was money, whether it was a gift, whether it was, maybe, a fling in bed, or whatever it was, she didn't need you anymore; you were no good.

"It doesn't take her long," he said. "When she goes after something, don't get in her way or she'll walk right over you to get what she's after."

Jim suspected Sueanne of abusing his son before they were

divorced, yet he let the boy go back to his mother to start a new life. And Jimmy knew well what his mother had done secretly to him in their house in Prairie Village, yet he happily chose to go to her. He remembered that old life well; like a convict, he had for years nothing to do but remember. Time stopped when Sueanne left.

If Jimmy had not met his mother's expectations at nine, perhaps now, at seventeen, he could do so. She seemed to care and to care intensely; she had given him new purpose and energy that spring. This time he would do it until he got it right. The bad mother whom he feared had suddenly appeared to rescue him, only now she was good and rich.

Jimmy could see that Suzanne loved her mother and had gotten along well with her. Suzanne could help him and he, in turn, could be the protective older brother she had long sought, a male on whom she could rely.

7

When Jimmy first moved into his mother's house on Friday, the fourth of May, 1979, he felt as if he were a visitor who had to be on his best behavior. Ed gave him a car to drive back and forth to Raytown High School so that he could complete the last three or four weeks of school. Ed and Sueanne had been married almost exactly five months.

Jimmy looked on the Hobson family as if he were a stranger. He had plenty of practice as an outsider, living so much in other people's homes, and he felt he had become a sharp observer of others. "I was happy at first," Jimmy said. "When I moved in, it seemed pretty much picture perfect, so to speak. Everybody was happy. Of course there was a lot of newness at the time; they were still getting used to each other.

"At first I thought mother had mellowed out," Jimmy said. She had told him of her years of counseling with Dr. Craft and how effective he had been in increasing her patience, her self-control. She was, he saw, less demanding, less angry. She was now able at times to be funny, even to be spontaneous on occasion; she

seemed reasonable and stable and strong. Her skills at getting her
way, Jimmy thought, "were more refined, more subtle."

Jimmy had never been very assertive; rather, he had a desire
to please the people he found himself around. Immediately
Sueanne began to teach him manners, to show him that he
could be graceful. In some ways that was easy. He had always
been very clean and neat in his appearance and he held himself
aloof from those around him; he was a handsome boy with dark
eyes and a sensitive, vulnerable face. He watched the faces of
others closely as if he remembered beatings. His mother would,
he hoped, make him a gentleman, for he was acutely conscious of
class; having fallen with his father, he sought to rise with her.

Sueanne seemed to be making up for the years she had abandoned Jimmy. She was generous to him, pressing things upon
him. He did not ask for clothes or spending money or jewelry:
these came without his asking, and if he asked, they would not
have come.

Ed liked Jimmy and Jimmy liked him. Ed was the peacemaker
in the house, the one who negotiated minor disputes. Before
long he began again to discuss more thoroughly with Jimmy his
plans to adopt him, to bring the whole family together. Ed saw
Jimmy's father through Sueanne's eyes, saw him as an abuser of
his wife and her child, and he wanted to help Jimmy escape
from his control.

Jimmy was made uncomfortable by Ed's directness and persistence in seeking to adopt him. He was made uncomfortable by
any demonstration of affection or devotion. Characteristically,
Jimmy would say neither yes nor no to Ed's offer to adopt him,
and he avoided any commitment.

Unlike his own father, Jimmy saw that Ed worked hard; work
was really his main recreation. He was a tough man, a man's
man. To Jimmy, Ed was a simple man who thought he was the
breadwinner and who wanted Sueanne to be the homemaker.

Jimmy felt closest to Suzanne, but he understood little about
her plans. Suzanne's invitation to Jimmy had changed the
dynamics of the family and she knew it. She was more pleased
than anyone in the house, for she felt that she was most responsible for Jimmy's being there. She had taken a chance, called him,

and things had worked out well. Jimmy had a grace and an aloofness she mistook for sophistication.

By comparison to Jimmy, her stepbrother, Chris, was immature and crude, blond and unfinished looking—like Ed. Right away she used Jimmy to keep Chris in his place. To intimidate her stepbrother, she told him about Jimmy's rough life, about the drugs he had taken, about his attitude toward school. She made clear to Chris that she would use her older brother to protect herself against him if he angered her. Suzanne saw Jimmy as a force to threaten Chris, to control him.

For Chris, Jimmy immediately became a threat down under him in the basement, one that Ed couldn't control. Yet Jimmy scarcely knew Chris at all and their paths rarely crossed, or crossed no more than they had for the last six months when Jimmy was living in Raytown. Their rooms were set at opposite floors of the house, Chris's at the top, across from the master bedroom and down the hall from Suzanne's, Jimmy's at the bottom, two stories below.

If Suzanne and Chris could affect little what their parents had done, at least they could vent their anger at each other and display what power they had. But now Suzanne's power was dramatically increased by her alliance with Jimmy.

At first Jimmy thought little about Chris. "Ed and Chris had a pretty good relationship," Jimmy said. "They seemed to try to get along well with each other. They had differences, as everybody will. They did things together around the house—games and stuff—and went hunting. The relationship between Chris and Suzanne was pretty common for two kids being close to the same age, attending the same school. They had their arguments, but they got along usually. They'd play together sometimes; they'd skate together. I was gone most of the time and I'd see Chris only occasionally throughout the day, so we never had a whole lot of time for activities together. I didn't dislike Chris; it would be more like than dislike.

"In May it seemed Chris and Mother were getting along pretty well. Within a month or two after I moved in, I started noticing peculiar things happening around the house. It became apparent to me there was a lot more tension between them than what I had first observed. They tended to avoid each other. That was pretty much it. That was about the first thing I noticed. Mother was kind of two-faced about it. She would be real nice and motherly toward him when Ed was around and when Ed wasn't around she acted like Chris wasn't there."

In July, two months after Jimmy had entered the house, the Hobson family took a three-day trip to Silver Dollar City in the Missouri Ozarks in the southwest corner of the state. The resort was on the edge of the man-made Table Rock Lake and was located on the site of an 1880 Ozark mining village. In high summer there were tours of caves and boat rides and there were women making dolls or quilting or curing meat. In the nearby restaurants in the late evening, the waitresses and waiters, gingham girls and plaid-shirted men, danced wildly and sang and mimed songs about chopping wood, bouncing dangerously near the customers' tables. The Hobson family all sat together in a line on one side of the table watching the performance. Jimmy had not been on a family vacation since Sueanne had left his father.

Chris was not there. "We sent Chris to a YMCA summer camp," Ed explained. "This was something you had to pay for in advance and everything. The times were already set for him to go to summer camp and I still didn't know whether I was going to get my vacation because I wasn't high enough on the seniority list."

Jimmy had a different view of why Chris wasn't there. His mother took him aside one afternoon in Silver Dollar City and "she said that she thought it was very nice and peaceful since Chris was not there with us."

He nodded agreement with her. "I would always say yes to whatever Mom said."

By midsummer Jimmy was not only driving Chris to Dr. Craft for individual counseling, but had a standing invitation to go to the weekly family sessions himself. Jimmy was very uncomfortable about going. He had never been to any counseling sessions before and it seemed something you learned to do, like tipping a waiter or waterskiing or speaking in public, and he felt he could not learn the skills the others had acquired. New things always seemed difficult for him.

When Jimmy did go, he was surprised. "Nobody in the family seemed to know anything about anybody else; nobody even looked at anybody else," he said. "Mom and Dr. Craft took charge. Chris would dump on his past life, and he told things against Ed. Chris was also upset about Mom. Mom spoke only to put down Chris.

"I sat quietly, hiding tears about my own life and my own problems. I wasn't about to open my mouth after seeing how Mom would attack Chris. Mom is a very intelligent, precise, domineering person. She takes control of whatever situation she is in." Jimmy found excuses not to go to counseling again; he didn't ever say directly that he wouldn't go, but he never attended another session.

Ed used to tell his coworkers at the mill, "Chris is afraid of the dark. He is a pussy! A pussy!" Chris was too clinging, too unassertive for Ed, though Ed knew he had protected the boy too much, especially during his long illness in early childhood. Yet from birth, Chris's life was filled with family conflict and he always showed daring and courage in family disputes that he never showed outside them.

In the counseling sessions Ed became the instrument both Chris and Sueanne sought to put to their own uses. Sueanne had learned as a child in the Sallee family that there was no middle ground between control and submission and now, in her new family, she sought control. The only one who defied her was Chris.

Chris did not so much desire to control Sueanne as to keep control of what he already had. He wanted to protect his relationship with Ed, the only stable point in his life.

As the year wore on, the counseling didn't seem to help the relationship between Chris and Sueanne. During his childhood Chris had learned to live through a crisis every few days; he had learned to live through Shirley's rages. Chris seemed to think he was back in his mother's house where Shirley, dying slowly, would turn a loaded .38 pistol on him and Ed and threaten to kill both of them, though of course she never pulled the trigger.

Chris misread Sueanne badly, mistook her anger and fear for Shirley's. He would not yield in all the small ways she demanded, despite the counseling, and he seemed set on enraging her.

"It was difficult to accept that I was afraid of my own children," Sueanne said later. "Good mothers aren't afraid of their own children."

At Ed's insistence Sueanne quit working so that she could help the family, in her phrase, "to meld." She wanted to melt them down, to weld them together, and she accepted the responsibility for doing this; it weighed heavily on her. Sueanne had always sought to limit her responsibilities severely because she took them very seriously. For the first time in many years she had a family, and now she must devote all her time and her great energy to it.

Chris wasn't the only child giving her problems that summer; Jimmy had problems, too. The first problem was Jimmy's thieving. He had gotten a summer job at the Oak Park Mall as a salesclerk for a department store, Stix, Baer, and Fuller, and was fired after only three weeks.

"I had stolen a little bit of money," Jimmy said, "somewhere between twenty and fifty dollars. It was slow down there in the area I worked and I'd play with the computer and I rang up a bunch of false sales. I never got anything from them. There was no money going in, so there was no money to take out. Mom and Ed were real upset."

"Evidently," Ed said concisely, "Jimmy had been lifting five or ten dollars out of the till each night that he worked, and they set a trap for him with marked money and caught him."

"One midnight we were awakened by two women," Sueanne said. "I thought they were Jimmy's girlfriends. We had girls coming by all the time, and I hollered out the window that Jimmy wasn't home and that I didn't appreciate them being there. When I went downstairs and opened the door, I found these two girls were detectives from the store. We had to pay Stix three hundred dollars for the money Jimmy stole." Stix did not prosecute and the Overland Park police were never called.

Once in the late summer of 1979 and once in the fall, Ed and Sueanne found drugs in Jimmy's room. "We caught Jimmy in several lies and there was times he was not acting normal," Ed said. "I searched his room. When we found stuff the first time, he told me he was keeping it for another kid. We had him write down the name of the kid and we said we would call him. And then he owned up to it and said it was his and we grounded him, took the car away from him for two weeks. The next time we found drugs, it was approximately the same thing. I got a pack of lies about five feet long before I could wade through to the truth. After I found stuff the first time, I searched quite frequently."

Sueanne recalled that Ed had found both marijuana and cocaine and that Jimmy had admitted using "pot, cocaine, uppers, and downers."

One afternoon Ed and Sueanne called Detective Darrell Urban, a juvenile detective, to go through Jimmy's room with them. Sueanne and Ed said they suspected their boy of using drugs and they needed his help. Urban, an experienced, wiry detective, well over fifty, went through Jimmy's room with them. They'd ask him where a boy would put his drugs and Urban would say, "Your guess is as good as mine. It ain't gonna be in plain sight," and he'd poke around at the top of the foil-covered furnace pipe dividing the ceiling of the basement room. Urban was a little puzzled because he didn't know what they wanted of him, maybe just someone to dump their troubles on. Finally he found a pipe that had the ashes of some substance in it and they wanted him to take it down to the station and have it analyzed. He told them it wasn't worth bothering with; since he had been hunting around with them, any evidence he found couldn't be used in court anyway because he had no warrant.

When they came back upstairs, they all sat at the glass-topped table in the kitchen. Ed and Sueanne sat at opposite ends of the table; Chris, who had come down from upstairs, sat in the middle, directly across from Urban. While Ed and Sueanne asked about drugs and droned on about what they could do with Jimmy, Urban watched Chris out of boredom. Juveniles were what he knew best and cared most about; besides, he liked to watch people who weren't watching him, in fact he made a habit of it in his business.

Chris kept his hands under the glass tabletop; when Urban spoke, the boy's hands were still, but when Sueanne or Ed spoke, his thumbs would steadily wind around each other, like the parts of a fishing reel. "Chris didn't seem at all interested in me,"

Urban said. "He was reeling in what we said for future use against Jimmy, or whoever, when the time came. Chris seemed like a conniver to me, the kind of kid who'd run off with any information he got and tell one bit to his mother and another to his father and something else to Jimmy. A conniver," he said, looking as if he were tasting something bad.

Urban was more impressed with Sueanne than with anyone else in the house. "She was a good-looking woman. She looked like she just stepped out of some magazine, she was groomed so well. Anyway, I just thought they were concerned parents, or maybe overly concerned parents. I told them to give me a call if they found any dope." They seemed naive to Urban and he couldn't understand what they expected him to do.

8

In the fall when Jimmy started his senior year at Shawnee Mission South High School, just a half mile straight down the street from where the Hobsons lived, he had hopes of performing well. In the spring of 1979 Jimmy had come to apply for entry to the school under the name of Crumm. In the fall, under the name of Hobson, he spoke with counselor Gerald Colwell in a large, pleasant room with yellow, concrete-block walls and a broad north window looking back toward the residential area of Overland Park. Colwell, a calm, lean, orderly man with a large, square, well-groomed face, was the counselor of the H's and he remembered Jimmy Hobson fairly well. The passion of others seemed to escape Colwell; a math major, he had quite logically chosen the role of counselor because counselors received summer pay. He did not become involved in the lives and passions of students easily.

"When I first saw Jimmy," Colwell said, "he dressed very nicely, kept himself very neat, a clean-cut, good-looking kid, very well mannered. He was courteous and very cooperative; he knew how to act. He either wasn't relaxed, though, or he couldn't be himself; he seemed to say what he thought I wanted to hear him say. I liked him and he seemed to like me."

Jimmy intended to graduate that academic year, with his age peers. The Ds and Fs he had accumulated at Raytown left him with no alternative except to take a heavy load of classes in the day and to make up in night school the courses he had failed.

Colwell met Sueanne for the first time in September and she made a powerful impression on him. In the fall of 1979 Colwell saw her more than any other parent. "Mrs. Hobson was a very attractive, smooth, well-dressed person," he said. "She was dressed beautifully and just looked fantastic. Very prosperous looking, too.

"In my conference with her and Jimmy after he had skipped a class, she really raised hell with Jimmy. For a parent to come in and raise so much hell about skipping one class—that is uncommon. Right there in the conference room, she'd angrily order her son to do things; she'd say, 'You're going to do that, Jimmy, that is the way it's going to be done!' I just don't see a parent doing that with a child of Jimmy's age. I'd say, 'I think you should back off of your son'—because he had not lived with her that long and she wanted everything instantaneously. She wanted him to be an excellent student and a perfect kid, and I said, 'Hey, it's going to take some time for this to happen.' She was putting way too much pressure on her son to become a perfect gentleman, and fantastic in school, and to change just like that. Jimmy wasn't given a chance to say much. It was mainly Mrs. Hobson and myself talking. He just kind of sat there. At the end I tried to give him a chance to say something, but he didn't."

Sueanne began to call Colwell almost daily as Jimmy's attendance and success declined. "She was trying to be a good mother and trying to help Jimmy be a fine young man, trying to get her son turned around," Colwell said. "She was so concerned about being a good parent to him after all those years without him that maybe she thought she had to do triple duty to turn him around. She was becoming impatient because he wasn't doing exactly what she wanted him to do and she wanted him to be the perfect student. For a parent to continually bug me all the time and come up and be so demanding about things—I don't know that I have ever seen a parent be like that in the fifteen years that I have been counseling, to come on so strong and hard. She wanted him to change just like that. She seemed like such a nice-looking person, but she came across so strong and so harsh; she seemed so hardened about it."

"School was important to her," Jimmy said. "She was always interested in the community, in how things looked to others." She had her will set on seeing that Jimmy graduated, had her will set on promptly and thoroughly cleaning up the mess he had made of his formal education.

"She was on me all the time," he said. "It was the same old shit as it had been when I was a little child living with her and my father. When Mother would ground me for life, take away the car and everything else, Ed would bring her around in a few days to let me out again." Despite Jimmy's petty theft and his trouble with drugs, Ed still trusted him, even confided in him.

9

Sometimes Ed and Sueanne would withdraw to their bedroom soon after supper for an hour or two and close the door. Once Jimmy came up the half-stairs to the master bedroom and knocked on the door. Sueanne came out immediately, closed the door behind her, and said that he could not come in, that this room was for private talks. Some evenings Ed would come down from the bedroom at nine or ten o'clock and ask Jimmy to go outside for a walk with him.

One fall evening Ed was angry and could scarcely speak for a mile or two as they walked fast through the paths in the woods. Sueanne had told him that they should send Chris to military school, in fact had insisted they send him. "Ed bitched and ranted and raved," Jimmy said.

"She threatened to divorce me if I don't agree," Ed said to Jimmy. "I'm not about to be separated from that boy. We've been through a lot together. She's got to be patient, goddamn it! She's got to be patient with him!" Ed saw nothing abnormal in the boy's behavior, nothing that warranted sending him away.

As usual Ed reacted not acted. He had to be told what to do or be caught in a corner before he'd do anything. He denied the validity of Sueanne's anger against Chris, denied he was too permissive with his son. He was puzzled by Sueanne's anger, by her complaints; they seemed trivial to him, normal things for a boy to do. Sueanne had a long list: Chris fought with Suzanne; Chris deliberately stuffed up the toilet so that the water ran out of the upstairs bathroom and onto the rug; Chris ate like a glutton; Chris embarrassed her by acting like a three-year-old in public and she refused to be seen with him. Chris needed the discipline of a military school and he needed it now, she insisted.

"Why can't she give him time to adjust?" Ed would ask Jimmy. "Was she always like this?"

Though Jimmy knew well her impatience, he thought he knew even less about her character than Ed did. To Jimmy also her passionate attacks on Chris seemed disproportionate to the cause. "She goes off on little things now, just the way she did when she was married to my father," he thought.

"Chris and I had lived completely different than Sueanne and Suzanne did," Ed said. "It's like taking a queen and putting her with a pauper. You've got to make some compromises someplace on both sides to make it work." He appreciated the difficulty of bringing the two families together, but his tolerance for family conflict was high. Based on his first family experience on the farm and his second with Shirley, he thought everybody was getting along well enough, even making progress.

Despite his quick temper he counseled patience. This was an ordinary family, he felt, or at least an ordinary family with stepchildren. Sueanne was making a family, putting together a family. It was difficult, but this was what Ed had wanted all his life. This was the best time in his life and in Chris's life. Ed saw progress in Chris's schoolwork and his behavior; even if Sueanne did not yet see it, he saw it, and Chris's teachers saw it.

Even though Ed was in fact the territory Chris and Sueanne were fighting over, Ed felt peculiarly immune to the conflict. In the months since his marriage, Ed imagined he was in charge of a family for the first time in his life. He had sold some of his farmland to provide for its needs. It was off his father's land they really lived now, eating it, drinking it, and wearing it.

Sueanne had lost her patience with Chris and knew it; she

told her friends of her frustration with him and asked them repeatedly for advice. To Beth Clarkson she would say how Chris tormented her, how she couldn't bear to be around him. Beth, outwardly less patient even than Sueanne, would counsel patience. "You've been married less than a year," she'd say. "You can't solve everybody's problems all at once."

Norma Hooker, drawing on her own experience with her children and her stepchildren, would say, "Look, Sueanne, Chris is twelve, almost thirteen. In five years he'll be out of the house for good. Take the long view. You and Ed will have the rest of your lives together. Don't force Ed and Chris to leave. Wait Chris out."

Ernestine Bean, who had brought three children from a prior marriage into her present one, told Sueanne, "Children test you, push you. Chris is a normal kid, but he'll drive you up the wall. Any parents who haven't felt like strangling their kids aren't normal parents."

Sueanne would complain almost daily to Margie Hunt-Fugate about her anger toward Chris. Margie would listen without instructing her and she never took the matter seriously.

But Sueanne had no intention of giving in to Chris, of waiting five years; she was a Leo with a strong Virgo shadow and she could not bear messes. If Ed would not send him away to a military school, if her friends had no suggestions other than tolerance and patience, she would try other ways to get rid of him. She had already tried counseling and cross adoption, and nothing had been done, nothing changed. In fact Chris became more insolent, more intolerable. She had come to fear him.

She told Jimmy she had again sought the help of Dr. Craft and had Chris diagnosed by a psychiatrist. "Mother told me Chris was 'a primate schizoid with suicidal and homicidal tendencies,'" Jimmy said. She told Jimmy that Chris was as disturbed as his mother, Shirley, that he needed to be committed to a hospital, to be committed the way Shirley had once been committed. She said she wanted him kept in Osawatomie State Hospital, thirty miles south of Overland Park down in Miami County.

Sueanne also told her friend Margie about her need to get

Chris out of the house; they talked one afternoon in Sueanne's condominium. "She said that he was a problem," Margie recalled, "that he'd been causing a lot of problems between her and Ed and that she couldn't put up with that anymore. Sueanne said Chris had been determined to be 'an extremely violent primate schizoid.' He wasn't mentally right. It had been determined that he should be put away, that he shouldn't be left in the home atmosphere, that for his own good, he needed to be put in an institution."

Whether Sueanne told Ed what she told Jimmy and Margie is not clear. At that time, though, in November 1979, Ed did make a decision and all family counseling stopped at once.

Powerless before the alliance of Ed and Chris, Sueanne felt helpless and frightened by her impotence. Chris had become her scapegoat, the reason that the family had not melded, the focus of her fears about her future and their future.

She did have advantages she had not fully used. Jimmy allied himself with his sister and his mother and sometimes he would talk to Chris about his behavior. He would reprimand Chris, carry to him the message that Sueanne herself was unable to deliver except in shouts and gestures at moments when she could not fully control herself or her anger.

Still, Chris would not yield to Sueanne; Ed protected him against any force Sueanne could use. Jimmy was now a force that she could control, a force down there in the small room in the basement, far from Chris at the top of the house, but available, for the change in his life that Jimmy sought depended wholly on her.

By late fall Sueanne's view that Chris was emotionally disturbed became a view held by her and her alone. Chris had been placed in Lee Shank's special education room at Indian Creek Junior High. Mrs. Shank was middle-aged, with bright dyed-blond hair and a short, plump body. At rest she seemed to be quite ordinary; in her work she was creative and energetic. Within days of Chris's arrival, Mrs. Shank diagnosed his problem and set him to work to correct it. Unlike what others had said, Chris had no dyslexia, no learning disabilities. Rather, he had emotional problems, a sense of guilt over his mother's long agony and over Tani's death. She talked with him about these problems, but she saw to it that he did his work, made clear to him that his troubled life did not excuse him from classwork. He began each day in her class, but his main work was done in regular classes and she checked to be sure it was done. Once, when Chris got into a fight in gym, he wanted to talk about nothing else for several days; she would not hear him out. She told him that no provocation was sufficient for violence and she put him to work. She would not discuss the incident at all.

By November Chris's schoolwork had improved dramatically. He had never before learned to study, but he did study for Lee Shank, and in a few months his grades had been raised from C's to A's and B's.

Chris seemed ignorant of the degree of hostility Sueanne had toward him. Apparently he had not understood it, had not taken it seriously. Sueanne yelled at him when he didn't do what he was told to do, or she'd grit her teeth, or smoke, or go up to her bedroom and seclude herself. Sueanne certainly frightened him, but she, angry as she was, paled beside his nightmares of the dying Shirley, whom he loved and feared.

"Does Mom like me?" Chris asked Jimmy one day in November.

"I said, 'I think so, yeah, I would imagine so,'" Jimmy recalled. "I didn't want to hurt his feelings because I wasn't for sure. I didn't think she liked him from the way she had talked about him to me. So, instead of hurting his feelings, I thought I'd just go ahead and tell him that." Chris seemed to confide in Jimmy, to trust Jimmy, a trust that he never quite lost.

Sueanne had managed to isolate Chris and Ed, to encapsulate the two the way an insect might. There were two groups in the family now, those of her blood and those of Ed's. Sueanne and Jimmy reported to Sueanne, Chris to Ed. Sueanne negotiated with Ed; Chris was beyond negotiations. Ed never really grasped that, nor did Chris.

Despite her feelings about Chris, Sueanne loved Ed. If she had not loved him, there would have been no great conflict in her marriage. True, she had married him for money. She had told the Hookers years before she met Ed that she would marry the second time, if she married at all, for money. Now his money was already as good as hers, but the money had become a sign of his love; she understood it as a sign and it enabled her to love him. She had come to love him. Curled up on his lap, leaning against his golden, hard body, she felt protected by him as she had never been by her father.

Chris knew he had escaped Sueanne's control, yet he was uncertain how she would next try to drag him down. He feared her and he threatened her. He had a contempt for her that he displayed as often as he dared. If she could not love him, at least he would get her attention.

Chris needed a woman's love and Norma Hooker, who saw him regularly at Skateland, gave him what she could of hers. To her and to her husband, Jim, he was "a sweet little boy. He'd do anything for you; he'd give you the shirt off his back." She knew Sueanne's frustration, her aggravation; she knew how irritating a twelve-year-old boy could be, let alone one thrown into a new family with a beautiful girl his own age. The Hookers felt they were closer to Chris than Sueanne was. "Once we took him with us to my parents' house in western Kansas," Norma said. "We thought it would give Ed and Sueanne some time, take him off their hands for a few days. My parents fell in love with him."

At Skateland the Hookers sometimes hired Jimmy and Chris, along with five or six other boys, to sell things and change records and clean up during and after skating parties. When he worked, Chris always wore a whistle around his neck, and when school acquaintances came up to talk to him, he would say extravagantly, with a wide gesture of his arms, "This is my world." Chris felt relaxed and in charge at Skateland.

Suzanne spent time at Skateland, too, though sometimes she and Chris would be dropped off at the rink and Chris would go on in to skate while she would go off with others in a car waiting for her. She would go out with her friends, then get back just in time to stand in front of the heavy steel door waiting to be picked up again.

To Chris, Suzanne seemed an extension of Sueanne and her values. Now thirteen and a half, Suzanne had a certain beauty, a kind of adolescent tightness with her small breasts just letting out from her lean body. She dressed well, with the style and richness of Sueanne, but with the rainbow colors of youth, not just in black and white. In a photograph or at a distance, with her mouth closed over her braces, she looked twenty, confident and elegant, and she ran with a rich crowd, "the snobs," as Norma called them. She no longer associated with the Hookers' daughter, Tammy, whose dark heaviness and lack of polish made Suzanne and her friends turn from her.

Chris envied Suzanne's finished appearance and the girls around her. Though he was only four months younger than she, he was rough, unfinished, still a boy riding bicycles in the long paths of the park and playing in the water down in the deep ditches of Indian Creek, with great elms and cottonwoods growing thickly along its banks.

He found out almost by chance how much status, the community view of Sueanne and of her family, meant to his stepmother. "Suzanne ran Chris down at Skateland before his friends," Jimmy said. "He wanted to get even, so he told his friends that Suzanne was taking her clothes off in the dark aisles at Skateland, that Suzanne was the easiest lay in town." Also, months earlier Chris had said that "Suzanne drank when her mother was out, that she was an alcoholic," and according to Jimmy, he repeated the charge periodically.

Sueanne met the rumors with rage and quickly traced them back to Chris. Chris, of course, wanted the credit for them, wanted his stepmother and his stepsister to know that it was tit for tat. One night Sueanne called Norma and told her that Ed and Chris were coming over to apologize. When they came over, both were upset, both somewhat angry at Sueanne, but Chris did apologize.

The Hookers were never clear about what Chris was apologizing for that night and they paid little attention to it. Norma herself blamed most of the problems on Suzanne, whom she didn't like at all. "Sometimes she'd say how she was going to get Chris in trouble on a given evening, and she did," Norma recalled. Chris, on the other hand, had a kind of invulnerable innocence about him, a gullibility that seemed to Norma charming.

Ed would condemn Chris, sometimes restrict him to the

house for what he would say to or about Suzanne. Yet he saw the rumors as the consequence of normal antagonisms, petty adolescent fights over territory. "Chris and Suzanne got along like my sister and I did when we were growing up," Ed said. "That's the only way I know how to explain it. You know, oh, they had their big squabbles and their little squabbles, and the real bad problems were when Chris would get one of Suzanne's records and it would get scratched or Suzanne would borrow Chris's baseball glove, and it would get dirty, or they would borrow each other's tennis racquets without asking. At twelve and thirteen years of age, these are major disasters. That's just the way children are. They'd be bickering back and forth, and a few minutes later we'd be sitting at the kitchen table drinking coffee and they'd be outside in the back of the house throwing a football back and forth or playing tag or hide-and-go-seek. They'd gripe about cleaning the bathrooms. 'Well, he'd messed it up; she'd messed it up.'

"Suzanne was a lot like her mother. Clothes had to be hung up in the closet just so, to keep from being wrinkled, and she was real prissy about the bathroom, and Chris would clean the bathroom—he's just a little sloppier. These are the natural disasters that our family had between the children. This is what stopped the clock, you know."

Jimmy also saw the relationship between Chris and Suzanne as "a pretty common one for two kids being close to the same age, attending the same school. They pretty much hung around the same sort of places. They had their arguments and stuff, but they got along usually." Suzanne had talked with Jimmy about her problems, "about the normal stuff of them having arguments, and then little ways they got back at each other."

Jimmy, urged on by his mother, spoke with Chris about the problems, but these were "not strong talks. I just asked him what the thing was between him and Suzanne, what was his side of the story. There wasn't much I could say to him really. He was, at first, scared. And then he realized I wasn't going to jump all over him." After Jimmy talked with Chris, the rumors about Suzanne stopped for a month or two, then began again.

Suzanne viewed the bickering almost as seriously as her mother did. "When Chris and I got in fights," Suzanne said, "we'd go tell our parents and then they'd talk about it. Sometimes they got in an argument, sometimes they didn't. Chris and I got in fights; the fights may not seem a big deal, but to somebody my age and Chris's age, when we got in a fight, it was a big deal. We'd yell and scream at each other and we'd end up going and telling our parents. When Chris had spread rumors about me to my friends that I had done bad things up at Skateland South and I found out about the rumors, I told my mother, and Ed and she had an argument about that. I could hear them arguing upstairs. Mother told me all the time how Chris was getting in between her and Ed. They weren't getting along at all because of Chris."

"Mother said that Chris tried to control Ed," Jimmy said. Ed had become the no-man's-land each raided, but neither could occupy. Unexpectedly, with no more than unimaginative rumors, Chris had become, to his delight, the center of the family, the one who held together their most passionate desires and feelings.

Protected by Ed from Sueanne's wrath, and seeing her rage, Chris began a series of rumors at Skateland now aimed directly at Sueanne herself, rumors that Sueanne drank heavily, that Sueanne had lovers, and that he had come home himself and caught her with one. When Sueanne confronted Chris about these rumors, he threatened to tell Ed about them.

Jimmy could understand the power of Chris's threat. "Ed believed everything he said, and Chris lied a lot. Ed really couldn't understand. He couldn't make any sense out of it. Chris manipulated Ed, whipped him about, and Mom whipped him about."

Chris would not stop tormenting Sueanne. She had failed to get control of him, and now he would not release her.

Suddenly, after the threat to tell Ed, Chris and Sueanne had a different relationship: they gave up on each other. Now when Chris came into the room and Ed was not present, everybody would fall silent until he left. "She said it made her hair stand on end being around him," Jimmy recalled.

Alone with Chris, Sueanne knew a familiar kind of intimacy, when they seemed to feel the very circulation of the other's blood with an intense hatred. Like mortally angry lovers,

Sueanne and Chris would never be alone together in any room of the house. If one entered a room, the other would leave, not abruptly, not bursting out as from a trap, but calmly, slowly, silently withdrawing, backing away like a cat from a great dog. Neither would look into the face of the other. When they were in the house together, the position, the distance of the other, was measured; the very room the other was in was calculated, felt, as if there were something waiting, something leaking slowly toward them. It was a sensation both knew early in their lives, the weather to which they had long been accustomed.

"It was getting so that neither one of them would be in the same part of the house as the other," Jimmy said. "It was usually Mother that would leave. Like if Chris would come in the kitchen, she would leave the kitchen." Sueanne didn't do that when Ed was with her and things were better when he was there than when he wasn't.

Margie was with Sueanne much during the late fall of 1979 and the spring of 1980 and she said that if she were there in the kitchen with Suzanne, Jimmy, and Sueanne, when Chris would come in, "Everybody would shut up."

"Mother," Jimmy said, "was always complaining about the trouble Chris was causing and how he was causing unrest around the household. She told me he was a crazymaker, that Chris reminded her of her mother, and I understood she didn't have a very pleasant childhood with her mother.

"Chris didn't even eat with the rest of the family," Jimmy recalled. "He usually ate before us; sometimes he was busy and sometimes Mother had it arranged. She had him eat earlier because it was a small table. She didn't like the way he ate at the table, didn't like his manners; she said he was a glutton."

Before winter she began talking seriously with Jimmy about doing something with Chris. "The talks started out about two or three times a week," he said. "She'd say things were getting worse around the house and that something had to be done to get rid of him, get him out of the house. I guess she talked to Ed about it for a while. She said that she was checking into the possibilities. Something had to be done to get rid of him. I usually didn't say too much because at first she was just talking about him going to a military school or a mental hospital. When the talking started taking a more serious tone, I usually just hurried to get the conversation over with so I could leave."

Soon Sueanne became more direct. "She had been talking about getting rid of him for two or three months," Jimmy said. "At first she was kind of vague about it and then it just came right down to it: she wanted him dead. Well, after she started talking about him being dead, she asked me, 'Can I find somebody that would do it for a reasonable amount of money?' I said, 'I'd check into it.' I didn't check because I didn't know anybody who would do something like that. I told her I would, to get her off my back for a while. It worked for a day or two, then she'd want to know if I found anything out. She said that she would like to be rid of him before the Christmas season so she wouldn't have to spend any money buying him gifts."

10

A year had passed since the Hobsons' wedding and their December honeymoon in Miami, Oklahoma. On the first anniversary of the marriage, everyone in the family except Ed was filled with anger and fear that each member kept to himself or herself or shared with the Crumm side or the Hobson side. Chris felt fear now, too, and told his relatives on Shirley's side of the family about his fear, though he never talked about it with his friends or with Ed. Yet he knew nothing about Sueanne's plans and could not have imagined them.

Ed could not imagine them, either. In the early winter when Ed returned home from taking night classes, he said that Chris would tell him about the evening he spent with Sueanne. "He'd come in our room," Ed remembered Chris saying, "and sit on the bed with his mother, and they'd watch television together, and he says later, 'You know, Mom's real great.' And I said, 'I told you, just give it some time; everybody's got a few things they've got to work out.'"

Chris and Sueanne regularly embraced, Ed said. "Chris would kiss her practically every morning before he went to school. They put their arms around each other; they would do things together. They even signed up to take a cooking class together. I felt very good about their relationship." By winter Ed was the only one in the house not infected with fear.

Sueanne said of her relationship with Chris that winter, "Ed went to night school and Chris used to come in and get in bed with me and watch television with me on the nights that Ed went to school. Chris and I liked to read together. I was trying to teach him how to cook. He wanted me to teach him how to iron, but I wouldn't do that; I wouldn't even teach Suzanne how to iron. It's one of those nerve-racking things for me." Some of what she said was true; certainly they had signed up for a microwave cooking class they planned to take together in the spring.

Suzanne, ostensibly the one in conflict with Chris, was angered by him, though she did not fear him. Chris never physically threatened her and his rumors lent excitement to her life and drew her closer to her mother. She did not yet know of her mother's intention to kill him, though she knew of her hatred. She hoped for something more than ridding the house of Chris, hoped that she and her mother and Jimmy could live together without the others. She felt a bond with her blood relations. Her mother—the mother who laughed, who was funny and witty and social, who had many women friends—had changed in the past year. She wanted her old mother back. Unlike Sueanne, she blamed Ed and the marriage to Ed for the dramatic change in her mother's character. Suzanne disliked Ed greatly and Ed, she thought, disliked her. Chris and Ed were together against her and her mother. She did not hope to separate them as Sueanne did, but to rid herself of both.

Jimmy was afraid, too, afraid of Sueanne, for again he saw her as the angry mother who had left him. "Nobody could stand up to Mom," he said. "There was a wrong way and her way. There were never any arguments in the house. She said do it, you did it; you don't change her mind." She was on his case all the time, bitching about his work in school, nagging him about Chris. When he first came back to her, she gave him space to breathe. Every day now she seemed to press closer to him.

Sueanne gave Jimmy something, took it back, gave him something again, like a game of put-and-take with a baby. Jimmy could feel her putting and taking, and it paralyzed him. His greatest fear was that she would abandon him again, that his chance for the life that he had so long sought would be lost to him forever.

His mother's plans for him to kill Chris were dreamlike. He had no intention of killing Chris. What Sueanne wanted him to do seemed unreal, like a plot in the endless number of mystery novels she read by Chandler or Christie or whoever. Sueanne's fear of Chris seemed to him childlike, irrational, like fears in a fairy tale. Her plans were just words to Jimmy and she seemed naive about the anger and the violence required to kill someone. "Mother underestimated people's capacities for violence," he said.

Jimmy at first could not understand or believe the intensity of her fear. He had not seen Chris do anything violent. "Chris is afraid of you," Sueanne explained. "He won't do anything around you."

Repeatedly Sueanne would ask Jimmy to find someone to get rid of the problem. Jimmy remained as silent as he dared. "I never said no to her. Whatever she said, I said yes or nothing. Even then my blank expression made her angry."

Sometimes she would say to Jimmy, "You have a flip, screw-you attitude." At other times she called him "an emotional little bastard."

When Jimmy came home now, and Ed was gone, she would take him aside and she would speak to him in a low voice, emphasizing carefully each word in her accent of anger. Jimmy said, "She feared that Chris might sometime go off the deep end and run around the house hitting her or Suzanne or hurting someone. She'd say, 'It'd be awful bad if something happened to Suzanne.' She even feared he'd hurt her cats." Sueanne whispered to him, "Chris is un-okay."

Sueanne would speak of the clothes she had bought for him, of the car she would buy if he did as she wished. She had brought him to this house. She had done much for him.

By the end she would be near tears, helpless and desperate, as if her power were suddenly given to Jimmy. Then she'd say, "If you loved me, you'd do this one little thing for me."

No one had ever spoken to Jimmy with this intensity before; no one, except his mother in his early years, had ever given him that much attention. No one had needed him so much. She had the power to create an entire world for him, to draw him into her world, to expel him from it. When he left her room, the sense of that world faded slowly, like some strong aftertaste.

11

The pressure of Sueanne on Jimmy was exactly proportionate to the fear she had of Chris. She was driven toward Jimmy by her fear. She was relentless. She could not relent.

Sueanne had told Jimmy she wanted to get rid of the boy by Christmas. She had even begun to tell Jimmy stories about how she herself had tried to drug Chris, to poison him by an overdose.

Thirteen months after they were married, Chris was still with them, and the house was decorated for the family's second Christmas. Ed was a Baptist, a fundamentalist. Christmas for his family was so changed from what it had been four years before, so transformed, it made him thankful to God for rescuing him from the long dying of Shirley. In the past year Sueanne had made over the house. With new furniture, a redecorated living room, and a repapered kitchen, the whole house was almost finished, except Chris's room and the master bedroom. There was a sense of richness in the house, the richness he had gotten from the sale of his father's land and from his work on the greasy machines at the mill. Like the pauper with the queen, he had been lifted up to her class.

Jimmy, on the other hand, felt increasingly apart from the family, increasingly detached, playing the role of a potential killer with Sueanne, the role of a dutiful family member with Ed. His plans to change his life, so exciting six or seven months earlier, had been shattered. He was using drugs more heavily than ever before, sleeping much of the day at school, doing virtually no work in his classes. In his schoolwork he was in over his head from the first day and now he had no hope of graduating. He would not even take the semester exams; frequently, he did not go to school at all. Sueanne would still call Colwell at school, would still press Jimmy to account for his absences. Yet her obsession with killing Chris left her less energy to reform Jimmy's performance at school.

Jimmy also saw Suzanne being steadily drawn into the plot against Chris, being as consumed by it as he himself was. She became a messenger between Jimmy and his mother; if he succeeded in avoiding his mother, Suzanne found him out. There was no one he could talk to about the conspiracy except his mother and his sister.

Sueanne later recalled that Christmas as a time when the family was adjusting "better and better." She seemed to measure the adjustment by the balance she achieved in gift-giving: "There was less bickering, there was less petty jealousy between the kids. You know, 'So-and-so got a new blouse. I want a new shirt.' 'Chris got a new pair of shoes. I want a new pair of shoes.' Just petty crap, petty things like that. It was less and less. We tried to be equal as far as buying things for the kids."

The family spent Christmas at home, Sueanne said. "Chris got a new stereo and a backpack and clothing and plaid shirts and socks and underwear and a gift certificate from Tiger's Record Store. All the kids got gift certificates from Tiger's; they all liked records. I love animals, particularly cats, and Chris gave me a set of Kliban-cat Christmas place mats and napkins that have the big Kliban cat, with the Christmas bells and things. He used his own money because all the kids got allowances."

Jimmy got a gold neck chain and other jewelry. He gave his mother a light brown porcelain cat he had specially cast for her; it sat alertly with its tail curled around over its feet. Suzanne got an emerald ring, her birthstone, especially made for her at Kriegel's, and many gifts of clothing.

Norma Hooker brought her gifts to the Hobsons over to the condominium Christmas evening, and the children crowded around Aunt Norma to tell her what they had gotten. "Sueanne gave Chris much less than the others, though they all got too much," Norma said.

Between Christmas and New Year's, Ed took Jimmy and Chris out hunting on the farm of a friend near Lone Jack, Missouri, east of Kansas City. Hunting with his son was important to Ed and he hoped it would bring Jimmy closer to Chris and to him. "After Shirley died, my son and I went hunting and fishing almost every weekend," Ed recalled. "My son and I became very close. He was a companion to me. I enjoyed him very much. He was a very intelligent, very loving child."

Chris had a shotgun and Ed bought a cheap, foreign-made, 12-gauge shotgun for Jimmy to use. "I had a 410, but it wasn't good for bird hunting and stuff like that, so I bought the third one. Jimmy used it all day."

The hunting trip was unusual in Jimmy's experience—a father and his sons out in the woods. Out there with Ed and Chris, Jimmy felt accepted and he sought to please them. In the chill of the late-December afternoon, with dark coming down on the three hunters, what his mother was whispering to him in her master bedroom seemed to be part of another world.

The afternoon was peaceful. "I think we got a couple of squirrels," Jimmy said. "We also shot at pop cans and stuff. I thought Ed was all right, a nice person. When my mother first started talking about getting rid of Chris, I asked her, 'What about Ed? What would it do to him?' She said she could handle him."

"I'd been working a lot, an awfully lot of overtime," Ed remembered. "We talked about going hunting again. We never did."

12

By January, Sueanne and Jimmy would talk almost daily in her bedroom: "Chris got to be the only thing we talked about. Mother had an obsession about hating Chris. It showed on a minute-to-minute basis. She talked about making it look like a suicide or an accident or a possible drug overdose. At first it was just to see if I could find somebody to do it, but that soon changed. I guess she figured that I wasn't really putting too much effort into it or else I wasn't making any headway in trying to find someone. She decided that maybe I could do it myself."

By early February 1980, Jimmy and Chris went on a second hunting trip: "I was supposed to pick up Chris before he left for school and take him out hunting and shoot him," Jimmy said. "Make it look like he left for school and just never showed up. Mother had discussed it with me and told me that would be a good thing to do, to take Chris hunting and, once we got out there, to shoot him and get rid of the body and then come back. I was to kill him and dump him, then make it look like he had run away by leaving his bicycle or clothes at Metcalf South."

Jimmy had already quit going to school. Chris was now attending scrupulously and was a model student, to the surprise of his teachers. Sueanne said, "I gave Chris permission to get off this day, because he wanted to go and because things had gone so much better around our house that I was trying to show him extra love and extra affection by allowing him to do something that I knew his father would probably hit the ceiling about when he got home." She told Chris not to tell his father.

When his mother told him what she wanted him to do, Jimmy told her he would do it. The next day Jimmy invited Chris to go with him, told him that they would skip a day of school, that no one would know. This was the first time Jimmy had invited Chris to do anything alone with him and he was happy and excited to go out with his older brother. Chris seemed as ignorant as Ed of the plots against him.

Jimmy drove out to Lone Jack again and stopped less than a mile from where Ed and the boys had hunted a couple of months before. The February thaw had begun and the earth smelled again, the weak sunlight giving life to the scents. In the deep ravines there was a layer of snow and the creeks were thinly crusted with ice. Jimmy seemed uncertain where to look for rabbits and squirrels. At first he led Chris into the woods and the boy followed obediently, but Chris soon understood how inexperienced Jimmy was. Chris overtook him and Jimmy spent most of the afternoon following the boy.

Chris kept well ahead of Jimmy. Despite the distance between them, Chris never stopped talking, yelling things back to him that Jimmy could scarcely hear.

Though he had used it once before, Jimmy was uncomfortable with Ed's foreign-made shotgun. Jimmy kept thinking of his mother's plans, but she seemed far away, and actually killing the boy seemed ridiculous. "I thought about shooting him, but I didn't want to," Jimmy said. "I couldn't. I didn't even aim down at him when I was behind him as we crossed a deep ravine."

When Jimmy and Chris came back early that afternoon in their mother's white Datsun, Sueanne immediately took Jimmy up to her bedroom and closed the door. "My mother was upset with me," Jimmy recalled. "She attacked me for two hours, saying how un-okay I was, how ungrateful. She said, 'After all I've done for you, can't you do this one little thing for me? If you loved me, you would do it. After all I've done for you, you would do it.' I just didn't say anything."

While Sueanne cooked supper that evening, Chris sat in the living room on the couch under the paintings of tigers and lions and told his father quietly about the hunting trip. "Jimmy and I went hunting today and Mom let me skip school. I'm not supposed to tell you," he said. "Don't tell her I told you, Dad." They had lived so long together and had gone through so much that they kept no secrets from each other.

Ed was angry, but he didn't talk to Sueanne until a couple of weeks later because he had promised Chris he wouldn't tell. When Ed did confront Sueanne, she came over and sat on his lap and they talked quietly for a long time. By the time they were finished talking, Ed understood. "In the earlier part of the marriage," Ed explained, "Sueanne and Chris had had some problems, and I could see her letting him do things that she didn't normally. He hadn't missed any school; one day wasn't going to hurt him. Sueanne was very strict about the kids missing school. There for a while after Chris's mother died, he had a habit of getting up in the morning and saying, 'Oh, I'm sick, I'm sick, I'm sick,' to keep him from going to school, and fifteen minutes after you said he wouldn't be going to school, he'd be outside playing."

"By February Chris's grades were getting a lot better," Ed recalled. "After the first part of the year all of a sudden something just clicked. Sueanne and him were planning on doing a lot of things together and they were getting quite a bit closer together and she knew his grades were coming up, so one day really wouldn't hurt. In my own mind I could see what she was doing. I know my wife just as well as I do my son."

3

GETTING RID OF THE PROBLEM

1

After Sueanne sent her son Jimmy out in the woods to kill Chris and Chris came back alive, she began to consider again what she had done and what she would do. She had tried other ways to get rid of him and gradually and reluctantly had come to the idea of killing him. Now that she had come to it, her will was set.

Jimmy seldom attended school after the Christmas holidays; he would have had to take makeup exams that he knew he could not pass. He still associated with the few friends he had made at Shawnee Mission South and daily he used uppers and downers, marijuana, and any drugs or alcohol he could get.

In mid-February the winter broke completely and the snow melted. The spring coming on proved to be particularly beautiful and mild.

Suddenly on the sixteenth, Jimmy left the house for good, abandoned Sueanne to Chris. He had used a stolen credit card and Sueanne found out about it. "A group of people I ran around with would pass around stolen credit cards every now and then," Jimmy said. "I got in at the end of the line and got caught." One of Jimmy's friends had stolen the card from the purse of his English teacher in a lounge at the high school.

"Jimmy ran away," Sueanne said. "It was right after he was confronted with the stolen credit card and the stolen merchandise in his room. He bought a pair of leather boots, a black leather jacket, which he later said a cousin stole from him, and a pair of tennis shoes. Things he didn't need because he had them. When he walked into the family room, I looked at him and knew the boots he had on his feet were not boots that Ed or I had gotten for him. I asked him whose shoes they were and he said they were his friend's shoes, Junior Reyes'. I went downstairs and saw he had a brand new pair of tennis shoes in his closet. And this child had many pairs of shoes. He did not have one pair of shoes, all right? He told me the tennis shoes were also Junior's. Junior's feet are smaller than Jimmy's. By that time Ed was into it. He said, 'Fine, you give me Junior's father's name and address and telephone number, and if I can't get him on the phone, by God, we'll go over there and talk to him.'"

"Though we were the ones who called the police about the credit card, Jimmy felt that Chris had, in his quaint terminology, 'narked' on him," Sueanne said. "We also found drugs in his room again. Jimmy felt that he was going to go to prison for the credit-card theft and the drugs, so he just said to hell with it and left. He was very upset and very angry toward Chris because he felt that Chris had told on him about both the drugs and the credit card. Jimmy believed that everything he was in trouble for was Chris's fault.

"I think Chris did tell his father that he thought Jimmy was taking drugs," she added. "I don't believe I told Jimmy that Chris narked on him; we were the ones that called the police. I do know Jimmy told Suzanne that Chris had narked on him."

"Jimmy knew I turned him in for the drugs and the credit card," Ed insisted.

Jimmy's version of who in the family discovered his crime first is different from Sueanne's and Ed's. "My mother had told me that Chris was the one that was responsible for me getting caught using the credit cards. I was upset."

"Jimmy left," Ed said, "real quick one Saturday morning while I was at work. We had already talked to the police about the credit cards and the next thing I know Jimmy's stuff is packed and he's gone."

"There wasn't a whole lot said," Jimmy recalled. "Ed and

Mother didn't say much of anything. They didn't have a chance to; I just left."

Detective Urban found out Jimmy had been involved in a theft and he was assigned to investigate it. Urban knew a little about Jimmy and the Hobsons. He remembered the time Sueanne and Ed had called him out to their house the previous fall to look for drugs in Jimmy's room. Now Urban drove out to the Hobson condominium again to find out where Jimmy might be; Sueanne was there alone and said she didn't know.

While the juvenile authorities put Jimmy on their list of run-aways, Sueanne was protecting him from Urban. "A week or so after he left," Sueanne later admitted, "Suzanne and I went out and gave him some clothes at a Sinclair station on Metcalf." When Urban finally caught up with Jimmy weeks later, Jimmy told him that she knew all along where he was and paid him money to stay a runaway. Urban was angered that Sueanne, who had been so concerned about her son's use of drugs when he came to her home last fall, had been hiding him out, but he respected Jimmy's wishes and did not confront her. Taken in by Sueanne's profession of ignorance, Urban had wasted a lot of time chasing down Jimmy.

"When I caught up with Jimmy, he wasn't hostile," Urban said. "He was a gentleman." Jimmy readily admitted what he had done and was placed on probation under the supervision of the juvenile court, first under officer Jane Young, who was pregnant, then under Cheryl Schroeder after Young left to have her child.

What Sueanne gained, or thought she gained, by calling the police about Jimmy's involvement in the theft of a credit card while both were in the midst of a conspiracy to kill her stepson isn't clear. Neither Jimmy nor Sueanne could know how his moving out would affect the mother-son relationship. Whatever Sueanne intended, she was now more frequently alone with Chris and her fear of him grew.

Strangely, Sueanne condemned Jimmy for the theft of the credit card, but she did, in a moment of intimacy, share with him her own theft. She had claimed she lost her five-thousand-dollar ruby-and-diamond engagement ring and had told Jimmy she sus-pected Chris of taking it. The ring was insured by Hanover

Insurance Company; though investigators canceled her policy, the company paid her and she bought another ring. A few days later she told Jimmy she found the ring in her shoe. Smiling, she said, "I wonder how it got there. Chris must have put it there to irritate me. Isn't that strange?" Jimmy smiled back.

2

Jimmy fled to the Reffitts, to his aunt Dorothy's care. Her house had been, he said, "the only place I had ever been happy in." Dorothy's house was his third in less than a year and he was already planning to move into a fourth, an apartment of his own whenever he could afford it. At first Jimmy was excited by the change; he had escaped from a hard place, he thought, though in those first few weeks he was anxious about his crime until Urban caught up with him. Nonetheless, he was accustomed to this instability and felt at home in it.

The Reffitts soon knew about Jimmy's theft and begged him to face the police and end his dependency on his mother's money. Aunt Dorothy had observed a change in Jimmy since she last saw him. He had become greedy and materialistic, she thought; he had become the way she herself had always thought of Sueanne. Jimmy never saw his father during the six weeks he spent at the Reffitts', though Dorothy told her brother Jim that his son was now back at her house after nine months at Sueanne's.

While Jimmy lived at the Reffitts', his relatives served as a barrier to her visits. Now he himself would choose when he would visit his mother. Usually he would come in the daytime, when Suzanne and Ed were out and he could speak privately with his mother.

Jimmy thought at first he had escaped Sueanne's pleas and demands by leaving, but soon discovered otherwise. He found that now he was even more dependent on her for financial support and for protection from the police. He especially needed her support for his plan to move to the Oak Park Apartments in Lenexa, just across the street from the western limit of Overland

Park. He had a series of jobs but no job that would support him yet. Mainly he lived on the money his mother gave him.

Back now with his father's relatives, whom he had left with such energy and hope only nine months before, he was soon depressed by the change. Jimmy had little time for the Reffitts, little interest in them. They were resigned to all those constraints he sought to escape when he accepted his mother's invitation the previous spring. There was a slackness in the Reffitts, quite unlike the excitement and passionate energy he found at the Hobsons'.

Jimmy still had an intimacy with Sueanne that he craved, that nothing could extirpate, nothing could replace. They had already been conspirators, long been conspirators, even if the conspiracy had never been consummated, even if it were never to be consummated. Whenever they met now, and they met almost daily, she would say, "If you loved me, you would do this one little thing for me."

And he did love her; he did want to win her, to please her, to satisfy her. In many ways he felt he was much closer to her than Ed had ever been. Jimmy could never imagine, when Ed and Sueanne would go into the upstairs bedroom, the room directly across from Chris's, and close the door, that they would make love. She was too cold for that, too intimidating, he thought. And Jimmy had the intimacy of knowing much that Ed could not know, of knowing the most important thing for Ed to know.

What Sueanne was asking for was an act of love, an expression of a bond between them. He had her attention now, the attention he had long sought, and he had something to give her, providing he did not yet give it. But the deep pleasure of his power over her came well disguised to him, as did the pain and fear, for all his emotions were flattened and made distant by the entire lack of consummation in his life.

Underneath it all he did fear her. "No one ever stands up against her," he thought. When she would again propose her plans for getting rid of Chris, he would not say no; rather, he would remain as silent as he dared and seek to leave her, to get away as quickly as he could. Most of all he feared being abandoned, feared it even more strongly than at nine when she first abandoned him, for he had spent long years wondering where she was and what he had done or not done to deserve her leaving him.

Despite the fact that he was out of her house and hiding from the police, Jimmy saw Sueanne almost daily in March. "She was obsessed with Chris," Jimmy said. "She said he was a carbon copy of her mother and every day that Chris was alive was a day missed. Chris stood in her way; she wanted him dead, she wanted him taken out."

Sueanne had been hurt at first by Chris's refusal to acknowledge her power, her control. "She has to be on top," Jimmy said, "she has to be in control." Chris was the crazymaker, the only one in the family she could not get in place.

Chris was, Sueanne said with precision and finality, "unokay." She had a hatred of him that never seemed to leave her, that came on her alone or with her friends. Chris became the sole subject of every conversation she had with Jimmy. When Jimmy came, she would take him up to her bedroom and lock the door, offering things, demanding things, if he would find some way to kill Chris.

Sueanne came at Jimmy like a lover, came at him with almost a biological persistence. She came with gifts; she came with admonishments; she came with threats. It was, Jimmy thought, put and take, the pleasure of engagement and the control of withdrawal.

Yet Jimmy never knew how she would come at him. Sometimes he felt as small and helpless before her as he had felt as a child.

Sueanne's fear of Chris must have been equal to the pressure she put on Jimmy. Fear was gradually permeating her life, moving through it like the human smell that gets on the hands of lovers and undertakers and can't be washed off.

"She asked me to protect my little sister," Jimmy said. "I would do anything for my sister." Yet he still could not believe Sueanne's fear. He had not seen Chris do anything violent, had heard nothing except the rumors Chris started of things that had not been done by anyone, rumors of things that were far less damning than the things Jimmy himself had actually done.

He was angry that Chris had told about his theft of the credit card, about the drugs hidden in his room, angry that Chris had betrayed his trust. Still, he hardly knew Chris. Jimmy had spent increasingly little time at the condominium as the nine months he lived there wore on.

Jimmy always came now when Ed was gone, calling ahead as if he and his mother were secret lovers. The only sounds he heard when he came in the front door were from the cats. Though Ed and Jimmy hated cats, Sueanne's condominium was full of cats, seven of various breeds. She would say, "My cats are part of the family." The porcelain cat Jimmy had specially cast for her at Christmas was so lifelike that guests could sit for minutes glancing with increasing anxiety toward it, suddenly realizing with astonishment that it would never move.

There were paintings of great cats on the wall facing the door where Jimmy entered, a black panther above one end of the couch, a tiger above the other. The two paintings bracketed a mirror that appeared oddly shaped until a casual glance would finally bring into focus the thrusting head and mane of a lion embedded in its design.

If Chris were somewhere in the house, Jimmy would find his mother alertly sitting alone on the couch. One hand was open in her lap; her other hand was out of sight, grasping an eighteen-inch socket wrench wrapped carefully in an apron, and placed snugly between her and the couch arm.

If fear ruled Sueanne's life, it was only a part of Chris's. In March and April Chris felt he had more power in the family than at any time before. Chris had gotten Jimmy out of the house, and Sueanne now seemed quieter, less concerned about Chris, less easily provoked.

Sueanne even invited Chris to take a microwave cooking class with her in May. The class had been offered in an April advertisement in the *Kansas City Star* and together they filled out the enrollment form. At Indian Creek that semester he was taking "Foods," a course in which he did some cooking. He told his teacher how excited he would be to go with his mother to learn other ways of cooking.

At times Chris seemed to sense the threat that Sueanne and

Jimmy presented. He told his grandmother, Shirley's mother, that he was afraid of Sueanne and Jimmy. "I don't want to go home, because Jimmy's going to kill me," he said. Yet he could not hold his fear for long. He had just turned thirteen.

One of his teachers at Indian Creek wrote in April that Chris had "outstanding discipline, achievement, and friendliness." Only in the last three months had he made what the teacher called "drastic improvements in his behavior."

Yet she also wrote, "Chris has a tendency to want to disrupt the status quo after things have been running smoothly for a period of time. It is as if he has to live through a crisis every three or four months in order to survive. He feels that he can do anything he wants no matter what the task is. If he thought he could walk across water, he would attempt to do it until he was successful, even though it is known that this could not take place."

When Chris received his annual school photo, he tried to give one to Ruth Ann Matheson, a paraprofessional in special education at Indian Creek Junior High. "He was excited," she recalled, "and he asked if I wanted to have a photo. I said, 'Don't you want to save them and give them to your friends?' He told me he didn't have that many friends and started to cut a picture out and I said, 'They're really good. What will your mother think of them?' He said, 'There isn't anyone to care.'"

Chris seemed unable to form a clear perception of the strangers among whom he lived; he was filled with ambivalence toward them and he couldn't hold his anger or his hatred long. Though he had the desperate courage to face Sueanne, he was not a brave child and seemed overprotected by his father. "He did not like darkness by himself," Ed said. "As long as I was with him, it didn't bother him, but not by himself."

To Jimmy there was something childish about Chris's rumors and threats as his mother and sister repeated them to him; he himself had heard none except from them. One morning in March when he drove over to the condominium, Sueanne had a welt under her eye and she said Chris had hit her. She told her son that Chris had shouted, "I've gotten rid of Jimmy and I'll get rid of you and Suzanne, too!"

In late March Sueanne and Jimmy arranged to rent an apartment in a large complex just across the street from the Oak Park Mall, an enormous enclosed shopping center. It would be Jimmy's first place of his own. The previous summer Jimmy, of course, had worked in Stix, Baer and Fuller's in the mall until he began ringing up false sales. Though Sueanne's home now was four miles away at the eastern edge of Overland Park, she still lived and had lived for the past six years at various apartments and houses in a strip a mile wide cutting across the south edge of the city near 103rd Street; the mall and the apartment fell within that area.

Most of the renters in the Oak Park Apartments were from twenty to thirty years old and unmarried. The complex had several pools and tennis courts and generous open spaces around the two-story brown wooden buildings. From outside the complex felt like a small resort; little open taxis, really golf carts adapted for that purpose, carried the renters back and forth through it. Inside the buildings, the dark, narrow hallways and the worn look of the rugs and of the rooms made the apartments seem more like pleasant quarters for those spending a few months at a temporary job before going on to the real work of their lives.

Sueanne came across town daily with things for Jimmy's apartment. "You name it, she brought it," Jimmy said.

Sometimes Ed would drive over in his old Model-T Ford truck, its small bed piled high with furniture. Ed's pride in the truck had made it part of the family and he kept the truck immaculate. Chris and Jimmy had both helped him work on it and Ed tended it like a child of fourteen grooming a prize sheep or a cow for the county fair. Ed took pleasure in common work of any sort; he worked with an energy and enthusiasm alien to Jimmy, who was left standing around waiting uncomfortably. The things Ed gave Jimmy for his apartment were Ed's things mainly, though Ed seemed unaware of that, or at least he never spoke of it.

Sueanne discovered that Jimmy was now more accessible to her after the move, more dependent on her. She had plans, but no definite plan quite yet, no date. She always created elaborate plans; she could not bear a life without them.

She soon found a way to promise Jimmy a large sum of

money. In March she had filed suit against Jimmy's father for back child support of Suzanne. A hearing was set for May 7. What money she got she would give to her son. "Jim and I were divorced seven and a half years ago and he never paid any child support," Sueanne said. "I told Jimmy I would buy him a car, based on what we got from the settlement. I feel like the money is just as much his as it is mine, because when his father had him, he gave him nothing." Since Sueanne had legal custody of Jimmy, but hadn't actually seen him from the ages of nine to sixteen, she could not sue for his back child support. She asked sixteen thousand dollars for Suzanne's support; Jim counter-claimed that he didn't have to pay it because, in all those years, he couldn't find Suzanne, that he had looked for her and couldn't find her.

Jimmy—who had just been given a used brown van by his grandparents, the Sallees—was certainly interested in the offer of a new car, but the car always seemed contingent on the murder, not the civil suit. Sueanne had plenty to offer Jimmy, or to let him hope for, and daily she gave him a taste of her generosity.

There was something naive about Sueanne and her knowledge of the outside world, Jimmy said, even something naive about her knowledge of people's capacities for violence, about her own capacity. Certainly she seemed to behave as if she were locked back in the Prairie Village home of her parents, where nothing ever got out and became public knowledge, as if the whole world were like those rooms. In the midst of a conspiracy she had begun to seek through the civil courts a way to finance the conspiracy.

In the spring, Sueanne met with Lee Shank and the assistant principal, Delores Louis, at Indian Creek Junior High for a regularly scheduled conference about Chris. Lee Shank's appearance in repose belied her intelligence and energy. A superb teacher, her mind was clear and sharp. On issues of child abuse, she had assumed an important political role in the community.

Mrs. Shank reviewed Chris's progress before the meeting. Initially Chris had been referred as a special education student because of his chaotic life with Shirley, his emotionally disturbed mother. Pregnant with Chris in her forties, Shirley had not even wanted him to be born, Mrs. Shank knew. When Chris was six, his half-sister Tani committed suicide. Shirley had her first cancer operation when her son was three and she was dead before he was nine. Chris felt guilty, even responsible, for the deaths of his mother and sister, Mrs. Shank believed. Shirley's threats of violence had made Chris ambivalent about his mother's death. Naturally, the boy was distressed that he felt relief when she finally died.

Chris had no learning disabilities, according to Mrs. Shank. He was a "bright-normal child" and he seemed to get along with his peers fairly well. "At first Chris was not one of the better students, although all of our testing indicated that he had the ability," she said. "He really didn't have a lot of confidence in himself at that particular time. He started poorly, but he soon began to see what he could do.

"When the second semester began in January, we began to see some improvement," Mrs. Shank recalled. "He seemed a lot happier, more relaxed, willing to take responsibility for himself. We started to see some really good grades. He'd start on projects himself ahead of time. When an assignment was made, he'd begin to do some of the things himself, discuss the topic, decide on a topic, start gathering information, which made us very pleased with him. He was then making Bs, occasional As. We had a C or two in there, but we really were proud of him. He really had done a turnaround. He was cooperative; he wasn't fighting us; he was very friendly; he would talk to all the kids in the learning center and they all seemed to get along with him. He was not terribly outgoing ever, but a nice polite kid."

Mrs. Shank had good news for Mrs. Hobson, but this attractive, lean, well-dressed woman had scarcely taken a seat in the conference room before she began to attack Chris. She did not stop for well over an hour. "She was vitriolic," Mrs. Shank said. "She was as angry as I'd ever seen a parent. She said, 'Chris should be in an asylum, he's crazy.' Delores Louis and I had never seen a woman in such a rage. We were stunned. She seemed to hate the boy that we found so cooperative and sweet."

When Mrs. Hobson did calm down a little, she told them, according to Mrs. Shank, that Chris "was hard to get along with, that he caused difficulties between all members of the family. Originally she had wanted to delay the marriage until some help was gotten for Chris. Mr. Hobson had wanted them to get married immediately and she wished she had delayed it awhile longer because it had been a difficult situation." Neither Shank nor Louis could understand what had provoked the woman nor why she chose to speak so ferociously to them when they sought only to praise Chris.

3

To her friend Norma Hooker, Sueanne would speak often of her frustration with Chris. "I loved her as a sister," Norma said. "Sueanne and I were very strong women. We could tell each other to go 'right square straight to hell and stay put' and remain friends. Some nights when we sat and talked, she would say, 'The kids are driving me crazy. What am I going to do? I can't handle it. Something's got to be done.' Was she asking for help? Did we all miss the signs?

"She had said something about sending him to a mental asylum to me," Norma recalled. "I said to her, 'Sueanne, the kid's not crazy! He's just a little thirteen-year-old kid looking for security.' She said, 'My God, I can't take it, I can't stand him around.' I said, 'Sueanne, it's only five years, five short years, and Chris will be eighteen and Suzanne will be in college and Jimmy will be grown and you and Ed will have your entire lives ahead of you.' I never dreamed that she was that intent on really wanting him out of the house. Mothers, stuck in the house with kids, tend to get a little overwrought with children's behavior. Maybe this was her way of saying, 'Please God, somebody help me with this because I can't deal with it!' I took that just as moms talking together—'The kid makes me crazy. I'd like to choke him, or throw him out.'

"I'm not sure why she didn't divorce," Norma said. "Maybe she loved Ed so much that she really didn't want to be divorced from him. There was a point in time in Ed and Sueanne's marriage when she really wanted to have a whole, loving relationship." Even that spring she spoke to Norma about wanting to have Ed's child.

"Evidently, I knew two people," Norma said. "There was the Aunt Sueanne, who loved my kids, took care of my kids. We were very good friends. I was teaching preschool at the start of that year; I had twenty three-year-olds and I needed someone that could work with my babies. We needed an aid for my classroom and I called Sueanne. She came to the school, La Petite Academy, and she was hired. I've seen her sitting on the floor playing with the children in cardboard boxes, putting together puzzles, helping them eat their lunch. She was a gentle, gentle, loving person with those three-year-old children."

In the months Sueanne was teaching at Norma's nursery school, Jimmy moved out and the entire family was in turmoil. Norma said that one evening things got so bad at the Hobsons' that after an argument with Sueanne, Ed got drunk and drove the boy up to what was left of his farm near King City. The two spent the night there before returning to Overland Park.

If Norma saw Sueanne's tenderness, she also saw her anger and fear. One day in early April Sueanne came to Skateland to sell Jimmy's skates and Norma had coffee with her. Clearly Sueanne was angry at Chris and afraid of him. "She also voiced some fear of Jimmy," Norma recalled. "She was very nervous and agitated, a nervous wreck; she was just off the wall," Norma said. "She was afraid of something Jimmy would do; she didn't specify what."

Sueanne also continued to speak to Margie Hunt-Fugate of her anger and frustration with Chris. She was even more open with Margie than Norma. "I wouldn't say Sueanne was my best friend, but we were very close friends," Margie said. "I saw her several times a week. She said she had tried to put him in an institution, but Ed wouldn't have anything to do with it; he refused to let Chris leave the home. She didn't name a specific institution. She said it had been determined that he should be put away, that he shouldn't be left in the home atmosphere, that for his own good he needed to be put in an institution. She asked me if I knew anybody in the Mafia, if I had any idea what it would cost to have somebody taken care of, or if I had ever heard the name Sorrentino connected with the Mafia." This, Margie said, "was around the first of April, maybe the end of March." Margie didn't take Sueanne's request seriously.

The whole time Chris lived with the family Sueanne spoke of getting rid of him. "Sueanne said she hated Chris and she wished that he was gone," Margie said. "She wanted him out. She said that he'd been causing a lot of problems between her and Ed and that she couldn't put up with that anymore. In the family room one morning, while Ed was upstairs out of earshot, Sueanne told me that Chris had told her that he had gotten rid of Jimmy and he would get rid of Suzanne and her, too."

Margie listened silently to Sueanne's complaints and fears. She herself had been divorced and was now living alone with her two boys. Margie accepted rage and turmoil as part of any family she knew and she did not presume herself qualified to give Sueanne advice.

Placed on probation, Jimmy, now only two months before his eighteenth birthday, was assigned to Cheryl Schroeder, a probation officer for juveniles in Johnson County. Sueanne began to attend the probation meetings with Jimmy. In late March Schroeder wrote, "The credibility or validity of Jimmy's statements are not determinable at this time. . . . Jimmy feels that he is fairly mature and can be on his own and care for himself, however, I am not picking that up from the parents at all. They have allowed him to go and co-sign for an apartment that he will be moving into April first."

Schroeder's notes of her next meeting on the eighth of April were more elaborate. She met with Sueanne and Jimmy to discuss the details of the probation requirements. "We reviewed the recent theft charge and agreed that Jimmy would be responsible for approximately seventy-two dollars of the charges made on the victim's account," she wrote. "Jimmy stated that he would sell his van in order to make restitution. According to Schroeder, they also discussed the Scared Straight Prison Program. Jimmy remarked that it would be "interesting yet a little bit scary."

In a handwritten note Schroeder added, "Family dynamics: Jimmy aligned with mom—stepdad aligned with his stepson. Mother would like to leave marriage." Later that day Schroeder typed out her perceptions more fully. "The mother came across as supportive of Jimmy and what he had been through. Both Jimmy and his mother seemed to form a coalition together against Chris in the home and were angry that the dad supported Chris. The mother would very much like to leave the marriage, but said she couldn't do that at this time, due to financial reasons. She was glad Jimmy was getting out and not having to deal with the problems in the family."

Schroeder explored the possibility of counseling. "Mrs. Hobson stated that she had been in counseling with Dr. Craft for three years and made considerable progress. Jimmy agreed to counseling and agreed to contact Dr. Craft."

It was as if Sueanne's child-support suit against Jimmy's father, her talks with Lee Shank, Norma Hooker, and Margie Hunt-Fugate, and her meetings with Cheryl Schroeder were exclusive encounters, private exchanges, as if one audience was forever separated from another. Certainly what Sueanne said to Schroeder was accurate. The relationship between Ed and Sueanne was deteriorating rapidly from everyone's point of view except Ed's, since Ed measured it against Shirley's violent oubursts. There was a level of rage Ed could tolerate that Sueanne found intolerable.

"Chris was causing problems between Ed and Mom," Suzanne said. "They got in fights all the time. I could hear them talking or yelling. All the time. Serious problems. Mother said to me that something had to be done because Chris was causing too much of a problem."

From February on, Suzanne was drawn increasingly into the conspiracy. Her life was consumed by it. She had been a superior student, but her schoolwork began to suffer and she attended classes irregularly; frequently she stayed home with her mother. Sueanne complained openly to her daughter about her frustration with Ed's refusal to discipline Chris and about Jimmy's inability to control the boy or get rid of him. Suzanne knew of her mother's plans before anyone else in the family except Jimmy and saw them forming, dispersing, relentlessly re-forming.

Suzanne was also angry at Chris, very angry. She disliked Ed, tolerated him only because it made things easier for her mother, and she wanted both Ed and Chris out of the house. Her mother's plans to kill Chris never seemed quite real to her, but she did what she could to support them.

The mother Suzanne knew from the years before her marriage to Ed had had many friends, was funny, witty, and powerful. Suzanne wanted her real mother back, the mother who scarcely emerged at all now in her obsession with Chris. Her mother had become nervous and frightened, almost helpless. She blamed Ed more than Sueanne or Chris, for Ed had done nothing to control his son and his attacks on her and her mother, even though there was no truth to the rumors Chris had spread about her.

Jimmy told his sister that it was Chris who had told Ed and Sueanne about his use of the credit card. Suzanne held that against Chris, too. She knew also of his threat to get rid of her and Sueanne, though she didn't take it quite as literally as her mother.

Chris had drawn the Crumms together, made them a separate family within the Hobson family. When Suzanne and Jimmy conspired together, or Suzanne carried messages to Jimmy about the conspiracy, she felt an intense intimacy with her mother and brother, blood relations planning to murder one who was not of their blood. That intimacy gave Suzanne a vast advantage over Ed, who did not know, and over Chris, who suspected nothing.

4

That spring Sueanne asked Jimmy to teach her how to use a gun. "She said that she wanted Chris gotten rid of," Jimmy recalled, "and she meant killed, and then she asked if there was any way that she could help or if I would teach her how to use a gun." Ed had more than a dozen rifles, shotguns, and pistols stacked in a brown cardboard wardrobe closet at the end of the basement stairs across from Jimmy's room. Jimmy politely refused to teach her because, he said, "I just didn't think it would be the right thing to do."

Jimmy claimed he saw one attempt his mother made on the life of Chris. Sueanne and Jimmy bought ice cream at a Dairy

Queen just off Roe Boulevard near where they lived. "We bought ice cream for everybody and she put eight Quaaludes in Chris's portion and we took it home," Jimmy said. He thought she "got Quaaludes from one of her friends. When we got home, Mother dumped the ice cream in a big bowl and gave it to Chris and we all ate our ice cream and he complained about the taste. Chris was saying it was bitter, that it tasted funny, and she was screaming that he had to eat all of it. He ate all but a little bit."

When Chris was finished, Jimmy said, "He asked me if I wanted to go out in the backyard and kick the ball around, so I went with him and he started kind of stumbling around like he was drunk. He said he felt sick and then he went upstairs and went to sleep. He slept for quite a while. After he went up to bed, Mother said, 'I gave him eight Quaaludes in that bowl of ice cream. Do you think that will kill him?'" Chris awakened fifteen hours later, Jimmy recalled, and "Mother was disappointed that he woke up."

Later Sueanne told Jimmy that she had once put cocaine in a piece of bubble gum, "but there wasn't enough to do anything to Chris." Jimmy laughed at her naive attempt, and no one, not even Jimmy, seemed to believe that she would be silly enough to think that the cocaine would kill Chris. Compared with Jimmy, she knew very little about drugs. Perhaps she made up the story to convince her son that she herself was also trying to kill Chris; Jimmy didn't know.

Even after Jimmy no longer lived in the house, his talks with Sueanne on his visits took place in her bedroom. The plans she discussed with Jimmy were quite vague. She would talk about hiring someone to kill Chris, but not the details of how it might be done. At one point she asked Jimmy if he would run down Chris with their car as the boy was bicycling around the neighborhood. Both spoke the language of murder, of "doing one little thing," of "getting rid of the problem," a language that to Jimmy, at least, seemed far from any action, far from any shared passion that would enable him to do it.

When Jimmy finally moved into his own apartment in the Oak Park complex at the beginning of April, the Reffitts no longer stood in Sueanne's way and she was knocking on Jimmy's door morning and night, bringing him things. She talked of ways to kill Chris, of her arguments with Ed over the boy, and of Chris's snitching on Jimmy. As a guest in his apartment, she had more control because Jimmy couldn't walk out so easily and leave her there and she could come unexpectedly at any time. His mother paid his rent, supported him, and she could in a moment withdraw that support.

"This was my first stab at independence," Jimmy said. "I didn't want to give it up." Jimmy now assented or remained silent in response to his mother's demands. "I always said yes to whatever Mom said. You don't change her mind. There was a wrong way and her way. There were never any arguments in the house; if she said do it, you did it. You have to understand that."

Sueanne told her son that Chris repeatedly threatened her life and Suzanne's. In truth Jimmy never made up his mind about the reality of those threats. What he had actually seen Chris do and say to Sueanne—as opposed to what she accused Chris of doing and saying—was to him embarrassingly insignificant, too insignificant for him to mention: stopping up a toilet so that it flooded the bathroom, executing an order so slowly that it aggravated Sueanne. For Jimmy the threats Sueanne reported from Chris paled beside her threats.

After the arrangements Sueanne had made with Jimmy for the murder of Chris on the hunting trip fell through, and after her own attempts to kill him had failed, Sueanne knew and Jimmy knew that neither could kill him alone. She repeatedly asked Jimmy if he knew of anyone who could help. Jimmy at first said he would look around for someone, but didn't do anything, in part because he intended to wait out her desire to kill Chris and in part because he didn't know anyone who might do such a thing.

Jimmy had few acquaintances in Overland Park. He spoke of the area as if it were a foreign land. "I don't know a lot of people out there," he said.

At Shawnee Mission South he had met a few boys, yet he could call no one there his best friend. Those he did know were frequently boys who were "doing drugs" and who themselves were in trouble at home or at school, boys who seemed to have tenuous attachments to families. Jimmy couldn't remember the last names of the girls he had met, even the girl or two he had dated. Jimmy said, "In those last months out there I was on junk street, running with the tribe."

5

Though they scarcely knew one another, Jimmy had met Paul Sorrentino at Skateland almost a year before. Paul was a short, dark boy of sixteen who seemed even shorter than his five-foot-four height. He was thick-bodied, with a sensuous, round face. Yet he possessed an energy, a bounce almost, and a kind of aggressive impudence. He was, the girls said, an incredible skater; everyone knew him for his daring on the rink, and at Skateland other skaters would sometimes stand around to watch him perform. Unlike Jimmy, he had many friends; the girls especially liked his openness and his direct sexual interest in them, and among them he already had a reputation as a lover, "an Italian stallion."

Older women seemed to like Paul, too. Anne Gresham, a counselor nearing retirement at Shawnee Mission South, the school Jim and Paul attended, considered him a friend. She found Paul open and honest. In her report of a conversation with him, she wrote, "It is very evident that Paul needs a mother-image in his life."

Jimmy knew almost nothing about Paul, and Paul had scarcely even noticed Jimmy. Jimmy's first impression was that "Paul was a romantic," that he was attracted by the life described in *The Valachi Papers*. Once Paul boasted that he wanted to follow in the footsteps of a relative who was "a hit man for the Mafia" back in Boston.

One spring night Jimmy ran into Paul at a party and asked him what he would take for killing someone. "He seemed like the kind of guy who would do it, so I just came right out and asked him," Jimmy said. "He said he would, right off."

A few weeks passed before Jimmy again talked about the murder with Paul. When he asked Paul how much he would charge for the murder, he said he had a motorcycle in a garage for repairs and the mechanic wanted three hundred and fifty dollars to repair it. "If I do it, I want my bike fixed," he said.

Jimmy brought back the offer to his mother and she said that it seemed reasonable. Paul himself thought his request modest and reasonable. More money might be noticed by his father, Paul thought, and more would be easier for the police to trace. Three hundred and fifty dollars seemed just about right to him.

Paul's father, Patrick Sorrentino, a publisher's representative, traveled a great deal. He had been a police officer in the East before he took a job in Kansas City. What was now left of the Sorrentino family was living in a rented town house in Overland Park. Paul's mother had divorced his father several years earlier, then remarried. Pat had gotten custody of the three children, Michelle, Paul, and Mark. He had taken all the children with him to Kansas City. Michelle, the oldest, assumed the mother's role in the family. Mark Sorrentino was two years older than his brother, Paul, and Jimmy claimed he knew Mark a little better than Paul.

The boys had been causing Pat a lot of trouble and Pat didn't care much for the children his sons associated with. Paul had already had numerous run-ins with the police before, though one wouldn't know it from looking at the fact sheet the detectives kept on juveniles. Paul had once been involved in a motorcycle theft ring and Detective Gil Hernandez had let him off when he informed on his friends. Every detective in the police department had a snitch and Paul was Hernandez' snitch. He had been let off of four or five felonies by this time because he served Hernandez well. Paul, at sixteen, had found a way to work the system. He had, after all, been around police since he was born.

Both Paul and Jimmy had worked for the Hookers at Skateland South and they had first met there. The Hookers knew the Sorrentinos well; both families lived in rented town houses in the Rigg apartment complex on 102nd Street in Overland Park. The Hookers liked Pat very much and Norma said he was "a very good-looking, loving, Italian father, the epitome of a good father. A salesman, he had to travel a lot and he did what he could for his family. Whenever he left, he'd come down to the rink and say good-bye."

Norma liked boys and she was especially attached to Paul. Her birthday was the same day as Paul's. "We were birthday buddies, Geminis," she said. "He was always respectful, always dressed neatly. There wasn't anybody who knew him who didn't love him. I was very protective of Paul, very supportive, because I loved him as a son."

Pat would never talk about Marie, the mother of his children and the wife who had left him, or the life he had led in the east. The Sorrentino boys never went back to Boston to visit their mother. Only Michelle returned regularly. Paul told Norma he missed the fun they used to have as a family and he missed the snowmobile they had and the winter-long snow. Paul himself would say that he would not wish his family situation, with his mother gone, on anyone, that he wouldn't want to live in a family like his family.

Paul, the youngest, was particularly close to his father. They would often go out hunting together. Pat never raised his voice against his sons when Norma was around, though Jim Hooker said that Paul behaved because Pat would bust his nose if he didn't.

"Paul was ornery, but well mannered," Jim Hooker said. "I trusted him implicitly. On Halloween when Norma and I had to work at the rink, I had him go around with my little girls to protect them from strangers and check the candy and food. When he worked here, he worked hard; he was very helpful, and he'd do anything to please.

"Yet he had that ornery streak," he said. "One night he farmed my yard, cut deep tracks in it. He got hold of his father's car and drove 'round and 'round through my yard. The funny thing was, I was standing right there on my darkened patio when he was doing it and I called his father before he got back home. I got laughing so hard I could hardly talk, but Pat wasn't laughing. Pat said, 'Oh, you've got to be kidding! I'll be waiting for him.'"

"Paul," Norma said, "was the kind of kid who would walk down the middle of the street in a white suit, and if there was one speck of dirt in the street, it would smear itself all over that child. The other kid could be walking beside him and he wouldn't get one bit of nothing on him. Paul was the one that was always standing there with egg on his face, and bless his heart, he was always just honest enough, dumb enough, naive enough to admit it, to tell it like it is. Poor old Paul, he'd just come out with, 'Yep, I done it.' Like the night he farmed our yard and Jim was standing there on the patio watching.

"The kid did little piddling things, snag stuff in stores for instance," she said. "If the ax was going to fall, it was going to chop Paul's head off because, bless his heart, he was always in the wrong place at the wrong time. If somebody got garbage on somebody, he would be the one to come up stinking."

Lee Shank was Paul's teacher at Indian Creek the year before Chris enrolled. She, too, loved him and remembered him; Paul would often come back to visit her and invite her to parties he gave that he knew she'd never attend. She also thought he was looking for a mother and said he had had no attachment to his own mother after he was eight years old. When he'd come back to Indian Creek now, he'd burst noisily into her classroom and inspect the work of the children at the learning stations as if he owned the place, but he had a charm, a sense of humor, a desire to please, that let her forgive him, accept him.

Pat Sorrentino, too, she said, had the same kind of charm, but when she had a conference with him concerning his son, he boasted about his importance, boasted blatantly, and tried to use long words and business jargon to impress her. She found him, she said, "a little seedy, faking it, anything but prosperous. He was here for a conference about his son, but he wanted to tell us what books the school should buy without any knowledge at all of what it needed."

At Shawnee Mission South Paul was just barely hanging on in classes, getting Ds or Fs. He was always the boy in trouble, always skipping school, always involved in some theft or dispute, and always surrounded by friends; everybody knew Paul. Even at fifteen or sixteen he was heavily involved in drugs and alcohol and petty theft.

Paul described himself the way Jimmy did, as a "pleaser," the exact word Jimmy used to describe his own character. Both boys sought to please everybody, Paul more noisily and overtly than Jimmy. Both were abandoned by their mothers. Jimmy sought his mother, never attaching himself to anyone else; Paul sought to please a series of women, especially teachers or mother figures like Norma Hooker. In many ways he would do anything for a woman and most women and girls responded readily to his need of them.

Chris, Paul, and Jimmy suddenly lost their mothers at nine or ten years old. Like Jimmy, Paul was killing for a mother, pleasing a mother. Paul and Jimmy were planning to kill a boy as uncertain and as full of fantasies about a mother's love as they themselves were. The two boys were allying themselves with the murdering mother against a son like them whom neither knew personally except as Sueanne created him. Powerless to take revenge against the mothers who abandoned them, they agreed to kill a boy as helpless and as innocent as they were, agreed to destroy a boy who echoed their own family dramas.

At first Jimmy wanted Paul to do it alone. "I talked to Paul about it and he said, yeah, he'd do it. And I was going to get it set up where it would just be him and Chris and then whatever happened there. I kind of wanted to feel like I didn't have any part in it. And then it came about that I was supposed to go with him." Sueanne insisted that Jimmy be there; anyway, she said, Paul didn't have a car and Jimmy could use her Datsun when the time came.

Once Paul had been recruited, Sueanne asked Jimmy daily when the murder would be done, when he would set a date. She had two boys to kill Chris, and she wanted it done right now. "If you loved me, you would do this one little thing for me," she said when they met in her bedroom or his apartment.

"It couldn't happen soon enough for her," Jimmy said. "She was always nagging about it."

Nearly a month dragged by and nothing had been done; Sueanne herself decided to set a date. She learned that Ed had a Labor Relations Board meeting on Thursday evening, the seventeenth of April. On Tuesday she told Jimmy about the meeting. Ed would be home late, she would see to that, and they might do it Thursday night. Chris played racquetball on Thursdays right after school; they could pick him up at the racquetball club and do it, she said. Jimmy called Paul and he said he was free that night, that Thursday would be fine.

6

On Thursday Ed got up to go to work at the mill at his usual time, well before six. "I saw Chris in the morning before I went to work," he said. "He was asleep in his bed. I opened the door and looked at him as I did every morning." Ed picked up the lunch Sueanne prepared for him each morning and left for work. "I called Sueanne around eleven o'clock. I normally call her on my lunch hour," he said. Ed remembered fondly those conversations with Sueanne; her being there at eleven for his calls was something he came to depend on. He told Sueanne that he didn't know when he would be coming home, that he would phone her when the meeting ended. At three-thirty he showered and left work; he was at the Labor Relations Board by four-fifteen.

Jimmy and Paul had also been busy that afternoon, though they never got over to the Fox Hill Racquetball Club to get Chris. "I picked up Paul from school and we rode around for a while and got high on marijuana," Jimmy said. "I didn't want to do it and I told Paul that and he said all right. I dropped Paul off at his house and then went home. I tried to lay down and take a nap and it didn't work, so I got up and got ready to take a shower, and go out, and my mother called. I guess that would be about five, right along in there. She was very upset and wanted to know what the hell was going on. She said, 'Chris is sitting downstairs in the kitchen eating ice cream and I've already gotten rid of his billfold and some of his clothes, and if Ed comes home now and finds all this missing, he'll kill me. It's too late now for you to back out.' She said she was leaving and that she was going to arrange to meet Ed at Burger King for a hamburger, and not to worry about him, that he'll be gone and that Suzanne will be upstairs out of the way."

Jimmy's version of what happened early that Thursday

evening differs from the recollections of Suzanne and Sueanne. Jimmy didn't describe their last meeting in the parking lot outside his apartment. Either it didn't happen or he didn't remember what happened or he refused to tell about it later so that he would not implicate his sister. Suzanne, fully aware of the plan to take Chris out in the woods and kill him, had stayed home from school that day to help her mother. Suzanne and her mother had been over to Jimmy's apartment near the Oak Park Mall many times that Thursday. Except for the last meeting, Suzanne couldn't remember one time from another. Usually Suzanne would go in and get Jimmy and bring him out to the car; sometimes she and her mother would both go in. Jimmy's roommate, whom he scarcely knew, was out working.

Suzanne was a go-between that entire day. Both mother and daughter knew how shaky Jimmy was, how difficult it would be for him to do it. They came repeatedly to reassure him, to tell him how much they needed it done.

Immediately after she called Jimmy, Sueanne and her daughter drove over to his apartment. Sueanne parked on the far side of the large, empty blacktop lot, the side nearest the street. Suzanne went in to get Jimmy and silently walked him to the car. When the two approached, Sueanne got out of the dark blue Lincoln Continental to meet Jimmy, and Suzanne got in on the passenger side and closed the door.

Sueanne had come at six o'clock, an hour before sunset. It was a beautiful, mild April evening, with a red sun going down behind them. Standing close together beside the car, they spoke quietly. Jimmy stood uneasily in front of her, not looking at her, avoiding her eyes. She was nervous, too; she talked when she was nervous and she did almost all the talking. She said Jimmy had to get rid of Chris, that he was causing too many problems, that Jimmy and his friend had to take him out and get rid of him, that this was the night to do it. It had to be done, she said. Get rid of him.

They talked no more than ten minutes. Sueanne had to be back when Ed called and she was not sure how long his union grievance hearing would take. She didn't threaten or bribe Jimmy. He already knew he was to get a car and the murder would get his mother off his back; he hoped that if he killed Chris, he might get away from her for good. "Get rid of him, you've got to get rid of him," she said. Jimmy stood awkwardly before her for a long time; finally he said softly, "Well, we'll go out and get rid of him."

As Sueanne drove away from the parking lot she remembered that Chris's billfold was still in her purse. She had lied in her phone call to Jimmy; to prod him into action, she told him that she had already gotten rid of the billfold. Sueanne was, of course, not foolish enough to throw away the billfold until she heard directly Jimmy's assent to kill Chris. Even then she knew it was a risk; Jimmy might back out again, but she could wait no longer.

Sueanne wanted to make sure Chris would be sought as a runaway, perhaps one to whom some violence had been done, for this runaway was never coming back. If his billfold were left in the house, the police might believe the boy had been taken from it by force and ask other kinds of questions.

Sueanne had already purged the billfold of Chris's notes and addresses, tidied it up. She left only his social security card, his junior-high photograph on an Indian Creek identity card, and a color photograph of her and Ed. In the photograph Ed is wearing a tan V-neck sweater; the collar of his white shirt opens out over the V. He looks vaguely and proudly toward an object to the side and well above the camera. Sueanne is wearing a red V-neck sweater with three gold chains of varying lengths. The longest chain curves down just above her small breasts; attached to the chain is a medallion. She is looking directly at the camera with dark eyes strongly accented underneath by eyeliner. The lower half of her face is smiling.

On her way back to the condominium, Sueanne drove in the main entrance of the Metcalf South Shopping Mall. She quickly climbed the wide stairs to the top level, stopped in front of an exclusive women's clothing store, and threw Chris's black billfold under a weeping fig tree growing in a pot beside a bench. Suzanne, following a few steps behind, watched her do it.

"I called Paul and told him that we had to do it that night," Jimmy said. "I drove over and picked him up and then we went over to my mother's house." Paul was waiting for Jimmy when he got there. When Paul came out the front door of his town house, he had a 20-gauge shotgun with him. "He put it in the back of the car, in the hatchback of my mother's Datsun," Jimmy said. The special license plate on the car read SPIRIT, named after Sueanne's only female cat, who, she said, "has four brothers and can't stand any of them."

Jimmy didn't remember what time he got to the house, but it must have been not long after Ed's call at seven. Apparently Sueanne waited to see if the boys would show up. "It was dusk," Jimmy said. "We pulled in the driveway and my mother was coming out of the garage in the Lincoln. She said that Chris was in the kitchen and Suzanne was upstairs, then she drove away. Paul walked on inside. I went down to the basement toward my old bedroom. I stopped at the bottom of the stairs and picked out from Ed's gun case the same shotgun I had used on hunting trips with him and Chris, then got a shovel from the garage and put the gun and shovel in the back of the car."

Sueanne didn't have a clear idea of how the boys were going to abduct Chris and she wanted Suzanne out of the way. Before she left the house, Sueanne told her daughter to get in the shower when Jimmy and Paul came to get Chris. The three had talked about it for so long, so intensely, that to Suzanne that night their coming for Chris seemed as silent as a dream; she heard nothing and she wanted to hear nothing. Chris, Suzanne knew, expected nothing, had no idea his stepmother and stepbrother and stepsister wanted him dead.

On the glass-topped kitchen table, where Urban had watched him connive six months before, Chris was working on a poster for a science project due the next week at school. To the relief of Lee Shank, Chris had finally begun to plan ahead, to finish major assignments. While Jimmy was getting the shotgun and the shovel Paul was telling Chris about a drug scam they were going to do, how they were going to meet a truck transporting drugs and take the drugs by force. "Do you want to come along?" Paul asked.

Chris didn't ask any questions and Paul wouldn't even have had to tell Chris any story if he didn't want to. Chris was invited on an adventure with his older brother for the first time. Perhaps Chris thought that he would reveal his ignorance about such things if he asked to have the adventure clearly defined. Not asking made him one with them.

"Chris was so gullible," Jimmy said. "When I walked back inside, Chris and Paul were walking toward me, talking about making money. We were in the house probably three to five minutes. I drove, Paul sat on the passenger side, and Chris was in the middle of the backseat." He was eagerly leaning over between the two boys, included in their conspiracy.

"We went to the end of I-435, then south on I-35," Jimmy said. "When we started driving, I saw a sign that said 'Wichita' and I leaned over to Paul and I whispered to him, 'Why don't we just take him to Wichita?'—with the intention of putting him on a bus to go someplace for a while. Paul said that was fine with him."

Now night was coming on, a clear, beautiful spring evening with the sun just down, the temperature mild. Nobody had brought along a jacket. Jimmy wore a red flannel shirt, blue jeans, and dress shoes; Paul, a T-shirt, jeans, and heavy boots; Chris, a long-sleeved red sport shirt, jeans, and white running shoes.

I-35 angled sharply southwest out of Johnson County and passed for several miles through a series of small towns strung out along it. On the urban stretches of the Interstate Jimmy and Paul were at home, but they were basically city boys, and the open spaces south of the town were strange to them. They rarely entered the farmland outside the city and they thought of the people who lived out there with amusement and contempt. They were now, Jimmy said, "out in the sticks." The traffic thinned quickly. The air became noticeably chillier the further out they went, and they closed the windows against the night air and the darkness coming down.

Paul and Jimmy spoke guardedly. "When we were going down the highway Paul said it was getting too late, that we might just go ahead and do it so he could get back because he had school the next day. Paul said, 'We're pushed for time, pull off here.' We turned off the Interstate and we were driving around on gravel roads, probably an hour or two. We didn't have any idea where we were or where we were going. We just drove around."

Jimmy started down a dirt road. Just after dogs rushed out at them from a darkened house, the car started scraping its bottom. Jimmy kept going, keeping his wheels on the hard, dried mud pushed up by trucks during the rains last month.

"We came to a dead end," Jimmy recalled. "As I was turning the car around Paul said, 'This looks like a good place.' He meant it would be a good place to do the killing. I stopped the car. There was a creek at the end of the road and there was a sign that said, 'Bridge Washed Out' or something like that; there were no houses or people around that I saw. It was dark and we had our headlights on. We got out of the car. I opened up the hatchback and Paul took out his gun and Ed's shovel."

The three had driven a mile into Miami County and had wandered around until they came to Big Bull Creek. The bridge was out because a large dam was being constructed further downstream on Big Bull, though the gates closing the dam were not yet built. They had come upon an area that was to be flooded periodically—a wildlife conservation area in low water, a holding area during high water. The road running toward the creek had begun to deteriorate; where the road ended, an untilled field came down to touch the trees along the banks of the creek.

They had no plan to execute, yet things suddenly became quite simple and all three seemed to know exactly what to do. "Paul told Chris that we needed to dig a hole big enough for the truck carrying drugs to get stuck in," Jimmy said. "Paul took the gun and shovel with him and walked a ways up or down the street." There was, of course, no street, but instead unmarked terrain. Paul walked about a hundred feet south with Chris following. Jimmy left the headlights on, but "Paul and Chris weren't lighted up that much because I couldn't get the car pointed in the right direction."

The trees had grown fat and thick along the creek, sucking all the water they needed in all seasons. Though just starting to let out their leaves, the trees already presented an impenetrable barrier. The creek turned abruptly at the point Chris and Paul had reached and the trees cut the boys off darkly on all sides except for the gap opened by the dirt road coming across the flat toward the ruined bridge. The silence of the night was unusual to all of them and the stillness was broken only by dogs barking far away and the sound of a whippoorwill back for spring, its calls coming relentlessly over the quiet, defining it with the unnatural rhythm of a machine.

Despite the unusually warm spring, the grass had not grown enough to obscure the contours of the land. Chris followed Paul up a slight rise until they were stopped by a great branching elm. "Chris and I went over to the left side of the field that's facing the creek and I started digging," Paul recalled, "but the ground was too hard, so we decided to start digging over by the creek." The land rose sharply as it met the bank of the creek. Paul had chosen a spot tight against the trees and underlaid thickly with small roots; he had to keep digging around the larger roots and cutting through the smaller ones. Paul had never done much digging before and his arms soon tired.

"Paul and Chris started digging the hole, taking turns with the shovel," Jimmy said. "I was high on marijuana and walking around. I walked up the gravel road a piece, cut across the field, and came back toward the creek. It was a dream, it was like a dream. I mean it was happening, but I was kind of just a part of it, I was just there. You know how a dream is, where you see things and you're just there, but you're not partaking."

When Paul tired, Chris took up the shovel with enthusiasm; he wanted to prove that he was one of them and he dug the hole as quickly as he could. The beams of the car's headlights were coming toward him thinly as he dug. The light blinded him to all but the task; Jimmy and Paul now stood back a little way out of the light, talking quietly.

Paul and Jimmy could hear Chris puffing, digging as fast as he could to impress them with his strength. He stopped once to catch his breath and leaned on the shovel. "He asked why again, and we just told him the hole had to be dug," Jimmy said. "While Chris was digging we were off to the side. Chris dug a long hole, five or six feet long, two or three feet wide, two feet or so deep. When he had gotten it that far, I squared off the edges. Paul said, 'Let's get on with it,' and I picked up Ed's shotgun. We had loaded the guns before we even got in the car."

Jimmy asked Chris to lie down in the hole. "He was told to try it on for size, to see if it was big enough," Jimmy said. When Chris got down in the hole, it wasn't quite long enough; he was already nearly five-foot-nine, taller than either Paul or Jimmy. When Chris had lain down in the hole, Jimmy said, "If you move, we are going to kill you," and Chris got scared and sat up.

"At that point Jimmy and I were standing behind Chris and Chris was sitting up in the hole," Paul said. "He had his back to us and we spontaneously started counting off 'one,' 'two,' 'three.' I said 'one' and Jimmy said 'two,' and by the time I said 'three' Jimmy had walked around Chris's right side and was now in front facing him. I was still behind Chris, and Jimmy pointed the gun at Chris and they started to argue. Jimmy was telling Chris why he was doing what he was doing, why he was going to shoot him. He said, 'This is for hitting my mother and my sister, and for getting me kicked out of the house.' Then I shot Chris in the head from ten feet away and he held on to his head. And Jimmy shot, and Chris fell back, and I came around to Chris's left side."

"I heard him whimper after I fired," Jimmy said. "I said to Paul, 'He can feel it. Put him out of his misery.'"

"I shot him two more times, in the face and in the heart," Paul said.

Once the deafening sounds had died out, the clarity, the order, and the calm, almost unconscious, cooperation of all ceased. "I was a babbling idiot for about the next hour and a half," Jimmy said. "Both of us covered him up; we were on our knees, pushing and using the shovel and kicking and everything we could do to dirt. I wouldn't say it was all covered up, but it was the best we could tell because it was dark."

"We made the grave pretty even," Paul said. "As a matter of fact, we piled the dirt up a little bit. After I did it, I started shaking all over. I just went into a frenzy." When they had gotten the guns and the shovel back in the car, Paul turned around and saw Chris's hand sticking out of the grave. Paul ran back to the grave for the last time. "I put dirt on top of it, and stomped on his fingers, and put more dirt on top."

"We hopped in our car and hauled ass," Jimmy said. But the confusion of getting in was nothing compared to the difficulty of getting out. Their purpose in coming in was to get lost; now they had to find a way back. The dam and the preparations for the dam cut off most ways of access back to I-35; there wasn't a straight road out of the area, even if the two were capable of finding it. "I drove around for a long time, and wasted a quarter of a tank of gas," Jimmy said.

The boys asked directions twice. "We stopped at a big brick house," Jimmy recalled. "I didn't have my lights on when I pulled up to the house. There were two storagelike barns on the side and one in the back, and they had dogs. A young girl answered the door; she was baby-sitting evidently. It was a nice house for being out in that area, a real nice house; it had one of those fancy wrought-iron front doors and a chandelier in the front hall. You know how little girls are when they give directions; they weren't that good. Later we stopped at another house, a white house; a car just pulled into the driveway, so I stopped. The car was a rod; it had the wheels and the headers on it. The guy in the car was older than me, twenty-four or twenty-five, well built, long hair, about shoulder length, and I think he had a mustache and a beard. I was finally going in the right direction; he said keep going down the road and you'll hit it. We got on I-35 way south of where we left it."

"It took an hour or two to get from the creek back to my apartment," Jimmy said. "We got back at about eleven o'clock. We took the shotguns into the apartment with us and set them in the closet. We got high on marijuana for a while longer and drank and at about midnight I drove Paul home. When he got out of the car to go, Paul said, 'Boy, that was easy.'"

4

RUNAWAY

1

By late afternoon on Thursday, the day of the murder, Ed was at the National Labor Relations Board in downtown Kansas City, Missouri. "I was a union steward at Ralston Purina and we were having some labor problems," he said. "I didn't figure I'd be there past five-thirty. I knew it wasn't going to be real late because the attorney we were talking to had basketball tickets that night."

Negotiations broke off in the early evening, just at sunset. "I phoned Sueanne as we were walking out the door at seven," Ed recalled. "Because I didn't know what time I would get home, I figured she'd fix supper. She said, 'Why don't we just meet for a hamburger someplace? I didn't fix anything because I didn't know what time you'd be home.' I says, 'Where do you want to meet?' She says, 'The Burger King on Metcalf.' I says, 'Okay.' She loves Whoppers. We usually ate hamburgers at least once a week, or something like that. Normally I would come home and we would leave from there. It was a kind of rare thing to meet somewhere for supper on a weekday."

The Burger King was at eightieth and Metcalf, fifteen blocks directly north of the Metcalf South Shopping Center. Ed got there a little before seven-thirty and Sueanne was waiting for him in the parking lot. They sat across from each other in the orange-and-brown plastic booths and ate Whoppers, looking out on the White Horse Motor Lodge and the green-tinted windows of Regan's Restaurant across the street. The sun had been down for a half hour and lights were on. When Ed got there, he could still see clearly outside.

Ed was tired and they spoke little. The meeting exhausted him more than tending the machines at Purina. "Sueanne asked how things were going at the Labor Board, and we chitchatted about that. She knew the hours we were putting in to try to get the problem taken care of down there. She was just her usual self."

He couldn't remember any conversation about their family. "We didn't sit there and drink coffee and smoke cigarettes after we ate," he said. "We just drove home. I had a bunch of papers I had to go through." Ed followed the Lincoln home in his small Model-T truck.

"We got home at eight-fifteen," he said. "It was fairly light out yet. Suzanne was in her room watching TV. I didn't see Chris anywhere. Within a few minutes I asked Sueanne when was the last time she saw Chris. She said, 'Around six o'clock he was outside playing.' Chris was supposed to come home every night and do his homework, if there was homework to do. And then he could go out and play, or whatever he wanted to do. He'd play for a few minutes after he got out of school, but normally it was coming home and doing his homework. Because if I caught him out there outside playing and it was nine o'clock at night and I saw him doing homework later, we had a little talk.

"We went upstairs and turned the TV on in the bedroom and I laid on the bed," Ed recalled. The bedroom, in the midst of being redecorated, was messy; the walls were half-repapered and the closet doors were being sanded down. "I had a stack of reports I had to go through and I had to go over testimonies and I was very busy. The TV was playing, making noise, and I was going over the paperwork."

By nine-thirty Ed was irritated and concerned. "Again I asked Sue when was the last time she saw Chris. She said at six o'clock he was outside playing. Chris hadn't come in or anything, hadn't called, or whatever—or at least hadn't let us know where he was. It was dark. It was warm out, very warm, but it was dark—but he'd get to playing and playing and playing. There have been times that he would come in at nine-thirty, quarter of ten. He had to get his shower and stuff so he could get to bed and get to sleep. I went back to the papers for a little while and just something wasn't right, so I got up and asked Sueanne again, I said, 'When did you see Chris?' She says, 'Well, he was outside playing at six o'clock,' and I said, 'Okay.'

"Well, I started looking around the house and walked outside. I thought maybe he would be outside playing with some of the kids, and there was nobody out there, and so I started again looking, walking around the complex that we live in, trying to keep my eyes open. I walked out to see if his bike was there. I know he used to go down to the creek there behind the house; it's a couple of blocks down there. I ended up walking down there and back. There's a big park down there behind our complex. I walked around behind our condominium because a lot of times they played out between the two sets of houses. I walked around the house and hollered outside."

While Ed was hollering and walking around the house, Chris was just squaring off the sides of his grave. Jimmy and Paul counted down and shot him at approximately nine-thirty.

"By that time I was very concerned, and I started searching inside the house to see if I could find any idea of what happened," he said. "If his baseball glove was gone, or if his ball bats were gone, or what. Sueanne didn't go through the things like I did, but I really didn't pay that much attention to her. I remember her being there. I know she looked in the closet, I think it was, and found out we had a jacket missing. I ended up searching the whole house and the whole neighborhood. I found a shotgun missing, a 12-gauge single shot, the one that Jimmy used the last time we went hunting."

Ed never asked Suzanne about Chris. As far as he knew, she stayed in her room the whole night.

"I called the police at ten-thirty," he said. "I told them I wanted a policeman to come over. Sueanne was wondering what was going on, but I don't recall her saying anything. She looked worried because she could see I was getting upset."

Officer Briley from the Overland Park Police Department came over to the house a little before eleven o'clock and spent an hour with Ed. "According to Briley, the boy was going to have to be turned in as a runaway, and there was no evidence of anything else, and I told him, I says, 'My son didn't run away.' I knew Chris. I was all Chris had to an extent. Oh, he had a half-sister in Tulsa and he had a grandmother Eva, but other than that the only thing Chris had was myself and Sueanne and Suzanne. There was no place for him to run, for one thing, and he had no reason to run away. The only problems he complained about was the part of two kids bickering back and forth."

If Ed was the only thing Chris had, Chris was all Ed had left of the first thirty-five years of his life. His parents were dead to him long before they were buried; Tani was dead; and his grandparents whom he loved had died just after Shirley. He had been building a new life, yet, as Sueanne later said, "I knew that without Chris, there would be no Ed."

"Sometime that evening," Ed recalled angrily, "Sueanne said, 'Well, Chris may have run away.' I said my son had no reason to run away. I knew he didn't. I knew he didn't. And I still know he didn't. And I knew that every day of the week. Later, when the police officers would come by, I said there was one thing I could tell them: I knew my son didn't run away. Chris and I loved each other very much. He had no place to go and he had no reason to go. He wanted for nothing."

After Briley left, Ed searched alone. "I walked along Indian Creek all the way to Nall Street because I know Chris used to play in the creek some. I thought maybe he fell or got himself hurt or got pinned down there. I was up all night. I didn't go to work the next day and I spent all the next day going."

2

At midnight, after returning to the police station, Briley wrote a brief report: "Upon arrival contact was made with Mr. Hobson who advised his son had left the residence earlier this evening and had not returned. This is unusual for Chris on a school night. Mr. Hobson advised there had been absolutely no problems lately with Chris. Chris does well in school and has been in no trouble. The only friend Mr. Hobson advised was a Bob Flack. Contact was made with the Flacks who advised they had not seen Chris today and have no idea where he might be. Mr. Hobson advised that there are two pairs of tennis shoes missing from Chris's room. Mr. Hobson also realized that a 12-gauge shotgun was missing. He stated that Chris does not handle guns unless his father was present. Information conveyed to the dispatcher for computer entry. No photo. No further action."

3

The next morning while Ed was out of the house searching for Chris, Sueanne got up uncharacteristically early and phoned Jimmy. "She said something like, 'How did it go last night?' or 'What happened last night?'" Jimmy recalled. "Mother said that Ed was out looking for Chris and that if there was anything in the apartment that would identify that Chris had been there or anything about the night before, I was to get rid of it. She didn't ask if it was done or not. I didn't tell her the details. I didn't want to. I just said it was over with. I might have told her a couple of other things like, 'He's way out,' but nothing in great detail. She understood he wasn't coming back because she was the one that told me to make sure he didn't. It was the type of thing that was taken for granted by her, not by me. She didn't lose any sleep over it."

Sueanne herself went out looking for Chris that morning. When she came to Indian Creek Junior High, walking in under the long, curving concrete entrance on a fine early spring morning, she had Lee Shank called up to the front office. When Mrs. Shank saw Sueanne, she was astonished; at their previous meeting she was immaculately dressed and groomed. "Mrs. Hobson looked ten years older that morning," Mrs. Shank said. "She was wearing bedroom slippers and her hair was straggly and her eyes had deep circles under them. She was extremely nervous and very concerned about Chris."

After talking to Lee Shank for ten minutes, Sueanne hurried

back to her car. "I drove around Cherry Hill, which is the housing addition close to Indian Creek, hunting for Chris," Sueanne recalled. She didn't call Jimmy that morning, she said, because "Ed tried to call him several times."

Sueanne was home by noon and immediately phoned her friend Margie Hunt-Fugate. The woman Margie spoke to didn't seem at all like the distraught person Mrs. Shank saw a few hours earlier. "She wanted to know what I had to do that day," Margie said. "She was in a very good mood; she said that Chris was gone; she said that he'd run away that night. I was surprised that she and Ed weren't out looking for him. She said that Ed couldn't take off work; he'd get docked. She wanted to know what I had to do that day. She said, 'Let's go out.' She was at my apartment to pick me up within an hour. When she got there, she said, 'Let's go out and celebrate, he's gone.' We went out to the Brookridge Country Club on 103rd Street where I worked because I had to get my schedule and my paycheck. When we got there, she stopped at the bar downstairs and she said she wanted to have a drink to celebrate Chris's being gone.

"Later we picked Suzanne up after school," Margie said. "We stopped by my apartment again for a minute and then we went out to Belton, Missouri. She said she wanted to check on a job that she had run across in the *Thrifty Nickel,* one of those little newspapers made up of classified ads. Then we went to a restaurant out there where I knew the bartender, Marsha Rainwater, and had two more drinks toasting Chris being gone."

Margie knew the demands of raising children. Though she loved her two boys, she understood how difficult they had made her life. Laughing, Margie drank to the new life just beginning for Sueanne and her family.

That afternoon in the bar it was to Margie the men were drawn rather than to the more finely featured woman dressed conservatively in white, who looked the epitome of the Johnson County homemaker. Certainly Margie's intense blond hair gave men pause. She had a strong, clear face that let men know where they stood immediately. Margie liked men and she was alert to their interest. Sueanne seemed more interested in Margie than in men, more comfortable with her than with them.

"Sueanne was a lady," Margie said simply.

At this moment of transition, of change and crisis, Margie suddenly became Sueanne's chief support and confidante. In the darkened bar of the restaurant, fifteen miles from home, Sueanne was safe and she knew she was safe.

In the weeks that followed Sueanne began to treat Margie as if she were a member of her extended family. "She gave me a lot of Chris's stuff," Margie said. "The first thing that she gave me was the blue suit that Chris wore to their wedding because I have two boys; they were a bit younger than Chris was at the time, but she said they would eventually grow into it. Then she gave me sheets off of his bed, the cover that was on his bed, some odds and ends, other clothes, a desk with a lamp and chair that he used in his bedroom, his dresser, and some metal shelving that she had in the house. After Chris disappeared, she decided that she wanted to completely redo his room as a study."

Margie was not as surprised as she might have been at these gifts, for Sueanne had always been generous to her and to her other women friends. Each could speak of a coat or a fur stole or a television set Sueanne gave away—an unexpected gift for which the woman had no means to reciprocate. In the past year Margie had been an audience for Sueanne's good fortune in marrying Ed. Margie had seen Sueanne change from a woman who lived on credit or on the generosity of a lover, to one whose husband had land to sell in northeastern Missouri.

Perhaps Margie saw an opportunity in Sueanne's crisis. Sueanne now owned her own home and drove a Lincoln Continental. Margie herself had no car and bicycled to her job at Brookridge Country Club when the weather permitted. Certainly Margie was led to believe Sueanne had come into a lot of money.

Sueanne had always dressed well, meticulously, even in the years before she met Ed, and she was always paying off bills for the expensive furniture she purchased. Now she could buy the best clothes and the best furniture. "Her house was beautiful, it was perfect," Margie said. "It looked like a Hallmark shop. Everything was hers completely; she decorated every wall, every knickknack shelf. She spent a lot of money and a lot of time on furniture, except for Chris's room. Chris's room was the bare necessities and that was it. There was no decoration. I asked her, 'Why didn't you do anything about Chris's room?' She said, 'Well, I bought him a mirror.' And that was it. The room was the basics."

Though Margie had seen Chris often, she had never felt close to him and she accepted Sueanne's view that he was a trouble-maker. When Sueanne gave her his things, she didn't ask questions. Besides, Chris was not Sueanne's child really, but Ed's; if he ran away, that was Ed's problem.

4

Almost immediately Suzanne began to live as if Chris had never existed. She would simply tell her classmates he ran away, and she would behave, and sometimes feel, as if that were what had happened, or as if no one in the family really knew what had happened. "The next day Mother said that Jimmy went out and took care of him, and she did not elaborate," Suzanne said. "I didn't know what to think. I didn't know if they just beat him up real bad, just enough to put him in the hospital, or not. When Chris didn't come home after a few days, I figured they killed him."

After a day or two Sueanne wouldn't talk to her daughter at all about the murder. Even to Suzanne she would admit no complicity. Sueanne now told her daughter that she had nothing whatsoever to do with Chris's death. Amazingly, her mother seemed to believe it. She left Suzanne alone with her feelings about the stepbrother she had helped kill, alone with her guilt and her responsibility.

5

The three members of the original Crumm family, consumed by the conspiracy since February, now seemed to be prevented from sharing it, even with their co-conspirators. Jimmy didn't have much time to celebrate. After dropping off Sorrentino at his town house after midnight, he returned to his own apartment, drank some more whiskey, and slept for a few hours before his mother called at six-thirty in the morning. Sueanne told him that Ed was out looking for Chris and that he was trying to get in touch with Jimmy. She told him that he should get rid of anything that would tie him to what happened last night, and he remembered he had Ed's gun in his closet. He had thrown the spent shells out along the Interstate on the way back; now he had to get rid of the gun.

"I panicked," Jimmy said, "and I started getting rid of it piece by piece. The shotgun came apart; you had to take the screws off—the barrel and stock, the firing pin, and that metal stuff. I put the pieces all over, in trash cans around my apartment complex and in that area. Ed's gun, the 12-gauge, was not in the house for longer than three hours, that's how much sleep I had. Because I was on probation on the credit-card scam, I wouldn't keep a gun in my house."

Paul had also left his shotgun in Jimmy's front closet. "I wrapped Paul's up and took it back to him and put it in the shed behind the house where his motorcycle was kept."

Ten hours or so after the murder, Jimmy had cut himself off from the guns and the shells and most of the physical evidence of the crime. Yet the white Datsun with the license plate SPIRIT was out in his parking lot. At four on Friday afternoon, after Sueanne had returned from the restaurant in Belton, Jimmy called her and drove over to the Hobson condominium to return her car. When he went inside, he found his mother upstairs in the bedroom. Neither wanted to speak about the killing; both seemed reassured by talking calmly and quietly in this familiar place.

Jimmy had stayed a little longer than he anticipated. As he walked out to get into his old brown van, what he was trying to avoid happened. Ed had been out looking for Chris all day and he wanted to talk to Jimmy. "Jimmy was there when I got back home," Ed said. "I blocked the driveway so he couldn't pull out before I talked to him. It was in the evening, five or six o'clock. I asked, 'Have you seen Chris?' He said, 'Yes, I stopped by last night about seven o'clock and got some ice out of the refrigerator and he was sitting at the kitchen table doing his homework. I just came in and got some ice, spoke to him, and left. He was sit-

ting there when I left.' That's all he told me. I asked him about
the shotgun; he said he hadn't seen it. Within a few minutes he
drove out; how long he was there prior to me coming home, I
don't know."

Jimmy had more compassion for Ed and more fear of seeing him
than he had for anyone else. He knew that Ed liked him; he also
knew Ed had not had anything he could call a family before and
that he had tried to give him a sense of family. Ed had even confided in him. He had treated him well, better than his mother had,
better than he expected. In return he'd murdered his only child.

When he killed Chris, Jimmy had been in his apartment less
than two weeks and Ed had helped him move in. Even during
the weeks after the murder, Ed repeatedly loaded up his Model-T
truck and drove across town, taking things to Jimmy. Ed and
Jimmy spoke a couple of times after their meeting outside the
condominium on Friday, the eighteenth of April.

"I asked him both times I saw him, 'Have you seen Chris, or
have you heard from Chris, or have any of your friends said anything about Chris?'" Ed recalled. "Jimmy says, 'No, I'll have my
friends go look for him.' He appeared fairly nervous. Not real nervous, but a little hesitant, I guess you'd call it. He wouldn't look me
in the face. Ninety percent of the people I have talked to, if you are
looking them straight in the eye, don't lie too well. I felt that
Jimmy possibly might have known more than what he was telling
me. I did not think of him being responsible, but then I didn't
know what there was to be responsible for either."

Jimmy had much to do during the weeks following the murder
of Chris. His mother had promised him a car and he began looking for one to buy. When Paul asked Jimmy what he would be
getting out of the deal, Jimmy told him, "Remember all my skipping of school? Ted Reyes and I go out and drive cars at lots all
day—I'm getting a new car, an Oldsmobile Cutlass."

Sueanne didn't tell Jimmy when he was to get the car. "I
didn't know for sure, I just went out looking. I looked every-
place—through papers, car lots, everywhere. Every car lot that I
knew of, I went out there. Mom and I discussed several models
and there were three or four cars I really liked, but I never made
a definite decision on one."

While Jimmy was looking for a car, Sueanne had decided to sell the white Datsun. A few weeks earlier in the *Thrifty Nickel* she had advertised the car for thirty-four hundred dollars. On Wednesday, the twenty-third of April, Jimmy drove out to Raytown in the Datsun, Sue in the Lincoln; she sold the car for twenty-one hundred dollars.

"I followed her out there in the other car when she sold it," Jimmy said. "I rode back in the Lincoln Continental with her. She said it was a lot more peaceful around the house now that Chris was not there." He remembered that Sueanne had first whispered this to him last summer in the motel at Silver Dollar City.

On the drive back to Overland Park after selling the car, enclosed in the quiet, heavy luxury of the dark Lincoln, both felt truly secure. The murder car was gone; Ed's shotgun was broken into pieces and the spent shells thrown out along the highway; the half-buried body of Chris was rotting away in the sticks in the record heat of a magnificent April day. The chief conspirators knew how difficult it would be to connect them to those small explosions in the woods.

No one could even torture out of Jimmy where the body was; he didn't know how he got there, and once there, he didn't know how he got out. Now nothing but language seemed to connect Jimmy and Sueanne to the crime; the language of murder that they shared and still shared seemed vague, almost immaterial, almost spiritual. Sueanne had spoken only to Suzanne and Jimmy; Jimmy only to his mother, Suzanne, and Paul; Suzanne only to her mother and Jimmy.

Certainly Sueanne had seemed confident the day she sold the car. "She told me that she was picking out the curtains to make Chris's bedroom into a sewing room," he said. His mother was off his back finally and he was protected by the power she had. Jimmy felt that day an intimacy with her, a mutual dependency, an equality even, that he had never before experienced with her or anyone else.

Sueanne dropped him off at the Oak Park Apartments. Here he intended to start a life of his own, life as an adult. Alone, away from his mother, and out of the plush, soundproof Lincoln,

Jimmy felt much less certain of his safety. He had always felt alone, felt, or thought he felt, little need of others, despite his passion to please; besides, those he loved had always disappeared. Now he had only his conspirators to confide in. Of those he cared only about his mother and his sister, and they would also disappear.

Jimmy knew virtually nothing about Sorrentino; in fact, he had chosen Paul because he knew little about him except that he "looked like the kind of guy who would do it," a remarkably precise delineation of his character.

Ted Reyes, a boy of seventeen, whom Jimmy was with more than anyone else after the murder, said his friend never told him about killing Chris. "We noticed that Jimmy was acting funny there for a long time, you know, and we always asked, 'What's the matter?' Jimmy goes, 'Nothing, just, you know, problems.' He was nervous; all's he said was just 'problems.' He'd come over to our house, eat dinner with my family, and I didn't know what to think; I was reading the newspapers about the brother and the stepbrother and I didn't know what to think. He was more or less a radical person at the time, hyper. I'd go over with him to his house where his mother was at; he just told me, 'Wait in the car; I'll be right out, and it won't be long,' and usually it ended up to be about forty-five minutes I was sitting outside."

Jimmy tried to keep busy looking for a car to buy, painting the house of his friend Ted, hunting for a regular job, and getting drunk or high on drugs every night. At night, especially, he was afraid. He always had had recurrent dreams, dreams that he didn't ever have to write down to remember. Now in a dream he would be shooting with others at a dark figure in a hole; or he would find himself in a hole with dark figures standing above him, shooting down at him.

He also feared things outside him; at night he slept with earphones on and listened to stereo music so that he would not hear the knock when it came. He had an urge to call Urban, to tell him what he had done. In fact he called Urban almost every day in those weeks, ostensibly to discuss his probation. In the weeks right after the murder, he said extravagantly, "I lost thirty-five

pounds. I stopped smoking because it began to taste like gunpowder; finally, everything I ate tasted like gunpowder. I'd brush my
teeth to try to get the taste out of my mouth."

6

On Wednesday, the twenty-third of April, six days after the murder, Sueanne deposited fifteen hundred dollars from the Raytown
Datsun check in the Hobson account and took six hundred dollars
in cash. She told Margie about the sale. "I was really surprised that
Sueanne wanted to sell it because that was the car that Jimmy
drove," Margie said. "Even though he didn't live there, he still
drove her car all the time, and one day, all of a sudden, she just
drove it out to a Datsun dealer and sold it for cash, for far less than
what she could have gotten for it had she waited and advertised it
another week or two. She once told me she thought it was worth
about three thousand because she thought maybe I'd want to buy
it or knew somebody."

Sueanne knew that Sorrentino wanted his money, wanted his
motorcycle fixed; Paul spoke to Jimmy several times about getting paid. Leila Anderson, a high-school friend of Paul, recalled
Paul's end of a phone conversation with Jimmy a week after the
murder. "Paul said first, 'Well, what about the Datsun? Why
don't you just buy that? I am really economic wise; either get a
little car or get a motorcycle because you can't go out in a truck
and do all of the things you can on a motorcycle.' And then
Jimmy, obviously, over the phone must have said, 'Well, she's
already sold it,' because Paul said, 'She's already sold it? Why
didn't she give it to me?'"

Unlike Jimmy, Sorrentino couldn't bear to be alone, couldn't
live without others. His junior-high counselor noted that Paul
"made friends easily and had a lot of friends, but at the same
time, he was intolerant of kids who were somewhat different: a
kid who was slow as far as learning new things; an individual
who was retarded; the type of kid that juveniles would call a
'nerd'; and other children suffering from emotional problems."

Less than a week after the murder, on the last day Paul

attended high school, he spoke with Anne Gresham, his senior-high counselor at Shawnee Mission South. She had had many conversations with him before and he considered her a friend. "Paul would get himself in trouble just because he felt like it," she said. "A lot of times he told me he just didn't have anything better to do. The last time I spoke with Paul I could tell there was something troubling him and that he'd better get it worked out. I told him that he shouldn't keep that type of problem inside and that he should at least talk to his friends about whatever it is that's troubling him."

Paul didn't even wait a week to tell his friends about the murder. Jerry Boring heard it first; he was seventeen, one of two teenage sons of Jack Boring, a bankrupt real-estate promoter who was well-known in Kansas City because he regularly appeared to hawk his properties on local television. Jerry had known Paul for three years and they had played together on the high-school soccer team. Jerry said, "We were out at Shawnee Mission Park on Thursday afternoon, the twenty-fourth of April, sitting out on the dock talking to a couple of girls. The girls left and, when Paul and I were leaving around four-thirty, Paul said, 'J.B. ought to know what to do.' We had had a couple of beers, and he goes, 'J.B., I don't know what to do.' And I go, 'What do you mean?' and he goes, 'I killed someone,' and I go, 'No, you didn't,' and he goes, 'Yeah, I did.' Then he just started laughing, and he's always a joker and he lies a lot. You never know when he's telling the truth, and that's all there was to it.

"I didn't think another thing of it," Jerry said, "but when I heard the boy was missing, I was wondering. And when I heard later four people swear Chris was still around and someone saw him at Worlds of Fun, then I thought Paul was playing a bad trick. Kids, even junior-high kids, began to come up to me and say, 'Did Paul do that, or what's going on?' And I go, 'I don't know,' because I didn't know what happened."

In fact, Jerry began to tell others about Paul's confession the afternoon he first heard it. "I told Leila Anderson about it, but I wasn't sure, and told her not to ask Paul about it as if I told her, because I wouldn't want Paul getting mad at me for spreading false stuff. I asked Leila to talk to Paul to see if it was true. One day I was ready to tell Paul's best friend, Brad Brown, but Brad had said he had already heard. After that one day that he told me and I said I didn't believe him, I said, 'Paul, I don't want to hear about things like that!' I heard a lot of things, but I never heard anything more from Paul. I didn't want to hear no more because I didn't believe him. He did say that he and Jimmy Hobson committed a murder. A couple of days later I told Paul he ought to go see a priest; I said, 'Paul, you've got a pretty good friend you can talk to.'

"I didn't get any more than that from Paul," Jerry said, "but what I heard on the street was that Jimmy and Paul went out there and Paul chickened out and Jimmy took two shots and Paul tried to stop Jimmy and knocked him out and Paul looked over at the boy and saw two shots in his face, and shot him in the chest to put him out of his misery."

Little more than a week after the murder, everybody in the Boring household seemed to know about it, including Jack Boring, who overheard his son and a friend talking about the case. Mr. Boring, who thought his son Jerry was involved, cried until the boys reassured him by giving him all the details they had. Jerry recalled that in the Boring house, "all it was was discussion on this—my mind had gone berserk on this case."

Certainly Jon Boring, nineteen, the older brother of Jerry, knew. Brad Brown, Paul's friend, had heard Jerry and Paul talking in the car on Monday, the twenty-eighth of April. "I know who the people are who killed the kid," Brad said to Jon later that day when the two were in Jon's bedroom watching TV. "Man, you're going to freak out: Paul Sorrentino and the brother's stepbrother."

"I told the rent-a-cop, Steve Martin, at Shawnee Mission South, me and Brad both did," Jon said. Apparently Martin, a security guard, considered Jon and Brad's report just another rumor. "I told my dad what I had heard from Brad the next day," Jon continued. "We couldn't picture this lady getting away with it and still living with that man. My little brother didn't know nothing about me telling the police officer or me and Brad knowing. We didn't want Jerry to know that we turned in his friend.

"Friday night, the week I heard," Jon recalled, "I was at a kegger out at Brian Moore's and my little brother was with Sorrentino, so I went up to Sorrentino and I pulled him aside. I was pretty drunk and I just go, 'Hey, Paul, what's going on?' and I go, 'Let me ask you a few questions about this real quick, just between you and I.' And he goes, 'Okay, I'll tell you the whole story, but I'm not going to tell it again, so don't ask me to stop and say things about it. Just let me say the whole thing once.'"

Jon said, "We sat on the hood of a car and Paul goes, 'Man, the kid didn't fit in the family. There was a big conflict between the mother and her real son and the little boy being the father's real kid—he being the spoiled brat and him always being the daddy's boy—so the mother had always been mean to him and real bitchy to him, and that's what I heard from the guy that lived down the street from the kid.'"

"I asked," Jon said, "'How could you guys do something like this?' Paul said, 'I don't know, man, I was all fucked up. It was about eight-thirty at night and I was super blown away; the last street I remember was 247th. We told him we were going to bury some pot and stuff. We dug the hole about two, maybe three feet under the ground. So the kid was sitting there and digging and his brother goes, 'Chris, lay down and let's measure the hole to see how big it is.' So Chris laid down and his brother said, 'I'm going to blow your fucking head off.' Paul said Jimmy's brother started laughing at him and getting out of the hole and his brother winged him right up alongside the head, and after that Jimmy handed Paul the gun and Paul said he took three shots.

"After that I go, 'Well, what did you think?'" Jon recalled. "Paul goes, 'Well, you know, killing a boy isn't as bad as you think it is'—and right there this guy has to be a loony or something. He goes, 'If I had to do it again, I would do it.'

"All I knew was what I heard from Paul," Jon said. "I heard a million other stories at South. People were asking me what I knew about it. As soon as something breaks out at South, it's just wide open; you could sit there with a microphone and get a hundred different stories in five minutes. I was hearing stuff like it was the father that had the kid killed. Shawnee Mission South is so phony it's unreal.

"The first I ever met Paul he was getting dragged in the office for smoking a cigarette in the eighth grade," Jon remembered. "Later there were guys that had their cars ripped off and stuff and his name was brought up about it. He's a kleptomaniac. Still I thought he was a nice guy. He had good manners, always dressed as well as he could, always seemed nice, but I knew he had a problem, klepto, that's all. Otherwise I never knew him to get in a fight with anybody. Always treated his girlfriend real good and everything. He was a nice guy, you know."

Even Jimmy wasn't as discreet about the circumstances of the murder as he later professed to be. On Thursday, the twenty-fourth, Bruce Layn, a classmate of Paul's, stopped over at Paul's town house to visit, as he frequently did. Bruce said, "Whenever Jimmy would come over, the two would go off, like up to Paul's room. One time we were downstairs and Jimmy came over and Paul's brother came home. Paul's brother, Mark, said something about somebody being up at the Oak Park Mall saying that Paul did it. Paul and Jimmy were asking Mark questions about the rumor. And then, like fifteen minutes later, me and Paul and Jimmy went upstairs. And we were sitting there watching Paul's TV, and Paul clicked three shotgun shells out of a gun he had in the back of his closet, and he gave them to Jimmy and said, 'Here, get rid of these.' Paul said him and Jimmy had been hunting, and I could believe that because me and Paul went hunting all the time. Jimmy left real soon. Then Paul told me that he had killed Jimmy's little brother."

Paul told basically the same story as Layn. "Jimmy said he heard some talk about the murder and that he didn't like what he was hearing. We went upstairs to my room and I gave him the shotgun shells. I said, 'Get rid of these,' and he put them in his pocket and he left."

Paul was full of conflicting emotions, boasting of the murder to one friend, saying how easy it was to kill to another, expressing remorse to a third. His friends felt a sense of excitement around him in the days after the murder and he became the subject of gossip in larger and larger groups. Paul always enjoyed being the center of attention; he did whatever it took to make him so.

In the weeks after the murder Paul dropped out of high school and began drinking and partying relentlessly. Yet once he came back to visit Lee Shank, his teacher, at Indian Creek Junior High. As he usually did, he burst into her classroom unannounced. Like a school inspector, he arrogantly circled the room examining the work of other students until Mrs. Shank intervened. He seemed in an ebullient mood, yet clinging, not wanting to leave. He asked Mrs. Shank to come to Brian Moore's kegger on Friday, the second of May. As always, she found him charming and endearing, though she politely declined his invitation.

Paul wanted his motorcycle repaired and he wanted it done right away. A week or so after the murder, Sueanne and her daughter came over to visit Jimmy in his apartment and Jimmy brought up the payment. Jimmy said, "Paul was wanting to know when he was going to get paid, and I asked my mother. She said it would be soon." Jimmy also talked to Sueanne about it a couple of times on the phone. "Once I was over at Paul's house and he was wanting to know again when he was going to get paid, so I called her on the phone and asked her again, and again she said it would be soon. Paul seemed to be satisfied with that, but he was in a hurry to get his motorcycle fixed."

Paul recalled the phone conversation. "After Chris had died, I was in Jimmy's apartment with him and I said, 'Well, what's the word on my bike?' He said, 'I don't know.' I said, 'Well, can you find out?' I only heard half the conversation, his side. It was a rather short conversation. She said something and he agreed, and he hung up the phone. I said, 'Well, what's the word?' Jimmy said she said it was coming soon and to give it a little bit more time. It would be just a little while longer before she got the money all together. Jimmy wanted to know about his car, too, but the real heart of the conversation was mostly about me, what I was going to get paid, because I kept pushing and pushing, trying to get them to get it together.

"She has expensive things, if you've ever noticed. She wears a lot of expensive rings. They're all insured, but she had lost one and collected insurance on it, then later the ring turned up in a shoe and she kept the insurance money, so that's why I kept pushing Jimmy. I thought he was stalling me for the payoff. I believed him that she had the money. She had plenty of money. So I thought he was kind of pushing me off to one side and stalling." Paul never once spoke directly to Sueanne about the conspiracy to kill Chris either before or after the murder.

Jimmy didn't tell Paul the real reason the money wasn't forth-coming. Apparently Sueanne didn't want to be tied to the murder until she was certain Chris's body was not going to be found, certain that the police had abandoned any attempt to find the boy. Words alone linked her to the murder and she didn't intend to take any compromising action. "She was going to get the money in a week or so," Jimmy said. "The police were still searching for Chris; he was listed as a runaway at the time and there were all these little sightings coming up. People kept saying they saw him running around in Nall Park or wherever."

Certainly Jimmy warned Paul about keeping his mouth shut. A week or so after the murder Jimmy heard "that Paul bumped off my little brother. I overheard some people talking at a party." As soon as he heard, Jimmy asked Paul about it. "He said he didn't tell anybody, but I didn't believe him because I had already heard the rumor. Paul kept his mouth open, couldn't keep it shut. Paul's always wanted to blow his own horn; I say he's stupid for doing it."

7

Juvenile Detective Steve Moore was assigned the case on Friday, the eighteenth of April. On the nineteenth he spoke with Ed and Sueanne Hobson at their condominium. "Ed was concerned about what we were going to do about finding his son, trying to follow up leads or any information. He told me it wasn't the nature of his boy not to return home and he was worried; from the first time I met him, he was worried. I tried to explain to him that a lot of young people run away, and if this is the first time it's ever hap-pened, other parents feel the same worry. He felt maybe a little relieved, but not very much." Though Sueanne was present, she hung back a little and Moore talked mainly with Ed.

For the next four days Detective Moore did little to search for Chris. Ed called Moore a couple of times a day; when he didn't get any answers to his questions, he began to call Moore's superiors, insisting the police pursue the runaway more vigorously.

On Tuesday, the twenty-second of April, Chris's billfold was discovered in a planter out in front of Harzfeld's on the second level of the Metcalf South Mall. At eight-thirty in the evening an airline pilot for TWA, following his wife and his daughter around the shopping center, stopped to rest while they went into a bridal shop. His daughter was to be married soon. "I had just sat down and put out a cigarette and I saw a wallet laying under a small bush," he said. "I looked through it and saw the boy's picture and name on a school ID. Indian Creek was where all my children had gone to school, so that sort of imprinted it on my mind."

The pilot gave the billfold to a clerk behind the perfume counter at Harzfeld's. The clerk's teenage son had lost a billfold a couple of weeks before and a man found it and returned it to her. She said to herself, "One good turn deserves another, so I'll call the school and report it." She called Indian Creek the next morning and spoke to Delores Louis, the assistant principal. "Ms. Louis told me that the young man was missing and they were so happy to, perhaps, get something or hear something of him. They'd call home and tell his parents."

Ms. Louis phoned Ed Hobson at the mill and he called Detective Moore immediately. Moore and Urban drove over to Metcalf South to pick up Chris's black billfold that Wednesday morning, the twenty-third of April. In his report Moore noted its contents: "Contained in the wallet was his Indian Creek Junior High School photo-identification card, social security card, and a photograph of his mother and father. The wallet contained no money or other forms of identification. It should be noted that the wallet was completely clean of any other type of miscellaneous papers, phone numbers, or photographs."

At four that afternoon, as soon as he had finished work, Ed Hobson drove down to the Overland Park police station to pick up his son's billfold. Moore wrote in his report the next day, "During conversation with Mr. Hobson on 4-23-80 it was noticed that he was very nervous, depressed, and upset. He felt that his son is possibly the victim of some serious crime and was desiring to know what steps the police department was going to take in discovering his whereabouts. He was told that the situation would be discussed with supervisors of the police department, and, if no further leads were developed, the possibility of a field search and notification of the media would take place on 4-24-80."

When Ed got home that evening, he told Sueanne as she put his dinner on the table that Chris's billfold had been found at Metcalf South. According to Ed, she said, "Good." She didn't ask any questions or say anything else. She gave, he said, "a sigh of relief or something like that. I don't know. Things weren't very good right then."

Only now did Moore begin to act. A week had passed since Chris was first listed as a runaway; Moore had not spoken to Sueanne or Suzanne or Jimmy. When the case was first assigned, Moore had asked Ed to talk with his family because he thought they'd tell Ed more than they'd tell a detective. He especially thought that Ed would learn more from Jimmy because the boy was on probation and would be wary of a strange detective. In fact, Moore didn't even learn Mrs. Hobson's first name until two weeks after the murder.

Once the billfold was found, Urban immediately told Moore, "You're going to have to cover your ass." Moore had only been a detective for six months and he welcomed Urban's advice.

"Since I knew a little bit of background of the family, of Jimmy especially, and I knew some of Jimmy's friends, the department kind of asked me to ride shotgun," Urban said. "I'd been here for twenty-two years looking for runaway kids. We went along, and went along, and it became seven days and Mr. Hobson was beginning to call up after five days, putting the pressure on, beginning to go on up the line to the sergeants, the lieutenants, the captains, the chief, saying, 'What are you doing? That's fine, my boy. Let's do this. Let's do that.' I says, 'Steve, we're going to have to turn up a lot of damn stones, we'd better be doing something. You can ask nice questions now, but you've got to turn chicken-shit later on and kind of put a little bit of pressure on some people. You're going to have to ask what the hell is going on. You're going to have to put more pressure on Chris's peers, and whatnot.'"

Detective Moore spent a busy Wednesday evening. Several times he had asked the Hobsons for photographs of Chris, but the family had not provided one. A couple of hours after Ed left to go home, Moore drove over to the condominium and got Chris's school photograph from him. Ed also gave Moore Chris's small, black address book with numbers of the boy's friends and relatives. In it, Moore found the phone number of Chris's half-sister, Lailoneh Teed, who lived in Tulsa. He called a detective in Tulsa and told her to check out Lailoneh to see if she was harboring Chris; he asked her to arrive unannounced in case Chris was there. The Hobsons hadn't called her and Lailoneh was very distressed by the news of her brother's disappearance. She was irritated at being treated like a suspect, but she allowed the detectives to search her apartment.

"Ed told me that Lailoneh was odd," Moore said, "but he didn't try to stop me from contacting her. He was a little embarrassed by her more than anything else."

Moore also called several friends of Chris listed in the boy's address book. Bob Flack, a classmate of Chris, told Moore that Chris had never said anything bad about his parents, that he seemed happy when he last saw him, and that he'd help the police search the woods, show them where he and Chris played.

On the morning of Thursday, the twenty-fourth, a week after the murder, Urban and Moore drove down to Indian Creek to talk to administrators and teachers about Chris. Because a shotgun had been taken, Moore feared the boy had blown his brains out in the woods growing alongside Indian Creek. The teachers told of Chris's good progress in his schoolwork. Moore wrote, "They thought that he was in good spirits and did not show any signs of depression." On the other hand, the Indian Creek administrators, when asked if Chris would commit suicide, told Moore that "on a scale of one to ten, ten being the highest, Chris ranked a seven."

Moore and Captain Ron Jackson, Moore's immediate supervisor, set up a field search for the area around Chris's residence in the parks along Indian Creek. Reporters were notified of the search in order to get as much publicity for the runaway as possible. From eleven-thirty to one the police used a helicopter to search the area and found nothing. "We were going to fly around and see if we could find a body laying around someplace or see Chris running from us in the area of Indian Creek," Moore said. "About three in the afternoon we assembled together thirty or forty police officers and started a ground search, going through the woods and trying to find anything at all, clothes or a shotgun or a body. We found two sets of clothing."

At six-thirty the detectives brought back to the Hobson house for identification a red plaid shirt and a pair of blue jeans and a few other pieces of clothing. A photographer from the *Kansas City Times* took a shot of Sueanne and Ed examining the clothes. In the photograph Sueanne is holding the tips of the collar of a plaid shirt, looking down at it intently. Ed has a pair of worn jeans thrown over one shoulder as he studies the shirt. Sueanne in her concentration appears slim and soft with her short hair tightly curled around her face; only her mouth seems posed. Her oval ruby ring with stair-step diamonds is clearly visible. She is wearing a white blouse and from her neck hang several gold necklaces of various lengths, each carefully draped inside the other. Her long, lean neck draws the eye toward the perfected face above the white blouse as if to something fragile and beautiful.

Thursday evening Moore wrote, "This detective contacted the subject's parents and advised them of the disposition of the two searches. They were told that they would see their son's name in the newspapers and on TV, and possibly would be receiving phone calls. They were told that if they received any phone calls or information about the boy, they were to notify this police department immediately. They thanked this department along with this officer for taking a genuine interest in their son's welfare."

If the field search produced no evidence of the runaway, it did elicit numerous rumors about Chris. While the search was on, a high-school boy said that he saw Chris and a friend riding ten-speed bicycles on the paths of Nall Park just south of the Hobson condominium. To Moore's irritation many spurious sightings of Chris were to follow and he had to investigate even the most frivolous.

After the twenty-fourth, Steve Moore and Ed Hobson began to see a lot of each other. "Ed and I were getting to be pretty good buddies," Moore said. "We even talked about going out and getting drunk a couple of times. I'd even mention, 'You get your kid back, then come on over to the house; you and I'll sit on the back porch and just get totally bombed and I'll fall down the steps.' He'd ask me to come over after work and we'd shoot the breeze. I've never met anybody quite like him. He was a really colorful character and a nice guy. He was always real polite around me, a gentleman, but he was pissed that his kid wasn't around, and after you'd talk to him—and he was fairly rational—he'd say, 'Look, my kid never ran away, my kid was a pansy, my kid is a pussy. I don't want to belittle my kid, but he's a mama's boy. He wouldn't go out at night.' Well, maybe he was a pussy, measuring him by Ed's idea of what a pussy is and what it isn't.

"Ed couldn't care less about the house and the furniture," Moore said. "There's a lot of men that are like that; they let the women do what they want in the house. The women can come and go when they want; they can go buy this, they can go buy that, as long as it is within reason, as long as it doesn't interfere. Ed would play with his cars and tinker, and he'd go to work and come home, bring home the paycheck. But if a major decision or a major crisis occurred, you knew exactly who was in charge. It was him. There was no doubt in anybody's mind, it was him. He kept coming to the police department; he was taking care of it.

"It was his son, not hers," Moore noted. "I thought that was kind of strange. The stepparent will generally always be there to support the other parent and to show the other kids, 'I'm really with you, with your dad.' I'd call Mrs. Hobson on the phone and she wouldn't say much. I said to Urban, 'This is really ridiculous. Ed comes up here all the time checking on me to see if I'm working on his case, and I couldn't get the kid's picture out of his wife for a week.'"

After the field search Moore began to take a little more interest in Sueanne. Moore had plenty of leads once he'd talked to the media. "I imagine this was quite a load on her mind," he said. "She's watching this young detective calling all the time, coming over all the time, sitting at that glass table where you can see everybody's legs and feet."

Certainly Sueanne became more anxious after the field search and after Chris's picture appeared in newspapers and on television. She was not quite as peaceful as she had professed to be on the drive back from selling the Datsun the day after the billfold was found and the day before the field search. Right after the field search Jimmy came by unexpectedly to visit his mother. She was with Margie in the living room beyond the main entrance to the condominium. "I came walking in the front door and my mother had her back to me," Jimmy recalled. "Margie said 'Chris!', like she was recognizing the person walking in the door. I could see Mom jump in her chair. Then she turned around and saw it was me."

Moore also had a surprise for Sueanne. A couple of days after the field search, Denise Hanson, a girl of thirteen, whom Chris thought was his girlfriend, but who wouldn't say he was her boyfriend, said she had seen Chris at Worlds of Fun. Moore had to investigate. "That was the biggest crock. Here was this sweet little girl saying this stuff to her friends about how she had seen Chris up there at the park, and she got backed into a corner. She was shooting her mouth off and some adults heard about this, then her parents found out. Then a policeman comes to the door. She's not gonna go back on what she said.

"Denise kept a diary," Moore said, laughing. "She never could locate that information in her diary. I wouldn't examine a little girl's diary, anyway; there's probably a twenty-fourth amendment to cover that."

Before Moore checked the Denise Hanson rumor out, he phoned the Hobsons and Sueanne answered. "I said, 'Hey, I want you to know I think we found Chris,' and she just about dropped dead. She said, 'What?' I'll never forget that. That was the most distinct 'What?' I've ever heard. Right after I got off the phone, I went over and told Sergeant Jarvis, 'I know I'm a new detective, but I want you to know that Mrs. Hobson just about lost it when I said I thought we found Chris.'"

Later Moore was puzzled by Sueanne's reaction when he finally asked to talk to Jimmy. "It was the only time she ever questioned me. I needed Jimmy's phone number; I wanted to go talk to him, and she wanted to know where, when, and why I wanted to talk to him. It kind of startled me. I felt like a younger person looking at her as an older person, and when she turned around and questioned what I was doing, it was kind of like my supervisor questioning what I was doing, and giving me the inference that whatever it is you did, you screwed up, and I remember that feeling very well. It was like I was having to report to her. I got a little miffed. It was like, I said to myself, 'I'll show you! I'll get ahold of him anyway.'"

8

If Sueanne were concerned about Steve Moore's visit, Jimmy was terrified when the detectives suddenly came down on him. On Saturday morning, the twenty-sixth of April, Urban and Moore went out to the Oak Park Apartments to talk to Jimmy. "We were playing the angle that Chris was there," Moore said. "We set it up so Chris couldn't bolt. Urban phoned from a booth and said, 'Jimmy, go to your front door; there's a policeman there.' That must have just scared the shit out of Jimmy.

"When we got in the apartment, Jimmy was wearing a bathrobe and the sucker was shaking like he had the DTs," Moore said. "Our whole approach was that he had a little kid there: 'Just tell us where he's at!' We talked for a while after we determined that his brother wasn't there and I asked him, 'Do you know where your brother is?' And he said, 'No.' And we just started talking, just shooting the breeze. He just got a new job selling memberships in this club; you join this club and you can buy knives and appliances, and things like that, at a discount, and he showed us his little sales presentation. He was holding his little pamphlet in his hand and it was waving and shaking back and forth as he gave his pitch. I thought it was because he'd never done sales like this before. When he got done, he said, 'How will I do, Steve?' I said, 'Oh, you'll do real well, real well!'"

"I think this young man was living in fear for two and a half weeks," Urban said in his Kansas drawl. "His eyes were bugging out. He acted as if to say, 'I'm jumpy, but I've got to control myself. I've got to act nice. Act like a gentleman. Don't let nothin' slip.' He searched for words when he was speaking to us. Moore mentioned that there was someone who saw Chris up at Worlds of Fun a week ago. Old Jimmy lets out his breath in a sigh of relief. At first he was very guarded and hesitant; after Steve told him about the sighting at Worlds of Fun, he came down, like he was in a more relaxed state. I thought, 'This young man is scared shitless of something.'"

9

Sueanne and Jimmy had several legal matters pending. The motion filed against James Crumm, Sr., on the fourteenth of March, 1980, to "reduce past child support payments to a judgment of $16,600" had not yet been heard. The hearing in civil court was set for the ninth of May.

In addition Sueanne and Jimmy's contacts with Cheryl Schroeder, his probation officer, went steadily forward through the latter part of April. Schroeder wrote on the day of Chris's murder:

4-17-80: This officer called Mrs. Hobson to find out if they had received the prison forms to sign out for the "Scared-Straight" prison program Jimmy is to attend and to let her know I needed them back immediately.

4-28-80: Jimmy called this officer to report that his mother had signed the prison forms and that he would bring them by the next day.

4-29-80: Jimmy came in as scheduled. . . . This officer asked Jimmy about his brother, Chris. Jimmy stated that apparently

he had run away, because he had some of his friends out looking for Chris, and they had seen him at various places, such as
Worlds of Fun. I told Jimmy I thought it was funny that they
had put the picture in the paper if they thought it was a runaway. Jimmy indicated that the mother had done that before
when Jimmy ran away. Jimmy stated that the brother took the
shotgun with him when he left and that people had seen him
with the shotgun. I asked Jimmy why he would take the shotgun with him and Jimmy didn't know.

The last entry was undated. Schroeder noted that she had
attempted to contact Jimmy on the third and fourth of May
because he had not yet signed and returned the forms for the
"Scared-Straight" prison program he was to attend.

10

Two weeks after the murder Moore and Urban had no idea at all
of what had happened to Chris. "Usually in a runaway there was
something to go on, some of the friends would know something,"
Moore said. "Here there were no leads, no nothing." Most likely
Chris had killed himself, they thought.

John Douglass, a senior detective in the crimes-against-persons
unit, summarized the view that the Overland Park police had at
the time. "It hadn't flagged our attention as being anything really
unusual," Douglass said, "with the exception of the fact that a
shotgun was missing and he was missing, and there was no reason,
really, for him to be missing."

Of course there were many who did know. The entire Boring
family knew a week earlier and at least two dozen teenagers had
heard directly from Paul or indirectly from the Borings about
Paul's involvement.

Leila Anderson, a friend of Paul and the Boring brothers, was
doing some detective work on her own. She first heard about the
murder from Jerry Boring on Tuesday, the twenty-ninth of April;
on Wednesday she asked Paul what happened and he told her.
Anderson, a heavy, bespectacled girl of eighteen, was well-

known to the police as a juvenile offender; among other things, she had been caught passing forged checks. Still, passing checks wasn't at all like murder. On Thursday afternoon, the first of May, Leila called the Overland Park police station and said, "I want to give some information about a murder."

"Automatically they funneled the call to me because that was my area of work," Douglass said. "I was aware of what was going on in the case, but hadn't been actively involved until Leila Anderson called me. She tells us this incredible story about the Hobson case over the phone. As an investigator, I learned not to put a whole lot of stock into what any one person said without trying to verify it. And I thought that it would be pretty easy to verify what she had to say if we could get her in to talk to us. She agreed to come in that afternoon."

As soon as he got off the phone, Douglass walked upstairs to the juvenile division and told Moore about Leila's phone call. Moore was astonished and skeptical; he began to tell Douglass what little he knew about the runaway case. Before Moore was half-finished, Leila arrived.

Douglass and Moore began interviewing her at four o'clock that day. Douglass did most of the questioning. "Leila, why don't you tell us what you know about what's happened?" he said. "Why don't you start from the very beginning and tell us in story form?"

In a soft, sweet voice she began, "Okay, day before yesterday, Jerry Boring came to me and said, 'I need to talk to you.' We are real close and he gets into a lot of trouble, but he's not involved, okay? Well, he is indirectly now. But he came to me and told me that somebody I knew was paid off to kill a little kid that was missing. The mother paid her son to kill his stepbrother and Jimmy asked this other person to help him."

"Who is the other person?" Douglass asked gently.

"Paul Sorrentino. Well, Jerry didn't tell me any more about it because he didn't really know about it. So yesterday I went over to Paul's house and I acted like I didn't know anything. And Paul goes, 'Well, we need to stop by Jimmy's. Is it okay if I drive your car over there?' And I went over there and we were sitting there when Jimmy and Paul started talking about his stepbrother. I didn't even put two and two together because, when I heard it from Jerry, I thought it was just a little story; it sounded good and he was going to spread it around. There are quite a few kids who know about it, but Paul's been denying that he knows anything about it." She paused for a moment, puzzled. "I don't even know the kid's name."

"His name is Chris," Moore said.

"Chris? Okay. Jimmy says, 'Well, Chris is crazy if he wants to come back home, you know. The little kid has to be totally deranged for taking a gun with him anyway.' And Paul says something about, 'Yeah, did you see the picture in the paper and the police looking for him by Shawnee Mission South carrying guns.' And Jimmy and Paul are playing this up really big in front of me. And then we left Jimmy's house and we got in the car and I said, 'Look, Paul, Jerry told me about it.' And he goes, 'Well, Leila, not very many people know the whole story.' And I said, 'Well, I'll listen.' And he told me if I did anything, told any-one—Paul goes, 'Well, if I can do it once, I can do it again.'"

Patiently Paul told her what happened that night. "On the seventeenth Jimmy and Paul went and picked up Chris after play-ing racquetball," she recalled. "They took him out to 248th Street. Paul says it was way out in the country. And they had the gun the whole time and he told this little boy—who obviously was pretty ignorant in the first place for going—that they were planning this big drug scheme involving a lot of money, and this kid goes, 'I want in on it.' And he trusted his stepbrother obvious-ly. And they said we need to dig a hole that's big enough for a truck to get stuck in so they can't get by where we are going to stash the stuff. I guess that Paul and Jimmy both tried to dig the hole and they were just too damn lazy and the ground was too hard and the kid said, 'Well, I'll do it.' In other words he dug his own grave. And they said, 'Well, lay down in it to see if it's long enough.' And then they said, 'If you move, we are going to kill you,' and the kid got scared and Paul shot him in the head first, and the kid sat up and held on to his head, and then Jimmy shot him, and then Paul shot him in the face and the heart to make sure he was done. And then they covered him up. They said they were out of there by nine-thirty-seven or something like that.

Paul said, 'There is no way anybody could prove that we did it.'"

Paul seemed detached and Leila listened with growing disgust to his cold view of the killing. "I go, 'Paul, you're sick, you know! You have to be definitely ill. You, nobody, has the right to take a life.' But God, he goes, 'Well, Leila, I don't want people to think I'm crazy.' I said, 'You killed somebody. What gives you the right to do that?' And then I was afraid because he more or less threatened me, and I just laughed it off, and I said, 'Yeah, but Paul, you know you can trust me.' And I myself cannot live knowing that a little kid has been murdered."

"Did he tell you why they did this?" Douglass asked.

"His excuse for it was everybody in the family hated him but Ed, the father. And he's the kind of kid that—this is exactly how Paul put it to me—'If they had three quarts of milk in the refrigerator, this little kid would drink two and three fourths quarts of it and leave a fourth of it for the rest of the family for the rest of the week.' And that's another reason that got me stirred up, because that's no reason to kill somebody."

"Did they describe all this to you?"

"No. He just said it was out in the country and he said 248th. I can find out the cross street if they don't know that I've come up here to the station."

"How can you find it out?"

"I'll ask Paul. Well, everybody has overheard it. Mr. Boring has overheard the whole thing, and he was in tears thinking that his son Jerry was involved. And everybody doesn't know what to do because they are afraid of Paul and Jimmy—I mean if his mother can pay Paul off to get rid of her stepson, why can't she pay him off to get rid of anybody else who's going to turn them in? So everybody is pretty paranoid about what they are going to do. Bill Bray told me that Jonny Boring was talking to him, and they went to night school last night, and they were all talking about it in the car, and Jerry Boring was denying that Paul had anything to do with it. Bill said something about how Jonny told him where it happened and where the dead kid was. And I can find out. And I told Bill and my friend Brian Moore the whole story. And Brian and I were going to come in here together, because Brian said he could just no way live with himself knowing what was going on, and I was up all last night. See, before I heard it from Paul, I thought it was nothing. But when I heard it from him himself, and he said, 'I shot him in the head first—'" Leila sat quietly for a moment looking down at her lap. "I can find out more."

"How soon?" Douglass asked quickly.

"Tonight or tomorrow, I'm sure I could go up and talk to him and have him tell me more."

"I don't want you getting into trouble," Moore said, anxious to protect the girl.

"I'm just scared; my parents don't know what's going on."

"How old are you?" Douglass asked.

"Eighteen. And I don't want them knowing because I don't want them hurt. And I told Brian last night, if it came down to it, I would testify against Paul." Leila looked directly at Douglass. "I would do the whole thing if I knew for a fact that I could be protected."

For the first time that afternoon Douglass was angry. "Let me tell you about Sorrentino. Okay? Sorrentino is a penny-ante little crook. Without a doubt he is not a big-timer; he's not a big anything. He is a penny-ante little crook. Now there is every possibility in the world that he is trying to take advantage of the situation of the kid's disappearance."

Douglass knew something that the others didn't. He knew that Sorrentino had been Detective Gil Hernandez' snitch; Hernandez had let him off numerous felonies for providing information on other juveniles. If a snitch was lying to the police, he was also lying to the boys he informed on. Sorrentino was a habitual liar and Douglass suspected he was lying again.

"I know he did it," Leila said.

"If he did do it, and we can find out that he did it, and you do have to testify against him, he is not going to hurt you. We are not going to let him hurt you," Douglass said.

"What if he gets out?"

"He's not going to get out," Douglass emphasized.

"He's not going to get out, not for cold-blooded murder," Moore said.

"I told him that. I said, 'Do you realize what you've done?

That's premeditated murder.' I go, 'Do you realize what is going to happen to you?' And he just goes, 'Well, Leila, the only way I can live with it myself is to blow it off.' I go, 'You can't do that.' He was driving my car, so I couldn't say, you know—"

"Stop and let me out," Douglass said, finishing her sentence.

"Yeah. I was just trying to humor him; now I'm scared. If he can do that—"

"What kind of frame of mind is he in over this whole thing? Is it really bothering him?"

"I know that it bothers him, but he tries to block it out mentally," Leila said.

"Did he tell you what he did with the money he got, or how much money he got?"

"He hasn't gotten it yet. He made an arrangement that all he wanted was somebody to pay off the motorcycle for him and, like, three or four hundred dollars cash over that for spending money. Okay? Like it was no big deal. He goes, 'If you knew the kid, you'd do the same thing.' And then I thought it was kind of humorous what he was doing to my car. He was driving and there was a bird in the road, and he honked the horn for the bird to fly off so he wouldn't hit it. And I turned around and I go, 'You can murder a kid, but you can't run over a bird.' The guy is sick and he needs help."

Leila fell silent again, then said, "I don't know. Maybe it wasn't my place to come in here."

"I think it is. I'm glad you came in," Moore said encouragingly.

"I know what it's like to be in trouble," Leila said.

"You have been in trouble, but this is trouble, what you are talking about. This is *trouble*," Moore said.

If there was a body, Douglass wanted to find it; nothing could happen until it was found. Douglass resumed the questioning. "When they were talking about going out, did they say that they were very far from the road? Did they walk back in the woods?"

"He said they had him covered up. He said I can tell you the exact time he was dead. I said, 'What's that?' and he said nine-thirty-seven. He goes, 'We were back in the car by nine-forty-six.' So it can't be very far from where they parked. They took the kid's coat off of him before they shot him. It was set up obviously; Paul said it was set up a long time ago."

"Are they running around telling everybody about this?"

"Well, you see, Jerry Boring has a really big mouth. When he gets the news, he goes and tells his friends. Paul and I used to be pretty close—well, not real close—friends. But I knew him well enough and I trusted the guy. So I went up to him myself and I asked him to tell me the whole deal."

"Did he act surprised that you wanted to know?"

"He asked me who I heard it from. He said, 'Listen to me, if this gets out and around, we are going to get caught for it.' I laid it down that I wouldn't say anything. But that's not me."

"Are you going to be able to maintain your composure around him?" Moore asked, concerned about the threats Paul had made.

"Oh, yeah. I'm pretty good at acting, you know. I can put on a pretty mean front."

"I just want to make sure that you can do it," Moore said.

"He told you this was around 248th Street?" Douglass asked, going back to their problem of finding a dead body.

"I can find out. It could be 148th Street, but he told me 248th Street."

"Is there anyplace out there that kids go to? To drink beer, smoke their dope, or anything like that?" Moore asked.

"I don't know. I go about halfway down the road, and I get paranoid, and I turn around because it gets real dark, and I don't like it down there. I don't know. I don't hang around Paul. I've only gone with him one night with a bunch of people and I've seen him at parties of my friends, but I don't know where he goes to have his fun and do what he does. I know that Jimmy's mother is paying them off. Paul told me that the mother had hated the kid since she got remarried."

"It's not her kid, anyway, it's his dad's, isn't he?" Douglass wondered.

"Uh-huh."

"Do you remember when Jimmy got into trouble with credit cards and was arrested?" Moore asked.

"I just met Jimmy yesterday," Leila said.

Moore turned to Douglass. "Jimmy called Darrell Urban today on the telephone. He calls Urban quite frequently, maybe because he wants to tell Darrell what's going on. Darrell said he receives a phone call every day from the boy."

"What about the credit cards?" Douglass asked Moore. He knew little about Jimmy Hobson, even less than Leila, and most of what he did know had come from Moore a half hour earlier. Until now he had paid no attention to the runaway case; that was a juvenile matter, and besides, there were runaways every night.

"Okay," Moore said. "Urban investigated and charged Jimmy Hobson with unlawful use of credit cards and something to do with some dope. And Jimmy told Darrell after he was arrested that the Hobson mother, Barbara—I think that's her first name—paid Jimmy to remain a runaway." Moore had been working the case for two weeks and he didn't know Sueanne's name. "Darrell promised Jimmy that he would never tell anybody about his mother meeting him and paying him. Even though Jimmy was a runaway and a report was filed, Mom knew where he was at and was leading Urban on a wild-goose chase and was paying the kid to stay out of the house. It was like she wanted to get everybody out of the house so that it was just her, her husband, and her money. She's really materialistic. Extremely." Moore liked clear motives; they comforted him. Douglass cared more about acts.

Moore also told Douglass about his talk with Jimmy at the Oak Park Apartments. "I went over and saw Jimmy last week, last Saturday, and I asked him if he knew where his brother was. He told me, 'The last time I saw Chris was on the seventeenth. I went in and said "Hi" and "Bye" and left. I haven't seen him since then.' I said, 'Well, you know, I have talked to your mother. She is out to get your stepdad for about seventeen to thirty-nine thousand dollars in back child support. She is suing him.' He said, 'Yeah, I know. She likes money.'"

"Paul told me that she was really rich," Leila said, "that she had money and all this other stuff, and then I was driving up to South yesterday to pick up some of Jerry's things, and we drove by those apartments. See, I didn't even know who the kid was; I just saw the picture on the TV before I walked out the door this afternoon. I didn't think anything of it until the day before yesterday. And we drove down Nall and Jerry said, 'Yeah, that's where they live.' Paul was in the backseat and goes, 'That's where they live, right there.' I think, 'If she has so much money, why doesn't she live in a real nice home or whatever?' The lady has got to be a little bit crazy. And Paul told me that after he did it, he went into a frenzy and he couldn't believe that he did it. And he was really messed up at the time that he did do it, or else he couldn't have done it.

"After I heard it, I was sick to my stomach all yesterday," Leila continued. "It didn't bug me until I heard it from him myself. But I told Paul, I said, 'If you need an alibi—' And what I'm waiting for him to say is that he is going to tell you guys that he was with me all that night. And he's going to nail himself right there. I told him this big scoop that my dad was in really big with all the policemen out there, that they wouldn't even question him if he were with me. Because he doesn't even know the trouble I've had with the police over other stuff I've done."

Paul's callous attitude toward the murder irritated Leila. "Paul doesn't have any conscience at all. It's bugging him, but he's throwing it off like nothing happened, like it's another scam that he's pulled off. He was laughing at the point that the kid dug his own grave. And he said, 'I remember turning around and seeing his hand still sticking out after we had covered him up.' And they went back and covered him up more, but the grave is only three, four feet deep. And it's been there for two weeks."

The three sat silently for a few seconds then Leila offered again to help. "I could find out whose car they used."

"Don't do that," Moore said. "That's asking too many questions. All we want you to do is to find out where the body is at."

"I'm really nosy."

"They know that's your nature?" Moore asked.

"Yeah. When I know something, I want to find out the whole deal."

Douglass was much less concerned about the risks she was taking than Moore. He interrupted her. "Certainly whatever you can find out will be of great help. The most important thing we want to find out is where the body is."

"If you can find us where the body is, that's all we need," Moore said. "Did they say how they dug the grave?"

"He did it, the little kid did it. When they told me, I guess I had so many questions that I just didn't know where to start, and I was just kind of numb on the whole deal. And when I realized what he told me, then I got scared that if it came down to it, and if I didn't say anything, then maybe I am an accessory in some way. Because I know something."

"You're okay now," Moore reassured her.

11

Leila talked with Paul Thursday evening and again the next day. When she returned to the station Friday afternoon, she had little more information than when she left it. Moore and Douglass proposed to tape a phone conversation between her and Paul. Leila agreed to do it enthusiastically. The detectives decided to try right then.

"We set up the tap on the pay phone in the hall," Moore said. "Douglass was in an adjoining room listening in and running the tape machine, and I was waving my arms at Leila like a train conductor and reaching around to signal to John to pick up the phone. We hadn't done this a hell of a lot, you know. We got him at home on the second ring. I couldn't believe it."

To the surprise of the detectives Leila was quite calm, much calmer than Moore himself. Immediately she told Paul that she intended to go out and find the body to make sure it was properly covered.

Paul reacted angrily. "Don't even fuck with it. No one knows. No one knows enough. Just shut up. Everything is cool. There has been no problems."

"Huh?"

"There has been no problems. Don't go back to the scene of a crime. Goddamn!"

"Listen to me. Okay?"

"No, listen to me! Don't do it," Paul said emphatically. "Leave it alone."

"No, listen to me for a second, would ya?"

"Uh-huh," Paul said.

Leila spoke deliberately, carefully eliciting details based on the information Moore gave her. "Okay. The last time it rained was the seventeenth."

"So?"

"Okay, if you guys put wet dirt over him—" she began.

"It was dry when we put it on him."

"It was dry?"

"I think so. Yeah."

"You think or you know?" she asked as if she were a lawyer.

"It was moist," he said.

"It was moist. Okay, when it dries up, it will go down."

"It's going to harden when it dries," Paul insisted.

"It's not, either."

"Yeah, it will."

"I'm not going to argue with you," Leila said in a voice that suddenly assumed a nagging tone.

"It's going to harden," Paul repeated.

"Okay, it's going to harden, but it's also going to sink."

"A little bit," he agreed.

"A little bit, yeah. Well, if you already looked back—"

"We made it pretty even. As a matter of fact, we piled it up a little bit," he said.

"All right, fine," Leila said in a bitching tone, "but you even told me when you looked back, his hand was still sticking out."

"But I buried that already. I put dirt on top of it, and stomped on his fingers, and put more dirt on top."

"You stomped on his fingers and put more . . ." Her voice trailed as if she were going to lose control. "All right, fine. A dog can smell that," she persisted.

"Well, that's cool."

"They are going to dig it up," she said.

"They're not even going to begin to look out there!" Paul's voice was loud and agitated. "A dog smells lots of things. A dog even smells a snake hole. It's just a goddamn field where farmers grow corn and wheat. I'm not going to worry about it. There's no problems. But if you feel like there's a problem, yeah, you can cruise out there."

"Okay, I need to know how," she said matter-of-factly.

"I don't know how. Jimmy doesn't know either. We had to stop and get directions to find Antioch. We didn't know where we were."

"Okay, you went clear down Antioch then." Leila confused the town of Antioch with the street of the same name.

"Something like that, yes," Paul said. Apparently, he encouraged her confusion.

"And you went down to those fields by the dead end of Antioch?" Leila asked.

"I don't know where it is," he repeated.

"Okay, so if I took Antioch all the way down, then I'd find it?"

"Hopefully. I really don't know," he said again.

"Okay. Well, I'll check it out that way."

"All right. I mean, you know. If you smell something, you know he's ripe."

"That's disgusting!" Leila said.

"Well, you probably will smell him; he's been there two or three weeks. His body has maggots all over him," Paul said.

"Okay, if that is the case, then a dog has dug him up."

"Maybe. Hey, a dog doesn't just dig up bodies," he said.

"Okay. Is it down by the dead end where there are no other cross streets?"

"There is one cross street," he said.

"One cross street. What is it?"

"I don't know. I wish I could tell you, but I really don't know how to get out there."

"Okay, but you just kept going straight across on that cross street? You didn't turn?" she asked.

"When we got to Antioch, we took a right, I believe."

"And you went all the way down Antioch and that's the last place you turned?"

"Yeah, until we got to my house."

"Until you got to your house!" Leila yelled. "I'm talking about where you left him, not the way back!"

"Yeah, I know, but that's the only way I can remember to get out there—by the way back." Paul's voice was now flat and tight in response to Leila's frustration.

"All right. I'm going to check it out. Don't tell Jerry Boring what I'm doing. Tell him I'm going to be late if he calls to find out where I am."

"That's cool."

"I just want to make sure because my butt's in this, too. And I don't want my ass in a sling," she said.

"Nobody knows. So just keep it quiet."

"I'll keep it quiet, but I don't want my ass in a sling for what you two did," she said angrily.

"Well, you won't."

"I know I won't, but this way I'm just making sure."

"All right."

"Well, I'll give you a call in a little while," Leila said. "Are you leaving tonight?"

"I'm going to try to find a way to Brian Moore's party, yeah."

"Well, I can take you," she said.

"All right. We'll see you later," Paul said.

As soon as Leila left the station, Douglass and Moore listened to the tape of the call. The phone call was an "admission against interest," the best evidence the detectives could get, the most difficult to challenge in court. They knew the call was all the evidence against Sorrentino they'd ever need.

Douglass was excited, Moore excited and angry. Neither could sit down. Moore didn't know Chris, but he had come to know his father; sooner or later he'd have to tell Ed that his boy was murdered.

Douglass was more interested in the character of Paul. His impression was that Paul "was starting to realize that too much was already coming out; it was like trying to grab a bagful of feathers that's blowing in the wind."

Late that afternoon Moore and Douglass replayed the tape for the detectives still at the station. Unfamiliar with the case, the other detectives laughed, saying in the midst of hearing it, "That bitch! Can you believe it, the way she led him on? What a bitch! God fucking damn, she was good at it!"

Sorrentino's anxiety convinced Moore of Paul and Jimmy's involvement in the murder. Douglass, skeptical by nature and new to the investigation of the runaway, remained unconvinced.

He told Moore that he should be wary, that he still suspected that Paul was "trying to build a reputation by saying that he'd done Chris in."

Neither Moore nor Douglass could believe Sueanne's part in the plot. There was nothing about Sueanne Hobson in the taped phone conversation. "Sorrentino was building himself up," Douglass said. "He wanted to portray this image of a contract killer; he wanted to tell his friends, 'Hey, look at me! I've made it! I've taken the first giant step to becoming a Mafia hit man.' He wasn't too concerned about talking about Mrs. Hobson; he was wanting to talk about himself."

Moore immediately called Detective Gil Hernandez and told him of Sorrentino's admissions. Hernandez was incredulous that his reliable snitch had killed a child. This time Paul had snitched on himself.

When Urban first heard about Leila Anderson's interview and her taped phone call, and he heard immediately, he said, "I was believing those kids were trying to figure a way out. I had no suspicion of Sueanne even then."

Urban had dealt with Leila before and knew her well. "She has been in and out of scrapes with this and that. She was a gal that figured out all the angles; she'd think, 'I'm going to tell you something to get me off the hook, if I'm involved.' If you couldn't prove it against her, she'd never tell you anything, but the minute you had her pretty cold on something it was, 'I'm going to sing a song to get myself off and get them buried.'"

On Friday and Saturday, the second and third of May, the police made frantic searches for Chris's body. Urban, in particular, enjoyed the excitement of the search. "Moore and I were talking about it. I goes and gets Herb Ford, a good friend of the chief of police, who has an airplane. I told him, 'I'd like to fly down Antioch, I'd like to fly down Metcalf, I'd like to fly the main north and south streets.' I'm thinking in my own mind, 'Here I am, a radical murderer, and I'm taking a kid out. Which way would I go?' We flew Metcalf and Antioch. Moore and I also went out and walked the ponds around and we walked every damn place along Metcalf, Antioch, and other through streets that showed similarities to the same locale that

Anderson and Sorrentino described. And we come up dead and we never did think of the little town of Antioch.

"Ford and I flew down to 166th and Antioch Street, and it was nice and clear. I was looking for a clump of trees, a low spot, or whatnot. There was a bridge out on 167th. Dead-end street! We were flying above this place, and I looked about a half a mile east up the creek, and I saw this nice little square. It looked like a perfect grave damn near concealed underneath the trees. We were flying about four hundred feet. I saw that one spot down there and I said, 'That is it! That is it! No use lookin' anymore.' We came back and I jumped in my car, and I goes hotfooting it down there, and I look at this place. Some farmer goes out and takes a load of manure and dumps it out in a nice little square! From four hundred feet it looked like a nice, dark mound of fresh dirt. Boy, did I get the raspberries for that." Urban choked with laughter. "It was a sad story, you know, a sad story!"

Neither Urban nor Moore could imagine that Paul and Jimmy had gone out so far. Like the two boys, they thought of anything past 160th Street as the sticks and neither gave any thought to the town way out south. Even if they had, they wouldn't have found Chris's body.

12

On that Saturday, while the police were searching carefully, twenty miles north of the scene of the murder, Ed and Sueanne had dinner with Sueanne's friends, Ernestine and Philip Bean. Ernestine remembered that Sueanne "looked like death warmed over" that evening and that they left fairly early. Later Sueanne picked up Margie at the Brookridge Country Club after her shift as a bartender and drove her back to the condominium. Filled with anxiety over his son's disappearance, Ed needed to keep busy and he was repapering the master bedroom until midnight.

Earlier that day Ed had left a message for Steve Moore at the police department. A secretary wrote it out for the young detective: "Ed Hobson wants to talk about what might be done with Chris when found." Ed had told the secretary that he didn't want

Chris kept in detention by juvenile authorities. He wanted his son to be treated in a respectful, friendly, and gentle manner until he could come and talk with him.

13

All day Saturday Jimmy had been painting at Ted Reyes' house and he was tired. "I got back to my apartment about seven, then I got cleaned up and left a little after dark. Paul was having a party that night and I stopped by early in the evening. I'd had a dream of the body being found. I just went over there and said to Paul, 'They found the body.' I didn't know it at the time, but it just was something that I felt, and he says, 'So when do I get my money?' "

5
ARREST

1

On Saturday afternoon, the third of May, Barry Carpenter, four-teen, and his friend Mark Burger, seventeen, students at Gardner High School in rural southwestern Johnson County, drove a couple of miles down to Big Bull Creek to fish. They drove east down a rough, gravel road and descended into the floodplain of Hillsdale Lake. They reached the creek at the point where a bridge was out; a truck had fallen through it the year before. The road dead-ended there and they parked near the abutments of the ruined bridge.

At two o'clock they took their poles out of the car and began to walk along the creek looking for a place to fish. The day was sunny and warm. The creek was still high from the spring rains and they were up above it at first, walking in the thick brush underneath the elms and cottonwoods and pin oaks growing along it and in it. The leaves of the trees had the intense green of midspring. The grass and weeds had not grown past the knees of the boys; by midsummer they would reach the height of a man's head.

When the boys wanted to walk quickly, they would go out in the plowed field that began fifty feet from Big Bull's banks. After walking a few minutes, they'd carefully make their way back through the heavy brush to the creek. After several attempts, they found a spot where the water widened to thirty feet and deepened, and they sat down to fish.

Barry, the younger boy, said later, "If I remember right, we wasn't catching too much, so we decided to go look for some snakes or lizards or whatever we could find. We didn't find any snakes or lizards, but we found some baby mice. We wanted to keep the mice, so we decided to go try to find something to put them in. We went to look for a jar. Lots of people dump stuff down there and that's when we noticed something. We just stepped right up on him; we walked on the fresh dirt. We thought it might be trash, so we poked at it with a stick, but it was hard and wouldn't turn over. We just seen the blue jeans and a little piece of red material."

The boys scrambled out of the brush and ran back to the car. Mark drove to Barry's home and Barry told his mother, Emma. Emma Carpenter immediately called the Miami County Sheriff's Office. At four-thirty the boys and Emma drove back to the bridge to meet Dan Morgan, a Miami County patrolman. Morgan drove in from the east and had to wade across the creek to get to the boys.

"When we got close to it, we could smell a real strong odor and the boys stood back and pointed out what they had found," Morgan said. Morgan, a balding, heavy, round man, soon realized that there was a body under the dirt. "It wasn't really all that obvious, but we seen what appeared to be an arm and what appeared to be a knee and then you could make out more or less an outline of a grave." He assumed the boy was murdered. "It would be kind of hard for somebody to put his self that far underground," he said dryly.

At five o'clock Morgan called the county dispatcher and told him to contact the sheriff and the coroner. Ron Orton, the deputy sheriff, arrived a little after five, the Miami County coroner, Dr. Robert Banks, at five-fifteen. By six o'clock, a Kansas Bureau of Investigation agent, the coroner, and five police officers from Miami County had assembled at the grave site. Under Dr. Banks' direction, they began to dig out the body. Everybody helped dig except Banks and the funeral director, who arrived later. Orton carefully photographed the murder scene and the stages of exhumation, even catching, in the rich, spring light of late afternoon, Barry and Mark watching the work go forward. The police had driven the boys back to the abutments of the fallen bridge on which they now sat. When Dr. Banks had seen enough, he had the dispatcher call Dr. James Bridgens at Shawnee Mission Medical Center in Johnson County.

Dr. Bridgens, a thin, wiry man in his sixties, was the most famous forensic pathologist in Kansas. In his thirty years as coroner he claimed he had done ten thousand autopsies, more than the living population of Miami County. His recollection of every notorious crime in the area made easy the work of reporters and detectives. When Bridgens testified in court, he had a grisly humor that horrified judges and juries and lightened the day for reporters. And when prosecutors would ask him whether the bullets he held were the same in every respect as those he removed from a dead body, he would say, "Yes, except for the smell," and the jurors would squirm in their boxes.

Finding the way to the murder site at Big Bull Creek was difficult for everyone except Miami County officers. Jimmy's trouble in finding a way out of the area could easily be understood by any outsider. One Kansas Bureau of Investigation agent who was sent to the grave site searched for two hours and never arrived. Dr. Bridgens was met by a police car near the town of Antioch and the officer led him down to Big Bull. "We drove over an unbelievable, winding, tortuous, rough dirt road, ending up on the banks of a stream somewhere—which reportedly was in Miami County," Bridgens said. By the time he got there at six-thirty the body was already uncovered.

Bridgens, who easily commanded a courtroom, took charge wherever he was. "I made a cursory examination of the body at the time it was still in the grave. I recognized that this was no place to proceed much further and more facilities would be needed than were available in Miami County. I decided to take the body to Shawnee Mission."

What the two teenage boys had seen was a knee and an elbow that Jimmy and Paul had left uncovered in their frenzy to get away. The grave itself was less than two feet deep and not more than five feet long, a poor fit for Christen, who, at five-foot-nine and a hundred and forty pounds, was already well grown, taller and heavier than either of his killers.

In the narrow, shallow grave in the soft yellow afternoon light, what Bridgens saw, laced in the roots of a cottonwood, was a dead boy dusted with dirt. The boy's head and body were turned to the south, his back toward the road he had been driven in on. His hand was under his head, his elbow sharply bent toward it; the head was tipped down into the hand that sought to clutch it. The other arm rested lightly across the boy's stomach. His upper body twisted gracefully away from the angle of his legs, as if the boy had chosen the position after many hesitations. The legs and the pelvis were tightly covered with faded, worn blue jeans; the well-formed legs were precisely parallel and had the kind of elegance and strength one sees in the legs of young women. His arms were covered by a long-sleeved shirt that showed gently red through the dust. His shoulders and chest were broad and strong, yet bloated by decay. The boy's face was unrecognizable, flattened and bleached a gray white. Like a Pietà, the oval of his head was made beautiful by the strong anonymity of form.

Everyone perceived the boy's helplessness before the remote violence, before those small, distant explosions in the woods. Bridgens vaguely recalled reading about a field search for an Overland Park runaway boy. None except Bridgens knew anything about the boy's sudden power to change lives. Miami County abutted Johnson County, but was far from its wealth and sophistication; the suburbs of metropolitan Kansas City had not yet penetrated that far south.

By seven-fifteen the body was out of the grave; by seven-thirty the hearse was on its way to Shawnee Mission Hospital. Bridgens began the autopsy at eight-twenty and didn't finish until nearly eleven.

"I had great help, you know," Bridgens said ironically. "Many inquiries from prosecutors, police, the KBI. Knowing that an adolescent had been missing from Overland Park for a period of some days, I immediately contacted the police department. They came back with a description—height, weight, clothing that he was wearing—which was identical to the clothing that was on the body. The height and weight were consistent with what we

saw. I told them to notify their detectives that we probably had
the boy. After the detectives arrived, we proceeded with the
examination."

2

That Saturday night Detective John Douglass was giving a poker
party at his home in Olathe, Kansas, eight miles south of
Overland Park. Most of the cardplayers were coworkers, including Lieutenant Ron Jackson, Douglass's immediate superior.
Douglass lived in a new split-level brown house set tight against
other houses on a treeless street. He had small children, yet the
rooms were clean and orderly and well furnished. Like Steve
Moore and most of the detectives in Overland Park, Douglass
had graduated from a small, local, Roman Catholic college. He
sought order in his home and in his work; he was intelligent and
ambitious and he had a taste for power. The prosecutors could
depend on him.

"About nine o'clock," Douglass recalled, "I got a telephone
call from the coroner, Dr. Bridgens, who said, 'We got a dead
body out in Miami County. Rumor has it that it might be a little
boy that you're looking for. Can you give the particulars on him
and I'll tell you if it's him?' I said, 'Well, if he was buried in a
field and has a shotgun wound in the head and a shotgun wound
to the body somewhere, and he's wearing a red shirt and blue
jeans, he's ours.' Bridgens said, 'Well, that sounds like him. Are
you coming down?' I said, 'Yeah, I'll be down in just a few minutes.' After I told Jackson, half the card party stood up and went
to the autopsy."

Douglass had Moore and Urban called immediately. On the
way to the autopsy he began to plan how he might assemble
teams to arrest simultaneously the two conspirators Sorrentino
had named in his talks with Leila Anderson. Simultaneous arrests
might give him three separate statements; if he could get three,
he could use one against the others.

Moore, who also lived in a new home in Olathe remarkably
similar to Douglass's, was at a church square dance with his wife.

Moore and his wife had gotten a sitter for their baby son that Saturday night. When he got the message to call the station, he was sure his snitch was calling and he answered reluctantly and petulantly.

Urban lived within a half mile of the police station and was at home when the dispatcher called. He decided not to go to the autopsy; they were all the same to him and they spoiled his day. Within minutes he was at the station waiting for orders.

Less than a half hour after Bridgens called, Douglass, Moore, and several other policemen were at Shawnee Mission Medical Center. When they came into the autopsy room, the smell of rotting flesh was overwhelming, more like taste than smell. The police watched and photographed while Bridgens, like a slow, cautious butcher, manually split apart Chris's ribs, sawed open his head, and tore his torso in pieces.

One of the detectives wanted to leave immediately and said that he could identify Chris by sight. Bridgens said laughing that he himself wasn't nearly that good at it and he kept him there. Bridgens seemed to enjoy the audience and the tension.

Steve Moore hadn't been to an autopsy before. He was angry. All the talk had come down to this. Moore had been a juvenile detective for less than a year and Chris was his first runaway to come up dead.

"Chris was the first boy I had come to know after he was dead," Moore said. "Later, whenever I got to feeling sorry for the killers, I thought of the autopsy; once or twice during the investigation I'd even take out my copies of the photographs of him in the grave and of his broken body after Bridgens was through with him."

By ten o'clock the police had had enough. "At the autopsy it became apparent that everything that we had heard so far was true," Douglass said. "It pretty much corroborated the story Sorrentino told Leila Anderson—the number of shots, where he was shot."

It had all been language before, but the dead body defied language, Douglass thought. Sorrentino was hardly reliable, a snitch held in contempt by the police. At sixteen he had already lived a life of elaborate deceit and betrayal. No one except one of the killers could know the details of the boy's death. They would find the truth about the rest of Sorrentino's story tonight, he would see to that.

When Douglass, Moore, and the others got back to the station, Assistant District Attorney Larry McClain and Lieutenant Jackson brought them together in the assembly room, a shallow, yellow-walled room, with a lectern on a table in front of a wide blackboard. Jackson gave Douglass the assignment he coveted; he was ordered to create three teams of interrogators. Douglass himself would lead the team interrogating Sueanne Hobson. He planned the timing of the arrests carefully; he wanted to be sure that no conspirator would be able to communicate with either of the other two.

Steve Moore and Darrell Urban were upset. Moore, especially, considered Chris his case; he had been given the runaway case and had been working on it for more than two weeks. He thought Douglass had intruded on his territory, assumed an authority he had not earned. Moore was also irritated by Douglass's elaborate, slow organization of the three arrest teams. "He did it as if they were SWAT teams," Moore said. "What did he expect out there?"

Underneath Douglass's calm organization of the arrests was a sense of excitement, elation, for when had he had a chance to catch three murderers at once and to feel that he would win, that he would nail them all? "It seems almost morbid to get excited over a death, but we knew we were getting close; we knew that our efforts were going to pay off," Douglass said. "The pieces were starting to fall together; we had the missing part, the body. I was up for it."

Moore felt sadness and anger more than elation. He was thinking about what he would have to tell Ed and remembering the smell of the dead body. Douglass had never met Sueanne, never been made a fool of by her. Moore wanted her; he wanted to get even for the way she had treated Chris and Ed and himself.

More than an hour had passed since the detectives had returned from the autopsy, yet no arrest teams had been sent out. Suddenly the dispatcher left his phone upstairs; he walked quickly down to the assembly room and stepped up to the lectern at its center. When he had waved the room quiet, he said, smiling broadly, "Paul Sorrentino just called. He's locked himself in handcuffs and he wonders if someone could come down and get him out."

At first they all thought it was a bad joke, then the room erupted in laughter and Douglass's time to plan was over. "Sure we will! Fucking-A," somebody shouted.

Laughing, Moore looked up dramatically and said loudly to everybody as he left, "Thanks, Big God! Somebody's looking after us tonight. God fucking damn!"

3

It was eleven-twenty when Detectives Darrell Urban and Jim Hight, and Patrolman Paul Douglass, John's younger brother, came to get Paul in the set of dark brown town houses just off 103rd Street. Sorrentino was sitting out on the steps of his town house in handcuffs, his legs spread wide, his elbows on his knees. When Hight hurried up to him, he seemed calm and unembarrassed. His five-foot-five-inch body was muscled enough but appeared crudely squared off on all sides; he looked squat and heavy.

Paul had done many favors for the police, especially Gil Hernandez, and his black hair, dark eyes, and fleshy, rounded face exuded confidence that these men were friends. When Urban got out of the patrol car, Paul shouted, "Hello, Darrell," but Urban, thin and wiry, scarcely gave him a look, let alone a greeting, as he ran past him up the stairs to the party that he could hear going on behind Paul. He told the patrolman to keep everyone in the town house while he got the names of the teenagers at the party.

Urban hurried through the first floor, found the stairway, and raced up it, going clear through the house to find Paul's brother, Mark, making love to a girl in the farthest room. From the dark Mark yelled, "Get the fuck out of here!" Mark quieted down immediately when Urban found the light switch and told him who he was. Amused, Urban calmly took the lovers' names, ages, and schools. While they scrambled to get into their clothes, he acted as if he didn't even notice what they had been doing. He then worked his way back down through the house, recording the names and addresses of the rest of the guests so that he could interview them later. Urban had hoped to find some drugs he could use against the kids in the interviews, something he could threaten them with, but he couldn't find anything out in the open and he didn't have a warrant. He was disappointed that he hadn't found any drugs and even more disappointed that Jimmy Crumm wasn't there.

Mark told Urban that his father, Pat Sorrentino, was vacationing in Jamaica, that he hadn't seen his mother, Marie Sorrentino, for several years. Paul's handcuffs, Mark said, were from his father's old job as a policeman.

While Urban worked the house Hight told Paul he'd have to come to the police station to discuss Chris Hobson, a runaway. Hight coldly narrated Sorrentino's reaction to his request on the police report he wrote the next day: "At the mention of Chris Hobson's name, Sorrentino became visibly nervous. His respiration rate increased. His olive face turned an extremely pale color, and he became what some might call excitable. He immediately wished to discuss the case at that time." Paul agreed to come without force; he went quietly to the station in his father's handcuffs.

Urban's language was less restrained than Hight's. "Hit man for the Mafia! He said to his friends that he wanted to be a hit man for the Mafia!" Urban mocked. "The Italian stallion was scared shitless."

4

When they got back to the station, Hight took Sorrentino on in to be interrogated. Urban and Paul Douglass were met in the parking lot by two uniformed officers waiting to assist in the arrest of Jimmy Crumm and they immediately joined them. John Douglass sent out two cars. Urban and Paul Douglass were in an unmarked car and wore plain clothes; the other members of the team were in uniform and in a marked car.

Urban, of course, knew exactly where to go; he drove quickly through the maze of apartments just across from the Oak Park Mall. He and a uniformed officer went to the door of Crumm's ground-floor apartment. The apartment was located in the middle of a large two-story building, one of twenty buildings set in rows like barracks. Paul Douglass went around the back to cover the sliding glass door that opened onto an unfenced, concrete patio.

Urban was unarmed. When he knocked, Jimmy opened the door promptly. "I asked him if he would voluntarily come down to the police station," Urban said. "He asked me what for. I said we would have to discuss it when we got to the station."

Jimmy's friend Ted Reyes ran out the back door when he heard the caller was a detective; Douglass caught him and brought him back in while Urban was still talking to Jimmy at the front door. Urban took the name of Reyes, then let him go, and made a mental note to talk to him later.

When they got out to the parking lot, Jimmy sat in the front seat with Urban, Paul Douglass in the back. Urban said, "Jimmy was maybe a little bit nervous, like, 'What was this all about?' Jimmy asked why we was going to the police station and I said, 'Wait till we get there and we can discuss the whole situation then.' We made some small talk. Jimmy was a very nice gentleman."

Jimmy and Urban got back to the police station a little before midnight. Paul was already being interviewed in Captain Jackson's office in the entry to the juvenile division. "Where Paul was, the door and most of the walls were glass," Urban said. "If Jimmy had looked in that direction as we entered, he could have seen Paul." Urban took Jimmy down a little way to a small, windowless room and left him there unguarded. The beige room was furnished with a light brown table and four chairs. Urban wanted orders from Captain Jackson or John Douglass before he would begin interrogating Jimmy.

5

At the time Jimmy was entering the juvenile division, Douglass and Moore were arriving at Sueanne's house. They were followed by a car of uniformed policemen. When they entered the house, Douglass simply said that they wanted Ed and Sueanne to come with them to the station. Even at midnight Ed was busy redecorating the upstairs bedroom and he came down to greet the detectives with his hands covered with plaster. Neither Ed nor Sueanne asked any questions.

Suzanne, in her bedroom when the police arrived, walked halfway down the stairs as her parents were leaving and burst into tears. "Suzanne looked down at me and she started crying; I felt she knew," Moore said.

Margie Hunt-Fugate, who had been talking in the dining room with Sueanne, went up to comfort Suzanne. Margie had known the girl for a half-dozen years and Sueanne asked her to stay with her daughter until they returned.

The detectives separated Ed from Sueanne immediately and did not give a reason. "Under the circumstances we felt Ed shouldn't be in the same car with her because we didn't know how he was going to react," Douglass said. "We kept them apart, and Steve and I brought Sueanne up to the station. We kept it very quiet in the car because I wanted her to think. I felt that once we had all the information laid out in front of her, she would break down and tell us about it." Sueanne spoke little on the way to the station. Ed, in the marked car with Patrolman Steve Turner, was greatly concerned and wanted to know if they had found Chris; no one would answer his questions.

Margie recalled that evening vividly. "Sueanne came by and picked me up at work, and then we stopped by her house and sat in the dining room drinking iced tea and talking. When I got to the Hobsons', it was approximately ten o'clock. We'd been sitting there about an hour and all of a sudden a bunch of policemen came to the door and they said that there had been some new developments in Chris's disappearance and they wanted to talk to Sueanne and Ed. Sueanne asked me if I would stay there with Suzanne while they were gone.

"After they left, Suzanne was really upset and she was crying; she was just about to completely come apart. I didn't know what was going on. I asked her and she wouldn't reply. She wouldn't tell me what upset her so much about it. We waited up for about an hour, hour and a half, and then we both went up and laid down. I laid down in the master bedroom and Suzanne went to her bed."

6

When the detectives got to the station, Douglass took Sueanne to an interview room and Moore led Ed to a public waiting room on the floor below. Moore had not yet told Ed his son was dead; he had grown fond of him and hated to do it. He thought he'd talk to Sueanne first. Now all he could tell Ed for sure was that Chris was murdered and he wanted to wait until he knew who did it. Moore was confident that after an hour with Sueanne, he could tell Ed what Leila Andersen had told him two days ago.

Ed seemed enervated without Sueanne. "He always reminded me of a guy in a marriage where the wife takes care of everything," Moore said. "He goes out and works. He goes out and has a few beers when he wants, goes hunting and fishing with the kids, works on his truck, and she takes care of everything." Now that Sueanne no longer could lend him support, Ed had no strength to face the night alone.

Douglass put Sueanne in an interview room in the adult criminal department a floor down from where Jimmy and Paul were being interviewed. The room was identical to that Jimmy was in—a windowless room, plastic chairs, a light brown Formica table. When the door was open, Sueanne could see a portion of a long rectangular room divided into small cubicles by portable gray screens. The small rooms as well as the larger ones were meticulously clean.

Now that all the suspects had been picked up, Douglass had to make some political decisions. Several officials from the Kansas Bureau of Investigation and from Miami County were at the station, and both groups wanted to participate in the interrogations. Since Chris was murdered just across the Johnson County line, Douglass had to use some of the Miami County people as interrogators, though all the Miami officers were kept ignorant of even the basic facts in the case.

As the night wore on, Moore especially found the puzzlement of the Miami officials amusing. He enjoyed the boredom of Undersheriff Niesz and Deputy Ron Orton. He thought of them as hicks. "They'd stand up and stretch themselves in the doorway frame; they'd walk around half-asleep. They knew nothing, nothing at all."

When asked later what role he had in the Johnson County interrogation, Niesz said, "None that I can recall." The following day these "hicks" would play a dominant role in producing new evidence in Miami County.

Detective Jim Hight, Douglass's friend who knew little about the case, was assigned to Sorrentino; Douglass asked the sheriff of Miami County, Chuck Light, to help. Urban and KBI Agent David Wood were assigned to interrogate Jimmy. If they did little else, Sheriff Light and Agent Wood could serve as witnesses for Hight and Urban when the case came to trial. Moore and Douglass would take Sueanne Hobson. Douglass knew she would be difficult and he didn't want an outsider getting in the way.

7

Well before midnight Hight began the interview with Sorrentino. Sorrentino waived his right to remain silent, his right to legal counsel, and his right to have his parents present. Detective Hight wrote: "Reporting Investigator outlined for Mr. Sorrentino the known facts of the investigation and bluntly told him he was the prime suspect in the shooting death of the victim. Sorrentino adamantly denied these accusations and it was not long until it became increasingly apparent that no useful information could be gained from him. In essence, Sorrentino, after being told of the evidence against him, advised he had made up the story about killing Chris Hobson in order to get additional attention from his friends. He stated that this had had the desired effect, and he was really not sorry that he had made the story up."

Hight was frustrated. "Reporting Investigator pointed out to him it would be highly coincidental, if not impossible, for him to have made such a story up and to have the self-fulfilling-prophecy effect that this particular fairy tale had created." Hight told Sorrentino that "the location of the body was basically accurate. The manner in which the victim died was basically accurate. The number of rounds that were fired was basically accurate. And the indication of criminal conspiracy to commit this homicide involving the victim's stepmother also seemed to be accurate. Sorrentino stated all this information was false and all other persons in the case aside from him were lying.

"He further stated that this was his revenge against the police department for all the times he had been 'hassled' by them. Sorrentino admitted he had been involved in criminal activity in the past and had never been arrested on an unjustified basis.

"Sorrentino," Hight continued, "was obviously agitated and contradicted himself on several occasions." Hight asked him to take a lie-detector test and he refused. By midnight, Sorrentino was told that he was under arrest for the murder of Christen Hobson.

Hight had not yet given up. He played the tape Douglass and Moore had made of Sorrentino's conversation with Leila Anderson. "Sorrentino," Hight wrote, "once again looked shocked; however, in this officer's opinion, he recovered his composure relatively well and at once denied it was his voice that was on the tape. Mr. Sorrentino continued to insist that the police department had fabricated this tape and he repeatedly wanted to know who the female talking on the tape was." When Sorrentino asked for a lawyer, the interview ended. That night he was held briefly in the Johnson County Jail, then transported to Miami County before dawn.

Hight and Sheriff Light were not quite done with their work. At their request Larry McClain, the assistant district attorney, drew up a warrant permitting them to search the Sorrentino town house. They were to look for Paul's shotgun, his shells, and a pair of shoes to match tracks made at the murder site. At four in the morning they woke a judge to sign the warrant. When they got to Sorrentino's house, only Mark was there. Mark let them in and led them to a shotgun hidden deep within a closet in his father's bedroom.

8

Douglass had never been much concerned about Sorrentino. The Leila Anderson tape was unlikely to be challenged in court. "We got the telephone call and that was our evidence," Douglass said. "Once the body was found, that completed the circle around Sorrentino."

When Sorrentino asked Hight for a lawyer at midnight, Jimmy's interrogation had not yet begun. Earlier that evening Jimmy had dreamed of Chris's body being discovered; now his dream had come true. Repeatedly, Jimmy had confronted Paul about the rumors he had started concerning his role in the murder. Though Jimmy did not yet know it, once arrested, Paul admitted nothing. Ironically, it was Jimmy who confessed immediately, even before formal interrogation had begun. Jimmy was worn down by the anxiety of discovery—sleeping with his stereo earphones on, eating food that tasted like gunpowder, losing weight steadily. The fourth of May, the day he confessed, was precisely one year from the day he first moved into his mother's condominium in Overland Park.

Darrell Urban, unlike Moore and Douglass, had not gone to college, didn't live in Olathe in new houses on four levels, and wasn't ambitious. He had been in the police department for over twenty years, and though he was in his midfifties, he looked older. He looked like a lean, clean-shaven, chain-smoking garage mechanic. He planned to retire in a couple of years, to do some carpentry and cut lawns in his old neighborhood not far from the station, a neighborhood of small, clean houses built close together, dwarfed by great elms and maples. He lived consciously a small life.

Working as a juvenile detective a decade before, he came down to Shawnee Mission South and told the teachers how they should treat their students and how he treated them when he encountered them in his work. He gave them an illustration. If he found a student with a taillight out on a car, or one who didn't stop precisely at a stop sign, he'd confront them and let them off if they'd enlist in his army of people who would report more serious offenses by other students. "I'd put them in my debt real fast," Urban said. His bluntness and bullying offended some teachers and he was temporarily broken back down to patrolman after that talk.

Even though the teachers didn't like him, Urban had made firm alliances with high-school principals. When Jimmy used a credit card stolen from a teachers' lounge, he got the principal to give him the names of suspects and he singled them out. "I'd breathe in their faces a little bit," he said. "I wouldn't charge them with anything, but I'd make them think I could charge them."

Once Urban dressed up like a janitor at Shawnee Mission South and hung around the lockers until he saw a dope deal go down. He chased two boys through the school. "They never saw a janitor move like that, and they still thought I was a janitor after I caught 'em." Urban wanted Steve Moore to breathe in some faces a few days after Chris disappeared, but Moore didn't have the intricate lists, and he didn't know Assistant Principal Tiegreen at Shawnee Mission South well enough to get the lists.

Urban had been straightforward with Jimmy on the credit-card theft. "The first time around I gave Jimmy the straight skinny," he said. "I thank God for that." Urban thought there was a straight skinny, and he gave it when he knew it, or when he thought he knew it. Though Urban's mind easily fixed on the point of view of others—Ed or Sueanne or Jimmy—and took it as his own, still, there was something to be said for the obvious, and underneath all this talk the most obvious things to Urban were the trust Jimmy had in him and the half-decayed body of a boy.

He knew that this might well be his last murder case. He had waited for orders that night and Douglass had given him the assignment he wanted. Neither he nor Jimmy had lied to each other, he thought. He believed Jimmy trusted him and he would use that capital now. Urban knew there were three murderers waiting in little rooms around the station and several prosecutors busy downstairs in the large assembly room giving instructions, and he knew this was the most complex case he'd ever been involved with. He knew he'd be testifying for years in the long series of trials that lay ahead.

Urban and Wood started interviewing Jimmy at midnight. "Get it off your chest," Urban suggested. Jimmy refused to let them turn on the tape recorder, but agreed to make a statement. Urban read him his rights. He made sure to add the phrases for juveniles that the prosecutor had written out for him on the back of the rights form; one phrase acknowledged that Jimmy had a right to call his parents before he spoke. Conveniently, Urban didn't mention that his mother was sitting downstairs directly under him not more than ten feet below.

Jimmy signed the waiver of rights after David Wood, the KBI agent, patiently printed it out. Wood sat across the table from Jimmy, Urban beside the boy. Urban was frustrated by Wood's painfully slow writing; he was giving Jimmy too much time to think. "We'll never get done this way," he said. "Let me try." The rest of the statement was in cursive in Urban's hand; Jimmy refused to write any of it, though he was willing to dictate it. The four-page statement, written on yellow legal paper, took more than an hour to complete. Jimmy asked only for cigarettes and water; as always, he was polite and appeared to be calm.

After finishing a page, Urban would read it back to Jimmy and the boy would sign it, sometimes deleting or adding a word; Urban would make him initial each change. On the last two pages Jimmy initialed the beginning and end of each paragraph, whether or not any changes were made. Jimmy dictated the following statement:

> My mom called me one day and said she needed to talk to me. When I saw her, she had a welt by her eye. She said Chris had hit her. She said that Chris said, "I have gotten rid of Jimmy. You and Suzanne are next."
>
> Chris had threatened Suzanne and my mother. My mom said something has to be done to Chris.
>
> I talked to her a few days later and she said that if I could find a way to get rid of Chris she would buy me any car I

wanted. I said I would think about it and check around. I knew I could not do it myself, so I called Paul Sorrentino and asked if we could get together.

I explained to him the situation and told him he would be paid well. He said yes. I said I would get back to him.

About a week went by and I talked to my mother again. She said Chris had done various things and something had to be done immediately. She had been trying that week to do it herself and she couldn't. She asked if it could be done this week. I said I didn't know. I talked to Paul Sorrentino and he said yes, he could do it this week. I told him tomorrow evening we would do it. I picked up Paul Sorrentino after school. We stalled around and killed time for a while. Then I decided not to do it. I dropped Paul off at his home and went home. My mother called me and asked me what had happened. She said it was too late now to back out, that she had already gotten rid of his billfold and some other things. I called Paul Sorrentino and we went and picked up Chris Hobson at 5425 W. 103 Terr. and we drove towards Wichita on I-35.

When we got out in the sticks, we pulled off the highway, drove around until I got lost, and decided to do it.

We got out of the car and we told Chris Hobson that we needed a hole dug and told him to start digging. He dug the hole and I told him to try it. I tried to pull the trigger and couldn't. Paul Sorrentino pulled the trigger on his gun. I shot into the woods. Paul Sorrentino shot two more times. We started covering him up with our hands and a shovel. We hopped in our car and hauled ass.

Jimmy's narrative ended. On the fourth page he responded to specific questions, clarifying what he had said already and providing details.

Paul Sorrentino had a shotgun and I had a 10-gauge shotgun, single-shot. I don't know what Paul Sorrentino did with his gun. I threw my shotgun in the river over the A.S.B. Bridge the next day.

Chris Hobson went with Paul Sorrentino and myself willingly. There was no force used.

My mother threw Chris Hobson's billfold away.

My mother was going to pay Paul Sorrentino's repair bill on his motorcycle for doing this job.

My mother was going to buy me a new car for doing this job. She talked me into this.

This is all I wish to say. I will sign this four-page statement because it is the truth to the best of my knowledge.

The interview ended at seven minutes after one on Sunday morning.

9

What Jimmy, Urban, and Wood were creating was known to the other two teams of interrogators before it was half-done. Information from Jimmy's confession began to enter the accusations of Hight against Sorrentino and of Douglass and Moore against Sueanne. Assistant District Attorney Larry McClain sometimes delivered the information and sometimes the interrogators went out to get it themselves. Before one o'clock, according to Hight's report, "McClain informed Mr. Sorrentino that other investigators had obtained a signed, written statement from James Hobson, which further implicated him in the shooting death. Sorrentino stated that obviously Mr. Hobson was lying, although he could give no reason for it."

Douglass had already used his knowledge of Sorrentino's involvement and Leila Anderson's tape against Sueanne. He also went out and got an oral report on Jimmy's confession. By twelve-forty, Douglass told Sueanne, "Your son was brought in here separate of Sorrentino; he was kept isolated. It's the information that I have just received that your son told us exactly what happened, and is in the process of telling detectives now what happened. And he also implicated you. Information is becoming very, very potent."

10

At one-thirty Urban finished interviewing Jimmy and the boy went out to urinate in a rest room down the hall. Moore was also on the way to the toilet after the first stage of the interview with Sueanne. When Moore came in, he was surprised to see Jimmy and stood at the urinal beside him. Jimmy remembered him from the week before when Moore and Urban had come to his apartment. "We were both taking a whiz," Moore said. "I asked him right out, 'Jimmy, are we supposed to believe all this crap about your mother planning the murder and her paying people off?' He turned his head right toward me and he said, 'Steve, it's all true. She did those things.' That was the first time I felt she really had done it and that Douglass and I were on the right track."

Jimmy went back into the interview room and stretched himself out on the seats of three chairs he had lined up. Urban turned off the light, closed the door, and left him there alone. It was now almost the middle of the night. Urban liked Jimmy. He was an attractive, well-dressed boy with dark eyes and the tightly drawn features of his mother, a polite, well-behaved boy even on this night. "He was a gentleman," Urban said to Moore, his highest praise.

A couple of hours later, after arrangements were made and a transportation order issued, Urban drove Jimmy to the Johnson County Jail in Olathe. Deputy Ron Orton, the man who had photographed the grave ten hours earlier, and Undersheriff Neisz picked up Jimmy in Olathe, then went on down with him to the Miami County Jail in Paola. On the way down to the jail Niesz said casually to Jimmy, "If you ever care to discuss the case, we'd be glad to talk about it with you."

11

Sueanne's interrogation began at seventeen minutes after midnight. She waived her rights with a nod of the head and a signature. Unlike Sorrentino and her son, she permitted the detectives to tape the interrogation.

"The information that we have indicates that that night your son and Mr. Sorrentino deceived Chris, took him out to a field, used a shovel from your garage, shot him, and buried him," Douglass said. "The information that we have was that it was because they were paid to do so by you. The information we have strongly implicates you in this particular matter."

"I wasn't—I was with my husband," Sueanne said, sobbing quietly.

Douglass asked if she knew the murder was going to happen, and she denied such knowledge, still crying. If he could not get her to admit the whole at once, he would begin with the part. "Did you talk with your son about purchasing a motorcycle or car in the last few days?"

"No. No, but the car deal with Jimmy is, we go to court May seventh. I am suing my ex-husband for back child support. We were divorced seven and a half years and he never paid me. He also, from what Jimmy has told me, beat Jimmy. I told Jimmy I would buy him a car, yes, based on what we got from the settlement. Because I feel like the money is just as much his as it is mine, because when Jim had him, he gave him nothing." Sueanne was no longer crying.

"Had you and Jimmy discussed the death of his stepbrother?" Douglass asked. "Have you discussed it with anyone? Did you talk at all about anything like that, even in jest?"

"All I have said many times—and I have said it in front of my husband—if Chris would do something wrong, I would say, 'I'm going to kill that kid or break his neck.'"

"I know what type of boy Chris was," Moore said sympathetically. "He was the type that would make you pull your hair out and bang your head against the wall."

"Yes, but we have been in this for so long, we have gone through family counseling, things were getting better."

Immediately Douglass had tried to get Sueanne to admit to some knowledge of the conspiracy and failed. He had thought this would be easy, that he would get her to admit a degree of involvement at once, for he had "potent information," much more than he had for any of the other confessions he had taken over the years. Despite her tears he was surprised by how quickly she regained her composure, how subtly she evaded answering.

"It's down to the point now where all of the information seems to verify, except your nod of any acknowledgment of it," Douglass said. "I can understand your feeling that way, but I've sat across this same table with a great many other people in the same position. I work crimes against persons on a day-to-day basis. My opinion, based on the information that we have, is that you are involved in this, and I think you need to give us some kind of indication about what, if any, that involvement is."

"No, sir," she said, slightly raising her chin.

Douglass again lowered his expectations. "Did you know about it after it happened?"

She waited more than fifteen seconds without answering, staring down at her hands in her lap; she seemed puzzled, humble, and wounded. For Douglass her control, the long pause under such pressure, seemed remarkable, yet he was thrilled, for now he guessed that she did know. Still he had to get her to speak, to take a position. If she didn't speak, he had only the words of two murderers to use against her in court.

Douglass could not wait her out. "Did you know about it after it happened, Mrs. Hobson?" he asked softly.

Sueanne was sitting at the end of the table near the closed, windowless door; Douglass was five feet away on one side of the table, Moore directly across from Douglass. At that moment, in a room exactly like this, her son was sitting above her dictating his confession. She waited more than six seconds before answering. "Do you know what it's like to have a seventeen-year-old son that you love desperately, and that you want to help, and you try to keep him out of trouble, and you want them to make something of yourself—themselves—and you want them to forget the hurt and the pain? Jimmy told me some terrible things that happened to him when he lived with his father, and he himself has a terrible temper, and we tried to get him help, and he wouldn't take it."

She paused and looked directly at Douglass, who was leaning forward, shortening the distance between them. "If I answer any more questions without an attorney, is this going to hurt my son?"

Douglass now knew Sueanne was aware of Chris's death before his body was discovered; he must get her to admit at least that much. Words alone connected her to the crime, words alone would convict her, he thought. According to what he heard from Urban, Jimmy was not guilty because Paul killed Chris and Sueanne ordered it. Now Sueanne was saying she was not guilty because it was Jimmy who shot the boy. The whole family was innocent.

Still, there was the smell of Chris's dead body that Douglass couldn't get out of his mustache. He had to give her an easier way, let her take an easier path. Once she was safely on the path, he'd show her the prospects that opened before her.

"I can't tell you whether it will hurt him or not," Douglass said. "Jimmy's up there telling us what happened right now. I don't think you're going to be able to hurt him anything past that. Certainly telling you is one thing, and conspiring to do it is another thing. Did you know that he did it? Did he tell you that he did it?"

Again Sueanne was silent for more than fifteen seconds and Moore could not wait her out, could not breathe in that thick silence. He pulled out his black appointment book. "Did Jimmy wait till the weekend? Did he tell you that night? When did he tell you?"

She waited several seconds before responding. "I didn't see him that night. I don't remember. I honestly don't remember."

Suddenly she was crying again. Moore pretended to be sympathetic and asked her how long she had had these feelings bottled up inside her. After a pause she said quietly, "Too long."

Moore asked about her reaction to the false report of Denise Hanson that Chris had been seen at Worlds of Fun. "I called you around the twenty-second, twenty-third, which would have been a Wednesday, and told you that I thought I found Chris. Has it been a week, two weeks? And that's when I got the reaction from you which I didn't think was quite right. As if you already knew something had happened."

"I honestly don't remember."

"Why would Jimmy make up the idea that you were going to pay him and Sorrentino to kill Chris?" Moore asked.

"Jimmy expected a brand-new car, but instead he drove one of ours. And he told his sister that all hell was going to break loose. I told Ed and Ed talked to him and said, 'I didn't promise you a brand-new car.'"

"Do you feel that Jimmy's doing this to get back at you?" Douglass asked.

"I don't know. I know I've been through almost three years of therapy with Dr. Craft and I know that Jimmy feels like I abandoned him when I took Suzanne and left. And I know he hates me." She hesitated. "And I know he loves me."

"Did Jimmy tell you why it happened?" Douglass asked. "Why don't you tell us what Jimmy told you?"

"He said because Chris 'narked' on him—about using credit cards and taking drugs." Sueanne quickly provided a clear motive for Jimmy: revenge.

Douglass was irritated that Sueanne professed to know nothing about the murder itself. "I think if it happened the way you said, you should have much more information. You should know when he told you, you should know what he told you, and, certainly, as the boy's stepmother, even if you don't care for the boy, you would have asked some details about what happened. We have proved that we know who's killed the boy. Now we have to prove that you weren't involved in it."

Douglass attempted to put her in an impossible position; she had to prove a negative, prove her innocence. He asked her if she'd take a polygraph.

She nodded her assent, then interjected, "I've heard that they are not one hundred percent accurate."

For the first time Douglass almost lost control of his voice and he leaned over until his face was within two feet of hers. "I have worked a great many homicide cases, and the same thing that I've seen then is what I'm seeing right now. I'm seeing retreat and back up, retreat and back up. Everytime we ask you to do something that could obviously prove your innocence, you back up. I think that if you're innocent, by damn, we ought to prove that you're innocent. And I'll be glad to give you the benefit of the doubt."

"Please," Sueanne said politely.

12

Douglass and Moore went out to speak to Lieutenant Casida, the officer who was to give the lie-detector test. For a half hour they discussed the progress of the investigation with Casida and helped him formulate questions to put to Sueanne.

Casida was still not satisfied that he knew enough. While Douglass got Casida a copy of Jimmy's written confession, Moore talked to Jimmy again to get more information he could use to confront Sueanne.

Moore had delayed as long as he could; he had to tell Ed now. Ed was, Moore thought, just an ordinary, blue-collar guy caught in a hard place, and he had come to like him. Ed had had a bad first marriage and he thought his stepdaughter had been murdered; he'd never had much happiness in his life. For two and a half weeks Moore had held Ed's hand, talking with him daily, reassuring him. During those weeks Ed never said anything bad about anybody, even when Bob Wilson, Chris's uncle on the Teed side, made wild accusations against him.

Moore himself had thought Chris was a suicide. Yet he had encouraged Ed to think of his son as a runaway, had minimized Ed's fears. Ed always thought—"knew" was Ed's word—that Chris would never run away. A pussy afraid of the dark, how could he run?

Now a handsome man of thirty, clean-shaven, still lean, and filled with the exuberance and energy of a teenager, Moore himself had come from a troubled home where his father drank. More than once he had run away from home.

From his first meeting with Ed, he felt sorry for him. Now, after what he had learned in the last two days, he identified with him. Moore was his representative in the interrogation of Sueanne, and he imagined that he embodied Ed's anger.

After he talked to Jimmy for the second time, Moore told Douglass, as they whispered in the barren hallway in the middle of the night, "If she just killed him, that'd be one thing. But that she manipulated her son to do it, that just fries me!"

When Moore came into the waiting room, Ed was holding his head in his hands so that all he could see was Ed's blond hair. Before

Moore spoke, Ed looked up at him startled and afraid. Immediately Moore said, "I'm sorry, Ed, we found your boy's body tonight." Ed began to cry, repeating "no, no" softly, his hands over his eyes, his whole body shaking on the orange plastic chair in the glassed-in lobby. Moore went over to him and sat down beside him, his arm awkwardly draped over Ed's shoulders. Ed sat sobbing and shaking for what seemed to Moore a very long time.

Finally Ed took his hands from his eyes and looked up at Moore as if Moore alone could save him, as if he depended totally on him. Moore had never had to announce a death to anyone, let alone the death of an only son. He wanted to get the rest of it over with. Bluntly, he told Ed that his stepson, Jimmy, and Paul Sorrentino had murdered Chris. Still crying, Ed asked over and over again, "Why would they want to do something like that to my boy? Why?"

Moore hesitated; he certainly didn't have any idea of the boys' motives and he wasn't quite sure of Sueanne's involvement. "Ed, I think your wife planned it, then ordered them to do it, and paid them when they got done with it."

Almost as if he hadn't heard, Ed kept saying, "Why would they want to do that? What did he do to them?" He seemed to be talking to himself. Moore just sat there and watched Ed sob, not even touching him anymore. After a while he went out to get Patrolman Steve Turner and told him to take Ed home and stay with him until he called. Moore didn't know what Ed would do, but he didn't want a suicide; besides, they needed him as a witness.

13

Douglass was waiting impatiently for Moore downstairs in the assembly room and he asked about Ed's reaction. Moore was upset, almost out of control. "I just told this man that his son was dead, then I told him that his wife's son had killed his boy, then I told him that his wife had planned and paid for the whole goddamned thing! Did he react? What do you think? Fuck, no! He was a zombie!"

Before Sueanne took the lie-detector test, Moore and Douglass decided to meet with her briefly one more time. They had given her a long time alone to think. Douglass believed that she might confess under the pressure of the impending test. Douglass began with the billfold. Much of what Sueanne had done was just speech, but dropping the billfold was an act to further the conspiracy. Douglass wanted confirmation of an action, not just secondhand knowledge of the murder.

"Your son has told us that, the night this happened, you took Chris's billfold and you disposed of it at Metcalf South," Douglass said. "He also told us that two weeks before it happened, he talked to you, and you told him that Chris had punched you and given you a black eye."

Sueanne answered only the last assertion. "Chris has never struck me."

Moore had seen the body of the boy torn apart and been forced to stand beside it and smell it. He had had to sit there and watch Ed sobbing after he told him his boy was dead. He and Douglass had gotten nowhere with this woman.

Angrily, Moore interrupted Douglass's interrogation. "Okay, there's another problem I wonder about and this is relating to your *safety*, about *your* becoming a victim. And that is that your son feels that if you go home tonight and you face Ed, you will tell Ed the truth. And I feel that Ed would probably shoot you. Now you have that to worry about!"

"I don't believe that," she said. "I don't really think he would. Do you really think that he would?"

"When it comes down to the nitty-gritty, he's lost everything," Moore said. "And here he's married a woman who he thought he could trust, and he finds out from you, because you break down in front of him, that you are responsible for his only son's murder. There's no doubt in my mind, due to the past record and the way he's been, what he'll do to you."

"I'm not worried about him hurting me," she said.

"But I just want to let you know," Moore said.

Now it was Douglass's turn to interrupt. "I don't want you to get any impression that we're going to cause Ed to hurt you or let him hurt you. We're not going to let anyone hurt you." He was concerned that Moore's threat was endangering the admissibility of what she said, that his anger would do some legal damage to the state's case in the trials that were certainly coming. Douglass quickly ended the second interview and told Sueanne that the polygraph operator was ready.

14

After Sueanne took the lie-detector test, Moore and Douglass again talked to Casida. The detectives were disappointed in the results. Mrs. Hobson had lied about some things, Casida said, but he wasn't certain how much she had lied, wasn't confident of his judgment of her, especially on questions directly related to the murder. Casida believed she should be tested again a day or two later when she was under less stress.

With the preparation of the lie-detector test, the talks with Casida, and consultations with the attorneys in the prosecutor's office, Moore and Douglass had not talked to Sueanne for nearly three hours. When they began the third interview, it was four-thirty in the morning and they were exhausted.

"Casida detected deceit in much of the stuff you had to say," Douglass said. "He told us that finally he was able to pin you down on the fact that you had deposited Chris's billfold up at Metcalf South. It seems that we work, and we work, and we work, and we catch you in a lie, and then you say, 'Okay, Kings X, I lied, but here's how it really happened.' And we work, and we work, and we work, and we work and we catch you in another lie."

"I know—" she said.

Douglass didn't let her finish her sentence. He was frustrated; she should have confessed long ago with the evidence against her. Like Moore, he, too, was very angry now. "Listen, I wasn't born yesterday, and this isn't the first homicide case I've ever worked, and I've given you every benefit of the doubt, but I have seen tonight the death of a thirteen-year-old boy. I have listened to two other people tell me about how it happened, all of the details, all of the gruesome details of an execution-type murder, and their involvement and your involvement, and all I get from you is one story after another story after another story. Ma'am, I don't know how to put it any plainer. Don't you think it's time you told us what happened?"

"The car, I told you—" she began.

Douglass broke in, "No, I don't want any cockamamie stories, I want the truth."

"I'm not going to give you any cockamamie stories," she said. "I feel like I shot him myself, because if I had gone to Ed or somebody else . . ."

"I think you should feel you shot him yourself," Douglass said brutally. "I think you shot him just as much as if you'd walked in there and pulled the trigger and shot him in the face yourself. That's what I think. You sent those boys out to do exactly what they did, and not only did you send them out, you guided them through it. And then when they came back, or before they came back, you took that billfold and deposited it at Metcalf South, and you were fully well prepared to complete your agreement by purchasing your son a car and by purchasing or taking care of some other indebtedness to Mr. Sorrentino. That's what I think. And I think that's what you're feeling guilt about it. But that guilty feeling doesn't go away just because you want to wish it away."

"I feel guilty because I feel that if I had said something to Ed or somebody else the first time that Jimmy said something, made a threat, this would not have happened. I didn't want to admit that this had happened."

She expresses regret, she expresses remorse, but she never exhibits it, Douglass thought. "Why did you lie to us in the first place?"

"Because he's my son."

"Why did you lie to us about the billfold? That certainly couldn't have hurt him. The only person that that implicates is you and your involvement. And that billfold was there from the day he was killed. That billfold was at Metcalf South either shortly before or shortly after he was killed. Sorrentino doesn't know you from a bowl of soup, but he says it happened that exact same way."

Douglass narrated the substance of Leila Anderson's phone conversation with Sorrentino. He emphasized the fear Leila and the other teenagers who knew about the murder had of Paul and Jimmy. "The kids thought, 'If Jimmy's mother can pay him off to get rid of her stepson, why can't she pay him off to get rid of anybody else who's going to turn them in?'"

Then Douglass read verbatim Jimmy's written statement. When he finished, he said, "Sorrentino says you were involved in it; your own son says you were involved in it; you don't show truthful on the lie-detector test. Now, why is it that you can't tell us what happened?"

Sueanne had been silent for ten minutes while Douglass read from the documents he had before him. When she finally spoke, she told him the simple truth: "I did not pay those boys."

"What about the billfold?" Douglass asked. "You have admitted to us that you deposited the billfold at Metcalf South. Jimmy says that he couldn't back out of the deal because you'd already deposited the billfold."

"That is a lie."

"I just think that it's time we get this out in the open. You're ate up about it. I can see that it's been driving you crazy. It's still driving you crazy, and now it's driving us crazy!"

"I did not pay those boys. I didn't."

After a pause Moore asked quietly, "Did you have any idea at all what might happen?"

"Yes," she said. Moore was excited; he thought he had made progress, had gotten her to admit that she knew something about the conspiracy before the murder.

"Then why did you just let them go ahead if you had some kind of idea that they were going to do it?" Moore asked. "You don't have to tell somebody to go out and murder 'em to make 'em do it."

"The first thing that was said was right after Jimmy ran away from home, and Suzanne and I went out and gave him some clothes in February. We met him at a Sinclair station, and Jimmy was very mad and upset, and he was yelling that he was going to get even, and he was going to give Chris three shots in the face. And I didn't think he would do anything like that." Sueanne's answer was uncharacteristically long and emphasized Jimmy's vague threat.

"That is a long distance from what Jimmy says that you did," Douglass asserted. "He says, 'My mom talked me into doing it. My mom sent me out to do it; my mom said she would pay me to do it; my mom said, "You can't back out now because I've already deposited the billfold."' Now, what do we know about that that's true? Well, we know that you deposited the billfold. We know that the car that was used was your car. Okay, we know all of these things occurred, right down the line. Why shouldn't we believe the rest of what he has to say? The only thing that you have to say is, 'I don't know. I took the billfold down to Metcalf South, but I don't know when. They told me that the murder happened, but I don't know when.' No, I'm saying to you right now, in anything as traumatic as a homicide you will remember the date and the time and the place for the rest of your life. You don't come up with an 'I don't know.' You'll come up with, 'Yes, I know. He told me because we were at my house, and it was the day after, it was two days after.' Now I'm submitting to you the reason that you're not telling us is because you are involved in this."

"I am not and I don't want Jimmy to be involved in it. He's my son."

"Let's go back to Sorrentino. Let's just say that for some unknown reason, some phantom reason, your son has an illusion that you're involved in this, that you're involved in this in some way, shape, or form. But you're really not, it's your son's illusion because he's psychotic. That's what you've alluded to. What about Sorrentino—does he share the same illusion? Not only that, but a confidential informant overheard Sorrentino talking on the telephone to your son, talking about the payoff, talking about when the payoff was to occur, talking to your son and saying, 'Well, Jimmy, why don't you just get a new motorcycle, after all; let's be economical about this, you don't have to stick your mom for a brand-new car.' And then Sorrentino also saying in the next breath, 'You know, all I want is to get this thing squared away; I don't want too much money because my folks will start asking questions.' Now, where does Paul's illusion come in?"

"He could have gotten that from Jimmy," Sueanne said.

"No, you already had a deal worked out with him— that we know—because you told the polygraph operator that you had arranged to get your son a car and you'd also arranged to work out a great deal with Sorrentino." Despite Casida's warning about the reliability of the lie-detector test, Douglass was exploiting it to the hilt.

"I told Jimmy I would get him a car, depending on how much money I got out of the settlement when we went to court May seventh. The car was part of the divorce settlement. It was."

"Was Sorrentino part of the divorce settlement, or did you adopt him, too?" Douglass said cruelly.

Douglass realized that he was losing control and tried to get hold of himself. He would try again to feel his way into her position, come closer to her view of the family, convince her that he understood her problems.

"Let's talk about the situation. It was an intolerable situation—you had two families, two distinct families. You had a traumatic child, a child who had problems in school, a child who had problems getting along with his family, a child who had difficulty getting along with his friends. He was a pain in the butt; he was a pain in the butt to a lot of people; he was a pain in the butt to the people at school, and he was a pain in the butt to you. And that's easily enough documentable. He gave you a hard time at home, he gave Jimmy a hard time, and he probably bullied his stepsister, without any doubt. Now, is that what happened? Did he bully his stepsister?" Douglass had little understanding of Chris's character, a good deal of understanding of how Sueanne perceived the boy.

Sueanne answered that Chris sometimes bullied her, sometimes bullied Suzanne. She added, "But he also gave me things, and brought me things, and we also did things together."

Douglass sensed a weakness in her; suddenly he became a counselor, not an interrogator. "It's been my experience in things like this that they get completely out of hand before you know what happens. You build up a lot of hostilities, you build up a lot of resentment, you build up a lot of problems, and things just start to go in motion. Things that you may not really ever intend to work out that way but do. Now, I think that it's a situation like that."

"And how am I going to prove to you that that is not it, when everybody else is saying that it is?" Sueanne responded. "I didn't pay those boys. I didn't."

Douglass guessed wrong; she was having nothing to do with his sympathy. His tone changed entirely. "Now what you've told us is not consistent, it is not logical, it doesn't make sense. At least give us a story that makes sense." His voice and face sneered at her.

"I don't feel logical. You know, I just, I feel at, at loose ends . . . I . . . This is my son we're talking about."

"We're talking about you," Moore said.

"We're talking about you," Douglass repeated. "Did you put the billfold up at Metcalf South?"

"I put it there because I wanted it found and I wanted it to be okay. I didn't want Jimmy to be blamed, I didn't want him to be caught. I—I wanted everything back the way it was." This was her first admission to the detectives of any tangible connection to the crime.

"When did you put the billfold up there?" Moore asked.

"The next day. I took it out of his room. I don't want to admit that Jimmy did this; I don't want to admit that this even happened. This is my child and I cannot, I don't, I don't want to believe that he did it. I'm having a hard time dealing with that, because he's threatened Chris before and I feel like, if I had said something, this wouldn't have happened."

"I don't think you feel guilty because he threatened Chris in the past," Douglass said. "We hear people threaten other people all day long."

"You probably were sitting there having a conversation with the boys or with one of the boys, and you really didn't say yes, but you really didn't say no." Moore now was offering Sueanne an easier way to admit her complicity. "You didn't say don't go out and do that, but you didn't say go ahead and do it. The suggestion was there. You didn't have to say what you wanted done due to prior conversations, prior threats, knowing the prior history of how Jimmy felt against his brother, how he hated his guts, and how this little brother hated him, and how they would do anything to get back at each other. The jealousy was there."

"But not to that extent." Sueanne admitted nothing about her role, commenting only on the degree of hostility between the stepbrothers.

"It must have been there to that extent because we've got one dead person," Moore said. "Now, he comes up, you know, and you say, 'Something's got to be done! Something has got to be done!' and he says, 'Hmm, well, I'll take care of it.' And in the back of your mind you're convincing yourself that you're not a part of this; you're going to be so far removed from this thing, just like you're trying to convince yourself right now that your son didn't go out and do it. You're trying to convince yourself that you didn't put the 'okay' in his head. You didn't have to say, 'Jimmy, I want you to go out and shoot him, take care of him.' You just said, 'Something needs to be done.' I can look at John and say, 'John, something needs to be done,' and if we have had prior conversations about someone who's a pain in the butt, and he knows that I know what's going to happen, that is the act. That is the act, because he went out and committed it."

Moore paused; he was guessing now, but he was closer to the truth than he imagined. "Did you talk to Jimmy one night saying that something's got to be done with Chris?"

She wouldn't answer directly. "I did not make a deal with those boys. I didn't. I have tried to cover up for Jimmy. I have tried to cover up, I have tried everything."

"Then what keeps me from thinking that you wouldn't try to cover up for you?" Douglass asked.

"Nothing. You're right," she said. "It makes you feel like the other person has done nothing but lie the whole time."

"You've got the feeling I have." After a long pause Douglass said insidiously, "You can tell us, Mrs. Hobson."

"The whole thing—I tried up until tonight to act like it didn't happen. And it's hard for me, it's hard for me to deal with it, it's hard for me to admit that it happened, it's hard for me to admit to myself that it happened."

"Is it hard for you to admit that you probably allowed it to happen? Do you feel any way responsible for that?" Douglass leaned toward her. Sueanne didn't move at all.

"Yes. Because of the threats that Jimmy had made against Chris in the past. I have sat here and pussyfooted around."

"You have, but you haven't told us what the hell your involvement was," Douglass said. "You have pussyfooted around, I can tell that, and it's driving me crazy, because I get little tiny bits of incongruent materials. Stuff that does not fit together. Stuff that doesn't make a story, or doesn't even make a logical sequence of events."

"No, no, I don't blame you at all," she said. "But I did not make a deal with those boys. I'm guilty by association."

"No," Douglass insisted. "If you're guilty at all, you're guilty because you cooperated in this particular event."

Moore was wrought up; he was still irritated by Sueanne's treatment of him during his hapless investigation of the runaway. "I come over there three or four times. I'm showing you clothes, I show you we got forty-five officers out there, we got helicopters, we got things on the news. You know, it's just that the whole situation is just entirely inflated, and the whole god-damned time you knew what was going on and never said a word. And here I'm sitting there looking at your husband trying to tell him something about his boy."

"And I'm caught between my son and my husband," she said.

"When did your daughter find out about it?" Douglass asked.

"Right after it happened," Sueanne said.

Douglass almost slapped his head. What did Suzanne know? He had not thought of Suzanne until then. Would Sueanne permit him to interview her daughter? If he could not break Sueanne down, he would try later to get her permission to talk to Suzanne.

"Who told her about it, about his death, about Chris's death?" Douglass asked.

"I did. I told her what Jimmy had told me."

"Boy, I sure hope so, because we're going to have to ask her," Moore said.

"She worships, she just worships Jimmy."

"Doesn't she know the difference, though, between right and wrong?" Moore asked. "Don't you know the difference? There is a difference between right and wrong, you know; bloodlines only go so far."

"I wish I had told you last week, but I didn't and I'm here in this big mess." Sueanne's eyes filled with tears.

"Do you know why we think that you didn't tell us last week?" Douglass inquired bluntly. "We think that the reason you didn't tell us last week is you couldn't tell us, because you couldn't tell on Jimmy without Jimmy telling on you. That's why I think you didn't tell us last week. Now, let me say one other thing about Jimmy and the things he's had to say tonight. Everything he says has checked out to be true. Even down to the point where he says, 'Mom gave me money while I was a runaway so I could stay run away.'"

Sueanne was silent for several seconds and Douglass could not wait her out. "Why should I believe that Sorrentino's lying? He has nothing to gain from putting you in a crack, nothing at all. The only thing he has to gain from is if he goes out and does what he's supposed to do and benefits by getting the motorcycle. In his own demented way he benefits. And how do you benefit from the entire thing?"

Sueanne remained silent; Moore answered Douglass's question. "If Chris is no longer around, how do you benefit? You don't have to put up with a kid that's a pain in the butt. You've got a kid that has got your family all upset—your family, your offspring, not Ed's, *yours*. There's no longer a threat there; little Suzy can become Ed's primary daughter because she has been deficient, hasn't had the father-type image. Maybe now you can get your son back there at the house. Now you can have one big happy family—make up for all that time that you missed and that your family and kids missed in not having an entire family unit with a husband, wife, kids. You know, 'We've got the suburbanite family, now we've finally made it and got rid of our little pain in the butt.' The old golden ghetto routine."

"Detective Moore, I know how much that boy meant to my husband."

"I know, too," Douglass said.

"And I love my husband."

"We know that, too," Moore said flatly.

"He is the best thing that has ever happened to me. And I would not take the one thing away from him that he loves most in this whole world."

15

Douglass was exhausted and considered ending the interview. It was nearly dawn. They'd gone as far as they could and it wasn't far enough; Sueanne could be charged, but she wasn't going to be convicted on what they had.

The best evidence they had was her admission that she planted the billfold at Metcalf South. Douglass again asked Sueanne why she had dropped the billfold and she insisted that she wanted it found so the detectives would search harder for Chris. Douglass could not coax her to go further.

In his frustration Douglass again found himself answering his own question. "I don't believe you wanted it to be found for any reason like you're trying to make me think. There's no advantage to that. If you wanted me to find out about that murder, you could have planned a half-dozen other things that would have led us right there and you'd have never had to say a word. And the minute we brought you up here, you could've told us all about it. You wanted it to be found, all right—to think that he was robbed, to think that he was abducted, to think a whole lot of things. And I don't think you ever counted on us finding the body, and I don't think you ever counted on the fact that Jimmy would turn right around and tell everything he knew."

Douglass recessed the interview at five-thirty in the morning. When he walked out of the room, he felt she had defeated him. Still he was reluctant to go down to the assembly room and admit that to the prosecutor. Suddenly he remembered that Sueanne had said that her daughter knew of the murder right after it occurred.

"We had some good information," he recalled, "but the interview itself was frivolous. It hadn't produced the kind of information we wanted to have, that we thought important. The thought occurred to me that if the little girl had been around, maybe she heard something, saw something that would help us. But you're talking about the daughter of the person you're hoping to charge. It was very unlikely that even if she had any information, she would give it to me. I asked Sueanne during the recess if I could talk with her daughter. She said, 'Sure, you can talk to her tomorrow,' because she wanted to demonstrate how cooperative she was being. But I said, 'No, I want to talk to her tonight,' because my experience said, 'You talk to her tomorrow and you'll hear what Mommy tells her to say.' Sueanne said, 'Okay, you can talk to her,' but I still wasn't convinced we were going to get anything. I was very tired; I felt my chances of getting any information from this little girl was zero, but we could at least tell the district attorney we covered all the bases."

As soon as Sueanne consented to her daughter's interview, the three left the station and drove to her condominium. The prosecutors were going to charge Sueanne when she returned to the station and she was to pick up a change of clothes before she was jailed. Whatever happened at her house, Douglass intended to interview her one last time as soon as they got back to the station.

By the time they got to Sueanne's house, it was light. Douglass said, "Steve and I stayed right with her at the house because it was important that we see whatever it was she was going to tell a potential witness. Sueanne said, 'Suzanne's upstairs sleeping; I'll go get her.' We said, 'We'll go with you.' We walked upstairs right behind her; she opened up the door and called, 'Suzanne, wake up!' She looked up and Sueanne said, 'These policemen are here; they want to talk to you.' Then, as an afterthought, as we started to walk into the little bedroom, she said, 'Just tell them the truth,' and she turned around and walked downstairs."

Once inside the girl's room, Douglass realized he had left his tape recorder at the station. "I almost get religious over a tape recorder. I took a tape recorder with me anytime I thought there was going to be anything because it was much better than taking notes." Fortunately, Moore had a yellow legal pad with him.

Suzanne scarcely had enough time to sit up in bed and straighten her nightgown around her shoulders before the detectives entered.

Her precise, small face was the image of Sueanne's, what they had been looking at all evening. Despite their sudden intrusion she seemed quite composed and spoke without emotion. Douglass asked her to tell in story form what she knew about the murder. Immediately Moore and Douglass were astonished; it was as if she, too, were one of the conspirators.

"She was possessed at the time to tell the truth," Douglass said. "Her mother had told her to tell the truth; it seemed like the right thing to do. Once she really got started, Steve was so surprised and disgusted that he stopped taking notes. She told us about a meeting that took place a day or less before the homicide. I don't think she comprehended what the outcome could be at that point. Later on I'm sure she did. What she said there was more elaborate than what she said later at the station. She didn't require coaxing at the house."

The detectives were in the room only five or six minutes. Once they understood how much Suzanne knew, they ended the interview. Both realized they had to get back to the station to get the girl on tape before she comprehended the damage she was doing. While Suzanne got dressed they kept her away from her mother.

Margie found herself in an uncomfortable position that Sunday morning. When the detectives knocked, she was sleeping in her clothes in the Hobsons' master bedroom. Neither she nor Suzanne had awakened when Ed and Steve Turner returned in the middle of the night. "When I woke in the morning," Margie said, "I heard a bunch of voices, and I heard Sueanne in the bedroom with her daughter telling her to go and tell them the truth—to tell them everything that she knew and to tell them the truth. Sueanne came into the bedroom and asked me if I would stay with Suzanne all the time because they were taking her to the police station and I said of course. After that I got up and Sueanne went downstairs. The two detectives went in and talked to Suzanne in the bedroom just for a few minutes."

"On the stairway I asked Steve Moore, the detective, what had happened, and he briefly told me about their finding Chris and the charges that were being brought. I went upstairs where Suzanne was and she got dressed."

Moore was instantly attracted to Margie; she was the sort of woman who would wear enameled parrot earrings. When Margie asked him what was going on, he whispered, "You're not going to believe what you hear."

Before the detectives left, Moore told Patrolman Steve Turner, who had spent the night with Ed, to help Sueanne finish gathering up her things. Moore asked Turner to drive her to the police station in the marked car out in front of the house.

Margie accompanied Suzanne and the detectives in an unmarked car. The detectives needed Margie to witness their interrogation of a juvenile and Suzanne needed Margie's support. Suzanne trusted her; she had known Margie for five years, as long as any adult except her mother and her great-grandmother.

16

It was six-thirty Sunday morning and the streets were virtually deserted as they drove back to the station on Santa Fe Drive. As soon as they arrived at the station, Douglass hurried downstairs to pick up his tape recorder from Sueanne's interview room. He inserted a new tape, then ran upstairs to find a room in the juvenile division. By the time he got up there, Moore already had a room. Suzanne sat at the end of the table nearest the door. Margie had pushed her chair away from the table and back against the inner concrete-block wall. Moore sat on the inner side of the table, too, and Douglass quickly took his place across from Moore. They began the interview at six-thirty-eight.

"At your house when we were talking to you, you told us that about a month ago there began to be some real serious problems between your mother, your brother, and your brother Chris."

Douglass spoke slowly, quietly; he took his time. It was as if he were painstakingly writing the words in his head. His voice was disciplined and no longer had the biting tone it had assumed in the last interview with Sueanne. If Suzanne said again what she said in the bedroom a half hour before, the audience for the tape would be half the people in Johnson County and all the lawyers and judges. He was near to the nest and he was tense.

"Could you tell me what kinds of problems those were?" Douglass asked.

"Chris was causing problems between Ed and Mom," Suzanne answered.

"What kind of problems was he causing?" Douglass asked.

"I don't exactly remember, but they got in fights all the time," she said.

Douglass immediately took control of the interview, and Moore, realizing how crucial Suzanne's testimony was, let the experienced detective lead.

"And the fights were over Chris?" Douglass asked.

Suzanne spoke reluctantly once she saw the interview was going on tape; she was wide-awake now. She was sniffling and had a cold, but she was also crying at times. "She could feel the effect of the things that she was saying," Margie said later.

"Yeah," Suzanne agreed, after a long pause.

"How did you know this?"

"I could hear them talking or yelling."

"About how Chris was getting in between her and Ed?"

"Uh-huh. All the time."

"About a month ago—that would be about two weeks before Chris disappeared—were they having problems then?"

"Serious problems, yes."

"What kind of serious problems?"

"Well, they weren't getting along at all because of Chris."

"Okay. Did your mom talk about doing anything about it to anyone?"

"Um . . ." she began, then fell silent. She couldn't bring herself to go on.

"I know we are at the difficult part, but what did she say?" Douglass asked in a gentle, patient voice, almost whispering.

"She said something had to be done because Chris was causing too much problem," she finally admitted.

"Did she give any indication what that something was?"

"No."

"Did your mother talk to Jimmy about Chris on the day he disappeared?"

"Yeah, we went over to his house."

"Where did you talk to Jimmy?"

"Out in the parking lot of his apartment."

"What did your mother tell him?" Douglass spoke quietly, but distinctly emphasized each word.

"I don't know. They were out in the parking lot. They were talking about Chris and that they had to go out somewhere."

"When we were over to your house, you told us that you overheard part of that conversation. What did you overhear?"

"That Jimmy and whoever were going to take him out to wherever and get rid of him."

"What did they mean by get rid of him?"

"That's what they said. She told Jimmy that something had to be done. He said, 'We'll go out and get rid of him.'"

"Did she say anything about being gone that evening? Or getting Ed out of the house?"

"I don't know; they left for Burger King or something. She got him out of the house. She said that she was going to get Ed out of the house?"

"Was that so that Jimmy could take Chris out of the house?"

"Yes."

"Okay. Did your mom ever tell you before that something was going to happen to Chris?"

"What do you mean, a week before or what?"

"Well, anytime before that day."

"Yeah. I don't know. About a week before. She said that, well, she just said that something had to be done about Chris. She didn't say what."

"Did she ever say anything about why he didn't come home?"

"She said that Jimmy went out and took care of him. So I wasn't sure."

"Has your mom talked to you at all about this since it happened other than to tell you that Jimmy took care of Chris?"

"No."

"When your mommy told you that Jimmy took care of Chris, what did you think that meant?" Moore asked, joining in for the first time.

"I didn't know what to think. I didn't know if they just beat him up just enough to put him in the hospital or not."

"When he didn't come home, what did you think?" Moore continued.

"I figured they killed him."

"The day you were out there by Jimmy's apartment, did they talk about killing Chris?" Douglass asked.

"They didn't really say that word for word. They were just going to get rid of him. That's all they said."

"Did your mom tell you anything about what you were supposed to do that night?" Douglass asked.

Suzanne hesitated. "Umm—all I know is that I was supposed to stay upstairs. I don't know when Chris left or anything. She said to get in the shower."

"Did she tell you why?"

"Well, she said Jimmy was going to go pick up Chris."

"Can you think of anything else that's important?" Douglass had decided to end the interview and confront Sueanne with what he had learned.

"No," Suzanne responded.

Moore, though, did think of something important, quite as important as anything asked in seven hours of interviewing. He had not spoken for the first two thirds of Suzanne's interview and had posed only two questions to her before now. In the same quiet, restrained voice he had heard Douglass use, he asked, "Do you know anything about the wallet?"

"How it got to Metcalf South?" she asked.

"Uh-huh."

"My mom threw it up there."

"How do you know that?" Moore asked.

"She told me."

Now Douglass resumed the questioning. "How did she get the wallet?"

"It was in Chris's room."

"When did she get it?"

"That night," Suzanne said.

"When did she throw it up there?"

"That night."

The entire interview took twelve minutes. Elated, Douglass and Moore left the room immediately. What they had taped was a very direct dramatization of Sueanne's role in the conspiracy on the day of the murder and testimony that Sueanne herself had thrown the billfold up at Metcalf South that very evening. According to Suzanne, her mother had put the billfold in the planter hours before Chris was murdered.

17

In the minutes before Douglass began his final interrogation of Sueanne, he tried to understand her motives for dropping the billfold, tried to imagine her way of thinking. "If her mom took it up that night," Douglass said, "she had to know that Chris was going to be killed. Because if she didn't know that he was going to be killed, there would be no reason to take the billfold. And if she did know that he was going to be killed, she knew that he was not going to need it anymore. In fact, she told Jimmy, 'You have to go through with it because I've already put the billfold at Metcalf South.' She thought that she was just simply smarter than everyone else. That was her way of throwing everybody off the scent. She wanted people to think, 'His billfold is up there. He's disappeared without his billfold; something must have happened to him; you hear about people kidnapping little boys from shopping centers all the time. He must have gone up there, hung around there after being a runaway, went with a stranger, or just disappeared.' And he would have disappeared, except for fate. She was looking for a long-term solution. Runaways come home; this runaway would never come home."

Turner had taken Sueanne back downstairs to the room where she had been interviewed the night before. Now Douglass and Moore were as wide-awake as if they had had a good night's sleep. It was a lovely Sunday morning in May and they finally had enough to get a confession. What they had now was not coming from the mouth of a murderer, but from the daughter Sueanne doted upon.

Douglass and Moore planned to talk with her for a few minutes, set her up, then ask her about the meeting she had in the parking lot hours before the murder. They could think of nothing else but the parking lot. They could see her standing beside the Lincoln in a white dress pleading with her son to kill Chris. They couldn't get that scene out of their minds. "I wanted all that laid out," Douglass said. He planned to say, "Look, you've lied to us and lied to us. Both of your children tell us what you did and they have no reason—the little girl has less reason than Jimmy. She wasn't involved in it; she wasn't culpable, yet she tells the same story." Going in, he knew he'd break her down.

18

Margie and Suzanne were left alone upstairs in the juvenile division. Margie had said nothing throughout the interview. Moore glanced back at her occasionally and he could see the effect of Suzanne's testimony in her face. Still, Margie hadn't spoken or moved from her chair until the detectives left.

After they were gone, Margie walked over and closed the door again. She bent over to embrace Suzanne and burst into tears. Over and over again she said to her, "Why didn't you tell me? I could have helped. Why didn't you tell me? You knew it was wrong. How could you just sit by and watch your mother do that?"

Suzanne was crying, too, but at first she couldn't think of anything to say. She shrugged tentatively. "Once Mom gets her mind set on something, you can't stop her. You know that. She'd just get mad."

19

Douglass began the last interrogation of Sueanne at six-fifty-five. "Do you feel too fatigued to answer any questions? Do you feel physically incapable of answering any questions?"

"Oh, I'm tired, but I want to help," Sueanne said, drawing out her words. She was near tears.

"We talked to your daughter, Suzanne," Douglass said. "We

talked to her at your residence. Your daughter explained to us that she was informed that your stepson, Chris, had been killed, that she had been told this after the fact. She has also given us a detailed statement to the fact that on the day of the disappearance, you called up your son Jimmy. You went over to Jimmy's apartment and, in the parking lot, discussed the impending disappearance of Chris. She told us what was said. She told us that you repeated to Jimmy that something had to be done; you also said to her that they were going to get rid of Chris."

As Douglass spoke he studied her face; her mouth was closed and she was staring at him impassively. "Suzanne also overheard you tell Jimmy that you would get out of the house that night and you would get Ed out of the house. She's also told us that you told her to take a shower when Jimmy came over. She told us that you found Chris's billfold and that night you put the billfold at Metcalf South. Not two days later, *that night*, the seventeenth of April. In light of everything that we've said, there seems no doubt in my mind that you knew what was going to take place. That you aided and assisted in that particular act." Douglass spoke precisely, emphasizing each word, almost as if he were reading from a text.

"Now again, I want to ask you to tell me the truth. If you don't want to talk, you don't have to. But I think the time for the lying and the fooling around is over. I think now you should tell us the truth, or you should decide not to say anything at all." Frustration was in his voice again.

"You've already got me guilty," she said querulously.

Douglass exploded. "Ma'am, I don't have you guilty! The evidence has you guilty! Now, are you going to tell me the truth or are we going to play word games? Did you go over to Jimmy's apartment the day that Chris disappeared?"

"I believe I did, yes."

"Did you talk to Jimmy about the fact that Chris was to disappear that night?" Douglass asked.

"No, not that I recall."

"Did you discuss the fact that something had to be done with Chris?" Moore asked. At first Sueanne did not answer his question.

Until the very end of the interrogation only Sueanne and Douglass spoke. The two seemed in an intense, intimate world of their own creation and Moore did not choose to enter it.

"The truth, Mrs. Hobson," Douglass said.

"Yes. Yes. He was threatening Suzanne."

"Suzanne also said that Chris was the subject of many arguments between you and Ed. Is that correct?"

"Uh-huh."

"Did you tell Jimmy that you were going to have Ed out of the house that night?"

"No, Ed was at a union meeting that night."

"But you said you would make sure that he stayed out of the house."

"No, he was at a union meeting," she repeated in a patronizing tone.

"Why would Suzanne tell us that, if it wasn't the way it was going to be?"

Sueanne began to answer and Douglass angrily interrupted. "Now before we get going, I want you to understand. I've listened to your theory about the illusions that Jimmy has. And before you start off on the track that now Suzanne has a bunch of illusions, I want you to know that I don't believe that. You have already told me that you went to Jimmy's apartment."

"Uh-huh."

"Apparently you went there to talk about Chris. Right?"

"Uh-huh."

"All right. You said something has to be done."

"Oh, amongst other things," she added casually, as if she were speaking to a clerk.

"Well, Suzanne didn't say 'amongst other things.' She also told us that day, that Jimmy told you that he was going to take another person with him that night. And that the name Paul Sorrentino came up. To the best of her belief she thought she heard the name Paul Sorrentino. And in fact that someone else was going to go with Jimmy to take care of Chris. In Suzanne's words 'to get rid of Chris.'"

"Jimmy told me that he had a friend named Billy that would scare Chris so he would leave Suzanne alone. He would take care of it." This was the first mention of the name Billy in the interrogation.

"And you know that he was going to take him out and at least scare him, is that correct?"

"He said he might."

"Okay. When did you get Chris's billfold? Suzanne says that you got it that night and put it at Metcalf South that night."

"No. It was the next day. Because I was with my husband that night."

"Suzanne seems to indicate that you put it there on your way to meet your husband. And that is what Jimmy indicates, that you did it on the way to meet your husband. Not afterward."

"No, I went—"

Douglass interrupted loudly. "Mrs. Hobson, tell us the truth. Two hours ago you were telling us lies about what you are now telling as the truth. Now look. I am putting it to you very plainly: Tell us the truth or don't tell us anything at all. But, *please*, I'm getting awfully tired of having you lie to me. I mean it is demoralizing to sit there and have you lie to me over and over again. Tell me the truth. When did you pick up the billfold?"

"I picked it up the next day from his—from his desk."

"Why does it all sound like a big plan that day? Why does Suzanne tell us it's a plan? Why does Suzanne tell us that you go over there to Jimmy's apartment and talk about getting rid of Chris, telling her that it's going to be all taken care of, then the next day telling her that it was all taken care of?"

"Because she was with me when I went over there." Suddenly she confirmed offhand many of Suzanne's statements.

"That's right. She heard what was going to happen, didn't she?"

"Uh huh."

"And the things she said are true, aren't they?"

"That Jimmy and Billy were going to scare Chris so that he would not threaten Suzanne anymore."

"Did the mention of the word 'killing' him ever come up?"

"No."

"Did the mention of the word 'get rid of him' ever come up?"

"Probably. But not in that context."

"What other context is there? I mean, how do you get rid of a thirteen-year-old boy, besides getting rid of him and taking him out in the boondocks and blowing his head off?" Douglass spoke bluntly for impact, but she didn't blink; she just looked at him.

"You scare him so that he doesn't threaten," she answered blandly.

"So when it boils all down to is, you did know that Jimmy and this boy named Billy were going to take Chris out somewhere that night."

"And scare him," she added.

"And scare him. Why didn't you tell us that an hour ago? Or two hours ago? Why did you wait until we have talked to Suzanne, who was supposed to prove you innocent? Why did you wait until now to tell us that?"

"Because I'm scared to death." Sueanne's voice was shaky and she seemed about to cry.

"I understand that. I understand that. I really do. I understand. And you have reason to be." For the first time in this final interview Douglass seemed genuinely sympathetic.

"I didn't think it would go that far. And, after the fact, I could not do anything about it. And I was scared to tell my husband."

"I understand," he said barely above a whisper. "As we discussed before, many of these things start out and we never think they're going to go that far."

"I have never been involved with anything like this. And I was scared after I found out. I don't know what to do about it." Sueanne was crying softly.

"How far did you think it would go?"

"That he was just going to scare him."

"How was he going to scare him?"

"Threaten him that he was going to beat him up if he hurt Suzanne again."

"Jimmy tells us that you knew that it was going to go further than just to scare him."

"I know that." She added quickly, "I know you've told me that."

"So has your daughter," Moore cut in in a flat, bitter voice.

"Your daughter was under the impression that at the meeting

you knew and Jimmy knew and she knew you were going to get rid of him," Douglass said. "And when she said get rid of him, she assumed Chris was not coming back."

"Well, that's not what she said to me."

"That's what she just said to us. She had the feeling that Chris was not coming back. That Jimmy was going to get rid of him. And that's why she was told to be upstairs taking a shower when Jimmy came over. And that's why you were going to be out of the house and Ed was going to be out of the house and Chris was just going to be taken care of."

"No, it was just to scare him."

"And it went too far," Douglass said softly. "Okay," he whispered as if to himself, and ended the interview.

20

Sueanne was led out to be formally charged and jailed. Over the intercom the arresting officer called Suzanne and Margie down from the glassed-in waiting room to comfort Sueanne as the charges were drawn up. Moore was shepherding Sueanne through the routine police procedures. When Turner had brought her back to the station, she was dressed as if she were going to an afternoon luncheon. As she was standing before the desk waiting, Moore asked her what she wanted to do with her jewelry. He didn't need to be a jeweler to admire the blood-red ruby encircled by stairsteps of diamonds. Her rings and gold chains were worth thousands, Moore thought, maybe tens of thousands, how the hell would he know?

"You could leave them here in the safe, but that's not a very good idea," Moore said to Sueanne. "Things sometimes disappear around here. Why don't you give them to Margie?" Sueanne silently put the jewels in her purse and gave the purse to Margie.

She also asked Margie to find a lawyer for her. She told Margie that Ed wouldn't do anything to help her and she needed a good lawyer. Moore then walked her back through the building to the station's small municipal jail.

That Sunday before he drove back home to Olathe, Moore

took Suzanne back to the condominium, then dropped Margie off at her apartment. Margie was more concerned about Suzanne than about her mother. Watching the girl go up the steps of the condominium, Margie told Moore her fears. "Two days before Sueanne was arrested, in her car in front of my apartment, she asked me, 'If anything ever happened to me, would you take Suzanne in?' I said, 'Of course, but what about Ed, he's her adopted father?' She said Suzanne doesn't even like Ed; she's just nice to him because it makes things easier."

"That figures," Moore said.

Suzanne was thirteen and Margie was concerned that she was going to have to live indefinitely with a man she didn't like, even if he was her legal father. Margie seldom felt confused; she always converted doubt into certainty as quickly as possible, but she couldn't be certain about anything that morning. When she said good-bye to Suzanne, she didn't even know what to say to console her or if she needed consoling.

21

Douglass was exhausted and worried. He hoped he had followed the legal guidelines carefully enough so that Suzanne's statement could be admitted when Sueanne's trial came, if it came. Certainly what Sueanne told them wasn't enough to convict her; they would need the testimonies of Suzanne and Jimmy and Paul to make the case.

Sueanne's was the most difficult interrogation Douglass had ever done. He remembered that long night vividly. "She didn't get a lawyer because she figured she was smarter than we were, and given enough time, she would simply talk her way out of it. It became a mind battle between Sueanne and myself. We had a lot of information. By the time Jimmy started talking to us at the station, we had essentially all the information that we needed. I felt that once she was really confronted and understood that there was no retreat, she would confess to me. She surprised me, she surprised the hell out of me because she didn't confess. She came very close, she came very close several times, but she backed up just enough to cover up what she was getting into. She was tough."

In the interrogation there was a price for silence and a price for speaking. In this small room with two men, the woman, under enormous pressure to answer direct questions, repeatedly remained silent for fifteen or twenty seconds until the detectives yielded to the anxiety her silence generated and began to answer their own questions. The most remarkable revelation of Sueanne's character during her interrogation was in her use of silence. The power and control of silence, of the clear refusal to use language, became the central territory raided by the detectives, but more and more occupied by Sueanne. That tension dominated the interrogation.

During these silences Douglass said, "Sueanne looked down, looked very humble, looked very wounded, puzzled. In interrogations we anticipate a lot of reactions—hostility, aggression, even hysterics sometimes. People break down and cry. Very little of that with her, very little emotional range. And when she did speak, she could answer a question very indirectly, almost sound like she was answering the question, but not answering it. She could change the tone of the question, change the question itself in her response."

Nobody in the conspiracy ever said that Chris was to be killed; Jimmy and Paul were "to get rid of him," were "to get rid of the problem." The language of murder, the private language Sueanne had created, was the language she shared with Jimmy and Suzanne. It was the intimate language of the remnants of the Crumm family. The language was going to be challenged in court later, Douglass knew already. A jury would have to decide if "getting rid of the problem" could be equated with "killing the boy." By the end of her interrogation Sueanne forced the detectives into using her phrase at some cost to them.

Douglass never spoke to Sueanne again, yet he thought he had come to know her in that long night. "She's a cold individual," Douglass said. "She talks about how upset she was about Chris's disappearance and the fact that he was dead; she tells you that she knew he was dead and that she had nothing to do with it; she tells you that she found out the next day after he disappeared, yet she still gives away all his clothes and furniture. In this society that's incomprehensible."

"Start with Margie," Douglass said. "Margie and Sueanne had a common denominator: status, or the idea of status. Margie dresses to the hilt, wears a considerable amount of jewelry, likes to talk about dining in the finer places. That seems to be a common denominator among many of Sueanne's friends. If you're by yourself and you think you have status, it's not nearly as credible as if you're with someone else who tells you that you have status. Or between the two of you, you think that you do. It's even more credible if there's four or five of you. It's all a game, it's a mind tease over whether or not status is really there. But you can convince yourself, if there are enough of you and you can live the life-style you want to.

"How she lives and what she perceives herself to be are two different things. What she thinks she is, is all-important to her. She must have told us ten times, 'I wasn't raised that way; I wouldn't do those things; in my family we never fought; in my family we never did this; my family was always a step above; my family raised me in a different way.' She had a very high regard for herself. She felt that she came from a very socialite situation, almost aristocratic; that was her life-style. Whether it was true is inconsequential; she believed it to be true. She felt that she was a step above.

"Everything was very prim, everything was very proper, everything was socially acceptable, everything was just as Sueanne wanted it to be and that was the way she organized her world. Chris, on the other hand, wasn't like that at all. He grew up mainly with just his father. He grew up in a bachelor environment where order was not necessarily the prevailing mode of life, where the glasses were not all lined up in a row, where table manners were not necessarily the prime thing, where things were not exactly so. At the same time there was a very definite rivalry between Chris and the little girl Suzanne, and I'm sure Chris probably did his share to aggravate the situation, as any child would, because he saw a stranger moving in and taking over a lot of the affection. Suddenly he's the outsider; he's the outsider with his father because his new stepmother makes it that way. He's the cog in the wheel; he's the difference; he's the one that gets left out; he's the one that eats by himself; he's the one whose picture doesn't appear with everyone else's; he's the one who gets left home or sent to a boyfriend's house. It's not a tidy little family unit anymore. And Sueanne likes everything to be in order. He was the cog in the wheel and she just eliminated him. He stood in her way and she took him out."

Douglass knew that what he had gotten that night wasn't quite enough. Just a little more or a little less and a trial would have been unnecessary. "Sueanne had the capacity to change stories," he said. "I found it remarkable afterward. At the time it was extremely frustrating. She would modify her story, back up, change it. She started out by saying there wasn't any kind of problem at all—it was a very happy household and she couldn't understand why we would think that it was anything other than that. She altered her story radically numerous times—from her first words to the end—and every time swore that that version was exactly the way it was. Given twenty-five years, maybe she would have given us the truth. I don't know, but she wore me out.

"She'd just come up with something else that had just enough truth in it that it was hard to break down," he concluded. "Finally we boiled the story down to where she didn't send the boys out to kill Chris, only to threaten him and keep him from hurting Suzanne. She really didn't intend for them to kill him, she was kind of sorry that it happened that way, maybe. That was after being at it all night long."

22

All night Steve Turner, a short, heavyset patrolman of twenty-five, had been Ed Hobson's minder. At Moore's request he had driven Ed home. While Sueanne's interrogation continued, they drove back to the condominium, arriving there at one-forty.

"I'll remember that night until the day I die," Turner said. "I didn't carry any sidearms, but I did have a small pistol strapped to my leg because I knew there were a lot of guns in the house. We spent the time in the kitchen and the living room. It was a kind of gaudy living room, reds and oranges and blacks, with mirrors and pictures of cats.

"Ed and I drank coffee all night," he said. "Here was a man whose boy was killed and his wife had killed him. What worse thing could happen? Yet he was trying to comfort me, offering to cook eggs and bacon for me, offering orange juice. He was trying to take care of me as if I were suffering. After a while he lay down on the couch and I sat in a soft chair near the door. He was mumbling to himself a lot, turning over toward me, and then turning his face into the cushions. Every little while I'd say, 'Ed, are you going to be all right?' He was catatonic by morning.

"About six a car drove up," Turner recalled. "Sueanne came right on in followed by Steve and John. When he heard the door, Ed sat up for the first time in a couple of hours, then put his elbows on his knees and held his head. Nobody even looked at us; they all went right on upstairs. Ed didn't even follow them with his eyes; he and I just sat there staring at each other. I was as dead as he was. After a few minutes Sueanne came downstairs again, put her purse on a chair, and walked right over to Ed. She sat sideways on his lap, caressing his cheeks, whispering to him, and pressing her face right against his. He never put his arms around her, but he never pushed her away either."

6

FUNERAL AND WEDDING

1

The cemetery where Ed buried Chris was just off Metcalf, twenty blocks straight south of the shopping center where the boy's billfold was found. The internment was at four on Wednesday, the seventh of May, a day short of three weeks after Paul and Jimmy murdered Chris.

The heavy, black iron gates to the Johnson County Memorial Gardens were hung on two thick pillars of Kansas limestone. With their car lights on the mourners drove through the open gates and alongside a narrow spring bed of red and yellow tulips dividing the roads in and out.

Once inside, the mourners came quickly upon a small stone house, like the house Hansel and Gretel came upon in the woods. They parked just beyond it in a blacktopped lot. The lot was soon full. The rest of the funeral procession drove slowly past the lot and parked up the hill on one side of a gravel lane until that, too, was full.

The burial plot was quite near the entrance. A hill rose steeply beyond the open grave. There were no woods, no full-grown trees in this area of the cemetery. Large trees grew a few hundred feet farther up, and were newly leaved with the delicate green of spring. The graves were scarcely a foot apart.

The land rose steeply to the south and west, so the main view was north toward Interstate 435 and the business parks along it. There was a wasteland a half mile wide that began less than a hundred yards north of the grave; the land had been stripped for development. Beyond it were the backs of great brown or green office buildings and hotels; the buildings, covered with expanses of opaque reflective glass, were like burnished mirrors strung out along the Interstate.

Chris's classmates from Indian Creek Junior High had arrived early. They stood impatiently in a semicircle to the south of the grave in a thick line arching a little way up the hill. At first, when they had heard what had happened to Chris, they were afraid. For three days Lee Shank had talked about Chris's death openly in her classroom and the children would say to her and to each other, "My stepmother would never do anything like that. Do you have a stepmother? Do you think yours would?"

Yet this Wednesday in spring they had gotten out of school a little early; they felt far from any death, on this day at least, and they had trouble being as quiet as they thought they should be. Somber and well dressed, they looked particularly young and unfinished, especially the boys.

Reporters stood thirty yards away across the gravel lane. Television cameramen were shooting up toward the green tent that the gravediggers had erected over the hole that morning.

The black hearse was closely followed by Ed and Suzanne Hobson in their dark blue Lincoln Continental. Lailoneh Teed, Chris's half-sister, had driven up from Tulsa and she rode with them.

Early on the afternoon of the funeral Ed, Suzanne, and Lailoneh, along with three or four of Ed's friends, had gathered at the Hobson condominium. At midafternoon Margie joined the small group.

After Sueanne had been granted bail on Monday, Margie had invited her to stay in her apartment for a few days. Sueanne had talked with her daughter as soon as she was out of jail; she knew that Ed didn't want her at the funeral and she knew Margie wanted to go. She asked Margie to act as her representative. Sueanne instructed Margie to talk to Ed and find out how he felt about her now. She also wanted Margie to calm and console Suzanne as best she could and to bring back some suits and dresses.

Darrell Urban and Steve Moore had arrived at the Hobson condominium fifteen minutes before the mourners left for the cemetery. For Urban it was business—"I just came to see who was there, who wasn't, who laughed, who cried."

Moore, on the other hand, wore his best blue suit, as if he were going to church. He had had to tell Ed that his son was murdered and he felt his sorrow. He himself had a baby son.

For three days Moore had done nothing but talk to Chris's friends and teachers. He was coming to know the boy, coming to know how fond of him his teachers were. Alone among the detectives, Moore had come to realize that Chris was not just "a pain in the butt to everybody," as Douglass had said when they interviewed Sueanne on Sunday.

Moore also had been interviewing Sorrentino's friends and their parents; he discovered that several classmates and at least one parent had known about the murder and didn't tell anyone. Getting to know a boy after he was dead was an unnatural experience for Moore. Wednesday was a bad day in a bad week.

"This was the most disgusting thing I'd ever come across, and for days everybody I ran into was a puke," Moore said. "The little boy is dead and a bunch of fathers are calling high-priced lawyers fearing obstruction-of-justice charges against their sons, and I'm just trying to get convictions on the three that blew his brains out. Pukes!"

Ed, isolated in his grief, without friends except for a few acquaintances from work, couldn't find enough pallbearers to carry the body to the grave and asked Urban and Moore to help. In their unmarked car the detectives followed the hearse and the Lincoln out to the cemetery. They stopped three or four car lengths behind the hearse and walked awkwardly up to it.

The brown metallic casket was light enough as the detectives helped carry it up the rise to the grave site, but one pallbearer slipped halfway to the grave and the sudden jar broke the seal on it. Reverend Robert Craft conducted the graveside service. The pallbearers had to stand in a line just outside the green canvas tent during the short ceremony and smell the sweet rotting body of Chris.

"God, what a smell!" Urban said. "He was ripe! As soon as it was over, we got the hell out of there. We didn't stand around

Sueanne Hobson in handcuffs: the woman accused of conspiring to murder her stepson. *Photo credit:* John Sleezer

Ed Hobson, Sueanne's husband. He stood by his wife through the murder investigation and trial, and remains convinced that she is innocent. *Photo credit*: John Sleezer

Christen Hobson, the thirteen-year-old murder victim.

Ed and Sueanne Hobson studying clothes picked up in the April 1980 search for Christen Hobson. *Photo credit: © Kansas City Star*

Christen Hobson's tombstone. *Photo credit: Doug Koch*

Jimmy Crumm, Christen Hobson's stepbrother. He followed his mother's instructions.

Paul Sorrentino, Jimmy's friend and hired accomplice in the murder.

Johnson County District Attorney Dennis Moore. *Photo credit*: John Sleezer

Assistant Prosecutor Steve Tatum. *Photo credit*: John Sleezer

Sueanne and Ed Hobson holding hands in the court-house (top) and leaving the courtroom (bottom). *Photo credit*: John Sleezer (top) and *Photo Credit*: John Sleezer (bottom)

Sueanne Hobson awaiting sentencing with her lawyer, Scott Kreamer. *Photo credit:* Fred Blocher, © *Kansas City Star*

Associate District Judge Robert Jones. *Photo credit:* John Sleezer

Ed and Sueanne Hobson. This photograph was taken in July 1981, after Jimmy's trial and before Sueanne's conviction. *Photo credit: © Kansas City Star*

and talk to anybody; I didn't even look back to see what anybody else did. Goddamn, I can still smell him, still smell him!"

2

After the funeral Margie came back to the condominium with the other mourners. Ed was drinking heavily and Margie also began drinking. Sueanne's precision and control had grated on Margie that morning. Sueanne had told her, "Be sure to get the two white blouses in the third drawer of the dresser on the left as you come into the bedroom and the black suit jacket in the closet near the entrance. Tell Ed I told you to be sure to tell him that the thick green blanket is on the top shelf of the closet in case it gets cold again and that the cat food is kept in the basement just below the stairs." There was no hint of sadness, no tears, no remorse; it was as if nothing had happened, as if nothing were to happen that Wednesday afternoon. Not a word about Chris; life seemed almost normal.

Sitting in the living room where they had talked so often about the difficulties of Sueanne's marriage, Margie could not get out of her head that her friend had given her the murdered boy's clothes to give to her children, even the blue suit Chris had worn at his stepmother's wedding. Whatever Sueanne knew, whatever she did, she knew when she gave her those clothes for her children to wear that they were the clothes of a dead boy.

Everybody seemed to be laughing, Margie thought, having a good time, even Ed. Nobody seemed to care.

Margie went upstairs to say good-bye to Suzanne and found her alone in her bedroom. She bent over the bed and hugged the girl, but she didn't tell her what she had decided to do.

She had gotten Sueanne a lawyer, had put her up in her own apartment. She had been her messenger. Yet how could she disbelieve what Suzanne had told the detectives Sunday morning? To believe in Sueanne's innocence she would have to believe that Suzanne was setting up her own mother. Margie had waited long enough, three days was long enough.

Driving back, Margie made up her mind and she didn't intend

to ask questions. She burst into her own apartment in a rage, screaming at Sueanne, "Chris is dead and nobody cares! Ed is drunk and doesn't give a damn. You don't give a damn. Everybody is happy Chris is dead. Get out of here! Get the fuck out of here right now!"

Immediately Sueanne called Ernestine Bean and Ernie drove over from Grandview, Missouri, to pick her up. When Ernie got there a half hour later, Margie was still in a rage, throwing Sueanne's things out on the porch.

Sueanne whispered to Ernie that she shouldn't pay any attention to Margie. "Don't listen to what she's saying; she's totally off the wall." When Margie began yelling again that nobody cared about Chris, not even Ed, Sueanne, still calmly gathering her things together, said quietly to Ernie, "Did you hear that? She thinks even Ed is glad Chris is dead."

On the Sunday Sueanne was charged, Ernie herself had doubts about her friend's involvement in the murder. She phoned Norma Hooker Sunday evening and they talked for more than an hour about how badly Sueanne had gotten along with Chris in the months before he had been murdered. Yet she never called Norma again. Ernie had been the matron of honor at Sueanne's marriage to Ed; she was her oldest friend. She had never known her friend to lie to her.

Right away Sueanne told Ernie what Jimmy had told her on the phone on the day after the murder. "We have killed Chris. If you breathe one word to a living soul, we'll take Suzanne and Ed and you down the tubes with us."

Several days later Ernie asked Sueanne, "Did you take the billfold and leave it at Metcalf so they would look harder for Chris?" She simply said, "Yes." In the end Ernie believed Sueanne. "I know in my heart that the person I've known and loved for five years is totally incapable of a violent act."

3

After Margie had driven Sueanne out of her apartment and calmed herself down, she thought about Suzanne. Sueanne had said to her two weeks after Chris's disappearance, "Ed and Suzanne don't get along. If something should happen to me, would you take care of Suzanne?" Margie said yes automatically. Now Margie felt she had a responsibility to Suzanne, even if the request to take care of the girl came from her mother. What Sueanne feared had occurred. Ed and Suzanne were left alone together, and who could say what would happen, for surely Ed knew, or soon would know, that his wife's daughter had also conspired to kill his son.

Margie had known Suzanne and her mother for five years. She felt that Suzanne needed her protection and trusted her enough to accept it. Margie knew, or thought she knew, that Sueanne had involved her own daughter in a murder, that Suzanne had been made an important part of the conspiracy. Sunday morning in the police station Margie had been more stunned by Suzanne's role in the murder than by any other revelation the girl had made.

Why had Sueanne needed to involve everybody in her family? Why had Sueanne coldly given Margie herself things taken from the room of the murdered boy? She herself felt stained; she had happily taken the furniture from Chris's bedroom, taken his clothes. Sueanne had always been generous with her things, but knowing the boy was murdered, why was she so cruel as to give to her in the days after the murder many of the things he touched and wore?

She had not protested Sueanne's gift of the boy's clothes. The day after he had been killed she herself had drunk to his running away. Chris's existence, his disappearance, had seemed insignificant to her, irrelevant to her bond with her friend, and she had taken her friend's side unquestioningly.

In fact, the bond between Margie and Sueanne had become stronger in the weeks before Chris's body was found. As Sueanne's exultation wore away in the first days after the murder, her need to be with Margie increased.

Margie felt Sueanne's tension, though they rarely talked about the disappearance of Chris. She attributed her friend's increasing agitation to Ed's influence. Sueanne told her that Ed was almost crazy with anxiety about Chris and Margie assumed the strain he was under was also shared to a lesser degree by his wife. Now Margie knew she had assumed too much. The two men Sueanne had chosen to marry were weak and Margie knew quite well that Sueanne was a strong woman who had gotten her husbands to do what she wanted. Certainly Sueanne did not often share Ed's fears.

She realized that Sueanne all along had scarcely disguised her desire to rid herself of Chris. Margie had laughed when Sueanne asked her if she knew if the Sorrentino family was involved in the Mafia, if she knew a hit man to take care of Chris. The questions fit the roles each had played in their friendship, Margie thought; Sueanne naively believed that Margie, unlike her, led a wild, undisciplined life, that Margie knew men from the underworld. When Sueanne had told her that she wanted Chris out of the house, told her with increasing frequency and shrillness, Margie had not admonished her, had not even acknowledged it. She already knew well the tensions between stepparents and stepchildren, the enmity between them.

Margie didn't like to be duped; she prided herself on seeing through appearances. After Chris disappeared, she had believed Sueanne's explanations. She had trusted her. Yet it turned out that even Sueanne's thirteen-year-old daughter was part of the family conspiracy. Why had she not seen? She and Sueanne had celebrated Chris's running away. Sitting happily beside a strangely boisterous Sueanne, she had drunk to his disappearance, if not to his murder. Why had she herself been so callous? Sueanne wouldn't even burn the clothes of the boy she hated and murdered; she gave them to her instead.

Margie felt implicated in Chris's murder. She could understand that it was necessary for Sueanne to deceive Ed, but why was it necessary for her to be involved in that deception? That was gratuitous, malice on top of malice. All of Sueanne's flesh and blood had become conspirators, murderers, and Margie's sons were to wear the clothes of a murdered boy. Margie's boys were only two or three years younger than Chris and she loved them more passionately than she had ever loved any man. She had fought to keep them with her.

On the evening of Chris's burial Margie had become Sueanne's enemy. She was a formidable enemy, for she was unafraid of detectives, unafraid of lawyers and depositions, unafraid of Sueanne, who, like her, was not a woman to cross.

Once Margie had gone over to the side of the prosecutors, she could see better than any of the women who remained loyal to Sueanne the fate of Suzanne, especially the difficulties that faced her in the next two or three years. Jimmy was beyond saving, Chris and Jimmy both, but Suzanne was not. She knew there was no one to protect Suzanne, no one to care except her mother; the girl had long been separated from the Sallees and the Crumms, her grandparents. Ed and Suzanne had at best a tolerance of each other. Sueanne once told Margie that her daughter hated Ed; now Ed had reason to hate her.

The noisy wake was still going on downstairs while the girl remained alone, shut up in her bedroom. The murder was no longer a dream to Suzanne. It was Chris that they had buried, the boy who had slept in the next room for a year and a half. Like Margie, she, too, had misperceived the drinking and the shouts coming up from below as part of a celebration, a party. Chris was dead and nobody cared. She had not let herself think of Chris much since she was told that Jimmy had taken care of the problem. Of course, once Chris was dead, her mother would not discuss the murder with her and never admitted to Suzanne any involvement in it. Jimmy had done it; Sueanne herself had done nothing.

Because her mother denied her own participation, Suzanne remembered hers all the more vividly. Besides, Jimmy, whom she loved, should not be made to bear the guilt alone. The ritual of the funeral made the death of Chris seem real to her for the first time. The flowers, the hole they had dug, the smell of the body had penetrated into her room in a way that the language of the conspiracy had failed to do.

4

On the evening of the funeral Margie called Suzanne and got her on the first ring. When Suzanne heard Margie's voice, she was greatly relieved, for Margie was the only person she trusted other than her own mother. Immediately Margie told Suzanne that she had driven Sueanne out of her apartment and thrown her clothes out after her. "No loving mother would treat a daughter like that," Margie said. "You deserve better."

Suzanne felt her stomach fall, felt panic, as if the last prop of support were being withdrawn. She began yelling and cursing at Margie. "How could you do this? Goddamn you! Why are you doing this to me?" she said over and over, and then broke down crying.

Margie, herself in tears, could only repeat, "You deserve a better mother than that. You know what she's done. You deserve better."

Suzanne knew that she would never see Margie again, that her mother now would stand between them. The time when she could live with her mother seemed far away and Ed was a stranger to her still, more a stranger than Chris himself had been. When would Ed know what she had told the detectives Sunday and when would he guess how deeply she had been involved in killing Chris? Or was Ed himself involved in it in some way she was unaware of?

5

Jimmy, the brother Suzanne worshiped, was even more alone than his sister. Jimmy and Paul were kept in the juvenile section in the front of the Miami County Jail in two adjoining, graffiti-covered cells nearest the supervisor's room. Most of the bile-yellow metallic paint was worn off the walls and bars of the cells by human touch. Paul immediately began to draw on the walls of his cell with Magic Markers, creating great red-and-black serpents as elaborately intertwined as oriental tattoos.

Both boys were angry. Jimmy was angry that Paul had told everybody about the murder before his arrest. Paul was upset that Jimmy confessed as soon as he was arrested, that he told of Paul's involvement, and that he insisted that Paul alone had fired into Chris.

Paul bragged to his jailers about what he called the Mafia lawyer his father had found for him, a rich man's lawyer. He repeatedly refused to speak to Undersheriff Kenny Niesz about the murder.

Jimmy called out to the guard at noon on Sunday, the fourth of May, and said vaguely, "I want to talk with someone about my situation." The guard told Deputy Ron Orton and Orton phoned Niesz.

It had been a long night for Niesz and he had just gotten out of bed when Orton called him. It took him an hour to eat, get dressed, and drive down to the station. While waiting for Niesz, Orton cleared off the long, gray metal table where the guards ate lunch and set up a tape recorder.

After Niesz arrived, he called the juvenile division in Johnson County to get some advice. He couldn't find anybody there who knew anything about the case; the detectives he had met the night before were all at home, maybe sleeping. When Niesz expressed his frustration to Orton, Orton just laughed and said, "That's where I want to be. I got two hours' sleep before I started my shift. I don't blame the bastards."

Unlike Niesz, who kept people at a distance, Orton was gregarious and liked people unless they gave him a clear reason not to. On the drive down to Paola from Overland Park, Orton felt he got a good sense of Jimmy. The boy was attractive, soft-spoken, and polite; Orton already felt he could trust him. Jimmy didn't seem like any murderer he had dealt with before.

Niesz invited Orton into his little office that looked out from the courthouse square to the storefront of the *Miami County Republican*, the town's weekly newspaper. Orton's idea was just to sit down with Jimmy and see what happened, but Niesz wanted to talk about what they had learned the night before.

Both knew they had been condescended to by the people in Johnson County; Steve Moore seemed to know the most about Jimmy, but last night they felt especially uncomfortable asking him questions. They spent the night drinking coffee together in a corner of the assembly room or wandering about the halls of the Overland Park police station.

"We don't know enough to do this, but we're going to have to do it anyway," Orton said. "Let's hope Jimmy hasn't changed his mind." Jimmy's cell was only thirty feet away from the table they had prepared for the interrogation. Orton had to unlock three heavy steel doors to get to the boy and lead him in.

Jimmy sat at one end of the long table between the two offi-cers and the interview began at two-forty-five. At Niesz's request Jimmy read aloud and signed a typed statement waiving his rights. Without asking Jimmy's permission, Orton began to tape the interview.

"Tell us the truth here now, who actually did the shooting?" Orton asked.

"Will this tape be heard by other people?" Jimmy was wary.

"Only our county attorney and the sheriff," Orton reassured him.

"That's it?"

"I don't think we can honestly answer that," Niesz said, con-tradicting Orton. Niesz was concerned that Orton's comment might jeopardize the admission of the interview into evidence. "If it goes to a jury trial, the jury may hear the tape, I don't know."

"Only the jury, though?"

"Well, who would you be interested in not hearing it?" Niesz asked.

"All people concerned," Jimmy answered.

"Well, you mean like your parents?"

"Yeah."

"Or, what's your buddy's name, Sorrentino?"

"Yeah."

"No, it won't be heard by him, but it may be heard in a court of law."

"With him present?"

"I don't know whether he would be present or not; I don't think I can truthfully answer that. I don't know what's going to happen down the road," Niesz concluded.

"It is quite possible, Jimmy, that what you tell is already known by us, and we are giving you this chance to be completely honest and truthful about it," Orton bluffed. "So can you tell us the truth about it?"

"Paul did it," Jimmy said. His reason for not wanting Sorrentino to hear the tape was immediately apparent.

"Paul did the whole thing?" Orton asked.

"Yeah, I fired over him."

Orton and Niesz knew that Jimmy had claimed in his written confession given the night before that he had shot into the woods over Chris's head with a 10-gauge shotgun and thrown the gun into the river. They thought that if they got more information about the gun, they could establish whether Jimmy had actually shot Chris.

"Is the gun still in your room?" Niesz asked.

"No, sir," Jimmy answered. "I started getting rid of it piece by piece in trash cans near my apartment."

"Are you protecting somebody?" Orton asked.

"No, sir. The only person I'm worried about right now is me."

"That's the way it should be, and I would if I were you, too," Orton said. "You won't tell us where you got the gun?"

"It was Ed's 12-gauge shotgun," Jimmy admitted.

"Whose?" Orton was unaware of Ed Hobson's name.

"My stepfather," Jimmy replied.

"Your stepfather. Is there any reason why you are trying to protect him?" Orton asked.

"Protect him!" Jimmy said in astonishment. "I'm protecting myself from him, *from* him."

"Whose idea was it that you take the gun?" Niesz interjected.

"I guess mine—mine," Jimmy said hesitantly.

"Whose idea was it to kill Chris?" Niesz asked.

Jimmy did not answer for ten seconds. "Not mine," he said finally.

"Whose idea was it?" Niesz repeated quietly.

Jimmy was silent for fifteen seconds, staring straight ahead between the two interrogators. "This was all passed last night."

"We haven't read the reports from last night," Niesz continued. "Thought maybe we'd give you a chance to tell us."

"My mother," Jimmy said softly, and paused for several seconds. "She won't hear this tape?"

"I can't make any promises," Niesz said. "All we are trying to do is establish the truth, why a thirteen-year-old boy's life should be taken. What were you supposed to receive out of this?"

"My sister's security and a car," Jimmy replied.

"Who was going to buy you the car?" Niesz asked.

"My mother."

Orton was interested in the details of the murder. "How long were you guys out there at the shooting scene?"

"A long time. The hole had to be dug, and I just kept telling Paul, let's just leave him here and just go back. And he said no, we couldn't, not now. It's too late." Up to this point in his interrogation, Jimmy appeared remarkably composed, but when he spoke of the murder itself, his face paled and his voice thinned.

Niesz resumed questioning. "Where was Chris when he was first shot?"

"Laying in the hole."

"Why was he laying in the hole?"

"He was told to try it for size."

"Who shot him first and where?"

"Paul, and I don't know where."

"Who shot him the second time?"

"Paul."

"And who shot him the third time?"

"Paul; I fired the second shot, but I went like that, and raised up," Jimmy said, gesturing with an imaginary gun.

Jimmy paused and stared straight forward.

In the midst of his elaborate denial that he had fired at Chris, Jimmy recalled a question that Orton had asked twenty minutes earlier about the murder weapon. Ignorant of the circumstances of the killing, Orton had inquired, "Is there any possibility that you forgot to return Paul's gun to him?"

Suddenly Jimmy imagined that the officers were trying to tie him to Paul's gun. His tone changed abruptly; he feared they would find out what really happened. "Was something found in my apartment, can you answer me that? Was the gun found in my apartment? It could put me in one hell of a situation. It could mean that somebody put the gun there without my knowledge."

Orton led him on. "What if—I'm not saying that we have it—but what if we recovered a gun and it's got your fingerprints all over it?"

"It'll put me in a spot. It could mean that somebody put the gun there without my knowledge. Because I'm on probation, I wouldn't keep a gun in the house. I was the one that wrapped it up and brought it over to Paul's house; Paul should have had to handle it to unwrap it." Jimmy had imagined that his lie about shooting into the woods would be believed; now he fantasized that Paul had created a similar deception to implicate him.

At times Jimmy seemed to lie arbitrarily. He also told Niesz that he was not with his mother when she sold the Datsun.

"The reason I was not telling them the whole truth was that you get going along telling them about everything and you get feeling battered," Jimmy said later. "You don't want to feel like such a dog. And the reason I told them that I had not shot Chris was because I was still trying to convince myself that I hadn't. I just couldn't admit to the whole thing at once; all the little shit I did embarrassed me."

Even the truth seemed improbable enough. Jimmy told Niesz that he had not talked to his mother about the murder after it occurred. "I just said it was over with to her, and that was it."

"Did she understand he wasn't coming back?" Orton asked. Jimmy nodded. "How did she understand?"

"Because she was the one that told me to make sure he didn't."

"Just the type of thing that was taken for granted?" Orton asked.

"Not by me."

"By her?"

"Yeah, she didn't lose any sleep over it." Jimmy spoke in a depressed, resigned voice.

"What did you do with Chris's billfold," Niesz asked.

"I did nothing with it. You see, Paul and I were supposed to pick him up after school, and I chickened out. Then Paul goes, 'Yeah, that's fine, let's not do it.' Then my mom called me and wanted to know what happened. And I said, 'We decided not to do it.' She said, 'It's too late; I've already got rid of his billfold and some other stuff.' And she said, 'If Ed comes home and Chris says that, I'm dead.' And it was true; she would have been. Ed believed everything Chris said, and he lied a lot." Apparently, on the day of the murder, Jimmy was still emotionally committed to defending his mother in the face of an imaginary threat from Ed.

"Was there a little hatred between you and Chris?" Niesz asked.

"Yeah, for hitting my mother, for hitting my sister, for getting me busted, yeah."

"Did he snitch on you to get you busted?"

"Yeah, and I found out there still wasn't enough hatred there to pull the trigger."

In his confession Jimmy never spoke of meeting his mother in the parking lot on the evening of the murder or of Suzanne's repeated visits to his apartment that day, nor was he asked about her pressure on him on the day of the murder. Though he reaffirmed that he had killed in part to protect his sister, as the days passed he came to deny that his fear for Suzanne's safety was a motivation for the murder.

Later Jimmy denied ever believing that Chris had hit his mother or his sister. Whether he believed it on the fourth of May is questionable. In the weeks after his arrest Jimmy still seemed to be searching for an adequate motive, trying out motives—his own anger at Chris's snitching on him; his fears for his mother and sister's security; his desire for a new car.

"Were there any arrangements made on the purchase of a vehicle for yourself?" Orton asked.

"No. I just went out looking. Through papers, car lots, everywhere. Every car lot that I know of. There were three or four cars I really liked, but I never made a definite decision on one." In the interrogation Jimmy strongly indicated how important the car was to him. Over the next year he gradually minimized the car as a motive and shifted much of the blame for the murder to the emotional and psychological pressure his mother put on him.

Near the end of the interrogation Niesz awkwardly tried to summarize the murder. "So you had already—the three of you, your mother and Sorrentino and you—had already schemed this idea up. The reason you brought the guns along and the shovel and all was for the purpose of digging a grave, killing him, then burying him?"

"Yeah," Jimmy said sarcastically. "I didn't want to, you know, tell Chris to start walking west."

"Do you want to stop talking about this, Jimmy?" Niesz asked. "Does it upset you?"

"It upsets me." Jimmy added that he felt no calmer now than he had the night before, when he was scared and drunk, giving his statement to Urban.

Suddenly Orton asked, "Do you love your mother?"

"Yes. I know I shouldn't, but I do."

"Would you do anything in the world to protect her?"

"I would do anything in the world to protect my little sister. I'd give up my life for her."

"Would you do anything to protect your mother?" Orton repeated.

"Close to it," Jimmy said.

"Did you ever think you would get caught?" Orton asked.

"Every night and every day. Every time my mind wasn't someplace else. I knew I would, with my bad luck. I've had it all my life."

"Would you rather talk about something else? You know we can stop anytime you want to." Niesz sensed Jimmy's depression.

"Yeah, I know, but I slept pretty good this morning," Jimmy said.

"Does it make you feel a little better to kind of get it all off your chest?"

"I slept, so I guess it did," he said, referring to his confession to Urban. "I just can't believe this happened."

At four o'clock Niesz shut off the tape recorder. The three chatted for a few minutes, then Orton gave Jimmy permission to make several phone calls before he led him back to his cell. What Jimmy said that Sunday afternoon—in his narrative of the murder, in his contradictory presentation of his motives, in his ambiguous attitude toward his mother and his devotion to his sister—became central to the prosecution of the three conspirators and to the conduct of a dozen legal hearings over the next five years.

6

Ed Byrne, an Olathe lawyer, heard and read about the Hobson case in news reports on Sunday, the day Jimmy confessed.

Except on days when he had to be in court, Byrne always got up late; he usually came to his office at noon and stayed until eight or nine at night. He was a young, unmarried lawyer working in a storefront law office a block away from the Johnson County Courthouse in Olathe. When he got to work Monday afternoon, one of the three lawyers in his office building was waiting for him. The lawyer, who had done some work for Jim Crumm, told Byrne that his client had come to see him that morning and that Crumm wanted a criminal lawyer for his son, who was charged with murder. Byrne had declared himself a specialist in criminal law, but had tried very few criminal cases and no murders. Nonetheless, he immediately agreed to take the case. As soon as he did, the lawyer stepped out the door and ushered Jim into Byrne's office.

The first thought Jim Crumm had was whether this kid could handle it; Byrne looked scarcely older than his son. Of medium height, Byrne wore glasses on his small Irish face. Despite his reservations Crumm had little money and he had to take what was offered to him. He immediately hired Byrne as Jimmy's lawyer.

Fortunately, Byrne cared little about money. He was the youngest son of a man who had owned a chain of small restaurants in Kansas City. With several young children still at home, Byrne's father, at forty, sold the restaurants and began to study medicine; he became a physician at fifty. Byrne was as impractical, as uninterested in money, and as persistent and stubborn as his father; he had passion for his clients, perhaps too much passion. He sought out extremes and lacked the ability to veil his emotions.

That afternoon Jim Crumm narrated what he knew about the murder, which was little enough. He had been watching television with his brother Stacy's family when the announcement came Sunday that Jimmy Crumm, Paul Sorrentino, and Sueanne Hobson were arrested for the murder of Chris Hobson. He had not talked with Jimmy for months and had paid little attention to reports of Chris's disappearance. He immediately called Jim Koonce, his brother-in-law who was a patrolman in the Raytown Police Department, and asked him to find out what he could.

Koonce couldn't tell him any more than what was in the news-papers.

Crumm told Byrne what he knew and then slumped back in his chair and waited for help. He wasn't so much angry as disbelieving and filled with guilt. The only thing he wanted to know was when Byrne could bail Jimmy out.

7

Tuesday afternoon Byrne drove down to the Miami County Jail in Paola to talk to Jimmy. When he got in to talk with him, he approached the boy as if he didn't know anything at all about the case.

"Jimmy, what happened? What's gone down?" he asked.

"I don't know," Jimmy said. "I don't know why I'm here. What can you do to get me out? Can you get bail for me?"

"I'll do everything possible to get bail for you," Byrne promised. Jimmy had no explanation at all for his being there. It was as if he had been hit by a bus, as if he had done nothing, knew nothing.

Despite his meager experience with criminal cases Byrne had already encountered this stage of ignorance and denial; frequently the accused treated his own lawyer as if he were an agent for the prosecution. Byrne had to earn Jimmy's trust, so he didn't challenge the boy's assertion of innocence. He already had read the written confession Jimmy had signed early Sunday morning and he heard about the taped one later that day. He told Jimmy not to talk about the case to anyone but him and his father. Despite his situation Jimmy seemed to be putting up a brave front before Byrne, an invulnerable one; he almost seemed to swagger. They had little to say to each other that day. After a half hour Bryne told him he would be back later in the week for the bail hearing.

When he was leaving the jail, Byrne ran into Dave Gilman in the cramped entryway to the sheriff's office. To Byrne's surprise Gilman was now Sueanne's lawyer. Byrne had known Gilman since he was a child; the old lawyer was a good friend of Ed's father, Dr. Byrne. When Gilman came in, he shook Ed's hand and said, "Ed, isn't it terrible about that poor boy. He needs help. We need to get him help. His mother tells me that he's been just about crazy for years. He's got this story that his mother was involved in his murder of Chris. Do you know that? I think we can prove he's crazy and put an end to all this nonsense. I need to talk with the boy."

Byrne, thirty years younger than Gilman, didn't even consider the offer or its implications at that time. Byrne was shocked by Gilman's brazen attempt to get control of his client and he felt as if Gilman were condescending to him. "Nobody is going to talk to my client. Not you, not anybody," he said. Gilman, Byrne thought, wanted to settle it like a civil suit, right there in the dark entryway. He thought how lucky he was to be there at that moment; if Gilman had been there an hour earlier, Jimmy would have talked to him. Byrne now knew the approach Sueanne and Gilman were to take and how she sought to escape indictment: Jimmy was to recant his two confessions, claim insanity, and the rest of his family would back him up.

Later that week at the bail hearing in Paola, Byrne spoke eloquently of this abused boy and how he had suffered from ill treatment by both mother and father. He spoke so well that he feared judge Hinkle would grant Jimmy bail low enough that his father could pay it. Byrne's argument before the judge was really designed to gain Jimmy's confidence, no more. As soon as he had understood Gilman's defense of Sueanne, he decided that he didn't want Jimmy out on bail. His mother surely would get to Jimmy if he were out. In jail he could deny her access to the boy and he intended to do so.

Byrne was relieved when the judge denied bail. His impassioned plea for bail had earned Jimmy's respect. Nonetheless, the boy still proclaimed total ignorance of the acts he had confessed to twice in two different counties in the past week.

Byrne needed Jimmy's cooperation. He planned to argue before the court that the boy be declared a juvenile. Unfortunately, the boy's eighteenth birthday was only two weeks away and Byrne knew his chances of succeeding were not good.

8

In Johnson County on Monday, the fifth of May, Ed Hobson filed a divorce petition charging Sueanne with "extreme cruelty and gross neglect of duty." By the end of the week Ed was granted temporary custody of Suzanne and a restraining order enjoining his wife from contacting him or mortgaging any property held jointly.

Ed had suddenly become a public figure and he made himself available for interviews. He spoke to reporters of Sueanne's treatment of Chris and about the difficulties the family had. The Hobson case had much more interest to reporters than Tani's suicide or the defilement of her body. Besides, the three conspirators all lived in a large metropolitan area where the media would compete to keep interest in the case alive. Sueanne's arrest, the involvement of her son in the murder of Ed's son, and Ed's filing for divorce from her were front-page stories. Ed denied the reporters nothing. He told them about Tani's murder, as he called it, and about his and Chris's suffering when Shirley died, and his love for the boy.

The press, following Ed's lead, portrayed him as Sueanne's victim as well as Jimmy and Paul's. The three conspirators had destroyed the sole child of his loins in the midst of the only happiness he had ever known. It was as if his public display of sorrow relieved his private grief.

Late Monday afternoon, the day Sueanne was bonded out, Ed granted an interview to newspaper reporters at his glass-topped kitchen table. His hair was disheveled, his eyes red and swollen from weeping. He drank whiskey and smoked steadily while he talked. Dr. Robert Craft and his wife, Delisha, were there to console him. At the end of the visit Craft, an enormous man dressed in running shorts, asked Ed to pray with him before leaving. Ed and the Crafts formed a tight circle, each of them clutching one of Ed's hands as Reverend Craft prayed that God would give him strength to bear the trial. The circle awkwardly collapsed into a triangle as they hugged Ed. His head was hidden and his shoulders were heaving under his white short-sleeved shirt as he sobbed audibly.

After Bob and Delisha had gone, Ed spoke despairingly about

his plight. "One thing about it, there ain't a hell of a lot left. I've given up on fair play a long time ago. What can happen next? There's work, but what does that mean? I don't have the knowledge to comprehend what's going on. I just don't understand it. I didn't know there was anything wrong. Sueanne and Chris had ups and downs the last year and a half, but I didn't see anything abnormal. Christen was prone to some adjustment problems, but at the time I couldn't see it being as drastic as maybe it was. Maybe I was blind.

"Chris and I had grown very, very close," he said. "I loved him very much—and I still do. He was a happy boy. He used to spend hours up there in his bedroom studying. He wanted to be a computer programmer. We talked about him going to college, about him getting a master's degree."

When reporters asked about Sueanne's relationship with Chris, Ed spoke cautiously, reluctantly. Sueanne and Chris were not close, he said. "I think Chris wanted them to be, but I don't think they were. I think he made efforts in his own way to get close to her. I know he wanted to be friends."

Ed was less cautious about his own relationship with his wife. "Sueanne was normally very happy, very kind, very loving. I don't hate her; I still love her. And I just don't understand."

What Ed had to say about Sueanne was ambiguous and hesitant. He didn't attack her publicly as the murderer of his son. He was perplexed, as stunned and perplexed as when she had sat on his lap and stroked his cheeks at dawn Sunday.

On Thursday, the eighth of May, the day after Chris's funeral, Ed gave a formal deposition that seemed devoid of anger toward Sueanne, devoid of direct accusations of her. That afternoon Detective Douglass and District Attorney Dennis Moore sat down with Ed in Moore's office on the sixth floor of the courthouse and presented the evidence they had against his wife. Already the prosecution knew they had to win him to their side. Inexplicably he was wavering.

In the meeting Ed spoke openly of what he knew and what he did not know. Yet there was, despite the tenor of his divorce petition accusing his wife of extreme cruelty, no expression of hostility toward Sueanne proportionate to what they had expected. The detectives and the prosecutors were more upset about his wife's actions than Ed was. He seemed as impassive and calm as if he were speaking to a group of bankers about a loan. Ed would say evenly, "Well, that makes sense now," and "Now I understand that for the first time." The prosecutor's dramatic revelations to Ed about Sueanne's role in the conspiracy to kill Chris seemed to generate no anger toward her. They could see he was tired and deeply depressed, yet they were puzzled by his demeanor.

9

On the Thursday after the body was found Suzanne also gave a sworn deposition in the Johnson County Courthouse. What she said, after meetings with her mother and phone calls from her, resembled little what she had said early Sunday morning in her bedroom and at the police station. Suzanne claimed she could not remember what she had said that night, even when her replies were read back to her.

Yet in her conversations with her daughter Sueanne must have neglected one detail, for Suzanne again confirmed that her mother had dropped the billfold at Metcalf South on the very evening of the murder.

10

Immediately after she was released on bail, Sueanne began sending emissaries to the condominium to pick up things she needed, or pretended to need—women to clean the house and to help Ed and Suzanne manage, women to talk to Ed about Sueanne herself. Sueanne gave elaborate instructions to the women on how to satisfy Ed's needs—instructions precisely stated by her, tenderly performed by them.

Except for these emissaries, Ed seemed quite alone in his grief. Deanna Crooks, a loyal friend of Sueanne, would arrange to come at the hours when Ed would most likely be at the condominium; Deanna would always find time to ask about Ed's feelings. He would speak to her of how his parents were dead and Tani was murdered and that now his only son, Chris, was murdered, too. He would speak of how afflicted he was and how God would help him survive these afflictions. God would not give him more than he could bear; God was with him, Reverend Craft had told him. Ed also told Deanna that he had filed for divorce. She could see that Ed was drinking heavily again, drinking more heavily than he had since he had first begun to court Sueanne.

"I knew I had to talk to Sueanne," Ed recalled later. "I was confused. The only facts I knew was what was coming out of the prosecutor's office—facts, allegations, or whatever you want to call them. The prosecutors were pumping me full of stuff. I was very emotionally upset; I just lost my son. What they were telling me is the only thing I knew. I knew I had to confront her. I knew in my own mind there was definitely a big problem here someplace with everything I was trying to deal with."

It only took Sueanne three or four days to bring Ed around. As a result of Deanna's mediation under the direction of Sueanne, Ed agreed to meet his wife on Saturday afternoon, the tenth of May. Almost as if nothing had happened that week, Ed had straightened the living room and cleaned up the kitchen before Sueanne arrived. She drove over alone to the Hobson condominium and Ed and Suzanne came out to greet her. Suzanne embraced her mother, but Ed held back, not touching her yet. The three sat in the living room and talked for an hour about Suzanne's schooling and about the cats and about the redecorating they had done.

Ed had been drinking since late morning and looked tired and bedraggled. Sueanne was neatly dressed in a white summer blouse and skirt; her makeup was meticulously done and she seemed calm and rested.

Immediately after Suzanne left to visit a friend, Ed began questioning his wife. Apparently he still believed that Suzanne had no role in the killing. "Why didn't you tell me?" he began in a low, intimate voice, leaning toward her from his chair as she sat before him on the couch. "For weeks you didn't tell me."

"Jimmy told me he had nothing to do with this, nothing," she said. Ed remembered that she had suddenly burst into tears and covered her face with her slender hands. "I was trying to protect Jimmy because he said he didn't have anything to do with it. Jimmy said that Paul had killed Chris. He told me not to say anything. He told me that Paul said that if I didn't help and if I opened my mouth, that Paul would make it a package deal and he'd get rid of all of us."

"Look!" Ed said, half coming up out of his chair. "Why didn't you ask me for help? I could handle those boys."

"I was afraid of what Jimmy had told me. Jimmy threatened me, too. He said, 'If you tell on us, we will kill Ed and Suzanne and you before the police can get us.' I'd lost one boy. I didn't want to lose another one, and I didn't want to lose you, and I would have ended up losing all three." She spoke slowly, her voice breaking. Ed said he could see she was struggling to talk about it.

"I could have handled it. I talked to Steve Moore every day."

"And I was afraid that if I told you, you would have killed Jimmy and Paul. You would have! You know you would have! Where would I be then? No child, no husband, no nothing."

"Why did Jimmy want to kill my boy? What did he do to Jimmy?" Ed asked.

She admitted to Ed that she didn't understand the boys' motives. "All I know is that they were on drugs and they were drinking and they talked Chris into going out there in the woods to do something, I don't know what. They were going to make some easy money or something. When they got him out there, they killed him. I just don't know why. Jimmy wouldn't tell me any more about it. I just can't believe this happened. How could it happen?" Crying, she leaned back helplessly, her arms down at her sides, looking directly at him.

"That's okay, that's okay," he said quietly. "But there's still something you did that I don't understand. Steve Moore and the D.A. told me you took Chris's billfold up to Metcalf South. Why did you do that?"

"I couldn't get up enough courage to tell the police and I wanted them to keep looking for him. If they thought he was a runaway, they'd keep looking, and they did keep looking after they found the billfold, didn't they? I desperately wanted to tell you when you came back home that evening with poor Chris's billfold. Didn't you notice? But I couldn't, I just couldn't."

Ed kept asking Sueanne the same questions. According to his recollections, as the afternoon wore on he began to pace while she talked; at times he turned abruptly and looked directly into her eyes. She always burst into tears as she spoke of her fear of Paul and Jimmy and of her anguish at seeing Ed so distraught in the weeks he frantically searched for his son.

At this point Ed said he began to understand that she, too, was a victim of her son's plot. By evening they were sitting side by side and talking quietly; when she cried, he put an arm around her to stop her shaking. The next day, Sunday, was Mother's Day and Ed asked her to stay the night in the condominium.

"I knew her well enough to be very satisfied with her answers," Ed said later. One week had passed since Douglass and Moore had picked Sueanne up for interrogation.

On Wednesday morning, the fourteenth of May, ten days after Sueanne's arrest, Ed appeared at her bond-modification hearing. He told the court that he wanted his wife home; he said he felt no animosity toward her for any involvement she may have had in his son's death. He also directed his attorney to ask for a dismissal of the divorce petition he had filed last week. At Ed's request the court removed all restrictions on Sueanne's contact with her family.

After a couple of days Ed and Sueanne began to sleep together again in the master bedroom. The walls of the room were still half-papered. The redecoration of the bedroom had been abandoned the night Chris's body was found.

He was deeply depressed by the death of his son. He left early in the morning for work; as soon as he returned home, he started drinking again. Incessantly Sueanne discussed the outrageous charges the district attorney had filed against her. Neither was interested in the other's problems.

11

One thing that held the couple together was their mutual hostility toward Margie Hunt-Fugate. On Sunday, the fourth of May,

Sueanne had given Margie her purse filled with jewelry and Margie had taken it to her apartment for safekeeping. Soon Sueanne accused Margie of stealing the jewelry. In an affidavit Sueanne wrote, "At the time of my arrest, I was wearing jewelry which I owned and which had been appraised at approximately forty thousand dollars. The next day I was able to make bond and Margie picked me up at the courthouse. On Wednesday, the seventh of May, Margie told me she had placed the jewelry in a safety-deposit box. That same day Ernestine Bean came over to Margie's apartment to pick me up. At that time Margie told Ernie and me that the reason the jewelry was put in a safety-deposit box was to keep it away from my bondsman; I could have my jewelry back anytime I wanted it. I told her that I needed to take the jewelry with me to the office of Dave Gilman, my lawyer, on the following Friday and told her I would pick it up that morning. I went to Margie's on Friday to pick up my jewelry and no one was home. I tried calling Margie during the weekend, but no one was home. My husband, Ed Hobson, went over to Margie's apartment during the weekend, and no one was home. I have never seen Margie again and she has never returned my jewelry."

Since the funeral, the day she kicked her friend out of her apartment, Margie had been secretly helping Steve Moore develop the case against Sueanne. With the consent of the Johnson County district attorney, Moore kept Margie away from Sueanne's lawyers.

Margie and her children were staying with her sister, who lived in Oak Grove, Missouri. Oak Grove, a town of two thousand, was twenty miles straight east of Kansas City—"Way out in the sticks," Moore said. He had spoken to Margie several times and each time she denied having taken the jewels. He asked her if he could look in her safety-deposit box and she allowed him to do so. The box was empty. Though he had no warrant, Margie also let him search her Kansas City apartment from top to bottom.

After spending a pleasant afternoon talking to Margie, Moore drove back to Overland Park and wrote a formal report of their meeting. "Margie Hunt-Fugate advised this officer that she did not want to have anything that belonged to Sueanne Hobson. She

advised that the furniture which she received from Sueanne
Hobson, which came from Chris Hobson's room prior to the
corpse being discovered in Miami County, was to be returned to
the Hobson residence. She requested that someone come and pick
up these items. Inside a dresser that Sueanne gave her are numerous clothes, bed sheets, and other household laundry items. All
these items were given to Margie by Sueanne."

Margie also claimed that Sueanne had told her that she
received payment from an insurance company for a diamond
ring; in fact she had not lost the ring. Of course Jimmy had
already confirmed this allegation in his statements to the police.

Moore liked Margie; she had spunk. "If she didn't like you,
she'd tell you, right out, and if she liked you, she'd tell you too,"
he said. Though married and devoted to his family, he found her
sensationally attractive. He imagined her bicycling down 103rd
Street to her work as a bartender at the Brookridge Country
Club. "Goddamn, that must have caused a few cars to go over
curbs," he said, laughing.

"I don't know whether she took the jewels or not," Moore
said. "I wouldn't put it past her. Still, you've got to consider
who's telling you Margie took them. We had nothing to go on.
Nothing."

The prosecution wanted the dispute resolved; Margie was a
witness and they didn't want her testimony impeached. Despite
strong pressure from Dave Gilman, Sueanne's lawyer, the prosecution couldn't find the jewelry and had no way to determine
what happened. The closer the trial of Sueanne approached, the
less interest the district attorney showed in investigating and
prosecuting Margie, a star witness against her friend.

12

On Monday, the twelfth of May, Detective Moore met with Ed
Hobson. At Moore's request Ed brought his April bank records
to the station. After examining the statement, Moore discovered that Sueanne had deposited fifteen hundred dollars in the
Mission State Bank, part of the twenty-one-hundred-dollar

check she had received from Raytown Datsun when she sold her car. Six hundred dollars, the remainder of the check, she took in cash.

In the midst of studying the material Moore asked Ed if he knew what had happened to the money from the sale of the Datsun. Ed said only, "I'm not in the habit of watching how my wife spends money."

Moore also tried to contact Don and Ruth Sallee, Sueanne's parents. He had gotten an idea of her relationship to her parents rather quickly from Sueanne's bail bondsman. The day after her arrest Sueanne and her lawyer were trying to raise enough money to bail her out. When the bail bondsman phoned the Sallees, Ruth refused to help.

A week later the Sallees weren't in a better mood. Moore wrote, "Mr. Sallee has recently retired from the Marley Company, and has advised family members that he is very afraid of his daughter. He also does not want to become involved in the incident. Officer has information that the Sallees get their newspaper as soon as it is thrown early in the morning and when the mail comes, they dart out, get the mail, and run back into the house, not attempting to contact any of their neighbors."

In the midst of gathering information for the prosecution of the three conspirators, Moore got a phone call from Ed Hobson on Wednesday, the twenty-first of May. On Thursday Moore returned the call. The only one home was Suzanne; she told Moore that Ed had gotten drunk and gone on a rampage Wednesday night. Suzanne said that her mother and Ed were very angry, screaming at each other, until, finally, her mother called John Adams, a minister at the Leawood Baptist Church.

Moore called Adams immediately. He learned that Adams had spoken briefly with Ed late Wednesday. Reverend Adams arranged for a motel on Metcalf that night for Ed and he got Dr. Craft to drive out to talk with him. Craft told Ed that he and his wife should live separately until he could cope with his son's death, that he should seek counseling. By this time, in the neutral territory of the motel room, Ed was calm and readily agreed with Craft.

"Ed didn't think his wife had Chris killed," Adams said. "The reason for the separation is that Sueanne is worried about her freedom and her involvement in the case, while Ed is only worried and concerned about the death of his son." The reunion between Ed and Sueanne had lasted eleven days.

Moore was more concerned with Suzanne than with the melodrama of Sueanne and Ed. Moore wrote in his police report, "She was very upset and possibly on the verge of some type of mental breakdown. Suzanne has been torn between her mother and stepfather over this homicide. She requested that this detective give her the phone number of her friend, Margie Hunt-Fugate, so she could talk with her about family problems. This detective had Margie call Suzanne at home. After the conversation, Margie said Suzanne needed to be taken out of the home."

That Thursday afternoon Moore called a judge who handled juvenile cases and explained the girl's situation. The judge gave Moore permission to put Suzanne in a YWCA foster home temporarily. Before Moore could complete those arrangements, Sueanne returned home, picked her daughter up, and took her with her.

In frustration Moore called Reverend Adams to see if he would help in locating Sueanne and her daughter. He told the minister what he and the judge had intended to do. Adams said that Ed would be greatly upset by the loss of Suzanne, but without her daughter Sueanne herself might have a nervous breakdown.

In his report Moore concluded, "Adams said it was best to leave Suzanne with her mother in order to maintain some family structure. Sueanne and Suzanne were going to live with an old friend, Deanna Crooks, in Johnson County. After a month, if Ed regained his emotional stability, he was to be reunited with his wife and daughter."

13

Ed Hobson was a simple man, a man of black and white caught in a rainbow skein of emotion. Despite pastoral counseling and his belief in God, Ed remained deeply depressed. In one evening he had lost everything—his child, his wife, his family. He knew Sueanne loved him and he desperately needed to believe what she told him. He wanted to believe that it was Jimmy who killed his boy, that Sueanne and Chris loved each other, and that their family was happy until Jimmy moved in. He could not admit that he had been duped by her, that she, so loving to him, would coldly plan for six months to kill his child. What a fool that would make him!

Dennis Moore, the district attorney, claimed to know what had happened and told Ed. Sueanne also claimed to know what had happened and told him. Ed was unable to face his ignorance of the threat to Chris until Sueanne explained to him that she as well shared his ignorance. He wanted to hold to her, a woman who dressed all in black or white, colors he understood.

What Shirley first did to Ed after the death of Tani was what Sueanne did to him later, except on a larger, more complex scale. Now the antagonist of Ed was not some brilliant, shadowy murderer who could devise and dictate Tani's extraordinary "suicide" note but, if the district attorney could be believed, a member of his own family. Because Shirley denied Tani's suicide, Ed denied Tani's suicide. Because Sueanne denied her conspiracy charge, Ed, too, denied her charge. The longer Shirley sought to reopen Tani's case, the more vehemently Ed insisted that the facts of the case were what Shirley said they were and nothing would ever change his mind.

In the ten days he spent with Sueanne in the middle of May, Ed came to believe that she had not conspired to kill his son. Rather, the police, the prosecutors, the lawyers, the judges, and the reporters were conspiring against him and his wife, denying them justice.

Though Ed could no longer live with Sueanne, he remained convinced that she did not kill Chris. The prosecutors had baited him, pushed him this way and that; still, in the first days after Sueanne's arrest, he was curiously passive and neutral. He was unable to express anger against the woman the prosecutors charged with masterminding it all, the woman who admitted she had slept with him and eaten with him for more than two weeks while knowing his son was dead—and yet she did not have the courage to tell him the boy was murdered. Through all this Ed understood that Sueanne loved him, but he became uncertain of his love for her. Without a woman he loved, or hated, to move him, he himself seemed unable to move. Encouraged by his lawyer to save what was left of his inheritance from his father, he contemplated filing for divorce again.

14

Suzanne was unable to finish the school year at Indian Creek Junior High. She was shunned by many of her friends and was constantly tormented and humiliated. Students who had never spoken to her started rumors that she was a bitch, like her mother. She was forced to complete the spring semester in her home under the supervision of a visiting teacher.

She felt as guilty as Jimmy. What neither the students nor the prosecutors suspected was that she had been totally involved for three months in her mother's plans to kill Chris. Now in May she was actively engaged in her mother's defense against the charges of murder and conspiracy to commit murder. For the next two years the center of Suzanne's life became the hearings and trials pursuant to the murder of Chris.

Suzanne was isolated with her mother at a time when she most needed the support of others. She was cut off from any communication with Margie and her brother Jimmy, and she constantly had to lie to her stepfather. Few of Suzanne's friends from Indian Creek dared to visit her. Even the Hooker children weren't permitted to associate with her.

Daily Sueanne began to coordinate her testimony with the testimony of Suzanne. The exact time Sueanne took the billfold from Chris's room and the hour she dropped the billfold at Metcalf South became the crux of endless discussions. Sueanne immediately realized that her maximum point of vulnerability was the billfold. Under oath Suzanne had already said her mother had dropped the billfold the night of the murder and the girl was worried that she would be charged with perjury if she changed her testimony now. Besides, if the prosecutors found out all the things she really did, she could be charged in the conspiracy, just like Jimmy. And Suzanne saw her mother take the billfold and saw her drop the billfold in the planter at Metcalf South.

Since the day after the murder, Sueanne never once acknowledged to her daughter that they were part of a conspiracy. She had, she said, taken Chris's billfold out of his room the morning after the murder so that the police would look for his body. "It was as if Mother really believed she was innocent," Suzanne said.

With the exception of Margie, Sueanne's enemies were also Suzanne's. Suzanne said, "If I heard it once, I heard it a thousand times: 'Margie took the jewels! Margie took the jewels! How could she just walk off with them and never be charged?' Mother always cared more about money than almost anything else. I didn't care whether Margie took the jewels or didn't take them, but I never heard the end of it."

Suzanne's fourteenth birthday was on the twenty-seventh of May. The day she first conspired with her mother to kill Chris, she lost her childhood suddenly and completely. Her mother depended on her as much as she depended on her mother. Suzanne was now her mother's loyal supporter and a powerful figure in determining her fate. In her first statement to the police on the morning her mother was charged, Suzanne had given the prosecution its most damning evidence and she had to play a crucial role in repudiating it.

Both Suzanne and her mother were still imprisoned by the conspiracy, paralyzed by it. In preparation for the trials to come they relived and fabricated details of their plot against Chris. In their imaginations they were relentlessly transforming the acts of four conspirators into the acts of two. Every day they had to do it again.

15

In the early summer, separated from Ed, Sueanne turned for support to Beth Clarkson. Beth accompanied her to meetings with bondsmen, lawyers, and judges. She was angered by the district attorney's attempt to get her to testify against her friend and she flatly refused to speak with the prosecutors.

Once, after a hearing, Sueanne mentioned that she had not seen Chris's grave because Ed had not permitted her to go to the funeral. That evening in Beth's crowded living room, giggling like two inexperienced thieves, they planned carefully how they might go to the cemetery without being followed by police or reporters. The next morning Beth took a circuitous route from Deanna Crooks's house to Metcalf, then drove straight south down Metcalf to the cemetery.

A light rain was falling when Beth parked the car near the caretaker's office at the entry to the cemetery. Beth covered her head with a newspaper she found in the backseat; Sueanne slipped on a tailored, khaki raincoat. The two walked directly to the grave; a hill, barren except for gravestones, rose sharply beyond it. The headstone Ed had ordered was little more than two feet by one and a half feet and was set close to the ground. Near the center was CHRISTEN A. HOBSON and below that "1967–1980." At the top of the stone, inside an incised rococo frame, a small lamp symbolizing the eternal flame was chiseled. In quotation marks, on either side of the lamp, were the words, "My Son" and "I Love You."

Neither woman spoke. Almost immediately Sueanne started to cry. Her whole body, thinner than it had been in years, was shaking hard and Beth had to support her physically.

Walking back to the car, Sueanne put her arm around Beth's shoulder and leaned into her. Embracing each other, the dark and slender women looked like sisters sharing a common grief. Only the clothes they wore and the perfected appearance of Sueanne reflected lives lived in different classes.

As soon as the two women got back into the car, Sueanne began saying like a litany, "I don't understand it. I can't believe it. I don't know how this happened. How could this happen? I tried so hard to bring the family together. How could this happen? Things were going so well." After she stopped crying, Beth started the car and drove out of the cemetery past the oval of bright flowers.

"What more could you do?" Beth said reassuringly. "You had no idea how crazy Jimmy was. Who could guess what the kid would do?" Still, Beth, who loved her and believed in her innocence, could think only of how impatient Sueanne had been that spring, of how desperately she had wanted changes made, of how she had wanted them made immediately.

Sueanne needed Ed now for a lot of reasons, not least among them being the financial support he could provide for her defense. But she was especially concerned about appearances. "How is it going to look if Ed divorces me?" Sueanne asked Beth.

"Not good, I can tell you that," Beth said bluntly.

"Ed won't understand. I love him and I think he still loves me, but he won't understand. If he goes through with a divorce, everybody will think it's because he believes I got Chris killed."

16

On Friday, the eleventh of July, the charges of murder and conspiracy that had been filed against Sueanne were dismissed. The prosecutor cited lack of available witnesses as the reason for dismissal.

Sueanne knew quite well what the prosecutor's plans for her were. She knew that Dennis Moore, the young, handsome, ambitious district attorney of Johnson County, appreciated the sensational aspects of the case and would not let her go that easily. He wanted to become the attorney general of Kansas, she thought, and he wanted the publicity her trial would generate. There was a cruelty and uncertainty about his mouth by which she understood him.

In the few days she spent with Ed after her arrest, Sueanne had learned how intensely the prosecutors had been gathering information about her involvement. Ed had told her of his deposition and of Margie's, had told her of the case against her that John Douglass and Dennis Moore had outlined for him. It was her they were after, Ed emphasized. Moore wanted Jimmy to testify against Sueanne, and if Jimmy wouldn't do it, he'd get Paul.

Dennis Moore was willing to plea-bargain with Jimmy, but Byrne, Jimmy's attorney, would have nothing to do with him. Byrne was bright, Moore thought, but inexperienced and lacking in common sense. What Moore could offer Jimmy was time, an exchange of fifteen years before parole for a minimum of seven and a half years. A more experienced lawyer would jump at the chance, Moore thought. All he wanted was Jimmy's testimony. Eventually Byrne would be forced to accept his offer, of that he was certain.

Moore handed Jimmy's case to Steve Tatum, one of a dozen prosecutors under his direction. Tatum was quiet, persistent, almost colorless, a perfect foil for the ambitious Moore. Tatum would prepare Sueanne's case for trial, and when the time came, Moore and Tatum would try it together. They needed either Jimmy or Paul to support the conspiracy charge; without them they could not risk going through a preliminary hearing and having the charges against Sueanne dismissed.

Child abuse had long been a concern of Moore. He had made it an issue in his last campaign, and when he was elected, he established a program in Johnson County to deal with it more aggressively. Sueanne was an abuser, the worst he had ever seen; she sent a child to kill a child for no reason he could fathom, and he wanted her.

17

Sueanne and her daughter lived with Deanna Crooks through June. In July they moved into an apartment in the rectory of Leawood Baptist Church through the intervention of Reverend John Adams. Though Sueanne had little money, she gave Deanna Crooks a rabbit coat and other clothes to reward her generosity. Apparently Ed had also been providing his wife and Suzanne with some money to live on.

On the seventh of August Sueanne and Ed were divorced, twenty months after they were married, three months after Chris's body was discovered. Ed filed for an emergency divorce; in Kansas an emergency divorce can be secured almost immediately if both parties can agree in advance on custody of the children and the division of property.

At the urging of Sueanne Ed had agreed to file for divorce in a rural county far enough beyond the metropolitan area that the chance of publicity would be minimal. Neither he nor Sueanne wanted public speculation about his motives. Following each other in separate cars, they took Interstate 35 out of Overland Park, past Olathe and past the Edgerton turnoff in the extreme west corner of Miami County, then down through open, rolling farmland broken up periodically by small, gray oil pumps, the levers dipping and rising like mechanical dogs running in slow rhythm.

It took an hour to get to Ottawa, Kansas, the seat of Franklin County, and to the courthouse square at its center. Sheldon Crossette, Ed's lawyer, and Dave Gilman, Sueanne's, were chatting outside the courthouse when Sueanne and Ed arrived. The ornate, red-brick Victorian courthouse, built in the early 1900s, was almost exactly like the one alongside which Jimmy was being held in Miami County.

In his first petition for divorce filed in Johnson County in early May, Ed had accused Sueanne of extreme cruelty. Now Ed charged only incompatibility and irreconcilable differences. Sueanne did not contest the divorce.

The reason Ed's lawyer gave for seeking an emergency divorce rather than waiting a few months was the emotional state of Suzanne. With an immediate divorce, Crossette said, "Suzanne could change schools and start afresh immediately. Suzanne suffers from peer interest and pressure. She could not complete the spring semester at Indian Creek Junior High."

Ed consented to do a remarkable number of things for a woman who was almost certainly going to be charged with the murder of his son. Sueanne was to get fifty dollars a month for the support of Suzanne; Ed would also pay his daughter's health insurance and her college tuition. Sueanne would get a 1964 Ford Thunderbird and "all the jewelry at the time of the marriage and all action related thereto." The last clause apparently referred to Sueanne's suit to recover her jewelry from Margie.

Ed also agreed to pay Sherman Bonds seventy-five hundred dollars, the amount it cost to provide the surety money on the fifty thousand dollars' bond his wife put up before her release from jail in May. He would pay credit-card charges of two thousand dollars, Gilman's fees of fifteen hundred dollars incurred in handling her criminal case, as well as a fee of two hundred dollars for work on the divorce petition.

In all, Ed would pay twelve-thousand dollars that Sueanne owed, nine thousand of it accrued as a direct result of her being charged with the murder of his son. He would also pay her initial deposit and the first six months of Sueanne's rent on her apartment in Grandview, Missouri. In addition to these debts, Ed got the condominium, now heavily mortgaged, his 1930 Model-T Ford with the license plate SUEANNE, and a 1977 Lincoln Mark V.

Sueanne asked and was granted her petition that her last name be returned to Sallee. A month later Suzanne also legally changed her last name to Sallee.

No one knew about the divorce for months and no one discovered the divorce petition for years. By any standard the divorce was amicable, even generous, given the circumstances. In the last thing said right before the divorce petition was granted, Sueanne declared, "Ed has lost his love for me."

18

Living in Grandview, Sueanne took a series of part-time jobs to support her daughter and herself. Suzanne became her main emotional support as the fall wore on, but both lives were suspended as they waited for the case to be refiled and for the date of Jimmy's preliminary hearing in Miami County to be set. According to Sueanne's lawyer, Jimmy's hearing and trial would be held in the spring at the latest. Her lawyer had already told her that the defense would compel her to testify against her own son. He also told Sueanne that her influence on Jimmy in the months before the murder would be the central issue in the trial. Suzanne Sallee knew that if her mother were called to the stand, she herself would be discovered and held up to obloquy again.

Sueanne told her friends that she had done what she could to preserve their marriage. To Beth Clarkson and Ernie Bean and Deanna Crooks she still proclaimed her love for Ed. Her friends understood what Sueanne wanted. When they managed to see Ed, they told him how much Sueanne was hurt by the divorce and by his lack of trust in her.

Ed could not forget what Sueanne had said so simply and directly in Ottawa the last moment before they were divorced. Once he had gotten home on the night of the divorce, he knew he had made a mistake and regretted what he had done. He knew that he loved her, knew that he would always love her.

"Sheldon Crossette told me that the only way I could retain control of my property with the circumstances that were going on would be to divorce Sueanne," Ed recalled. "From the time they found Chris I did not get any professional help of any kind. We got a divorce because of my emotional status, plus the advice of my attorney. I just didn't have my emotional stability; I was drinking heavily at the time."

The complex family web the murder exposed confused Ed utterly and he couldn't bear ambiguity or confusion. Suddenly, free of her and alone in the condominium, he was ashamed of divorcing Sueanne. He had stuck by Shirley through five years of illness and turmoil; Sueanne was what he had left of his family and he now knew that he should have stood by her.

Ed thought of their marriage as the happiest period of his life, the sweet spot in it. He had been proud of her looks, proud of the orderly home she kept and the orderly life she demanded, proud of the possessions she had acquired for him. The real killers were already imprisoned and Dennis Moore was trying to put the woman he loved in jail by making a deal with them, by letting them off easy when they had murdered his son for no reason at all.

If Sueanne needed Ed to demonstrate publicly her innocence, he needed to devote himself to her to avoid confronting her true nature and, perhaps, his own. He could not admit that she, living intimately with him, could so deceive him that she would conspire to abduct his only son as the boy sat at their kitchen table doing his homework.

"She didn't come back to me with open arms, once I tried to court her," Ed said. "I'd done a terrible thing to her and she wanted to be sure I wasn't going to do it again. She was hurt and angry."

Sueanne and Ed were married again on Sunday, the eleventh of December, four months after their divorce and two years after their first marriage. As quietly as they were divorced, they were remarried by a justice of the peace in a small town in Missouri on the edge of the metropolitan area. Ernestine Bean and Suzanne were witnesses. Though Sueanne was going to keep an apartment in Grandview, Missouri, where Suzanne was enrolled in school, the family returned to the condominium that evening. Ed hadn't put up any tree, but Sueanne would soon help him do that as they prepared to celebrate their first Christmas without Christen.

"She was the best thing that ever happened in my life," Ed said. "I realized the mistake I had made and I love the lady; she's a nice, wonderful woman and I married her back. I loved her very much and I knew I was wrong in divorcing her. I know she's innocent and she didn't do anything to deserve my divorcing her. If I thought she were guilty, I'd have killed her. She's a nice, wonderful woman and I married her back."

Since Ed's puzzling deposition the week of Sueanne's arrest, the detectives had doubted his usefulness. To them Ed's remarriage to Sueanne was only a curiosity; Detective Urban, in particular, found it amusing. Throwing his head back and laughing, Urban said, "She must have a snap-pussy. She kills his son and he remarries her. He's a goddamned pussy-whipped wimp!"

7

THE KEEPER OF HELL

1

In the two years since the Hobsons were first married, their condominium had been repapered and expensively furnished; it now resembled a series of showrooms at a conservative furniture house. Only Ed and Sueanne and Suzanne lived there now. Though they again called the condominium their home, Sueanne kept her apartment in Missouri where her daughter attended school; she herself sometimes hid out in the apartment from reporters and process servers. Yet things were simpler, for now their enemies, the sources of hatred and passion, were outside the family, where they belonged.

Ed and Sueanne were married just in time. The hearings on Jimmy's case were scheduled to begin in February. Ed became Sueanne's perpetual testimony of innocence. He would say angrily, passionately to whoever would listen, "If I thought she killed my boy, she'd be dead now. I'd have killed her myself."

Virtually no one who knew anything about the case believed Ed was involved in the murder. Still, no reporters or prosecutors disbelieved Ed when they heard him say he would kill Sueanne if he thought she was guilty. Dennis Moore, the Johnson County district attorney, and Steve Tatum, his assistant, were frightened by Ed's passionate devotion to her and they somewhat naively believed that once fully informed, Ed would see things properly and change his mind.

Ed's period of reflection, of doubt, was over. Once he had made up his mind, he would never change it. Sueanne knew that well and she was surprised only by how long it took her to convince him. Even during that terrible night of interrogation she knew he loved her and would stand by her. That night she had dared to touch his face the way a cat, its claws retracted, would gently touch the face of his master. She had dared to sit on his lap as a child would, to console him and be consoled. He and Suzanne were all she had, all the people she needed.

2

The courthouses in Olathe and Paola seemed much farther apart than the twenty miles that separated them. The Johnson County Courthouse was in Olathe, the fastest growing city in Kansas. The courthouse was located in what had once been the center of the town. The restaurants and shopping areas of surburban Olathe were off Interstate 35, a couple of miles to the east of the courthouse.

Surrounded by two-story office buildings and small retail stores, the Johnson County Courthouse, ten stories high and covering most of a square block, seemed even larger than it was. From outside, the courthouse was a beige brick building that looked like a dormitory at a university.

Inside were a half-dozen courtrooms of various sizes, a large jail, and offices for virtually every official county function. There was no center to the building, no open space within it to help visitors orient themselves. The halls smelled slightly of ammonia and wax and were filled with people who had never worn a suit and with lawyers who had layered haircuts and wore expensive suits and silk ties. The courtroom where Sueanne would be tried was perfectly square and the ceilings high, with little attempt at ornamentation of the walls; the backdrop behind the judge's bench was plain, an empty stage dwarfing the judge and the defendant.

District Attorney Dennis Moore himself seemed to smell of ammonia and wax. A polished, clean-shaven, tall man in his midthirties, he always seemed to have another interest behind his professed interest. Somehow Ed Hobson sensed that and he soon began to speak of Moore's ambition. With his large staff of lawyers, Moore was mostly an administrator and a public-relations man. He tried very few cases.

Johnson County Assistant Prosecutor Steve Tatum was assigned to work with the Miami County district attorney to prepare the case against Jimmy Crumm. Tatum was quiet and thorough, very bright, clean-shaven, and nondescript. Miami County agreed to hire Tatum and passed a resolution to pay him one dollar a year to help David Belling prosecute Jimmy.

Belling, Miami's district attorney, had been hired a month after he graduated from the University of Kansas Law School; he was the county's only attorney and he was paid little. Belling was a shy, short man with a crude face, blond hair, and acne, a heavy, awkward elf. Crumm's case was the first he had brought to trial and he welcomed Tatum's help.

The old courthouse in Paola, the only distinguished building in town, looked like a red-brick Victorian mansion. Four stories high and looming above the rest of the buildings around the square, it still seemed to be at the center of Paola. Looking out from an upper window in the law library, one could see the land stretching out flat and empty for ten miles to the west.

An oak stairway with elaborate wooden railings wound up to the library and down past the only courtroom. The bare oak floor and stairs swelled and echoed even light footsteps. The courtroom itself was more than two stories high with stained-glass windows stretching from the floor to an ornate ceiling with plaster designs. Ed Byrne, Jimmy's lawyer, thought it was the most beautiful courtroom he had ever seen. In winter the building smelled of wood and varnish and dust; in other seasons the windows were open to scents from flowering trees or fields outside the town.

In February, after the date of Jimmy's preliminary hearing was finally set, Byrne began to look for Sueanne Hobson. Her new lawyers, Hugh and Scott Kraemer, were uncooperative and Byrne knew he would have to subpoena her to get her to testify. In the weeks before the hearing Sueanne worked at the Pine Tree Condominiums and stayed, when she dared, with Ed in Overland

Park; infrequently Ed would stay with her in Grandview. She gave no interviews to reporters, in part for her sake, in part for Suzanne's.

Byrne told Jim Crumm, Jimmy's father, of his difficulty in tracing Sueanne. Jim called the friends Sueanne and he had had in common without any success. A week before his son's scheduled hearing, Jim was driving east along I-435 as it skirted the south edge of Overland Park and the southern suburbs when Sueanne passed his truck. "Goddamn! Goddamn!" he shouted. Always short of luck before, Jim was elated. He followed her as closely as he dared on her drive back to her apartment in Grandview. Exultant, flushed, he immediately drove to a pay phone to call Byrne.

The Grandview officers, now charged by Byrne with executing the subpoena, found out easily where Suzanne was going to school. The next day, as Jim watched, the police staked out the school. After she had dropped her daughter off, one unmarked car came in behind her, one in front. Quickly they served her with a subpoena to testify in her son's preliminary hearing.

After Byrne had failed to get Jimmy declared a juvenile, he weighed carefully what defense he might construct. He considered an insanity defense, but several psychiatrists had tested Jimmy and flatly declared him sane. The insanity defense did not look promising, yet Byrne was reluctant to accept Dennis Moore's offer to reduce Jimmy's sentence in exchange for his testimony against his mother.

Byrne was frustrated. He was convinced that Sueanne had abused the boy as a child, had called him back seven years later, and within months had persuaded him to act as a weapon to kill another equally abused boy. Surely a jury would recognize the powerlessness of Jimmy before a mother like that; surely he could show how abused Jimmy had been when he got Sueanne on the stand.

Yet in rural, conservative Miami County Byrne knew he was taking a chance; Jimmy would have had a better chance in Johnson County, where the jurors were more educated, more sophisticated. Unfortunately, the boy been unlucky enough to kill Chris one mile past the Johnson County line.

3

The preliminary hearing began on the ninth of February, 1981. Eastern Kansas was hit by a heavy snowstorm, the worst of the year. The reporters came down in four-wheel-drive vehicles. The Johnson County matrons following the case couldn't get down at all.

Byrne knew, of course, that Jimmy would stand trial in a couple of months. Jimmy's confessions, oral and written, were the crucial evidence against him. What Byrne wanted to do was to see if he could suppress Jimmy's taped confession, if not at the trial itself, then at least in the preliminary hearing, so that jurors would not be biased by newspaper accounts. If he could not get it suppressed, he would seek to close the hearing while Jimmy's taped confession was played. The judge ruled against both motions; he would neither suppress the tape nor close the hearing. Later Byrne tried to get Detectives Urban and Wood, who took the written confession, to indicate that Jimmy had not waived his rights voluntarily on the night of his arrest. This failed, too; Urban had done all with meticulous care, following the orders of McClain, the prosecutor.

The two days of Jimmy's hearing were framed by Ed Hobson, who was the first witness, and Sueanne, who was the last. David Belling asked only a few questions and Ed answered them in a gruff, depressed voice. When he was asked to identify a photo of his son, his voice broke and he cried. At the end of the direct examination Belling asked if Ed still had possession of Chris's billfold. He answered, "Yes, I do. I don't have it with me today. Oh, I'm going to keep possession of that wallet."

In Byrne's cross-examination Hobson immediately displayed anger as Byrne tried to get him to admit Sueanne's present address. "I don't think that's any of your business," he said. Ed finally answered and gave the Grandview address when Stephen Hill, the young, portly judge, told him he must answer. During the hearing Hill kept his distance from the disputants and intervened precisely and firmly.

Throughout Byrne's questioning Ed defended Sueanne. Byrne's intention was to focus his questions on the family and on

Sueanne in particular, to demonstrate the extraordinary pressure she put on her son.

In the preliminary hearing, whispering regularly with Steve Tatum, Belling let the questions on the family pass unchallenged. Tatum wanted Sueanne's conviction more than he wanted Jimmy's, but he needed to give Byrne and Jimmy a reason to plea-bargain with Johnson County. In the actual trial of Jimmy, Tatum planned to challenge every attempt to explore the dynamics of the family.

Byrne had, of course, never talked with Ed Hobson before. He wanted to know what use the father of the murdered boy would be to him in the trial. Byrne went directly to Ed's meeting with Sueanne in the weeks after the murder. He asked if Ed confronted Sueanne with the "allegation that your wife hired the murder of your son." Ed said yes, that he had, but "she said it wasn't true."

"Other than the one denial that Sueanne Hobson gave you, that she in fact did not hire Chris's death, did you have other conversations generally about the case?" Byrne asked. "About the discovery of the body? Jimmy's involvement?"

"We spent several hours talking about the issue, if that's what you mean. Then and for several days later." Ed answered angrily, speaking distinctly and quickly, flushing.

"Did she say, 'Yes, I'm sure that Jimmy murdered Chris'?"

"Well, she told me that Jimmy murdered Chris. He came to her the next day, prior to when I came home, and told her that he murdered Chris. Him and Paul Sorrentino murdered Chris, and if she opened her mouth, he would kill me and Suzanne before the police could get him." Ed said she told him these things about a week after her arrest.

"Did she tell you this early on in your first conversations with her or did she hold back for a while?"

"No, she came right out and told me exactly what I just got through saying once I started asking her questions. She specified to me myself and Suzanne. Now, whether she meant he would kill her, too, I don't know. She was very emotionally upset." Sueanne was crying, he said. "She was struggling talking about it. She still struggles talking about it."

Byrne asked Ed what Sueanne told him about Jimmy's motive. "She told me they were on drugs and drinking, and they talked Chris into going out there in the woods with them for something. They were going to make some easy money or something. Then they got him out there and they killed him."

"She gave no other motive, reason, or explanation beyond the fact that they were stoned. Is that right? According to her story?"

"That's the only thing I know of."

"To your knowledge did she ever advise the police of that?"

"I presume she told them that night at the police station."

"I take it you still are operating on the assumption that your wife related the same story to the police department. Is that right?"

"Oh, I know she was scared, nervous, upset, lied, a few other minor things at the police department that night, if that's what you're getting at." Hobson answered reluctantly; he preferred to attack Byrne.

"No, I'm not getting at anything. What I'm asking you is —"

Hobson interrupted. "I know my wife is innocent, if that's what you're getting at." Apparently he fully believed what Sueanne had told him about the motives of the boys and he believed that her account of her son's threats after the murder was the story she told the police on the night she was arrested.

Byrne ended his cross-examination by asking about Chris's room. Byrne knew that Ed and Sueanne were redecorating their bedroom the night she was arrested and that some of Chris's furniture had been given to Margie Hunt-Fugate. "Did your wife ever offer an explanation to you, Mr. Hobson, as to why it was that ten days after Chris's disappearance she decided to completely refurnish and redecorate the entire room that he'd been living in?"

"Why she what?" Hobson said, snapping off the "what" as a threat.

Byrne liked Hobson's anger; his display, his swelling neck, meant the nest was near. "Didn't she redecorate the room that Chris had been staying in? His room in your house after he disappeared? Did she never indicate to you why she was intent on doing that right at that point? Just ten days after Chris suddenly comes up missing?"

"We bought a rental property and we were completely rebuilding the inside of the house. The only thing we had left to do, at Chris's disappearance, was the master bedroom and Chris's bedroom. And we were starting in on the master bedroom, and when we got through with it, we were going to do Chris's bedroom."

"Sir, didn't you feel that coming only a few days after Chris's disappearance, your wife's sudden interest in redecorating and refurnishing was a very unusual event?"

"At that specific time, yes. But I . . . at that time, when I was going through it, no, I didn't. I just thought—we were talking about when Chris would come home; we'll take him out and buy him some new furniture and whatever."

"When you talked to Detective Douglass about it, you told him you thought it was a very unusual thing that all of a sudden your wife wanted to go out and spend one thousand dollars on furniture for Chris ten days after he doesn't show up at home. As you look back on it, it seemed kind of strange, didn't it?"

"After I found out he was dead, yes. But shock—I've done a lot of strange things in shock. Now I can look back at the last four or five months and say, 'Huh, you've done a lot of strange things, Ed.'"

4

Byrne had shown that Sueanne, knowing of the murder of Chris, had nonetheless duped Ed Hobson into planning to redecorate Chris's room. Sueanne also had told Ed her story of an arbitrary murder by the two boys on drugs and her son's subsequent threats, an account very different from what she told the police on the night of her arrest.

Clearly, Byrne's interrogation of Ed helped Tatum in the subsequent prosecution of Sueanne. What he had done for Jimmy, his client, was less obvious.

There was in Byrne a hatred of Sueanne, a sense of dealing with a witch, with pure evil, that sometimes overcame his judgment. That she had ordered her stepson killed was wicked enough, he thought, but that she had chosen gratuitously to involve her own son in the murder made her action irredeemable.

At the end of the second day of the preliminary hearing, Byrne called Sueanne Hobson to the stand. The prosecution, now thoroughly controlled by Tatum, attempted to constrain Byrne's interrogation of her. Tatum did not want Sueanne to lend support to what he feared would be Jimmy's insanity defense in his actual trial. He was aware of dangerous psychiatric testimony in the juvenile hearings and he was prepared to attack any attempt to get it in this hearing. Also, Tatum didn't want to violate Sueanne's right to avoid self-incrimination; this would further complicate her trial if it were ever held. When he took charge, he was much more aggressive than Belling, more precise, and Byrne spent as much time arguing with him as he did interrogating Sueanne.

Sueanne left her coat on when she took the stand; it was cold and drafty inside. Sueanne was naturally very nervous, but she was less wrought up than she expected to be on a day when scarcely anyone except the press and the principals involved showed up.

As a witness, Ed was excluded from the hearing. While his wife testified, he walked back and forth in the hallway adjoining the courtroom. Ed paced in a set pattern on the oak floors; on each round his intense, drawn face peered through the small glass window cut in the swinging door.

In order to get Sueanne to testify without invoking the Fifth Amendment, Byrne agreed to question Sueanne only about the period of time Jimmy was in her home in the year just before the murder. He asked her whether she saw Jimmy on the day of the murder. "I honestly don't remember," she said. Byrne tried repeatedly, but she recalled nothing about meeting Jimmy in his parking lot on that day.

"How was it," Byrne asked, "that your son Jimmy came to move in with you and your husband?" In his testimony the day before, Ed Hobson had said that it was she who asked Jimmy to move in.

Sueanne contradicted Ed. "My husband asked him to because Jimmy said that he had a miserable home life, and Ed felt sorry for him, and wanted him with us." Sueanne spoke slowly, placing a definite emphasis on each word. She was particularly sensitive about who issued the invitation; she had heard that many people who had read about the case were saying that she had called Jimmy back to her home with the sole intention of setting him up to kill Chris.

Byrne asked about Jimmy's emotional state from August 1978 when he was reunited with Sueanne to May 1979, the month he finally moved into the condominium. "He was very unhappy," Sueanne said. After he moved in, "he was moody and morose and angry at times. He was very down at times. Very unhappy."

"Was there domestic discord?" Byrne asked. "Problems between Jimmy and Suzanne? Problems between Jimmy and Christen? Jimmy and Ed? Family problems?"

"Well," she replied sarcastically, "none of us agreed on everything."

"Did you ever at any point after June of '79, notice any regression in his behavior?"

"He had mood swings," Sueanne said. "And if you want to call it regression, then it's regression. It was on a daily basis."

"So you never knew what to expect?"

"If you want to put it that way," she said. Byrne was thinking of Sueanne's comments to Jimmy on her own mother's moods and Jimmy's sense that he couldn't rely on any of Sueanne's moods.

Sueanne refused to look at Jimmy. Byrne would stand directly behind his client and ask a question to force her to look at him, and thus at Jimmy, but she would turn toward them and look directly over the tops of both their heads as if she were blind.

Byrne began to focus on what he thought would be his defense in the trial itself, Jimmy's insanity. He asked Sueanne what the symptoms would be if someone were mentally or emotionally disturbed.

"I would say," she responded, "they would have a short attention span. They would be depressed, dishonest, unhappy."

Byrne asked if she saw these factors in her son and she said that she did and that she thought he was emotionally disturbed. "I never thought his problems had gone away."

Finally Byrne asked her to respond to the Kansas test for insanity, the McNaughton Rule. "Did Jimmy know the distinction between right and wrong?"

"I don't know," she answered. With that the hearing ended and a trial date was set for April.

Byrne had made up his mind. He broke off negotiations with Dennis Moore and refused to exchange Jimmy's testimony for a reduced sentence. He thought that he could convince a jury of Sueanne's powerful influence over her son, convince them that this abused boy had become her weapon. If he succeeded, the strict Kansas test for insanity would not matter to the jury. A plea bargain was the easy way out. He knew an insanity defense would be dangerous and difficult, but it was primarily what interested him in the case.

5

Six months before Jimmy's preliminary hearing, Byrne had asked Dr. Alan Felthous, a Menninger psychiatrist, to give him an opinion of Jimmy's sanity. In August 1980 Felthous, along with his colleague Dr. Kim Smith, a psychologist, had conducted an evaluation of Jimmy's mental state.

Every day for a week in the summer heat, Miami County Deputy Ron Orton had driven Jimmy back and forth the sixty miles to the Menninger Clinic in Topeka. Orton came to like him and trust him. He wouldn't handcuff Jimmy. Sometimes he would even go into restaurants to get coffee and leave the boy out there alone listening to rock music in the air-conditioned car.

"Ron was the first person who trusted me after the murder," Jimmy said. "Sometimes he'd let me clean my cell and take things out to the trash in the evening without paying attention to when I'd return. I liked him a lot."

Byrne anxiously awaited the results of the Menninger evaluation. The McNaughton Rule made an insanity defense particularly difficult. Since June Byrne had sought psychiatrists who would support his view that Jimmy was legally insane. Some psychiatrists flatly refused. After his examination of Jimmy, Dr. William McKnelly at the University of Kansas Medical Center wrote, "I regret that I was unable to elicit any psychiatric finding which I could consider useful to the defense. Thank you for your referral of this tragic boy."

Dr. McKnelly was not the first or last psychiatrist who refused to testify in support of Jimmy's insanity defense. A month after the boy's arrest Byrne had approached Dr. Robert Schulman for another opinion. Kathleen Dillon, a lawyer working with Byrne on the case, spoke with Dr. Schulman and his staff by phone in late June.

The evaluation did not bode well for the defense. Dr. Schulman described Jimmy as a glib, slick psychopath. When questioned the boy showed little affect about or remorse for the murder. Jimmy condescended to everyone and he appeared to be an intelligent, complicated kid.

Dr. Schulman discussed the possibility that Jimmy was manipulated or seduced by his mother, but he concluded otherwise. Schulman seemed confused by the roles taken by family members. He found that Jimmy had a better relationship with Ed Hobson than with his mother, he blandly described his relationship with her, unremarkably, as inconsistent.

Schulman argued that psychopaths are intractable to treatment. To treat a psychopath at the Menninger Clinic would cost $60,000 a year, a sum that was clearly out of the question.

The motive for murder that Dr. Schulman emphasized was that Jimmy got involved because his mother promised him a car and "happiness." This wasn't, he believed, a Cain and Abel case, but a cold-blooded, calculated crime.

Byrne was unshaken by Schulman's report. Still, when Byrne himself talked with Jimmy, he felt that "there was nobody home." Jimmy seemed to have no fixed convictions, no moral center, no evil intent—he was a pleaser who would try to respond to the wishes of whomever he was speaking to at the time. Perhaps that's why the jailers liked him, he thought. Byrne didn't care what name other people gave Jimmy's emptiness or whether it met the narrow standard for insanity set by the old

McNaughton Rule—knowing the difference between right and wrong at the time of the crime. If he could hold Sueanne on the stand long enough, if he could make the jury feel she controlled Jimmy, he could make her the dominant figure everyone involved in the case already knew she was. If he could do that, the jurors would vote for an insanity plea. Still, Jimmy must be made sympathetic; that was harder than making Sueanne monstrous.

6

In August Dr. Felthous gave Ed Byrne something to work with. On the twenty-ninth, Kathleen Dillon spoke by phone with Dr. Felthous.

According to Dr. Felthous and his team of Menninger psychologists and psychiatrists, Jimmy presented conflicting images—a self-proclaimed Eagle Scout and a handsome athlete on one side contrasted with a thief and a murderer on the other. And Jimmy always said what he thought the listener wanted to hear.

Felthouse believed Jimmy was threatened by his mother and influenced by her at the same time. It was Sueanne's powerful influence over the boy that the two lawyers, Dillon and Byrne, wanted to develop in open court when the time came.

The boy was angry at his mother, but he still hoped for a loving relationship with her, even after the murder. Dr. Felthous strongly recommended that Jimmy "stay away from his mother forever." No matter how much he loved her, he was still frightened by her and he couldn't defy her or abandon her as she had again abandoned him.

Jimmy's dominant feeling, Dr. Felthous said, was not compassion for Chris, but regret for the consequences of his actions. He cried over the loss of his relationship with his mother. Four months after the murder, all of his sad feelings were for himself, not for others.

7

Despite the psychiatrist's inability to conclude that Jimmy did not know right from wrong at the time of the murder, Byrne's view of Jimmy was reinforced by the Dillon summary of the Felthous phone call. Felthous and Kim Smith completed their work in early September. In a report later put into the court record, the two wrote:

> There are no indications in the tests of psychotic disturbance. His fragmented identity allows him to comfortably hold quite disparate values at different times. Incongruities do not bother him. There is strong evidence that he has failed to consolidate his sense of masculinity, and on an unconscious level he views himself as neither male nor female but as a weird misfit. He does not act upon the stimuli of his environment in creative or thoughtful ways, but instead uncritically accepts them or reacts to them.
>
> Characteristic of borderline patients, his major defensive positions involve splitting and repressive mechanisms. Past behaviors which do not fit with his current sense of himself are dissociated and split off, having the mild impact upon him of a distant dream. Around intensely aggressive themes, he is apt to respond with a repressive, undifferentiated retreat from the event that likely keeps him from easily remembering the particulars involved. This tendency would make it difficult for him to recall the events of the alleged murder in detail.
>
> He seems to unconsciously regard people as objects of stimulation and/or gratification. This results in his often quite sincere efforts to carry out what they would expect of him and to fulfill those expectations as if to blend with or become a part of what he currently admires. Substituting for a more congealed sense of self, he unconsciously imitates others, attempting to put on "fronts" or facades just as he expects others to do. The driving force of his life is the need to compensate for his sense of being powerless and emasculated by becoming someone who has opulent wealth and is therefore admired by all.
>
> His Thematic Appreciation Test story about one person dropping his moral objections to another when he discovers

that the other has great riches suggests that he is very vulnerable to aligning himself with anyone he admires. This is likely to produce an "end justifies the means" mentality.

Later in the report Felthous described Jimmy's experience of his family:

The history suggests that the patient's father may have been emotionally unavailable for effective bonding and identification in early years because of occupational demands on his time. The patient likely yearned for acceptance from mother, his primary object, but was instead subjected to her anger and physical abuse. In early years the patient was terrified of her and given little reason to feel good about himself. Even so, she was his primary parent. Then she left. He felt abandoned. He did not hear from her again for years. Any earlier impairment in the development of object constancy must have been exacerbated by this event.

Neither could his father take care of him. Any realistic considerations of his father's situation paled before the emotional impact of abandonment. The patient likely learned to suppress painful feelings which he was ill equipped to handle.

He eventually moved in with his father and another aunt and uncle, but this was a mixed blessing. While it brought him a little closer to his natural father, it disrupted continuity of other significant relationships. He was again passed from one set of caretakers to another. This kind of disruption was repeated when he and his father moved out of his aunt and uncle's home. Living with his grandmother meant further disruption and abandonment. In addition to thwarting development of constant relationships, all of these different moves and different caretakers meant that he had to meet different expectations of different people. He failed to develop a solid sense of who he was and what he stood for.

His father eventually remarried, and the patient's relationship with his stepmother was conflictual. The patient felt disfavored by her and yearned to be accepted by a mother figure. He may have felt more distant from his father, who then had another object of his love.

Missing nurturance and a solid sense of self, he looked for acceptance by others and attached importance to superficial features, such as wealth and standard of living. When his natural mother reappeared, he saw hope for motherly acceptance, a sense of self, and increased self-esteem, if only through surname change and material benefits.

Living with his mother reignited his early childhood ambivalent feelings towards her. On the one hand, he felt angry at the way she depreciated him. He was terrified of her omnipotent power. He was perhaps even more terrified that she might abandon him again. Her talk of sending him to a military school fueled his early childhood fear of abandonment. He moved out but could not curtail his ambivalent bond to her.

He says he acceded to her persistent demand in order to get her off his back. Yet it is equally conceivable that he acceded in order to prevent another traumatic abandonment, a fear which the killing and related events unexpectedly realized. Psychological testing indicates that, given his eager susceptibility to the influences of valued others, his claim to have arranged for the murder because his mother demanded it is plausible.

What is particularly interesting in his Rorschach response is "the keeper of hell," a rabbit in the Richard Adams' novel *Watership Down*. This highly idiosyncratic response refers to someone who kills by letting out certain diseases for the good of the whole rabbit population. The keeper of hell is a killer providing a needed moral service. The unusual theme may well reflect his sense of participation in the act.

Felthous and Smith were relatively optimistic about Jimmy's capacity to respond to therapy:

It is felt for a number of reasons the patient is well suited for a good therapeutic response. His character structure is still uncrystalized. There is a part of him which values being aggressive, sleek, and clever, and which would like to use people and opportunities in order to gain the wealth that he desires. Should he not receive appropriate treatment, this part could eventually become the predominant aspect of his character structure. This would likely occur in a prison where some of the strongest figures are socially negative identities. Also, his current sexual confusion could lead to conscious acceptance of homosexuality in a prison setting.

There is, however, another part of him which values being an honest, respected, hardworking individual. This path is more difficult and uncertain because it involves increasing his frustration tolerance and his willingness to find other ways to make life meaningful.

At first the patient would try to behave and parrot back what he thinks his therapist wants to hear. This kind of change, however, would be transient and superficial. The therapist should focus on the disparities in the patient's actions and on his tendency to please the therapist.

Although there were no signs that the subject was psychotic or did not know what he was doing, he may have been intoxicated with marijuana with resultant poor judgment. But thoughts of killing Christen were entertained and shared well before the act. Of apparently much greater influence than the marijuana was his mother, who was seen as powerful, and irrepressible. Lacking a sense of identity and internalized values, and under social stresses, such as loss of mother's support, the patient apparently submitted to her morbid demands. It is my judgment that the patient should in the future have nothing to do with his mother.

8

In the weeks just prior to the trial, Byrne made efforts to get a stronger evaluation of Jimmy, one that would assert directly his legal insanity. In mid-April he had Jimmy admitted to the Mid-Continent Psychiatric Hospital in Olathe for a two-week period. Just before the trial began, he received a diagnostic report from Dr. G. Charles Welsh, the forensic psychologist leading the team of therapists.

Byrne found his man in Dr. Welsh. Welsh concluded his analysis of Jimmy in a blizzard of impressive jargon:

> Testing reported that the patient demonstrated physical symptoms so substantial as to imply somatic delusions, broadly based and felt frustration, depression of a psychotic nature and to a suicidal degree, obsessive-compulsive features, severe schizoid thought patterns, clear paranoid ideation, moderate anxiety, and moderate agitation. Pattern of data is that most typical of a severely confused and disturbed adolescent experiencing disassociative reaction and depersonalization. At the time of the commission of the crime the defendant did not appreciate right from wrong and could not conform his conduct to prescribed legal standards.

Once he saw Welsh's report, the Johnson County district attorney, Dennis Moore, quickly countered. The prosecution sent Dr. Gerald Vandenberg, a clinical psychologist, down to interview Jimmy on Saturday, the twenty-fifth, two days before the trial began. In his brief report Vandenberg wrote, "Testing presents a picture of a very bright young man with intellectual capacities well into the gifted or very superior range (99 + percentile)."

Vandenberg found Jimmy rather immature with low self-esteem. He concluded, "Jimmy is a currently depressed and somewhat anxious young man, acutely aware of the seriousness of his situation. His impulses are often undercontrolled and the patient's behavior may show a pattern of frequent acting out. Mr. Crumm is likely to be influenced by others. As Jimmy himself put it, he sees himself as 'a pleaser, too easily influenced; don't do my own thinking.' He did, at the time of the alleged crime, understand the difference between right and wrong and knew that what he was alleged to have done was wrong."

9

Jimmy himself didn't know whether he was sane or insane. He knew he had done what his mother told him to do, and he knew that he had been caught. He also knew that he could no longer watch movies where people were shot because then he dreamed he was in a hole and someone above was shooting down at him.

10

During the trial the Miami County courtroom was full every day. The trees were rapidly leafing out and the redbuds in the court-house square were in bloom. In the afternoon the bottom panes of the great stained-glass windows were opened to the north and south so a mild breeze could blow through.

A year had passed since Chris was murdered and it was spring again. Jimmy's trial was held from Monday, the twenty-seventh of April, to Friday, the first of May. A year ago during these days Chris was still buried in a shallow grave ten miles north of the courthouse.

Before the trial Byrne had gone out to see the grave. He had heard that Big Bull Creek had backed up into the area of the grave this spring and last, that the lake forming there from the new dam erected ten miles downstream had flooded the grave site. To his surprise he found the creek within its banks. The small hole Chris had dug for himself was still there, its edges smoothed by the water that had washed over it in the last year. The cottonwood tree whose roots neither Chris nor Paul could cut through was just now letting out its leaves.

11

The selection of the jury and arguments over the admission of Jimmy's oral and written confessions as evidence consumed the first day of the trial. Judge Fosse ruled favorably for the prosecution on each issue. The second day began with the state's summary of its case. Belling was present, but Steve Tatum, lean, polite, unpolished, was firmly in charge and made the prosecution's opening statement to the jury.

Tatum hated elaboration; he thrived on concision, directness, and order. Immediately he addressed the main concern of the prosecution: "As the evidence is presented it will, of necessity, show the complicated involvement in this matter of others. I mention Paul Sorrentino, Sueanne Hobson. You may feel strongly about the involvement of others in this case, as well you should. However, for the purpose of this trial, I am asking that you focus your attention on determining ultimately the guilt of James Hobson. Though you will see a pattern of a family emerge, the evidence will show that James Hobson was not legally insane, but committed a cold-blooded, chilling act. On the night of the murder Jimmy's mother called him and said it was too late to back out. Jimmy did not say no to his mother."

The first witness the prosecution called was Ed Hobson. Tatum wasted little time on him. Surprisingly Byrne's cross-examination of Hobson was also perfunctory. Hobson had been so hostile in his long interrogation in the preliminary hearing two months before that Byrne thought he might try to do serious damage to Jimmy's insanity defense. Besides, the father of the murdered boy was a sympathetic figure and Byrne did not wish to pit himself against Hobson before the jury.

Though Byrne had acknowledged fully Jimmy's participation in the murder and had stipulated that Jimmy fired at least one shot into Chris, Tatum insisted on calling a series of witnesses to demonstrate the brutality of the crime. He summoned Barry Carpenter, who had found the grave, and Ron Orton, who had helped dig up the body and who testified to its grisly condition.

Tatum also called Bridgens, the blunt coroner who had done the autopsy. Bridgens showed colored slides of the body he had broken open and elaborately described Chris's three shotgun wounds. He said that one blast blew away part of Chris's jaw; one penetrated his arm and pellets lodged in his chest; the third smashed through the back of his head and drove shot directly into the brain.

Tatum went through the prosecution witnesses in a day. Before the court recessed Tuesday afternoon, he played the tape of Jimmy's confession in the Miami County Jail nearly a year before.

12

The state rested its case early Wednesday morning. Byrne began his defense of Jimmy with a long opening statement to the jury. He spoke first of Sueanne's treatment of Jimmy. "Despite receiving custody of Jimmy on the day she received her divorce, she, in the most literal sense of the word, abandoned him," Byrne said. "Jimmy was living in Kansas City. You will learn that Sueanne was also there, and you will learn that there was no contact whatsoever. Not a visit, a phone call, a Christmas card, a birthday present, a telephone call, anything. Now, that is critical. The doctors will tell you that he is a boy searching for a mother, capital 'M,' whatever that means to you. You will learn from the testimony that if we had to describe Jimmy for eight years, up to 1979, it would be a boy searching for a mother. And he couldn't find her.

"You will learn from the medical evidence that Jimmy was an intense loner." Byrne was preparing the way for psychiatric and psychological testimony. "This shows a lot about his character, the character of a loner searching, searching for eight years. You are going to learn that during that period of time Jimmy went from one household to another. His mother abandoned him and his father was stuck with him. In a sense his father dropped the ball, too. So Jimmy goes to aunts, uncles, grandparents, maternal and paternal, and back with the father and an uncle, and the father remarries and he goes in with the father again, back and forth, never staying long enough in one place to find out or understand who he was or who he belonged to, if anybody."

Jim Crumm, seated in the front row of the courtroom, nodded assent and his eyes filled with tears. Unlike Tatum, Byrne was openly passionate and paced about the courtroom as he spoke. He was an energetic, emotional young man with a flexible voice, but it was a voice that expressed anger and frustration best of all. He was always alone against the others.

Byrne spoke directly of Sueanne's involvement. "Let me tell you right now, she is not on my side, and I don't know what she is going to say, but you have got to see her, because she is the key that unlocks the door to understanding what was going on in

Jimmy's mind when he killed Chris Hobson. That is why I am a little bit scared about it. If you don't understand this woman, and if I can't make you understand over the next couple of days what impact she had on him, the psychiatric testimony isn't going to help you too much, so please watch her carefully. Most witnesses you just listen to, and that is the end of it. This witness tells you as much or more in her eyes and on her face than her words ever could. Watch her and listen to her, but especially watch her.

"You will learn that Jimmy was happy when he heard from her," Byrne said. "This is the person he had been looking for all that time. When he moved in with her, she showered him with every kind of material thing—expensive clothes, coats, jewelry, spending money, the promise of an automobile. She lured him into her home with the promise and with the reality of all these material things.

"I am confident the evidence will show that it wasn't because all of a sudden she had some normal parental interest in her son. Chris Hobson was living at home, too. At some point, for some reason, Sueanne decided that little Chris, her stepson, the natural son of her new husband, Ed Hobson, had to go. I can't tell you why. I don't know why that happened, why she decided Chris had to go."

Byrne paused and pointed to Tatum. "Neither does he."

Byrne believed that when Sueanne had called her son back to her home, she had already concocted a plan to murder Chris. The very absurdity of Sueanne's involvement in the murder tended to make people feel she was innocent, Byrne thought. He himself had some doubts about her guilt. In the midst of preparing for the trial he'd say to his friends, "What if Jimmy all this time was just setting her up? What if she really did nothing at all? It's all talk, words." He had difficulty understanding Sueanne's motives. He was unmarried himself, uninterested in money, and had no grasp of the stress of raising children. Sibling disputes and a child one couldn't control were beyond his experience.

"Sueanne decided that Jimmy, her own son, whom she managed to get back into the house, would be the instrumentality," Byrne concluded. "Sueanne would be the brains; she would come up with the idea, the method, the process."

Tatum promptly objected to Byrne's going into "the mental state of Sueanne Hobson." Judge Fosse sustained the objection and Byrne ended his opening statement quickly.

13

To the thrill of the spectators Byrne immediately called Sueanne Hobson to the stand. The bailiff went out the large, swinging doors to get her and led her slowly back through the crowded courtroom. She was wearing a white suit.

As soon as she had been sworn in, Byrne walked over and stood behind Jimmy. "Do you see your son in this room?"

"He is sitting at the table by the woman in the red suit." She did not look at her son or at Byrne.

"At any time after your son was arrested in May of last year to date, have you visited with your son in the Miami County Jail?"

"No."

"Have you exchanged any letters with him?"

"No. I was told I couldn't have any contact with him."

"Who told you that?"

"My mother told my daughter who told me that his father was the only one that could visit him." Apparently Sueanne was still not speaking with her mother.

Sueanne was steadily rocking back and forth on the witness stand. To the reporters sitting in the rows of seats reserved for them in the front of the courtroom, she appeared to be heavily sedated. Despite her constant rocking she answered concisely, maintaining tight control of her language, accentuating each word. Certainly she was afraid; she knew that whatever happened here, she would soon be the prisoner in the dock testifying to maintain her own freedom. If this were the last stage of her son's prosecution, it was the first stage of her own.

Byrne attempted to document Sueanne's abandonment of Jimmy. "How often would you see Jimmy right after the divorce? Was it once a month, once a week, once a year?"

"I don't remember."

"Can you remember what year it was that you had your visit with Jimmy before he disappeared."

"I believe it was the latter part of '72."

"Did you ever go to your former husband and say, 'Look, I have custody! He is going to stay here with me'?"

"No."

"Did you make any effort to enforce the court order that gave custody of Jimmy to you?"

"I tried to get him back several times."

"How did you do that?"

"My daddy and I tried to get him back several times, and my parents hired private detectives to find Jim."

"And they couldn't find Jim?"

"That is what they told my parents."

"Did you ever go back to the court and ask for any kind of help?"

"No."

"Did you or your father have these detectives out searching for six years?" Byrne said sarcastically.

"No."

"When did you stop having these detectives search?"

"I don't know how long they looked."

"And did you continue with any efforts on your own to find out where your son was?"

"Do you mean by hiring detectives myself?"

"No!" Byrne was almost shouting out of frustration. "I just mean this, Mrs. Hobson, did you think that your son had just vanished off the earth, or did you think he was right there in town? What was going on in your mind?"

"I didn't know where he was."

Byrne turned to Sueanne's relations with her son after they met again in August 1978. "Did you talk about the past years? 'What have you been doing? Here's what I've been doing.' Or was it things that seemed to be bothering him in an emotional sense?"

"Yes," Sueanne answered unresponsively. "I answered any questions that he asked."

"Did he cry when he saw you the first time?"

"No."

"Did he say, 'Mom, I would like to move in with you'? Or did you just say, 'Jimmy, I want you to move in with me'? How did that come about?"

"He had told us some of the conditions under which he had been living, and was very unhappy, and we felt that it would be good for us and good for him to have him with us. The invitation was extended and it was up to him. He wasn't pressurized."

"How did Jimmy react to your invitation?"

"He was thrilled."

"Did he have clothes, shoes, sporting equipment, whatever?"

"He had very little clothing. It was old and ratty looking. Well, the first thing that Ed and I discussed was the fact that he didn't have any clothing, and we went right out and started in buying him things. He didn't even have enough underwear. Neither Ed nor I could stand to see him the way it was." For the first time Sueanne answered a question easily and fully. Clothes and possessions were important to her.

"Were you, in a sense, trying to make up for the absence of all those years?"

"Probably. Jimmy had told us that he had gotten very little and that anything he did have, his grandparents bought him."

"So you learned that he had some contact with his grandparents during these years?"

"Yes."

"Were you in regular touch with your parents, Mr. and Mrs. Sallee, during that period of time?"

"Not during the entire period of time."

"What periods of time were you out of touch with them?"

"Up until the beginning of '71 through '78, I believe."

Byrne was particularly distressed by the Sallees. For several months he had been trying to get Ruth Sallee to testify for Jimmy; Don Sallee wouldn't even talk with him. After Jimmy's arrest his grandmother phoned her grandson, Jimmy, once or twice a week, though she never visited the jail.

She would never meet with Byrne either. When he did call her, she would talk to him endlessly about the case. She would talk as long as he wanted to talk, talk rapidly and unceasingly until she wore him out; he could scarcely get a word in. Repeatedly Byrne said, "I'd like you to testify for Jimmy," but Mrs. Sallee would not commit herself to do it.

"We are private people," she'd say. "I have a bad heart," she'd say. If more than talk were required, this lean, intense woman in her sixties would commit herself to nothing.

Byrne was forced to subpoena Ruth Sallee for the trial. She was furious when she got down to Miami County on Wednesday. Her anger made her an unpredictable witness; Byrne was afraid to call her for fear of what she would say. Byrne, too, was angry that she had turned away from Jimmy when he needed her support most. In the end, like her daughter, Mrs. Sallee also abandoned Jimmy.

Byrne felt he was not getting anywhere with Sueanne. "How did Jimmy get along? How did he adjust?"

"Well, there were some arguments, but there weren't any big fights," Sueanne said.

"Just pretty normal?"

"Well, I don't know what normal is," she responded quickly. "I think jealousy was always there. I think children are jealous of one another."

While Sueanne testified, Ed Hobson again paced in the adjoining hall. As in the preliminary hearing, his anxious face appeared and disappeared in the small glass in the broad swinging door to the courtroom.

At the end of Sueanne's testimony Byrne focused on the days right before the murder. "Did you see Jimmy again after he moved out of your home in March of 1980?"

"Yes."

"How frequently?"

"Oh, I don't remember exactly," she said casually as if she were bored by the patter of a clerk.

Byrne was intent on questioning her, so intent that he did not notice her upper body rocking stiffly and continuously in a very tight arc. "Do you know that Chris Hobson disappeared on April seventeenth?"

"Yes."

"How many times, approximately, between the time he

moved from your home in March 1980 until April seventeenth
did you see him?"

"Oh, at least a couple of times a week."

"This is when he was out of your home, not living there anymore?"

"Yes."

"Where would you see him when you saw him a couple of
times each week?"

"At our home."

"Did you ever learn that he was living in an apartment in
Lenexa?"

"Yes."

"Did you ever go visit him there?"

"Yes."

"Frequently?"

"Oh," she responded, again drawing out the word as if she
were becoming impatient with these tedious questions, "I was
over there several times."

"Did you have occasion to see your son after April seventeenth and before Chris Hobson's body was found?"

"I don't know whether I did or not."

"You can't remember?"

"No."

"But you do know you didn't see him again after he was
arrested until he appeared in court?"

"Yes."

"Mrs. Hobson, before I release you from the subpoena today,
let me ask you, do you love your son?"

"Yes."

"Before you get off the witness stand, is there anything
you want to say to the court and jury in his behalf?" Byrne
asked.

The prosecution objected to the question and Judge Fosse did
not permit Sueanne to answer.

Tatum briefly cross-examined Sueanne. Before she stepped
down from the stand, Judge Fosse released her from the bond
imposed to secure her appearance in court.

Byrne knew he had failed to shake Sueanne and he felt exhausted, beaten. She had answered concisely and had contained her anger much better than she had done in the preliminary two months before. She had lied certainly, but Byrne had been enjoined against using statements from her police interview to counter her lies. Sueanne was tough, the toughest witness he had encountered in his short career. Not once could he catch her eye and she had never looked directly at Jimmy.

What Sueanne said provided little support for the insanity defense Byrne was developing. He now realized that in his opening statement he had attributed too much importance to her testimony, relied on it; now he had nothing except the psychiatrists.

Caught up in his despair, Byrne did not hear the scream, though the spectators and the reporters and the jury, sitting silent in its box, heard. After Sueanne had gone quietly out the swinging wooden doors and halfway down the oak stairs, she began to scream at the top of her voice, screaming and stomping her feet until she reached the turn of the stairs a floor below.

Her screaming and stomping on the uncarpeted stairs came at first through the door, then through the very floor of the courtroom itself as she descended further. Ed Hobson held her upright, awkwardly supporting her as he led her past the cameras gathered in the darkened hallway below and outside to the broad stone steps opening onto the noon light of a beautiful spring day.

That evening at their condominium in Overland Park, Sueanne and Ed watched the Kansas City news carefully as they had done for weeks. They didn't have long to wait. All that week the trial was the top local story. "Did I do that?" she asked incredulously when a reporter described her stomping and her screams.

Laughing, his arm draped around her thin shoulders, Ed said, "You sure did, honey! You sure did!"

14

After a fifteen-minute recess Byrne called Jim Crumm to the stand. In his midforties, heavy, with a rubicund face, Jim seemed older than his years. He was a softer man than Ed, more apparently submissive, a man who was reluctant to offend. His body hung loosely and he seemed depressed. He was sincerely bearing a burden of guilt, but displaying his guilt and his sadness nonetheless, as if to anticipate and thus ward off reproach.

"Do you know why Sueanne had requested the court to give her custody?" Byrne asked.

"Not for a fact, no, just, you know, my own assumption."

"But she didn't want him. Is that from day one, or did she take him awhile after the divorce and bring him back?"

"No, sir, that was from day one. She told me before the divorce she did not want him, that he was to stay with me, but she wanted legal custody of him."

"Did Jimmy stay with you at the house?"

"We stayed there six months, maybe, something like that. Then I was having a hard time with the divorce and drinking. Jimmy was upset that I was going to leave him with his aunt Dorothy, but, of the places, he accepted it." Tears were coming down his face as he spoke. He was ashamed, but he knew the more he could say against himself, the better it would be for his son. Jimmy had been sitting rigidly at the witness table; as his father spoke he covered his face with his hands and cried into them.

Byrne got Jim to speak of his disintegration after the divorce and of his neglect of Jimmy. Jim admitted that for several years Jimmy had not lived with him at all. He passed Jimmy from one aunt to another in the large, extended Crumm family, then to his grandmother Edna.

"During the period from the end of 1971 when you and Sueanne were divorced, until March of '79 when Jimmy moved in with his mother, had you seen Sueanne Hobson?" Byrne asked.

"Well, just a few times on occasion when I was making no child support payments, or things like this, and then that stopped around '73, and that is when there was no more contact. You know, all my relatives were still living basically in the same area. Everybody was still listed in the phone book." Byrne and Jim had made clear to the jury that Sueanne should have had no difficulty contacting her son, that no detectives were needed to find him, just a phone book.

Byrne didn't ask why Jim had not found Suzanne, why he really had not ever looked for her. After all, he hadn't killed anybody.

The rest of Byrne's questions focused on the year before the murder. In the period immediately before Jimmy was reunited with Sueanne, the boy had lived with his father and his new wife, Mary. "Did you see Jimmy again after he moved out of your house?"

"Jimmy would come by occasionally, yes, sir, to visit us."

"How often?"

"Oh, I don't know, once a month, once every three weeks, something like this. He would stop by and say hi, with his new car and new clothes, and see how things were going."

"Did you learn at some point that he had finally left the Hobson home?"

"Yes, sir, it was probably—I don't know, my sister Dorothy called and told me that he had moved out, and that he was going to get an apartment."

"Did you see him at any time during that time period after he moved out of the Hobson residence?"

"He came by occasionally, yes, sir. I don't know what else to say. He came by occasionally."

"Do you remember whether you saw him at any time after April seventeenth of 1980?"

"No, sir, I do not. I didn't see him that I remember anyway until the Monday that I came down here to the jail."

Jim was crying, his head lowered, his shoulders shaking slightly when he stood up to come down from the witness stand. Then Jim walked hesitantly toward his son. Both were crying; Jimmy, awkwardly caught between the chair and the table, half stood and embraced his father.

15

Dorothy Crumm Reffitt, Jim's sister, Jimmy's aunt, a middle-aged, heavy woman in dark clothes, took the stand next. Byrne asked how Jimmy came to live with her.

"Well, his mother and father got a divorce. His mother got legal custody of him. She did not want him," Dorothy said bluntly.

"During the two years that Jimmy lived with you, before he lived with his father again, to your own personal knowledge was Sueanne Hobson aware that he was living in the home?"

"Yes." Dorothy testified that Sueanne had never come to see Jimmy from 1972 to 1974, the years she kept the boy after the divorce.

"Did Jimmy ever come to live with you again at any time?" Byrne asked.

"Yes, in February or March of 1980, right after he left his mother, he again came and lived with us for about two months before this thing happened."

Repeated objections by Tatum were upheld by Judge Fosse and severely limited the subjects Byrne could explore.

After Byrne finished, Tatum briefly questioned Dorothy. "You just tried to absorb Jimmy into your already large family. Is that right?"

"Yes, but I didn't think it was rather large," she said.

"The four children that you had at the time?"

"Right. We had plenty of room."

"You tried to make a nice home for him?"

"We tried, yes, but Jimmy still had problems."

Dorothy's testimony supported her brother's: Sueanne had willfully neglected her son. Byrne attacked Sueanne's character effectively, but he had not yet provided any support for his insanity defense.

A month after the murder Dorothy and her son David, a little older than Jimmy, had told Detective Steve Moore how much Jimmy had changed when he returned to the Reffitts in February 1980. Moore's report of his interview was not admitted into evidence in the trial. Moore wrote:

After living with Sueanne and Mr. Hobson, Jimmy got into trouble with credit cards and drugs in the early months of 1980. Because of this activity, Jimmy left the Hobson home and stayed with his aunt, Dorothy Reffitt. During this stay, Jimmy advised his cousin, David Reffitt, that he was in trouble with the police. David discovered quite a change in Jimmy's behavior, and noticed that he was very materialistic, which is a trait possessed by Sueanne Hobson. Mrs. Reffitt stated the same observation, and feels that Sueanne is solely responsible for his change in behavior. Mrs. Reffitt and her son, David, were aware of the fact that Jimmy was in trouble with the credit cards, and they had knowledge through conversations with Jimmy that his mother had told him to stay away from home and was supplying him with money. Mrs. Reffitt told Jimmy that this was wrong, and that he had to face his responsibilities.

On April 8, 1980, Jimmy moved out of the Reffitt house into the Oak Park Apartments. Mrs. Reffitt has not had any further contact with the boy since that date.

Mrs. Reffitt, along with her son, David, advised that, when Jimmy was living at their home from 1972 to '74, he was a very good boy and was easy to get along with. He showed no signs of wanting any abundance of material wealth, nor did he show signs of any violent tendencies. They stated that after he had lived with his mother, who had abandoned him for a long period of time, he developed a desire to have material things. Both Mrs. Reffitt and her son feel that, because Jimmy had no mother during 1971 to 1978, he was reaching out to Sueanne and was trying to win her love. They further stated that they felt that Jimmy would do anything his mother told him in order to please her.

David Reffitt advised that he had talked with Jimmy about his brother, Chris, and it had been relayed that he did not like the boy and, at one point, he discussed taking him out and killing him. This incident occurred after Jimmy was caught using the credit cards. David further advised that Jimmy told him his mother did not like Chris, nor did his sister. This detective then concluded the conversation with the Reffitts and took no further action.

Certainly David Reffitt's statement suggested a clear motive for Jimmy's murder of Chris.

16

Tatum saw clearly what Byrne was doing with Sueanne Hobson, Jim Crumm, and Dorothy Reffitt. Under the guise of an insanity defense, Byrne was showing the jury that Jimmy was coerced into murdering his stepbrother by his mother. Certainly coercion was a better defense than insanity. Byrne should have taken the state's offer of seven and a half years, Tatum thought.

Soon, up in Johnson County, Tatum would be extracting the very same information from Sueanne that he was objecting to in Miami County. He didn't like protecting Sueanne from prying questions about her role in the conspiracy and he didn't like warding off revelations about her character from Jimmy's relatives. But Tatum had a clear, orderly mind that saw the complex of trials as a whole and his slow passion was invested in the legal process that would inevitably give Sueanne her turn. Byrne had spurned Moore's offer of a reduced charge and it would prove costly to his client. Tatum would see to that.

17

The rest of Byrne's defense of Jimmy relied on psychiatric testimony. On Wednesday afternoon, the third day of the trial, he called to the stand Dr. Alan Felthous, the young Menninger psychiatrist.

Despite his reservations about Byrne's insanity defense, Felthous had agreed to testify. Dr. Kim Smith, Felthous's colleague who helped write the report about Jimmy and testified in his favor during the juvenile hearing, would not agree to appear in defense of Jimmy. He did not consider the boy legally insane.

The latitude psychiatrists were allowed by law was much greater than that of lay witnesses. Byrne sought to take full advantage of the opportunity and he frequently permitted Felthous to speak without interruption.

Though other documents were available to him, Felthous's testimony was based almost exclusively on his week of interviews with Jimmy. "My impression is that Jimmy seemed pretty indifferent to Chris," he said. Yet Chris apparently had told the Hobsons about the stolen credit card, and because of that, "there was some discussion of sending Jimmy to a military school. He really saw his mother as the much more dominant parent. Any discussion such as that would come from her.

"Chris was something of a scapegoat for the family," Felthous said. "Sueanne felt very uncomfortable with him and didn't want to have anything to do with him. The sense is she was both frightened and angry at this fellow Chris, who, Jimmy says, reminded her of her mother. She stayed in the bedroom with the door locked as though trying to keep herself safely away from Chris. According to what Jimmy was told, Chris had a schizoid personality disorder with suicidal and homicidal tendencies."

It was Jimmy's belief, Felthous reported, that if he would kill Chris, Sueanne would buy him a sports car. If he did not do it, she would turn him in for breaking his probation by moving out of the condominium. "The most important thing is that Jimmy wanted to get her off his back," Felthous said.

"Jimmy has a very passive, impressionistic way of thinking," Felthous continued. "He does not think about things critically and creatively. Rather, he either accepts thoughts or reacts against them. In moving from family to family, he never really developed a good sense of who he was. While he does not have an internalized sense of values, in the sense that most people do, he does put a lot of emphasis on issues of power and wealth, and he has kind of a mixed attachment to these things. In other words, if he sees a person that appears to be powerful and wealthy, he admires that, and he wants to curry favor with that person so that he can get some of that power and wealth, but at the same time he is easily threatened by it."

Felthous also believed that Jimmy was confused about his sexual identity. "His sense of himself as a man is very shaky, and he feels very threatened by that. While he doesn't have a good sense of himself as a person, at least on an unconscious level, he doesn't have a good sense of himself as a man either. While consciously he would like to be regarded as a young man, unconsciously he doesn't really see himself as very male or female, but more of a weird misfit."

While Felthous spoke Jimmy drew figures steadily on a piece of paper and never once lifted his head to look at the psychiatrist. He was, of course, quite uncomfortable during Felthous's testimony, humiliated by the analysis of his sexuality before a crowd of spectators.

At times Gary Compton, Byrne's arrogant, fat private investigator, who sat beside Jimmy at the table, tried to coax the boy out of his depression. Regularly he whispered to him, "We're going to call you next. You're next, you know that, buddy?" Jimmy chuckled at Compton, whom he thought a crazy man, just barely the other side of the law from him, a daring man who would walk in and search the files of the district attorney in broad daylight without asking permission.

18

Felthous's view of Jimmy as a sexual misfit had been developed by Dr. Kim Smith in his testimony at the juvenile hearing seven months earlier. In a standard personality test Smith had asked Jimmy to draw a picture of himself. At the juvenile hearing, Smith testified, "Jimmy drew a hypermasculine, hyperathletic-looking fellow, which contrasted greatly with the swarthy, criminal-looking character that he drew for Dr. Schulman only two months earlier. That kind of disparity you just don't see, even with very young children. What they drew two months ago is going to be very much what they draw now. What I make of that disparity is, again, the fluidity or lack of solidness of his ideas about what men are like and what people are like.

"To Jimmy being a man means very much of a caricature of life," Smith continued. "It means being powerful, rich, and strong. He has a very simple, crude idea of what being a man or human being is. There's not a great deal of differentiation between men and women for him and that, I think, reflects some of his lack of identity. I don't think he really knows unconsciously; this likely irritates him for me to say that, but I don't think he knows whether he is really man or really woman at an unconscious level. I think that drives him to prove his powerfulness, drives him to see if he can prove himself to be a male by being powerful."

Smith believed that in prison Jimmy could easily become homosexual. "I hesitate to speak openly of that in front of Jimmy, but I suppose I must. I think it would be very, very likely for Jimmy to become interested in homosexual affairs. Consciously, Jimmy, I suspect, finds that irritating and not something he would want to do. Given the fact of how easily he is influenced and how much he can align himself and give up values to please, and secondly, given his basically predominant alliance and affection for males, which is stronger than one usually sees, it's very hard for Jimmy to find deep trust and affection for a woman because he tends to perceive women as very intrusive, very controlling, very powerful."

19

In his testimony at the trial, Felthous tried to explain to the jury why Jimmy had developed a strong sense of women as powerful and why he had so little sense of himself as an individual. Byrne let him speak without interruption.

In early childhood Jimmy did not have his father around. His primary caretaker in those early years was his mother, who, according to Jimmy, was ashamed to take him out in public and scolded him, screamed at him, slapped him in the face, and the impression is, it gave him not much of a reason to feel good about himself.

Then, at nine years of age, his mother left, and his father also left, and he was placed in the care of an aunt and uncle. It is kind of hard to appreciate what it is like for a nine-year-old to have a mother and father both leave, but particularly a mother who, while he feared her, he, at the same time, valued her because she was his primary parent.

So he really didn't develop a sense that those mother and father figures are around to stay for a while. Each time he had to adjust his behaviors, his outward personality, if you will, to the expectations of the people who were taking care of him. He didn't develop a good sense of who he was as an individual, of what he stood for, of what he wanted to pursue.

Jimmy is easily influenced by other people, particularly people he values that he sees as strong and important and powerful in his life. When I saw him, and he was then eighteen years old, he said, in effect, nobody could defy his mother; nobody could really go up against her. She would win any argument by intimidation. His stepfather couldn't stand up to her; he himself couldn't stand up to her. He didn't see that anybody would really stand up to her. He saw her as not only a very wealthy person, but somebody who could very effectively use other people and not encounter any resistance.

Also, in childhood, I think that he was quite frightened of her; as attached as he was to her, he was frightened of her. If he knocked over something, he would cower in front of other parents because that fear of her was generalized. It is possible that these early childhood fears were rekindled when he went to live with her again.

Felthous vividly described the psychological pressure Sueanne put on Jimmy in the last days before the murder, especially after he moved into his own apartment on the eighth of April. "Jimmy said that his mother visited him nearly every day or every other day and urged him to do something about Chris, urged him to arrange for the murder of his stepbrother. He said that he was really bothered by her frequent visits. But it was hard for him to ask her not to visit and, in fact, during the visits he said he had to somehow make it her idea to close the visit and leave rather than risk hurting her feelings. And he said that while she was offering some material inducements—'If you take care of Chris, I'll get you a new car'—he said that he was most interested in getting her off his back. In addition to the inducements and frequent extortions he says she threatened to turn him in for breaking probation."

20

Tatum began his cross-examination of Felthous by attacking the authority of the diagnoses he had assigned Jimmy: "Identity

Disorder of Adolescence," "Incipient 'As If' Personality Disorder," and "Incipient Borderline Personality Disorder."

"Now, psychiatry, by its very nature, is a very subjective type of situation, where you have to make conclusions based on variables that are presented to you. Is that correct?" Tatum asked.

"I think it is both subjective and objective. It is much more subjective than radiology, where people are reading X rays, because we are dealing with the complexities of the human mind," Felthous replied matter-of-factly as Tatum led him into a trap.

"Right, exactly. And in an attempt to make it more objective, make it more standardized, the American Psychiatric Association has developed the *Diagnostic and Statistical Manual III.*"

"Yes," Felthous agreed.

"How is a mental illness added to those lists of mental illnesses in that book? How do they decide?"

"There were a number of different committees that worked on this," Dr. Felthous began. "They drew on experts in various subspecialty areas in terms of diagnosis, and it involved a great deal of committee work, a great deal of trial of this method in the field by various centers across the country, so it really involved much more work than I am fully aware of."

"Sure. Ultimately, whether a new diagnosis is to be added to the list requires a vote. If there is a majority voting for it, it is placed in that book, isn't that correct, or do you know?" Tatum asked.

"I just don't know that for a fact," Felthous replied. Tatum, of course, was correct. Thoroughly prepared, he had brilliantly undercut the authority of Felthous as well as the authority of the manual from which the diagnoses were taken.

Tatum then tried to turn Byrne's dramatization of Sueanne's character to his advantage. He sought to equate Jimmy's character with his mother's.

"Did Jimmy appear to be familiar with psychiatric terms?" Tatum asked.

"He used some psychological terms. In my opinion I felt some of them were chic psychological terms, like referring to something as 'un-okay,' which is something his mother would do, as though that

implies some psychological understanding. So I felt that any understanding that he had would have been very superficial, and perhaps,
to some extent, imitative of his mother."

"And what understanding did Jimmy have of his mother?"

"I really don't know how much he may have had in a way of
insight into the psychology of his mother. He mentioned that his
mother may have regarded Chris much like her mother, that she
was very frightened and angry at Chris, although he did not
share those feelings. He said that he thought that his mother was
paranoid, but beyond that I don't know that he had much understanding of his mother's psychology."

"At least he conveyed to you that he understood his mother
was manipulative with him?"

"Yes, that she could be very manipulative of people."

"And in your report Jimmy said he had those manipulative
features himself. Is that correct?"

"That is one side of his personality. He has the potential of
being manipulative of other people for personal gain, yes."

Tatum took the opportunity to show how Jimmy had manipulated Felthous himself. "I believe when Jimmy described to you
how the killing took place, that he said at the last moment he
pulled his gun up so that Paul Sorrentino was actually the person
who did the shooting and the killing. Is that how he described it
to you?"

"He told me that he fired into the woods."

"If the evidence were to the contrary—and perhaps that
would be true of some other areas in the history that he gave
you—would the fact that he didn't fire into the woods be in your
findings at all?"

"No."

"The fact that he would lie about the history of the case
would not appear there?"

"If he would lie about that particular event, it would not
affect my conclusions, right. I wasn't expecting—I wasn't fully
expecting him to lie about that particular event. It is conceivable—" Felthous hesitated and looked away from Tatum.

"I understand it is probably difficult to put into words,"
Tatum said softly. Tatum was precise and respectful. He was a

skeptical, ordinary Kansan, one who would slit your windpipe without any pain at all.

21

The testimony of Felthous ended the third day of the trial. On Thursday morning, the thirtieth of April, Byrne called Dr. G. Charles Welsh to the stand. Welsh was a minister who had become a psychologist. Unlike the sleek, disciplined Felthous, Welsh was fat and dressed sloppily. The report he had prepared for Byrne was virtually unreadable, a crude, unrevised computer printout. Though the diagnosis of "major depression, with psychotic features" appealed to Byrne, he was angered by Welsh's devotion to jargon and his lack of attention to detail. The defense had paid for fifteen days of hospital inpatient evaluation and received a hopelessly garbled report. Yet Byrne needed someone to support unequivocally the insanity defense and he had heard from the lawyers that Welsh could be an eloquent witness.

Despite Welsh's limitations Jimmy relaxed and opened up to him during the weeks they spent together. With Welsh he was not afraid to show his emotions and cried easily; for the first time Jimmy admitted that he had shot Chris. Unlike Felthous, Welsh made it his business to know the facts of the case, to know what the detectives knew.

"I want you to tell me how you arrived at your opinion, explain it, and draw upon whatever sources you desire," Byrne instructed the witness.

"I would be more comfortable, if it is all right, to kind of go through the jigsaw puzzle with you all, because I can imagine what a puzzling thing this is for anyone hearing it for the first time," Welsh said. "It certainly was to us."

"Fine," Byrne agreed.

"The question in my mind became 'Who loaded and fired Jimmy Crumm?'" Welsh began. "That is the way I came to think about it. That is, what factors, persons, events in his life led him to the place, loaded him, in a sense, with ways of thinking, feeling, and behaving that would bring this boy to a point where, on that particular occasion, he would indeed fire that gun to kill his stepbrother?"

Immediately Welsh turned to Jimmy's mother for an answer. Like Felthous, he accepted the boy's view of the family. In his testimony Welsh portrayed Sueanne as someone who "tried to abort Jimmy by running up and down the stairs; here is a mother who doesn't want the child before he is born. The picture I get of Jimmy's early childhood is that he lived in a very troubled family, where there was lots of conflict in the marriage, where there was arguing, loud voices, throwing things, breaking things, accusations, blaming, hitting, father hitting mother—I don't know if mother ever hit father, but certainly father hit mother. Here is a little kid who is living with giants—because that is all we are when we are little kids and feeling powerless—observing all of this stuff on the part of the two most significant people in his life, the people that a child needs to make him feel loved and wanted and safe and okay. We are dealing here with an abused child."

Welsh speculated that when mother and son met again seven years later, Sueanne had implicitly said to Jimmy, "'I am not going to be so hard with you; I am not going to be so demanding with you. I am going to give you all of this stuff, lots of clothing and good things. I'm going to give you a lot of material things to make you happy.' The mother does, indeed, buy him a lot of stuff, almost to an outlandish degree—he had, I think, sixty pairs of slacks. She is not hard on him at first, though she does insist that he is going to have to do well in school and toe the line and be home at certain times— all of which seems to make good sense, good child-rearing tactics and policies."

Prompted by Tatum, the judge intervened to ask the witness the source of his information. Welsh replied, "The source of the things I just said in relation to Jimmy's mother is Jimmy."

Welsh confidently expressed his vision of Sueanne's treatment of Jimmy in the months immediately after the boy was reunited with his mother. For the next several minutes Byrne and Judge Fosse let Welsh speak virtually without interruption:

After the first month it appears the honeymoon was

over, that the sweet stuff has ended. Mother now becomes more hardened again. In Jimmy's words, "She really had not changed." She begins to express her perfectionistic ways again, very demanding in terms of his neatness, in terms of the way he behaves himself around the house. I am not talking about just the usual expectations that one would have of a sixteen-year-old boy, but very rigid kind of expectations.

At the same time she begins to talk with him about what a problem Chris is, what a nuisance Chris is, how she just has a terrible time getting along with him, how at times he almost drives her crazy because of his behavior, and how much better it would be without his being around. This kind of talk progresses in degree—that is, it gets stronger—over approximately a year. During this course of time Jimmy hears his mother telling him it would just be a good idea if somebody put Chris out of the way. And she progresses with this to the idea of "You put Chris out of the way."

Intermixed in all of this is an important dynamic going on between mother and Jimmy. Here is son wanting to be loved by mother, wanting to love mother. And mother gives a little bit and she takes it away; and she gives a little bit more, praising him for some things, and then, perhaps, ignoring him or rejecting him or landing on his case for something. This back-and-forth offering and depriving, offering and depriving, is historically the kind of behavior that is used in controlling people against their will. This is used as a brainwashing technique and has been used not only in wartime between countries—I have some familiarity with techniques of the Communist Chinese, for example, in the Korean War—but also some of the cults that we have in our day. I think the Jonestown thing is a good example of this, where there is one man that can exercise such control over these people that they will actually drink poison Kool-Aid.

Jimmy reported to me on one occasion his mother put Quaaludes in his stepbrother's ice cream. On that occasion he reported that to the stepfather, Mr. Hobson, who confronted Mrs. Hobson, who denied it, who then threatened Jimmy.

She threatened him in a direct way and a subtle way. The subtle way was, "How much do you know about poison?" He experienced this or perceived this as a threat. The direct way was threatening him that if he did not do what she required, she would get him into trouble, report him for some kind of parole violation. So he is living under threat and intimidation with this woman whom he wants to love and who he wants to love him.

Jimmy is not a plotter and a schemer. He is a follower, the kind of person who could only successfully carry something off at the direction of and in participation with someone else.

As Byrne neared the end of his direct examination of Welsh, he sought to counter the prosecution's portrayal of his client as a cold, sleek psychopath. "Did Jimmy show any emotion during your interviews with him?" he asked.

"I think about the first thing I said to Jimmy, after listening to him for a while was, 'You are cold,'" Welsh responded. "And that's how he came across to me. He had this hard exterior to him, which I interpret as being very guarded, which my clinical sense tells me is based on his own fear, his not wanting to expose himself. And he maintained this cold facade for, I suppose, the first two hours that I spent with him. Even when I got to the place of talking to him about the murder itself, he would talk about remorse, but I didn't see remorse. It was like the emotion, the expression of it, wasn't there. This is a fairly typical pattern of a person that is fairly depressed or is in some kind of psychotic state and not in touch with his feelings. Not that he is just hiding his feelings from me—he is hiding his feelings from him, usually because they are too fearful or painful for him to deal with."

On Friday, the tenth of April, the second day of Jimmy's evaluation, Welsh noted a dramatic change in the boy's affect. Late that day Jimmy first admitted that he had shot Chris. "He let go of the hard facade," Welsh testified. "His feelings began to emerge. He began to express in a genuine kind of way his confusion, his pain. He was remorseful. He was regretful. He was fearful. He was hurting emotionally. He was crying. He was visibly very upset, wringing his hands, pulling his hair, putting his face in his hands, all of these kinds of things, as the interview progressed. So what I am trying to point out is the contrast between the cold exterior on the one hand and the emotional individual on the other hand."

22

In cross-examination Tatum got to Welsh almost immediately. "Is your approach that of a counseling psychologist in this case, or one who is to evaluate the tests and render an opinion?"

"My motive in attaining the truth is that in this case justice be done; my concern is that this boy gets treatment. He needs treatment." Welsh was, after all, a Presbyterian minister.

Tatum calmly needled Welsh. "Is Jimmy an intelligent person?"

"Yes, he is a bright boy," Welsh answered.

"As smart as you?"

"No," Welsh said.

"You are brighter?"

"Much. May I have some more water, please?" Even the spectators groaned.

In a series of questions Tatum then established that Welsh had simply Xeroxed the diagnosis of Jimmy that was printed out by a computer in Atlanta, that the analysis of the data was all done without the intervention of human hands, for all anyone knew.

Tatum's main intent in cross-examination was not to attack Sueanne's influence on Jimmy, but to show that Jimmy was as dangerous and as manipulative as his mother. Tatum asked, "Do you see the same types of problems that James Hobson has in his mother? Do you see the cycle repeating itself? If you had Mrs. Hobson sitting there, instead of James Hobson, would you probably be coming to the same conclusion, that she is not really responsible for her acts?"

"I don't know," Welsh said, dodging the question. "I have never met Mrs. Hobson and I would want to know more than simply Jimmy's testimony about her to make that kind of evaluation."

"You would want to help her, too," Tatum said sympathetically, half asserting, half inquiring.

"Certainly, if she were in need of help," Welsh answered nobly.

By the end of Tatum's cross-examination Byrne was in despair. Though Welsh's views of Jimmy and his mother closely paralleled Byrne's, the witness seemed too defensive, too passionate, an easy mark for Tatum, who led him around with an arrogance he dared not assume with Dr. Felthous.

23

In his brief testimony Dr. Jan Roosa, Welsh's colleague who had helped diagnose Jimmy, passionately supported the conclusion that the boy was brainwashed by his mother. Dr. Roosa concluded:

He had undergone several months of intensive persuasion—cajoling, intimidating, mind transformation almost. Techniques such as these have been brought out by cults; we know people have been subjected to the point where they turn against their own parents. Over a period of time he was fatigued.

It was a constant kind of thing he ran into, with his mother continually talking to him about killing his stepbrother. Not only did he have to do it, but he owed it to her. He was selfish—the very charge that he was most vulnerable to, that he was selfish, that he hadn't pleased enough. She said this over and over again.

All of this was done by a mother who had rejected him and he himself had taken responsibility for her having done that. He blames himself for that as most kids do. If something hadn't been wrong with him, or if he had been a better person, she would have wanted him. The parents' actions are not parents' actions and decisions in their own right. They are caused by the wrongdoings of the child.

He was hoping that he could somehow gain her acceptance, that she could become a mother that he really wanted. He was extremely vulnerable to this constant repetition to the point where that was all that he could think of. This took over and became the predominant thing in his mind, so that he went ahead and did something which I am sure, under any other circumstances, he never would have done.

Byrne rested his case on Thursday afternoon, the fourth day of the trial.

24

On Friday morning the state called a psychiatrist, Dr. Charles Glazzard, to the stand to rebut the testimony of Felthous, Welsh, and Roosa. On Tuesday evening, in the midst of the trial, Glazzard interviewed Jimmy in his cell.

Dr. Glazzard was the last witness for the prosecution and an able one. He selected several statements from his interview with Jimmy to illustrate that the boy knew right from wrong. "Mr. Hobson said that his mother was a strict disciplinarian, and the father, also. He said, 'I deserved it when they did it,' suggesting knowing why it happened. When becoming involved with a credit-card fraud, Mr. Hobson said he turned himself in to the police, knowing that it was wrong and that he might be caught."

The witness then focused on the conspiracy. "When talking about his mother allegedly encouraging him to kill his brother, he said, 'I continued to put her off. I thought she is not right. I have got to leave her to get her off my ass.' He also said, 'I never was convinced I would do it. I backed out thousands of times. I said to Paul, "I obviously cannot do it." I knew it was wrong when I went down to kill my brother.'"

"Following the murder," Glazzard continued, "Jimmy immediately threw down his gun and, according to him, proceeded to cover the body so it could not be found. And on the night of the arrest he felt relieved; prior to the arrest he kept reliving the events, so that he did not feel right. He, in addition, said he was sorry that he did it."

Through a series of questions Glazzard had been able to get Jimmy to admit directly that he knew right from wrong at the time of the murder, the legal test for sanity in Kansas. "When Jimmy was telling me about his stealing the credit card, I asked, 'Did you know that was wrong?' And he said, 'Yes, I knew it was wrong.' I was at that point trying to determine whether he felt the same way about the night of the murder, and I said, 'Well, did you feel the same way on April seventeenth, that night with your brother?' He said, 'They are two different things. The credit card—I spent a few dollars, I charged a few dollars, nothing special.' So I said to him specifically, 'Did you, then, feel it was wrong, did you know it was wrong that night?' And he said, 'Yes.'"

In his cross-examination of Dr. Glazzard Byrne asked if the concept of right and wrong "could be things that you have learned from parents, for instance, or people in your home."

"It could be," he replied.

"So if a parent has taught you a certain value or has taught you something that is moral or immoral, that is where this aspect of right versus wrong comes in?"

"That could be."

"What would happen, Dr. Glazzard, if a person knew from some source, any source, that there is a law, a law in the law book, that says it is a crime to commit murder, and you will be punished if you commit murder, but that same person had learned from one of these other important sources that you are talking about, church or parents, that murder was moral under certain circumstances? What would happen to that person's mind?"

"I find it hard to imagine that the person could carry that kind of a discrepant position into what you are suggesting might be then an act or not an act."

"It would be an enormous discrepancy, wouldn't it?"

"It would seem to be."

"It would be very, very difficult for the mind to deal with it, wouldn't it?"

"Yes," Dr. Glazzard said.

25

Byrne and Tatum rested their cases before lunch. In the afternoon, before closing arguments began, Judge Fosse read a series of numbered instructions to the jury. Instruction No. 18 went to the heart of the case: "The defendant has denied criminal responsibility because of lack of mental capacity at the time the offense was committed. In law, this is called insanity. The defendant is not criminally responsible for his acts if his mental capacity was such that he did not understand that what he was doing was wrong because of his mental inability to distinguish between right and wrong. If you have a reasonable doubt as to the mental capacity of the defendant at the time of the alleged commission of the offense, then you should find the defendant not guilty because of insanity."

Byrne asked Judge Fosse to add to this instruction that "the burden of proving the defendent is sane rests with the state, the same as all other elements of the alleged crime; that is to say, the state must prove the defendant is sane beyond a reasonable doubt." Byrne's request was denied.

Ed Byrne's summation of the case to the jury was eloquent and passionate. Speaking without notes, he paced about the old, sunlit courtroom, coming toward the jury box, then walking back toward his client and standing near him as he turned and resumed speaking. Judge Fosse would turn his back to him at times when he spoke; at least Byrne remembered it that way. Throughout the trial he perceived Fosse as hostile to the insanity defense. Nonetheless, during Byrne's closing argument, Fosse quickly overruled all of Tatum's numerous objections.

In his closing argument Byrne focused on Jimmy's difficult life and Sueanne's abandonment of her son:

> You know, it strikes me as kind of ironical that on this day Jimmy is where he has been all his life. This is Judgment Day and you twelve are strangers to him; and in a very real sense, that is the way he spent most of his life, alone in the presence of strangers.
>
> I told you several days ago that there was one issue in this

trial, and that was the issue of insanity. I have never really been able to think myself of the words to use to describe it. A witness on that witness stand said it yesterday. It was Dr. Welsh. He said the question is not who killed Chris Hobson, but who loaded and fired Jimmy Crumm. That is what this case is all about.

How do we answer the question of who loaded and fired Jimmy Crumm? Apparently he was a child that Sueanne Hobson never wanted to begin with, because there is an indication directly in the history from Jimmy's dad that Sueanne tried to abort him, that she didn't want him, she didn't want this child, but he was born anyway. And she has to take care of him because Jim is on the road, or working, or drinking, I don't know what. He wasn't around and he admitted that to you, that he wasn't doing what a father should have been doing during part of that time. So the mother is the principal caretaker. And Dr. Felthous told you that from his personal history he determined that there was a definite pattern, from an early age, of physical abuse and, most importantly, emotional abuse.

There are several indications in the history that she may have broken his arm at some point. I don't know whether that is true or not, and I don't really care, because the pattern of emotional abuse is much more important, and that is throughout the record. Here was a little boy—I don't know, three, four, five years old—who she thought was too wild, too active, so pump some Rytalin into him, some kinds of drugs. When you are thinking about drugs, think about that at age four or five. She put something into him to quiet him down, to shut him up, to shut up this kid she never wanted to begin with.

Apparently this little boy had problems with his feet, and that is confirmed by Dr. Felthous. He needed orthopedic shoes and she got them for him; but, at least in his own perception, she was too ashamed to bring him out on the street because of the problem with his feet. In his own words to Dr. Felthous he said, "Finally my feet got better, and I got dingo boots, like all the other kids, and I got to be a normal kid, at least for a while."

As he went from family to family—the doctors described it to you—there was no constancy, no consistency. As he went from family to family he looked at it this way: "It's time to be moving on." This was his life. This was the way he knew life. This was the only life he ever knew.

His mother promised him a lot of things—clothes, a swimming pool, tennis courts, a new life, a new name, the Hobson name, a new beginning, a new identity—and that is irony, too. Some call him Jimmy Hobson and some Jimmy Crumm. I don't think he knows who he is now. He has never known. But she promised him a new identity.

He felt his life was in a rut, he felt he was going nowhere, he felt he belonged to no one. With this young man suffering from this illness, one day, God forbid, Sueanne Hobson comes back into his life. She offered him a lot more than material wealth. She did offer that, which would be probably of interest to any kid of that age. But, you know, that wasn't all that she offered him. All of the doctors, as they recounted for you his medical history, told you how Jimmy thought maybe things will be different now, maybe it won't be like before, maybe there won't be the yelling and the screaming and the abuse and the moving from family to family. "Maybe I can finally have a mom, just an ordinary mom and family life like everybody else has." When these prosecutors, ladies and gentlemen, tell you he killed Chris Hobson because he wanted a new car, you think about that real hard. You ask yourselves whether that was what this was all about.

What did the mother do with her affections? On and off. Affection and recognition and attention for a while that he had been deprived of all of those years, and then off of it again. "Do this and you will get love and recognition; if you don't do it, I will withhold it for a period of weeks, months"—this for a full year preceding the death of Chris Hobson.

So when Jimmy picked up Chris that night with Paul Sorrentino, he wasn't doing it because he was hoping to gain something, a car or some other material thing. He was doing it because he didn't want to lose again what he had been deprived of for eight years. He was finally somebody, Jimmy Hobson. "Here is my mom, here is my dad; here is my little sister, Suzanne, that I haven't seen since she was five." He is finally somebody, but there is always the threat hanging over him that his identity will be stripped from him unless he obeys her.

He is terrified of this woman's omnipotent power. He was sixteen, seventeen, and he had had no mother for all of those years, and his earliest memories of her were filled with all those bitter experiences that we have talked about—the leaving, the abandonment, and the threat of renewed abandonment. And he understood the power that she had, the power to deprive him, to deny him affection, recognition, individuality—the power to say, "If I go, you will be without a mother for all of these years."

I asked the question when I started, "Who loaded and fired Jimmy Crumm on April seventeenth, 1980?" I hope you know that the answer is Sueanne Hobson. Sueanne Hobson, in a very real sense, destroyed three lives that night. This is the obvious one, the boy in this photograph. But no matter what your verdict is, in another sense she destroyed the life of this boy who is seventeen. She also destroyed the life of another seventeen-year-old who has been sitting over in that jail for a year. What has happened to Jimmy, in a sense, is worse than what happened to Chris Hobson.

You are strangers to him. Do something for him that nobody else has ever done, not his mother, not his father, not anybody in his family. Give him an identity. Give him a starting point. Give him a chance to become something and somebody someday.

26

When Byrne had finished, Steve Tatum asked that the jury be permitted to stand and stretch before he spoke. He deliberately sought to destroy the mood Byrne had set.

In his closing argument Tatum dealt brilliantly and insidiously with Byrne's presentation of Sueanne's character. "I submit that the evidence that they say shows that his mother controlled him also shows that the mother and son are a lot alike, manipulative. Interested in material things and wealth—not controlling each other so much as having shared interests. I again submit this shows a picture of a psychopath seeking immediate gain and wealth and gratification."

Tatum picked up the billfold of Chris and displayed its contents to the jury. "We have talked so much about James Hobson that we have almost forgotten in the last three days Christen Hobson," Tatum said, holding up the photograph of Chris. "That is what is left for us of Christen Hobson and his life. An Indian Creek Junior High School card, a picture of his stepmother and father, a social security card. These things he was proud of. There's the picture of him, a young man. It's just about a year now since he was killed, a little over a year, and I want you to think for a little bit about him because we have been thinking so long about James Hobson—his problems and his hard life. Maybe we ought to think about Chris Hobson.

"Imagine him out there on this lonely deserted spot," Tatum said slowly, "digging the grave and seeing them get those guns, seeing Chris Hobson—excuse me—seeing James Hobson load that gun—he said he loaded it right up there by the grave—and then being told, 'Lay down in that grave.' Sometime right in there the cold realization of what was going to happen to him must have broken on him like a wave of panic. Whimpering, sitting up crying. James shot him, tearing his jaw out and his chest and part of his head.

"You know," Tatum continued, "I have got to believe when that dirt settled down around Chris's body and the warmth started going out of him, James Hobson had no idea he would ever get caught. 'We have done it. We have gotten away with it.' But an incredible quirk of fate occurred two weeks and two days later. The body was discovered, decomposed, still there out in that deserted countryside, a thirteen-year-old. And James Hobson should pay for his participation in that affair.

"Imagine James Hobson and his difficult life circumstances, a hard life of sorts," said Tatum. "I don't think it's extremely hard or out of the ordinary. He was always around loved ones. They are here with him." Tatum gestured toward Jimmy's father. "But I want you to see a picture of him standing at that grave site with that shotgun, pulling the trigger, in your minds. Envision that.

"I have seen tears shed for James Hobson in the courtroom," Tatum said quietly, standing beside the jury box. "I have seen him cry. Chris Hobson will never laugh or cry again or do all those things that a thirteen-, fourteen-, fifteen-year-old does as they are growing up and sharing life's experiences. There is no noise of doctor's voices coming around to say he had a hard life and he didn't know what he was doing. All I hear is the sound of his casket being lowered into the ground. Who is going to cry for Chris Hobson?"

27

The jury retired to consider the evidence; they deliberated from two-thirty to four-fifteen that afternoon. They hardly gave Jimmy time to get settled in his cell before they called him back to the courtroom. The jury found James Crumm guilty of murder in the first degree. Byrne made each juror stand up separately and declare his or her verdict.

Judge Fosse would sentence Jimmy later. Byrne knew that the law mandated that he serve fifteen years without eligibility for parole; he would have to tell Jimmy that evening. The sentence would be nearly as long as Jimmy had already lived.

8

WITNESSES

1

Paul Sorrentino, still in jail in Miami County and kept in a cell alongside Jimmy, had filed a petition in 1980 to be considered a juvenile, had it denied, then appealed it. During the appeal he was charged with first-degree murder.

Paul's preliminary hearing on the murder charge was held on the twenty-third and twenty-fourth of February, 1981, a couple of weeks after Jimmy's. The main witness against him was fat Leila Anderson. In a sweet, clear, modulated voice, Leila talked about how she had set up Paul in the police station the day Detectives Douglass and Moore taped her phone call. When she finished testifying, the prosecution played the tape of the phone conversation between Leila and Paul. There were other witnesses—the pathologist Dr. Bridgens; Bruce Layn, Paul's friend who knew about the murder well before the police; detectives from Overland Park—but, for the prosecution, the Sorrentino-Anderson tape, "an admission against interest," was sufficient. The defense did not call any witnesses and bond was set at two hundred and fifty thousand dollars..

After his own conviction in April 1981 Jimmy still refused to testify against his mother. In frustration District Attorney Dennis Moore began plea negotiations with Sorrentino in an effort to secure his testimony against Sueanne.

Sorrentino was never tried. On the sixteenth of June, 1981, he signed a plea agreement with the State of Kansas. He agreed to "testify truthfully and completely as to his knowledge regarding the circumstances of the killing of Christen Hobson." Though Paul had shot Chris twice, the first and last shotgun blasts, the prosecuting attorneys of Miami and Johnson counties, Belling and Moore, "recommended sentencing the defendant as an aider and abettor" of first-degree murder. If the terms of the plea agreement were met, Paul would be sentenced to seven and a half years in prison before he was eligible for parole.

On the nineteenth of June, Paul entered a plea of guilty in Miami County. On Tuesday, the twenty-third of June, in a brief courtroom appearance, he was sentenced to life in prison. Present were Pat Sorrentino, his father, and his brother, Mark. Paul's father was in an angry mood. As he left the courtroom he shouted at the reporters taking photographs of Paul. He yelled, "You don't need any more pictures. Leave the boy alone. Put the camera away! He just wants to have a cigarette. Put the camera in your bag!"

Before the week was out, Paul was transported downstate to the Industrial Reformatory in Hutchinson. Jimmy had already been at Hutchinson for two months. Though the two boys had different work details, they frequently ate lunch together. They didn't talk anymore about the murder, at least to each other.

2

Sueanne had first been charged on the fourth of May, 1980, with conspiracy to commit murder; the charges were dismissed on the eleventh of July for "lack of available witnesses." On the twenty-second of June, 1981, she was charged again. The charges read in part that on the seventeenth of April, 1980, Sueanne Sallee Hobson did "unlawfully, feloniously, maliciously, willfully, deliberately, and with premeditation, hire, procure, aid, and counsel James Hobson, also known as James Crumm, and Paul Sorrentino to kill a human being, to wit: Christen Hobson. . . . Further, beginning in the latter part of March, 1980, and continuing through the third of May, 1980, Sueanne Sallee Hobson, did then and there unlawfully conspire with persons, James Hobson, also known as James Crumm, and Paul Sorrentino to commit the crime of murder in the first degree."

Once Dennis Moore got Sorrentino to agree to testify against Sueanne, he moved faster than the defense expected. Sueanne's preliminary hearing was set for July.

3

Sueanne began to move quite as publicly and quite as quickly. She gave a series of striking interviews to local newspaper and television reporters in the month before her preliminary hearing was held. The first, a front-page interview in the *Kansas City Star*, was published on Sunday, the fifth of July.

Reporter Claudia Kuehl began her article melodramatically. "Who is Sueanne Sallee Hobson? According to the State of Kansas, she is a woman who carried the stereotype of a wicked stepmother to a macabre conclusion—coolly and deliberately plotting the murder of thirteen-year-old Christen Hobson. According to Mrs. Hobson, she is a 'sacrificial lamb' to a district attorney's ambition, an innocent now branded a social pariah, a once-trusting woman stripped of her naivete."

In the interview Sueanne attacked Moore and said he wanted to use her case to publicize his campaign to become the next attorney general of Kansas. She said, "They are sacrificing my husband, my daughter, my parents, and myself—because when this is over we will have nothing. We will have to start from scratch. I don't have anything to hide, and it angers me that I can't say exactly how I feel for fear they'll get up and lie even more than they already have."

Sueanne herself is being persecuted. "Mrs. Hobson said she will not leave the house without someone coming with her for fear of being wounded by a cutting remark, a scathing glance," Kuehl wrote.

"The fact that we have lost a child has been lost in publicity and name-calling and gratification-seeking for those in authority," Sueanne told Kuehl. "The general public does not care about my feelings. This has been so sensational and obscene and out of the norm. It was a big scandal and we felt that everyone *was* talking. And I'm sure everyone was talking. I think we have become an embarrassment to those people who have problems in their own home. We will never any of us be normal again. How can you? You can't go back!"

Kuehl reminded Sueanne that Jimmy would not talk, would not testify against his mother because he still loved her. "Why would Jimmy say that he loves me if I was this terrible person?" Sueanne asked rhetorically. "Jimmy lived in a fantasy world. Regardless of what he has done, I do love him. I will always love him. Ed understands this. He can put himself in my place and say, 'Oh my God, what if the situation was reversed.'"

"If there was any doubt in my mind at all that my wife was totally innocent, she would already be dead because I'd have killed her," Ed interrupted, issuing his implicit threat publicly for the first time. The threat became permanently associated with his character and for years he repeated it in virtually every interview he gave.

Surprisingly, Ed casually acknowledged to Kuehl that doubts about his wife's innocence had led him to divorce her a year earlier. "I was still emotionally upset," he explained.

"Who, finally, is Sueanne Sallee Hobson?" Kuehl wrote, returning to the melodramatic mood with which she began the article. "Is she, as some close to the case have contended, a calculating, icy murderer with instinctive acting skills? Or is the fragile-looking woman with a small, pretty face exactly as she described herself—outspoken and tactless on the outside, naive and insecure inside?"

On the front page of the Sunday paper in the photograph accompanying the article, Ed and Sueanne sat together on their couch in the condominium, both wearing white shorts with identical Kliban cat T-shirts, the fat cat covering half the chest of each. Their legs touched at the knees. Ed sat awkwardly, his left hand holding his right knee; his right hand rested in Sueanne's lap, and she clasped it with both hands. He looked directly at her. She sat on the edge of the couch, her elegant tanned legs and her lean body turned at an angle to his body. Her head, a little higher than her husband's, was turned slightly toward him, her dark eyes looking out just past the plane of his face.

4

On Wednesday, the twenty-second of July, two days before Sueanne's preliminary hearing in Johnson County, a long article on the Hobsons was published in the *Olathe Daily News*. The article was based on two weeks of interviews and a full page of the paper was devoted to the case. Because of its proximity to the Johnson County Courthouse, the *Daily News* was the paper of record read by the hundreds of lawyers and law enforcement officers who worked there. The sensational article, written by Andy Hoffman, transformed the way lawyers, prosecutors, and the public perceived the central figures in the case.

Hoffman, twenty-nine years old, was just a year out of journalism school. He was a handsome, intense man whose head always thrust forward beyond the plane of his body when he walked. His thick hair, half-grayed, strongly contrasted with his smooth unlined face.

As one of his first assignments for the paper, he had covered the Jimmy Crumm trial in Paola. Immediately Hoffman recognized the wide appeal of the complex family drama he saw acted out in Paola. Ed Hobson in particular interested him.

Hoffman entitled the article "Mysteries Surround Life of Ed Hobson." He began even more melodramatically than Kuehl. "If you are the judge deciding this Friday whether to send the mother of Jimmy and the stepmother of Chris, Sueanne Hobson, to trial on the charge of hiring two teens to kill Chris, you will hear again how the child was executed gangland style. But sitting alone in the courtroom is a stranger tale. He is Ed Hobson, the father of the murder victim and the husband of the accused conspirator. You will never hear in a courtroom many of the strange and bizarre tales that have surrounded Ed Hobson for the last eight years because a judge would rule them irrelevant, not pertinent to the murder of Chris. But aren't they? And you will begin to wonder if Ed Hobson is cursed and if he curses those who touch his life."

The article emphasized the violence in Ed's marriage to Shirley and in the death of Tani. Hoffman implicitly associated the violence with Hobson himself. He wrote, "To many the quiet demeanor followed by violent outbursts is typically Ed Hobson."

Rather than focusing on violence, Hoffman focused on Ed's threats of violence. "Through the quiet demeanor of Hobson explodes the violent undercurrent of a man at the end of his rope, a man on the verge."

Certainly Hoffman himself was afraid of Ed and he brought a photographer and a driver along with him when he interviewed him and Sueanne at the condominium. More than a year after the murder of his thirteen-year-old son, Ed Hobson was still angry. Ed greeted Hoffman warmly; he was wearing a T-shirt printed with a sentence directed at Dennis Moore: THEY PROMISED ME JUSTICE, I PROMISE THEM REVENGE.

Sueanne immediately came down from the bedroom to join them. She was wearing a shirt with the name and photograph of the rock group Rush printed on it. Though Hoffman had seen her in court several times, he had never met her. She was wearing red shorts and he was immediately attracted to her. "She was a fox," he said later, "definitely a fox!"

As soon as they sat down at the kitchen table Hoffman said, "I take it you don't appreciate much what Dennis Moore is trying to do."

"The prosecutor wants to make a deal with my son's confessed killer to convict a totally innocent person," Ed said abruptly. "If I didn't know my wife was absolutely innocent of all those charges, she would have already been dead. Oh, yes, if she wasn't totally innocent, I'd have killed her. I knew in my own mind I was confused because I didn't get a chance to talk to her before they arrested her. The prosecutors were pumping me full of stuff about her."

Sueanne sat beside Ed, tilting over a little away from him as he spoke. Ed's intense, rough face and his blunt features looked virile, but unmistakably lower class beside the delicate features of Sueanne. "I feel God has brought us safely this far," she said softly. "He won't desert us now; I have no doubts now that I'll be free."

Hoffman told Ed what he had heard. "According to my sources, the last time Chris was at his grandmother's house, he begged not to go home because he was afraid of Sueanne and Jimmy. Chris said, 'I don't want to go home because he is going to kill me.'"

"Then why didn't they get off their ass and tell somebody?" Ed yelled, half rising out of his chair. "If he told them that, why didn't they do something about it?"

Hoffman thought he saw an opportunity to exploit Ed's loss of control. "I don't want to cause any trouble here, but if you thought Sueanne was so innocent, why did you divorce her?"

Ed sat down slowly, leaned forward, and pressed his tightly crossed arms hard on the glass top of the kitchen table. "I knew in my depression over the murder of my son that I could not at that time make any kind of a fair judgment of anything. They're going to find my wife innocent. It's just the crap you've got to go through to get there. That's why I had her kept from coming home after the murder, because she could've walked in the door totally innocent—as she is—and I could have killed her. And I would have."

"That's right, oh, yes, that's right," his wife said.

"Nobody hurts my family," Ed said. "I have done everything I possibly can to protect my family. They can do what they want to me, if they're big enough, but they leave my family alone. Nobody steps on my toes that I don't step back."

"You need to step a little harder," Sueanne said.

5

The afternoon the article came out Sueanne called Andy Hoffman to discuss it. She said, "I didn't know those things about Ed. They make me afraid."

The public reaction to the *Daily News* article was immediate. Ed suddenly became the feared one; the extraordinary fear of the malevolent mother at the heart of the conspiracy was transformed by Hoffman's article into the more ordinary fear of this simple, vengeful male. Kathleen Dillon, the lawyer who had helped Byrne on Crumm's case, refused interviews with reporters because she feared retaliation by Ed. Even the prosecutors began to consider him a definite physical threat.

Detectives Steve Moore and John Douglass were puzzled by Ed's passionate verbal attacks on the police and the prosecutors. Months after the Hoffman interview, as if nothing had ever happened, Ed would have coffee and breakfast rolls with the detectives in the cluttered cafeteria in the basement of the courthouse during one of Sueanne's court appearances. Ed felt especially comfortable with Steve; though they never discussed the case, they talked easily and laughed warmly at each other's jokes. Yet Ed would say, smiling, "I've got to be careful; Sueanne doesn't like it when she sees me talking to you."

6

In June Paul Sorrentino began to talk with Douglass and Moore for the first time since his arrest. What he had to say was disappointing to the detectives. Paul matter-of-factly narrated Jimmy's offer to repair his motorcycle and the murder of Chris. However, to the disgust of the detectives, Paul admitted that he had never spoken to Sueanne about the crime and that all he knew was what Jimmy told him. The closest Paul came to implicating Sueanne was his claim that he overheard Jimmy's half of several phone conversations with Sueanne. The detectives didn't need an attorney to tell them that Sorrentino's testimony would be no help at all in convicting Sueanne Hobson.

Douglass saw a change in Paul in the year since his incarceration. "The bravado was gone. He realized that it was over, that the system had won, and that he was going to be penalized for it. And I think he was starting to be remorseful. Not necessarily over the death of this person, but at least remorseful over the fact that he was in a position that he couldn't come out of. There was a note of sadness, a note of finality to it."

7

Jimmy, convicted on the first of May, was sentenced in June. Before trial Byrne could have traded Jimmy's testimony against his mother for a lowered sentence; now the state had nothing it could give him and Jimmy had no motive for testifying. Byrne explained to Jimmy that Moore could call him to the stand and the judge could grant him immunity, and then hold him in contempt if he refused to testify. Jimmy told Byrne, "If I'm brought to court, I'll stand mute. I could care less. What more can they do to me?"

In May and June Byrne drove down to Paola weekly, trying to convince Jimmy to testify against Sueanne. Though Byrne was frustrated by the way Jimmy had been treated, he could not bear to see Sueanne go free.

"In our plea negotiations before Jimmy's trial the state somehow believed he would come around to testify against his mother no matter what they offered," Byrne said. "I don't know why. They needed him badly, too; he was all they had. From what Jimmy said, I knew Sorrentino wasn't worth anything to them."

Jimmy gave many reasons for refusing to testify, Byrne recalled. "He'd say he wouldn't do it because it was his mother and he loved her; he'd say he wouldn't rat on his mother. He'd say he didn't get the deal he thought he deserved—'They screwed me; I'll screw them!' He had many motives for not testifying. I thought the most important was one he wouldn't admit to. I'd say, 'You're afraid of getting up there in front of your mother and saying what she did, aren't you?' He'd say sarcastically, 'Oh, yeah, just terrified, scared shitless.'

"He had only just turned nineteen, a kid really," Byrne said. "Confronting her in court gave him real fears—not just over what she could do to him, but what he imagined she could do to him. I told him he should do the right thing and in early July he agreed to do it."

On the thirteenth and fifteenth of July Jimmy was interviewed in Hutchinson by John Douglass, Dennis Moore, and Steve Tatum. Byrne was at the first interview. When Jimmy was asked why he agreed to testify against his mother, he answered,

"Ed Byrne said it was the proper thing. I have no grudge against her, but I'm worried about Suzanne, concerned about her getting into a situation like me."

For Douglass and the others it was their first opportunity to talk to Jimmy and see the dynamics of the Hobson family. "I found that very fascinating," Douglass said, "because suddenly I had the chance to see for myself, to get an inside look at that situation. The way Jimmy describes his mother is frightening—the compulsiveness of her statements to him about doing away with this kid." What Jimmy told the prosecutors was the basis of what he was to say ten months later in Sueanne's trial.

"I still can't believe my mom was able to get me to do it," Jimmy said. "I thought after I killed Chris she'd leave me alone, that I'd get a car and get away from her for the rest of my life." He spoke decisively to the interviewers, spoke with energy, humor, even sarcasm. At the end of the interview he said, "I did it. I know I did it. I accept a hundred percent of the responsibility."

When Byrne talked with Jimmy alone, the boy was much less decisive. Byrne described his client's mood more than a year after the murder. "Jimmy was figuratively beating his head against the wall; he was infuriated at himself for getting into this situation and he'd keep trying out motives for what he did—he was disgusted with himself, angry, and this went on week after week for a very long period of time."

As soon as Jimmy agreed to testify against his mother, Ruth Sallee refused to speak to her grandson again. They talked for the last time on the twelfth of July. He had depended upon his grandmother; she was the last link with his mother's side of his family. He had been calling her a couple of times a week since his arrest and he was puzzled and hurt by her sudden refusal to talk with him. "I don't know what Mother did to win her over," Jimmy said sadly. "After all those years of excommunication, how did Mother get Grandmother back?"

In truth he had little to gain from testifying against his mother. Certainly his life in prison wasn't made any easier. "I caught hell from the other inmates for telling on Mother," Jimmy recalled. "Everybody in prison was put there by somebody else telling on them. There were scare tactics, some physical abuse. I wasn't particularly liked by other inmates; I was ostracized by them. Paul and I were pretty well alone for a time. If we wanted to talk to someone, we had to talk to each other."

8

Sueanne's preliminary hearing was held on Friday, the twenty-fourth of July. Before a crowded courtroom, Hugh Kreamer, Sueanne's attorney, made a motion to close the hearing because of the publicity the case had generated. Dennis Moore and Kreamer argued the motion for more than an hour.

Moore even called reporter Andy Hoffman to testify about the article he did on Ed Hobson. Hoffman was terrified when he had to get up off the front bench where the reporters sat and take the witness stand. Moore, an ambitious politician, loved publicity and he winked at Hoffman as he walked by the prosecution table. All Moore elicited from Hoffman were innocuous details about the circulation of the *Olathe Daily News* and the generous cooperation of the Hobsons during his interview.

Irritated that Kreamer had let Sueanne and Ed give numerous interviews attacking him, Moore asked Hugh why he didn't exercise "client control." He said that the Hobsons had sought this publicity; they had no right now to argue that legal proceedings, ordinarily public, should be kept secret. To relieved, intense whispers of spectators the judge promptly denied Kreamer's motion.

Virtually all the testimony taken in the daylong hearing was given by family members. Ed testified first, then Jimmy and Suzanne.

Chris's billfold immediately became a central issue in the hearing, anticipating the growing importance it would assume in Sueanne's actual trial. Ed had a surprise for Moore. "A week after her arrest," Ed said, "Sueanne admitted to me that she placed Chris's billfold up there at Metcalf South on Friday evening, April eighteenth. I saw the billfold Friday morning in Chris's room. She put it there Friday evening on her way to taking

Suzanne to skating." Until now Ed had never claimed that he had seen the billfold in Chris's room on Friday, not even to Steve Moore after it was found at Metcalf South a week after the murder.

Scott Kreamer cross-examined Ed for nearly an hour. Ed emphasized the closeness of Sueanne and Chris, the cooking class they had signed up to take, the television they supposedly watched in her bed. What Kreamer himself sought to dramatize was Ed's loyalty to her; he wanted to show that Ed himself was the best living testimony to his wife's innocence.

"Why did you remarry her?" Scott asked.

"Because I loved her very much and I knew I was wrong in divorcing her. And I knew she was totally innocent of all these charges."

"Had you felt, Mr. Hobson, that your wife had any part in the death of your son, would you have remarried her December seventh, 1980?"

"Scott, I'd have killed her," he snapped.

"And lastly, if you would please, just describe, the best way you can, what your relationship with Chris was."

"I loved my son, very much. He came before everybody— before everybody and everybody knew that. They knew without me [sic]—or without Chris there would not be me."

"And you have continued to live with your wife, Sueanne Hobson, side by side as husband and wife, correct?"

"Correct."

Sueanne was wearing a tailored off-white dress. When Dennis Moore asked him for the purpose of the court record to point out his wife, Ed said, "Sitting right there, a lovely lady."

Suzanne Hobson took the stand next; she was now fifteen years old and looked older and more poised than her age. She had dreaded taking the witness stand for months. Suzanne had been ill earlier in the day and her lawyer had come in to say how ill she was and how she would testify only if the judge insisted.

In the afternoon Suzanne appeared looking healthy enough and remarkably like her mother sitting down below her to her left at the defense table. Mother and daughter had talked daily for months about her impending testimony, especially about what had happened to the billfold and about the conversation she had with Jimmy in the parking lot. "We'd go 'round and 'round about it. When we'd get done, I'd be so confused I couldn't remember what had happened," she said. Both knew, of course, that the meeting in the parking lot was just one of many encounters that day, knew that Suzanne had repeatedly carried messages and pleas to Jimmy. Yet only the billfold and the meeting with Jimmy in the parking lot required refutation.

Sueanne still admitted no involvement in or responsibility for the death of Chris, even to her daughter. "She could never admit it, even to herself," Suzanne said.

Moore knew Suzanne's interview the night of the murder was critical to his case, perhaps even more critical than Jimmy's testimony. He also knew that she had changed her testimony dramatically from the night of May fourth to the deposition she gave on the eighth. Moore asked, "Did you tell the truth on May 4 to the officers at the Overland Park Police Department?"

"I didn't," Suzanne said.

"What did you tell them that wasn't true?"

"That my mother was involved." She went on to say that Steve Moore and Douglass threatened her. "They told me I had to tell them what they wanted to hear. They kept telling me that my mother told Jimmy to get rid of Chris, 'Didn't she? Didn't she?' And he [Steve Moore] must have told me that about fifty times."

"Did you ever tell anybody on May fourth, 1980, 'that Jimmy and whoever were going to take him out to wherever and get rid of him'?"

"Yeah, I think so."

"Was that the truth?"

"No, it wasn't."

"What wasn't true about it?"

"It just wasn't true. None of it."

"None of what was?"

"That statement."

"Are you talking about the whole statement or the sentence I just read?"

"Both."

"Did you ever say to Margie Hunt, 'These people have told me what I'm supposed to say'?"

"No."

Moore did get Suzanne to speak of problems Chris was causing, "fights, arguments, things, not fistfights" over disagreements "between Chris and I, stuff Chris had done, stuff I had done." He got her to confirm her statement in the interview on the fourth of May that Sueanne planned to keep Ed out of the house by meeting him at Burger King. She testified that her mother had ordered her to take a shower on the evening of the murder. "She told me because I had been on crutches that week that I should go soak my knee." Suzanne also admitted that all the furniture in Chris's room was moved out, though she claimed not to know whether this was done before or after the murder.

Much of Suzanne's hour-long testimony was also devoted to Chris's billfold. On the morning of Sueanne's arrest Suzanne had admitted her mother threw the billfold up there at Metcalf South on Thursday, the night of the murder. On the stand she said, "I don't remember what happened about the wallet."

As she testified Suzanne became increasingly confused. Once she said, "I don't remember what night it was gone because they found it Friday morning." Later she insisted that she herself "found it Friday" in Chris's room, an assertion she did not make again in subsequent testimony.

When Hugh Kreamer got Jimmy to the stand, he intended to show that it was Jimmy himself who was the problem in the family, that it was Sueanne who tried to hold the family together. Kreamer was trying out what he would do on a grander scale in the trial itself. He had been a prosecutor in Johnson County for years and he knew well how to interrogate a witness. Still, Jimmy was a more difficult witness than Kreamer had anticipated.

"Who was the one that tried to hold you all together more than any one person in the household?" Kreamer asked.

"Ed Hobson," Jimmy replied.

"And who else?"

"My mother, I guess."

"And what did she do to try to keep you and Chris and her and Ed and Suzanne living together in an harmonious fashion?"

"Well, she didn't do anything to keep all five of us together in an harmonious fashion," Jimmy said sarcastically.

"I believe you said, in the fall of '79, that your mother said, 'Something had to be done about Chris.'"

"Yes, sir."

"That's all she said, wasn't it?" Kreamer asked.

"First few times, yes."

"Because of what was happening around there between you and Chris, the place was getting kind of in a bad state, wasn't it, as far as the family? Chris was causing problems to Suzanne and you were causing everybody problems because you were evidently getting busted, arrested, thrown in jail. During this period of time you were screwing up in school, using drugs, stealing credit cards, and getting in other trouble, weren't you? And your mother tried to help you out, didn't she?"

"Yes, sir."

"Did Mr. Hobson know about it?"

"I guess, yeah."

"He tried to help you out, too?"

"Yes."

"Do you know your mother went so far as to adopt Chris through a legal proceeding here in Johnson County, Kansas, right up here, sixth floor above this place?"

"No, sir, I wasn't aware of that."

"In fact, Ed Hobson wanted to adopt you, didn't he?"

"It had been mentioned, yes, sir."

"Well, the papers were all drawn and are still sitting in the office waiting for your natural father to approve the adoption, aren't they? Or do you know this?"

"I don't know, sir."

"There was a consent form prepared for you to sign for the adoption, do you know that?"

"I'll take your word for it."

"Okay. Well, it was talked about between the family, wasn't it?"

"It was talked about, yes, sir."

Jimmy was humiliated by what he had to admit in the courtroom and he believed Kreamer sought to humiliate him. He had

owned up to killing Chris and it no longer distressed him to confess to his role in the murder. "What I couldn't take was all the
little stuff I did—having all that brought out," Jimmy said.

And Moore made him confront his mother. In Jimmy's last
moment on the witness stand, Moore asked him if he saw Sueanne
Hobson in the courtroom. Jimmy replied, "Yes, sir, I do. She's wearing the white dress right there at the defense table."

In his closing statement Hugh Kreamer focused on the difficulty the prosecution would have in developing a credible case
against Sueanne. Kreamer said bitingly, "Now I know that this
conspiracy charge is just kind of a free ride for the prosecutor to
get a lot of evidence before a court that he didn't get otherwise.
It's been called 'caring for the modern prosecutor's nursery.'"

There was no act, according to Kreamer. Language alone
seemed to draw Sueanne to the crime; only the conspirators
breathing together gave life to Sueanne's role in the murder.
And two convicted liars, two murderers, would be the chief witnesses against her.

Certainly Kreamer feared Suzanne's testimony. Moore feared
and desired it. He knew that the admission into evidence of her
taped interview with Douglass would be crucial. Despite their intimate knowledge of the case, neither Moore nor Kreamer knew how
closely Suzanne had conspired with the others to kill the boy. Only
the remnants of the Crumm family knew.

At the conclusion of the hearing Judge Earle Jones sat at his
bench for several minutes reading over his notes. Once Moore
caught Hugh Kreamer's eye and they smiled. Suddenly the judge
stopped reading, looked over the silent courtroom for a few seconds, then said, "It appears that certain felonies have been committed in Johnson County, Kansas, and, further, from the evidence,
the court finds that there is probable cause to believe that the
defendant, Sueanne Sallee Hobson, committed said felonies."

9

In the fall of 1981 and in the winter of 1982 the defense regularly
sought and received continuances in Sueanne's trial. The life of

what was left of her family was suspended waiting for the trial. All Sueanne's great energy was given to the case and she discussed her defense endlessly with Ed and Suzanne.

In 1981 Hugh Kreamer was diagnosed with lung cancer. By February he was undergoing chemotherapy treatments and there was little hope that he would live through the year. The Hobson case would be the last and the most sensational of the criminal cases he had tried. Yet his energy was gone. Even in the midst of a hearing, he would sink back into himself as he sat at the defense table, staring out the high windows of the courtroom, seeing only endless sky. "When Dad was healthy," Scott said, "he and I used to come in kicking ass and taking names." The energy came, only fitfully to Hugh now, but when it came he was masterful.

Sueanne, too, was ill that winter. She had a tumor in her uterus the size of a sixteen-week-old fetus and the doctors feared it was cancerous. Beth Clarkson believed that the prosecution of her friend had destroyed her health and Beth feared she would die. A surgeon cut out her uterus and found the tumor benign.

By February of 1982 Sueanne had fully recovered and the Hobsons again began a series of interviews. Tom Leathers was the owner of several small newspapers, magazines, and a cable television franchise. His primary audience was in Johnson County. For his magazine *The Squire*, he did a long interview mixed with commentary on Sueanne and Ed and he strongly supported their views of the murder case. Leathers wrote the article himself, and rather loosely, too, for he was always more interested in the impression things made on him than in the event itself.

In the Leathers article Sueanne and Ed angrily attacked Dennis Moore's conduct of the case; Leathers encouraged their attacks. He had become interested in the case eight months earlier and had interviewed the Hobsons on his local cable television station.

Leathers was a short, plump man of fifty with a large balding forehead, undistinguished looking, but with great energy. His sense of humor, even in the midst of controversy, didn't let him take himself or his views too seriously. A cause was a fitful passion, easily overridden by a new cause. Controversy seemed more a professional tool than the product of a cause.

Leathers dramatized the love and devotion Ed and Sueanne had toward each other, an emphasis he was to develop over the years he wrote about them. He shocked his readers by transmuting a story of malevolence and hatred into a testimony of love.

"Ed's the only one who's taken the time to know me as a person," Sueanne told Leathers. "He understands my likes and my fears—and knows that I'm an outspoken person. He can see beyond that outspoken facade. He's very protective of me."

"She's very warm, very loving, and caring," Ed said.

"Ed kept me afloat during it all. He knows me and he knows my problem is that I believe what everybody says to me. Ed never thought I was guilty or I would have been dead a long time ago. My husband has a bad temper. He believes in protecting his family at any cost. If he had even the most remote suspicion that I planned the murder of his son, I wouldn't be here."

"Nobody hurts my family," Ed declared.

"You don't tell him what to do. He does what he wants to do—regardless. And he doesn't care what you think. Ed is so protective and understanding. He always knows when I'm upset. And he could always pinpoint when I'm wrong. I've never feared that he wouldn't realize the truth. I told him why I said what I said and did what I did. And thank God he understood—as sick and warped and bizarre as the whole thing is. I believe God will do the right thing. He's with me."

"Moore filed charges against Sueanne when it looked like he'd have an election opponent," Ed interrupted angrily. "Then, two weeks later when no one filed to run against him, he dropped the charges. Then he brought them up again when he wanted to run for Kansas attorney general. Dennis Moore is through; he may not accept it, but he is. All because of this case. He doesn't have the guts or the knowledge to get anyplace else politically."

"Ed won't let Dennis wipe his feet on me. We have the facts and honesty and God on our side," Sueanne said.

Leathers ended the article with the Hobsons' attack on Moore. In a parenthetic insertion he noted that two days before the scheduled publication of this interview Moore heard about it and went to "court with a motion to prohibit further comment by Sueanne regarding the case." The motion was granted and pretrial interviews with the Hobsons were banned.

10

The trial was to begin on Monday, the twenty-sixth of April, 1982, a year and a day after Jimmy's trial and during the second anniversary of Chris's disappearance. It was high spring again, the most beautiful season of the year in eastern Kansas. The mornings in late April were unusually cool and clear and the trees had scarcely begun to leaf out.

At eleven o'clock on Sunday night Sueanne took an overdose of tranquilizers. When Ed came upstairs to go to bed, he found his wife unconscious, an empty pill bottle within arm's length. Immediately he called an ambulance. The medics took her to the intensive care unit at the Shawnee Mission Medical Center. The staff treated the case as a routine suicide attempt; they gave her an enema and pumped her stomach. Monday morning, the day her trial was to begin, Sueanne was still in the intensive care unit, though the hospital listed her condition as fair.

The jury was to be selected that Monday and a large panel of prospective jurors virtually filled the courtroom. Hugh Kreamer told Judge Robert Jones of the overdose and Jones dismissed the entire panel of jurors for the day. The rest of the day Jones struggled to keep the defendant's condition secret. He feared that publicity about Sueanne's purported suicide attempt might be seen as prejudicial to her case and warned the prosecution and the defense against revealing it.

By evening Jones knew he had failed. Reporter Andy Hoffman couldn't get anything from the lawyers on either side of the case, so he began calling his sources at the main hospitals in Johnson County. When he got down the list to Shawnee Mission, he called the pathologist Dr. James Bridgens. Bridgens made it his business to know everything and he immediately told Hoffman the details of Mrs. Hobson's sudden illness on the condition that Andy would not say he was the source. Within minutes Hoffman sat down with Judge Jones in his office and told him that he had a scoop: Tuesday morning the *Olathe Daily News* would publish details of Sueanne's drug overdose.

Judge Jones was silent. As soon as Hoffman left, Jones phoned down to the county clerk and told her to dismiss the panel. They would have to start again.

The next morning a new panel of untainted jurors was summoned at considerable expense to the county. Sueanne still complained of nausea, but she had sufficiently recovered so that, in Jones's judgment, the trial could proceed. Jones and the lawyers from both sides spoke to her at some length in his chambers before jury selection began.

When everyone was seated, Hugh Kreamer said to Judge Jones, "I've asked Sueanne if she had any pills with her, and she offered her purse up to be searched, and I didn't feel I needed to do it."

"They gave me an enema and something else, I don't remember exactly," Sueanne interrupted.

"I'm going to make a condition of your bond that you surrender to the sheriff this evening," Judge Jones said. "I'm going to direct that the attorneys surrender you to the jail at the conclusion of whatever proceedings or conferences they have with you. I understand it's not a jail cell; it's an infirmary room in the Johnson County Jail. You will spend the night there."

"Will I be able to take a shower and wash my hair and curl my hair and all that kind of stuff?" Sueanne asked.

"Yes," Jones responded.

Scott Kreamer argued that Sueanne should not be locked up. "She needs to be with her family during this time more than any other time. There isn't any evidence before anybody that she has tried to do anything other than, maybe, just go to sleep."

"Money is not the only concern, but there was a few thousand dollars that the county expended for a jury panel yesterday, and because of the circumstances, I just want to prevent a repeat of that," Jones explained.

Sueanne was concerned about her appearance. "Where will I be able to take a shower and curl my hair and all that kind of stuff? I don't want to go in the courtroom looking like death warmed over."

Judge Jones attempted to reassure her. "We'll make it so you can curl your hair over at Kreamer's office."

"I'll have to wear a sack over my head," she said.

"Just get a bandanna," Scott suggested.

"I don't want to go back to jail," Sueanne said plaintively. "The main thing that I'm worried about is my daughter has one month left in school, okay? She's had two years where she's never been able to finish school, and that worries me." She paused. "Will I be by myself?"

"Yes," Jones replied.

"Good. Do they have showers in jail?"

"Yes," Scott said.

"Amongst everybody else?"

You've been to camp, haven't you?" Scott asked.

"No, I haven't been to camp," Sueanne said. "I was always shy."

Judge Jones turned to Scott Kreamer. "The court is going to order that you not allow her to take any medication."

"I'm on estrogen; I take two estrogen at night," Sueanne interrupted. "I have to have it because I don't have any insides left."

"Okay, I understand," Jones said. "My wife just had a hysterectomy last summer, so I understand what you're talking about." Jones dismissed the defense and ordered all to assemble in open court in fifteen minutes.

The selection of the jury consumed the rest of the day. At least half the prospective jurors questioned admitted they were biased against Sueanne. After the panel was chosen, the Kreamers found it especially difficult to select alternate jurors who did not believe she was guilty. One of the panelists dismissed said that she had been a substitute teacher in Chris's class at Indian Creek "three days before the Thursday Chris disappeared."

11

By eight Wednesday morning a line of spectators extended from the doors of the courtroom all the way back down the marble stairs leading up from the cold, barren hallway. Most came in groups of two or three. Though many were fat, middle-aged women, well-fed men working evening shifts were there, too. The courtroom was high and spacious, but the seats were long, barren, wooden benches, like pews in a church; there was room for less than two hundred spectators.

When the doors were opened, the line moved slowly and security was unusually tight. Because of Ed Hobson's reputation for violence, an image mainly generated by Hoffman's article, Dennis Moore asked that Judge Jones order Ed to be searched each time he entered the courtroom. Jones agreed to do it, further increasing the public's conviction that Ed was actually dangerous and, in some way, involved in the conspiracy to kill his son. Of course the Hobsons took this as confirmation that Judge Jones was biased against them.

At nine o'clock the crowd pushed into the narrow hallway leading to the courtroom and past the bailiff. Already many of the seats were taken by relatives, friends, or secretaries of the lawyers and the Court. Dennis Moore's new wife was there and Scott Kreamer's beautiful, wealthy aunt. Judge Jones himself had his lean, attractive, red-haired wife sit separate from others in an old high-backed chair on the side of the room opposite the jury and well inside the balustrade that kept jury and lawyers away from the reporters and spectators who pressed against it.

Jones, a handsome man of fifty, tall, thin, with a mustache and a long patrician face, looked the part of a judge. His quiet demeanor flattered his power. Still, as Ed Byrne said, if Jones ended up saying the right thing, he started to say it far too many times. Frequently he couldn't find the end of a sentence after two or three tries. He had no gift for language, for fluent speech, but he had patience with himself and with others and was slow to come to judgment.

No cameras were allowed in the courtroom; on great white sheets of paper artists were sketching Sueanne Hobson and her lawyers for newspapers and television channels. At least thirty reporters, though intensely competitive and jealous of each other, huddled together like a separate school, turning coldly and contemptuously away from the intrusions of observers.

12

What everyone came to see was a family terribly at odds with one another—a husband who defended a wife charged with murdering his son, a son who accused his mother of ordering him to kill her stepson, and a daughter who accused her brother of murder.

The spectators didn't have long to wait to get to the family. The prosecution called Ed Hobson as its first witness and Ed walked quickly and firmly to the witness stand.

"Would you please point Sueanne Hobson out to the jury?" Moore asked.

"She's that lovely lady sitting there," Ed said, gesturing with his head toward the defense table.

Moore began with a series of questions attempting to establish the source of tensions between Chris and Sueanne. "You had been bachelors with Chris for a couple of years, is that right?"

"Right," Ed responded.

"And during that time you weren't always so tidy?"

"No, I'm not—I don't like housework very much."

"Was Chris a tidy person at first?"

"No, not really."

"Did that ever cause any conflicts with Sueanne?"

"Oh, you know, when we first got started, sure, you know."

"What did she say to you about Chris?"

"Oh, she says—well, I can remember a couple of things. Chris would take the dishes out of the dishwasher and he'd set them in the cabinet. He didn't line them up or anything like that, and these little piddly things, you know, would, oh, upset her to a great extent for a while until he started getting used to some of the things, and he'd bitch back and he said, 'Why does it have to be this way?' and I said, 'That's the way she did it. She does ninety percent of the housework and everything, you know, so this is the way she wants it and it's a good idea for you to learn it because this way you also learn to take instructions from—whether it be a schoolteacher or from your mother or what.' And that's one thing Chris always did, even before we got married, he always called her Mom."

"What kind of housekeeper was Suzanne? Was she like Chris or more like Sueanne?"

"No, she was a lot like her mother. She was real fussy about the bathroom and Chris would clean the bathroom—he's just a little sloppier."

"In 1980 what were your observations about Sueanne's relationship with Chris?"

"They were getting closer. There was a lot less tension around the house. The only one we were having any problems with was Jimmy."

"Right. Now this cooking class that's been mentioned that your wife and Chris were going to attend together, when was the cooking class supposed to begin, do you remember?"

"I believe it was either the last of—I think it was the last of April or first of May of 1980. It was one of these deals Sears had put out, I think, Sears or Ward's, it was a—you know, a basic microwave-type cooking class, if I remember right, and cake decorating because we'd just boughten a new microwave and stove combination and it was—as I said, I don't remember whether it was Sears or Ward's that put it out, but it was one of those, oh, like a sewing-class-type things you see advertised on TV and things."

"Okay. Had they enrolled in that class?"

"Yes, they had. Sueanne had."

"What other things did Chris enjoy doing with his mother?"

"Oh, cooking. Or they'd go out and pick up pinecones. So many little things. They loved to—Sueanne did not like to swim, Chris liked to swim, but they would go out and they had the hose there on the back porch and they'd sunbathe together and they would watch television together. I don't know, there's just so—"

"Things a mother and son normally like to do?" Moore interrupted.

"Well, yes. I saw nothing unusual at all," Ed concluded.

Many of the spectators were disbelieving, whispering to each other. "'I saw nothing—I see nothing,'" one woman mocked in a whisper.

"You said that Chris would kiss Sueanne Hobson before he went to school?"

"When I was there he did, yes."

"When did you normally go to work?"

"I normally went to work at seven o'clock in the morning."

"Did he go to school before seven o'clock?"

"No, he didn't." Ed paused for a moment, suddenly realizing the contradiction Moore had brought out; he added defensively, "I can only tell you what I saw."

In fact, Ed so thoroughly perceived that things had been normal in the household that, later, when Scott Kreamer tried to elicit testimony critical of Jimmy's treatment of Chris, Ed insisted, "I saw no big problems. Neither one of them ever came to me and had any hassle that I know of. Jimmy used to get a little disgusted about taking Chris down to counseling; we'd let him take him down since he had a driver's license and I was still at work and Sueanne was busy here and there. This was part of Jimmy's chores to earn his allowance—to take Chris back and forth to counseling."

Moore was particularly interested in what Ed knew about Chris's billfold and approached the issue obliquely. "What did you do on the eighteenth? The day after Chris disappeared?"

"Searched. I searched his room and found his billfold, found his school identification."

"When did you see it?"

"Oh, I saw it the morning of the eighteenth. It was in his desk. He got some shelves and he would put his books under here, and he's got three shelves here," he said, gesturing. "It was a wrought-iron desk with a wood top, had a little lamp on it, and he had it stuck back under some papers there. I found it underneath his bed; I found it in his pillowcase."

Moore interrupted, irritated by Ed's elaborate narrative. The plethora of details were either designed to show that Ed remembered vividly the moment of discovery or demonstrated, as they usually do in others, a well-made lie. "So sometimes he carried it and sometimes he didn't, is that right?"

"Well, normally if he was out of the house, yes, he would carry it, unless he was going out to play. He always carried it to school every day. But, I don't know, like kids play cap guns and stuff, he would hide things at times, you know, and he always—

his billfold was very special to him, so he would hide it at night. That was just fantasies-type things."

"Did you have any conversation with Sueanne Hobson about the billfold?"

"I can't remember having a conversation about it."

"All right. Mr. Hobson, you told me on April eighteenth you saw this billfold in Chris's room, is that correct?"

"Yes, it was."

"Did you ever find out how the billfold got to Metcalf South, Mr. Hobson?"

"Yes, I did."

"And how and when did you find that out, and from whom?"

"I found that out from my wife when we were talking about it a week after the whole thing happened."

"And what did she tell you?"

"She said that Jimmy threatened her and that if she didn't cooperate with him that he would kill the three of us—or two—" Ed looked puzzled; what he had told was one of many versions.

Moore broke in. "My question is, what did she tell you about the billfold?"

"Well, I'm trying to get to it Mr. Moore, if I can," Ed said loudly in his echo-chamber voice, his face reddening.

"Let me rephrase the question. Did you find out from your wife how the billfold got to Metcalf South?"

"My wife took it up there Friday evening."

"She told you she took it up there Friday evening?"

"Yes, she did. It was there Friday morning." Ed meant there at the house apparently.

"She told you why she took it to Metcalf South?"

"I guess so they would think Chris was a runaway, to keep the police looking for him, and to protect her son."

"Did you have any questions about her explanation?"

"No, I didn't—you know. No, I was—I really didn't. I don't remember having questions."

"You didn't have any questions about why she hadn't told you she knew what happened to Chris?"

"Oh, I knew that, I knew the answer to that. She had already told me that and I was very—I know me well enough to be very well satisfied with that answer."

"During the next several days, say the week after April seventeenth, did you have any conversation with Sueanne or did she suggest to you where she thought Chris might be?" Moore asked.

"Oh, she said, 'It's possible he ran away.'"

"What did you say to her?"

"I said, 'No, my son wouldn't run away.'"

"Did she seem satisfied with that?"

"Oh, she was very upset during this time. I was at the point where I was damn near refusing to go to work. She was very upset; it was a very emotional, trying time."

"Did Sueanne make any statements to you during this period of time as to where she thought Chris might be?"

"She said she thought maybe he ran away," Ed repeated.

"Is that the sum and substance of all the conversation you had with her?"

"Right, you know."

"When did she first tell you that she knew what had happened to Chris?"

"After he was found."

"How long after he was found?"

"A week."

"A week?" Moore pretended astonishment. "Did you have conversations with her between May third, 1980, when Chris was found, and the week that you just mentioned when she first told you what had happened to him?"

"No."

"You didn't see her in that week?"

"No, Mr. Moore," Ed said abruptly. He was irritated by the prosecutor's emphasis on the period when he doubted her innocence and first filed divorce papers. After a momentary pause he began to ramble. "I was very emotionally upset. The police were trying to tell me things that happened that I knew—I knew they were wrong in what they were saying, but I had—I couldn't comprehend anything at this time. I just lost my son. I came to your office, I believe it was the next Monday. I knew—"

"Mr. Hobson, stop, stop just a minute, please," Moore interrupted. "My question was, 'Did you have any conversations with her?' and I believe you said, 'No.' Is that correct?"

"That's right."

"How did she come to tell you a week after Chris was found that she knew what had happened to him, Mr. Hobson?"

"I asked her. It was in our house. The date I don't remember. It was approximately a week."

"And what did she say?"

"About what?" Ed asked defensively. "What did she tell me?"

"Yes, sir."

"She told me that the reason she didn't tell me what had happened to Chris was several things. Number one, Jimmy had threatened to kill Suzanne and I if she said anything. And she said he had already killed Chris. She also knew that if she had told me at this time, I would have found Jimmy Crumm and Paul Sorrentino and I would have killed them."

"And these were the two reasons—or were there others?"

"Yes. Later she told me that she was doing it to protect her son. This was her only son and her—"

"Did she tell you that at that time?"

"No, not at that time."

"When did she tell you that?"

"Oh, I guess it was a week, ten days later, maybe two weeks, someplace in that time there."

"When did your wife tell you that she first knew what had happened to Chris?"

"Jimmy called her Friday afternoon of the eighteenth. I presume the way she told me it was prior to Jimmy coming over to the house. He gets there five, five-thirty, six o'clock. I know I went over to his apartment that day and he wasn't there."

"So she knew on April eighteenth what had happened to your son Chris, is that correct?"

"The evening of the eighteenth, yes."

"And for the next seventeen days or sixteen days she didn't tell you what had happened to Chris, is that right?"

"No, she sure didn't."

"Even though you were very upset about what had happened to Chris?"

"Yes."

Ed's defense of Sueanne included within it a powerful indictment of her. Repeatedly he acknowledged Sueanne's silence during the two and a half weeks before Chris's body was discovered.

In his opening statement Moore called the defendant's silence a "charade of ignorance." Already that silence began to tell on the jury and the spectators. Ed portrayed himself as a man desperately searching for his lost son. He portrayed his wife as the woman who knew about the murder, yet feared to tell him because Jimmy and Paul threatened her family and, paradoxically, because she wanted to shield her only son. Apparently Ed perceived no contradiction between the silence Sueanne endured because of a threat and the silence she chose to protect the son who threatened her.

Relentlessly, Moore pursued Sueanne's silence. To many of the spectators and jurors it was as if the silence itself were a crime committed over and over again, hour by hour, for more than two weeks. The perception of the crime escaped Ed, its living victim, yet even the dumbest and least sensitive juror could understand her betrayal of trust and love. In the midst of Ed's professions of her innocence her silence was what the jurors and spectators would carry with them that evening when they left the courtroom. It was either a malicious act or an astounding failure of courage.

When Scott Kreamer cross-examined Ed, he made him into a character witness for Sueanne, not the father of the murdered boy. "My understanding of your testimony is that at some point in time after the body was discovered you had a conversation with your wife and she admitted to you that she had learned of Chris's death prior to the discovery of the body, is that right?"

"That's right."

"And she told you this?" Scott said emphatically, as if to demonstrate the forthrightness of Sueanne.

"Yes."

"And she told you that she'd taken the billfold to Metcalf South?"

"Yes."

"And she told you why?"

"Yes."

"And later on you divorced her?"

"Yes."

"And you knew all of her reasons for why she had done these things?"

"Yes."

"And do you believe her?"

"I believe her very much."

"And I believe she told you that she had taken the billfold because she wanted to protect her son?"

"That's right."

"And that she was frightened for the rest of the family?"

"Yes."

"Okay. Did you find anything about her explanation for not telling the police or not telling you to be inconsistent or incongruent?"

"No, I could understand her completely."

"Why did you remarry her?" Scott asked.

"Because I love her; I know she is innocent and she didn't do anything to deserve this."

"And you've lived together at the same home as husband and wife since that time, correct?"

"Yes."

In his last questions to Ed, Dennis Moore also dealt with Ed's devotion to Sueanne. "Mr. Hobson, do you love your wife?" he asked.

"Very much."

"And you would do anything you could to help her?"

"Except lie, Mr. Moore," he said sarcastically, ending his testimony with a small triumph.

Once, in the midst of Ed's testimony, Moore asked the Judge to declare him a hostile witness, a designation that would help him question Ed with greater freedom. In his response to Moore's request Judge Jones characterized Ed's testimony precisely: "He does not appear to be a hostile witness—although maybe an adversary to some extent, he is certainly not hostile."

On the whole Ed Hobson elicited sympathy from the jury. To the jurors he was a simple, passionate man who couldn't disguise his emotions. His awkwardness in attempting to remain loyal to the contradictory interests of both wife and murdered son only made him appear more sincere.

If he had suspected his wife's involvement in his son's murder, he would have killed her, he had said. No one who heard him say it disbelieved him. As usual, he was Sueanne's living testimony of innocence.

13

On Thursday morning, the third day of the trial, Lailoneh Teed took the stand. Moore assigned Steve Tatum to question Teed; throughout the trial Moore reserved the major witnesses for himself.

"Lailoneh, are you nervous?" Tatum began quietly. Tatum had spoken to Lailoneh the day before; he wanted to put the jury at ease, if not Lailoneh herself, and she agreed to describe her physical condition directly.

"I have cerebellar idiopathic tremors. When I'm under stress, it causes a lot of shaking, so, you know, it makes it look worse than it is."

"What is your relationship to Ed Hobson?"

"He was married to my mother, so my relationship would be he was my stepfather."

"What is your relationship to Christen Hobson?"

"Chris was my half-brother."

"And how did you feel about Christen Hobson?"

"Well, he was my brother and I loved him very much."

"Sunday night, April the twentieth, 1980, did you receive a phone call?"

"Yes, I did. It was from Ed Hobson."

"And at that time did you know that Chris was missing or gone?"

"No, sir, I didn't."

"What was the nature of that conversation you had with Ed Hobson?"

"It was about seven o'clock on a Sunday night and he called and asked if I had seen Chris. And I said, 'What are you talking about?' I didn't understand, you know. And he said, 'Well, Chris is missing and I thought maybe he had come to Oklahoma.' And I said, 'You're kidding! I mean, you know, what are you talking about?' And he said, 'Well, you know, he's been missing from home and I think—I don't know what's happened to him. I think he's run away and I thought maybe he had come up to Tulsa.' A couple of days later the police showed up and asked me if they could look around and I said, 'Sure, feel free. I have nothing to hide.' They came in and they went through the house and searched it and said, 'Thank you,' and they left."

"As a result of having the police come out and the conversation you had with Ed Hobson, did you try to get ahold of the Hobson residence yourself later that week?" Tatum asked.

"Yes, it was on a Thursday, the twenty-fourth of April. I tried about four or five times, and about the fifth time Sueanne did answer the phone. It was in the afternoon." The twenty-fourth was the day Detective Steve Moore organized a field search for Chris.

"Would you relate, please, for us the conversation you had with Sueanne Hobson at that time?"

"Well, I was upset because the police had come to my house and I called to talk to her about it or to Ed and to ask them what was going on, you know, and so she said, 'Well, that was just routine; it was just something that the police were doing.' I had talked to my aunt, who called me. I had heard something about a theft of credit cards and Chris had turned in the person who had stolen the credit cards."

"Are you talking about Jimmy?"

"Jimmy, yes. And my aunt was worried that something might have happened to Chris, foul play."

"And what, if anything, did Sueanne tell you about that? Did she say who had turned Jimmy in?"

"'First of all,' Sueanne said, 'Chris did not turn Jimmy in, we did, because we felt that he should pay for what he had done.' There was a mention of a shotgun and I made the comment, 'Do you know anything about the shotgun? The person that I talked to seems to feel that Jimmy might have had something to do with

Chris disappearing.' And at that time she said, 'Oh, yeah, Jimmy took him out in the woods and shot him and we turned his room into a disco.' I just said, 'Oh sure,' or something like that. I thought she was being sarcastic."

The spectators, accepting Teed's narrative on Chris, murmured at Sueanne's audacity. Lailoneh's testimony about Sueanne's sarcasm seemed too precise to be believable. Certainly Sueanne found it so, whispering to her lawyer and shaking her head.

"What else was said during the conversation?" Tatum asked.

"She said that Chris had taken some things with him and that she thought that he was probably at a friend's house. When he came back, she was going to hug him and kiss him and then probably hit him in the head with a two-by-four for making them worry so much. She said, 'If I hear anything, I'll call you.'"

Scott Kreamer briefly cross-examined Lailoneh. "Ms. Teed, who was the person you talked to who told you about Chris having turned Jimmy in about stolen credit cards Jimmy had used?"

"My aunt, Jerry Wilson."

"And what did she say to you?"

"She called me on the phone and she said, 'Have you heard that Chris is missing?' And I said, 'Yes, I have, Ed called and told me.' And she says, 'I think something's happened to him, you know. You knew about the stolen credit cards and the shotgun missing from the house and all of that?' And I said, 'No, I didn't know anything about this.' And then Aunt Jerry told about how, supposedly, Chris had turned Jimmy in for stealing a Mastercard and that she felt that, maybe, Jimmy had a personal vendetta against him."

"I believe you stated you have met Sueanne Hobson in all of your lifetime on just one occasion, correct?" Scott asked.

"I was on vacation and we had come for dinner."

"And how long were you with Sueanne Hobson on that one occasion?"

"About four hours."

"Four hours in your lifetime you've spent with her personally, right?" Scott asked.

"Yes, sir," she said.

In his last question to Lailoneh, Tatum sought to develop further Lailoneh's strongly negative characterization of Sueanne. "Did you try to get ahold of Chris from time to time?"

Kreamer objected immediately. In an argument before the bench Tatum told the judge that Lailoneh had tried to contact Chris several times during the Hobson marriage and was turned away by Sueanne. "Sueanne was not agreeable and would not assist her in seeing Christen," Tatum said out of the hearing of the jury. The judge sustained Kreamer's objection and Lailoneh was permitted to step down from the stand.

14

Suzanne was scheduled to take the stand next, but the lawyer who served as her guardian asked that she be given a grant of immunity against prosecution. After a half hour of discussion Judge Jones granted his request.

The girl walked to the witness stand hesitantly. She was wearing a full-length black leather coat over her dress; she looked much older than fifteen and greatly resembled her mother. Dennis Moore resumed the questioning. "Would you please describe for the jury the relationship you observed between Ed and Chris Hobson?"

"It was fine. They got along great," Suzanne answered casually.

"What did you think about the relationship you had with Chris?"

"It was pretty good, the normal relationship."

"Normal relationship?" Moore echoed.

Suzanne nodded her head up and down emphatically. Moore was irritated and his face showed it. Just like Ed had told him earlier, everything in the family was normal, but Chris just happened to come up dead.

"Did you have fights at times?"

"Yes."

"Did you have some good times?"

"Yes."

"What about the relationship between Chris and Jimmy?"

"Well, it was good sometimes, but mostly Jimmy ignored him."

"Did Jimmy get on him or just ignore him?"

"He got on him once in a while."

"What about?"

"Oh, things Chris had done and things that made him mad."

"Can you remember any of those things?"

"Just little stuff that made Jimmy mad. Anything made Jimmy mad, so it didn't take much."

"Did you make Jimmy mad?"

"Yeah."

"What did he do when he got mad at you?"

"He screamed and cussed at me."

"What did he do when he got mad at Chris?"

"Did the same thing."

"Did he ever hit you?"

"No."

"Did you ever see him hit Chris?"

"Not—I didn't—I never saw him hit Chris, no."

"Would you describe the relationship that you observed between Chris and your mother?"

"It was the best one in the house," Suzanne said extravagantly.

"He had a better relationship with your mother than he did with Ed?"

"Well, it was about the same. I mean, they got along fine."

"So you got along—" Moore began.

Suzanne interrupted. "Sometimes it was rough, but that's expected."

"What were the problems, though? I'd like you to be specific." Moore was frustrated by her curt answers, answers devoid of ambiguity and complexity.

"Well, when Chris and I got in fights and, you know, it was just stuff Chris and I—we got in fights and Jimmy and I got in fights."

"So what would happen when you and Chris or you and Jimmy got in fights?"

"Well, we'd go tell our parents and then they'd talk about it."

"Who would you go tell?"

"My mother."

"Who would Chris go tell?"

"Ed."

"What happened then when they talked about it?"

"Sometimes they got in an argument, sometimes they didn't."

"Were there any problems in the early months of 1980? Were there any problems between your mom and Ed at that time?"

"Oh, when Chris and I got in fights. I mean, they may not seem a big deal to you or anybody else, but to somebody my age and Chris's age, when we got in a fight, it was a big deal. We'd yell and scream at each other and we'd end up going to tell our parents."

"Did they do anything about it?"

"Well, it all depends on the situation. I don't really remember. They'd talk about it or they'd have a disagreement about it."

"Do you remember any situations at all?"

"Well, when Chris had spread rumors about me to my friends and I out found about them and I told my mother and they had an argument about that."

"What did Chris spread a rumor about?"

"That I had done bad things up at Skateland South."

"What kind of bad things?"

"I would take my clothes off."

"And that wasn't true, of course, was it?"

"No."

"Was your mom upset about that?"

"Yes."

"Was Ed upset about it?"

"Yes."

"Did it cause any problems between your mom and Ed?"

"Oh, just—they had a fight about it."

"How do you know they had a fight about it?"

"Because I could hear them arguing upstairs."

"Did Chris cause any problems between your mom and Ed?"

"Yeah, we all did. Chris did, Jimmy did, and I did."

"And you told somebody on May fourth that Chris was causing problems between your mom and Ed?" Moore began interrogating Suzanne about her statements to the police the morning her mother and brother were arrested.

"Yes, I did—and so was I."

"Did you ever tell anybody there had been some serious problems between your mom and Ed over Chris around April seventeenth, 1980?"

"Oh, yes."

"Was that true?"

"Yes, to me they were serious."

"Were you ever present at a conversation between your mother and Jimmy on April seventeenth, 1980?"

"Yes, I was there."

"Where was that?"

"In the parking lot of Jimmy's apartment complex."

"And who else was there?"

"Jimmy, my mother, and me."

"Would you tell me about what you heard in the conversation?"

"I didn't hear much at all. I was in the car."

"Did you hear anything?"

"Not really that—no, I didn't."

Moore approached the bench. "Let me hand her this statement and we'll see if we can refresh her recollection," he said softly to Judge Jones. He passed over a transcript of Sueanne's police interview the morning after Chris's body was found.

Despite objections by Scott Kreamer, Judge Jones ruled, "At this time the court feels that that would be an appropriate way to allow her to refresh her recollection."

Moore turned back to the witness and passed her a copy of the interview. Suzanne scarcely glanced at it.

"Suzanne, have you refreshed your recollection by looking through this statement?" Moore asked.

"Yes, once," she answered.

"Once what?"

"I've read through it."

"Well, have you looked through it today and do you remember what you said by looking at this?"

"I haven't read it today, no."

"Do you want to do that?"

"No."

"Why not?"

"Because I've already read it."

"So you remember what was said?"

"Yes."

"Now, having looked at this statement, do you recall any more about that conversation?"

"No."

Moore returned to the bench; he wanted Suzanne declared a turncoat witness. "Judge, you saw her refresh her recollection. She thumbed through that in two seconds."

Judge Jones responded promptly. "The court realizes the relationship of this witness to the defendant and the court realizes when she reviewed the statement and looked it over that she said she didn't need to. She went over it and didn't look at it that closely. From her reactions the court finds that she is a turncoat witness. The court will allow the state to cross-examine her."

Moore turned back to the witness. "Miss Hobson, did you make the statement that date at that time that 'Jimmy and whoever were going to take him out to wherever and get rid of him'?"

"Yes, I did."

"What were you talking about?"

"Well, I heard that something had to be done about Chris, meaning that Jimmy had to talk to him, but not in the sense of killing him."

"Well, who said anything about killing him?"

"The cops did."

"Who did you hear talking about something had to be done about Chris?"

"John Douglass and Steve Moore told me the morning that they came by to my—our house."

"You didn't hear your mom talking to Jimmy Crumm about that?"

"No, all I heard was, 'Something had to be done.'"

"Who said that?"

"My mom and Jimmy."

"All right. When was that?"

"I guess that day, I don't know."

"Suzanne, did you tell anybody about a conversation on April seventeenth in the parking lot at Jimmy's apartment?"

"Yes, I did."

"And was that when you heard your mom and Jimmy talking about, 'Something had to be done about Chris'?"

"Yes."

"Thank you, Suzanne." Moore was just barely able to control his frustration. He was pacing. "And did you say that you heard them talking and that you heard them say, 'She told Jimmy that something had to be done and he said, "We'll go out and get rid of him"'?"

"I don't remember that. All I remember saying is that—them saying that something had to be done."

"Would you like to refresh your recollection with State's Exhibit 15?" Moore again offered the transcript of the police interview to Suzanne.

Suzanne took the transcript and found the passage. "Yeah, it says, 'He said, "We'll go out here and get rid of him."' I don't remember saying that, but I don't ever remember hearing that." She was confused and upset, garbling her responses to Moore.

"Well, did you say that or did you not say that?"

"I don't remember."

"Did you say, 'I don't know, they left for Burger King or something. She got him out of the house, she said that she's going to get Ed out of the house'?"

"Right."

"Where did you get that information?"

"Huh? Well, I knew they were going to Burger King so Jimmy and Chris could talk."

"So Jimmy and Chris could talk," Moore repeated flatly in a tone that emphasized his impatience. "What were they going to talk about, Suzanne?"

"What Chris had—" She paused. "The problems Chris had been causing."

"And what kind of problems had Chris been causing that Jim was supposed to talk to him about?"

"The rumors that he'd been spreading—that he did spread around about me."

"Anything else?"

"No—well, just the problems we had been having, stuff Chris had done."

"Well, what else had Chris done, that's what I want to know," Moore insisted.

"Just all I remember is the rumors that he spread around about me."

"Did your mom tell you what had happened to Chris when he didn't come back on April seventeenth?"

"No."

"Did she have any conversation at all with you about that?"

"No."

"Did she say anything at all that Chris wouldn't be coming back?"

"I don't remember, she could have, but I don't remember."

"Did you ever ask her where Chris was?"

"Well, Ed—the cops were looking for him—"

"No, my question, Suzanne, did you ever ask your mom if she knew where Chris was?"

"No, I didn't ask her, but I heard her saying to Ed he probably ran away—or he ran away. I didn't know he was dead until the cops told me that morning."

"Did you say to Detective Douglass on May fourth, 'Oh, she said that Jimmy went out and took care of him, so I wasn't sure'?"

"That's what the detectives told me that she said that Jimmy had told them." Suzanne's layered response was very confusing.

Judge Jones interrupted. "The court will direct the witness to answer the question and the question is very direct."

"Yes," Suzanne finally admitted. She was terrified that she herself would be charged with perjury and, perhaps, even conspiracy.

"Did you hear any conversation between your mother and Jimmy about getting rid of Chris?"

"Getting rid of Chris, no, I don't remember."

"Did you hear any conversation between your mother and Jimmy about killing Chris?"

"No."

"No, or you don't remember?"

"No."

"Did you say to Detective Douglass on May fourth with regard to killing Chris, 'They didn't really say that word for word, they were just going to get rid of him, that's all they said'?"

"Yes."

"You said that?"

"Right, but that didn't—to me they didn't say 'kill.'"

"But I asked you a minute ago if they were going to get rid of Chris and you said you didn't remember that?"

"Right," Suzanne agreed. "But you said right then 'get rid of' as in the meaning of killing."

"Did your mother tell you where you were to be on April seventeenth, 1980, when Jimmy came to see Chris?"

"Yes."

"What did she tell you?"

"To be upstairs."

"For what purpose?"

"To take a shower."

"Why were you to be upstairs?"

"To soak my knee because I had been on crutches that week."

Suddenly Moore switched to the billfold. "Did your mom have any conversation with you about Chris's billfold?"

"No, I don't remember anything about the billfold."

"Did you make any statements to anybody about the billfold on May fourth, 1980, specifically John Douglass and Steve Moore?"

"I could have. Obviously I made the statement, yes, but I don't remember anything about the billfold. I didn't know anything about the billfold until they told me where it was."

"Did you tell John Douglass and Steve Moore on May fourth that your mom threw the billfold up at Metcalf South?"

"Yeah, I did, but—"

"That's enough, thank you," Moore interrupted. "Did you tell Detective Douglass on May fourth that your mother told you, 'She said that Jimmy went out and took care of him'?"

"I don't remember that."

"You're not saying you didn't say that?"

"No."

"Did you hear a conversation between your mother and Jimmy about Jimmy getting a car or some money?"

"Yes. About, maybe, three or four weeks before Chris disappeared."

"And who was present during that conversation?"

"My mother and Jimmy and I and I don't know if anybody else was or not."

"And what did you hear?"

"That the money that my mother got from the court hearing she had pending, that she would help him buy a car."

"Do you know when your mom threw the billfold—Chris's billfold—up at Metcalf South?"

"No, I don't remember."

"Are you saying, Suzanne, that the things you told Detective Douglass and Detective Moore are not true?"

"I don't remember, I don't remember anything—hardly anything—about that conversation."

Moore concluded his cross-examination and passed the witness over to Scott Kreamer.

Whenever Suzanne had a chance, she attacked her brother's character during her cross-examination by Moore, insisting Jimmy was the one who brought his problems and drugs into the house. She also stressed his anger and his loss of control. Suzanne betrayed Jimmy and she was filled with remorse. She knew that Jimmy had never discussed her role in the murder.

Suzanne did again indicate that her mother had dropped the billfold at Metcalf South, and because of clumsy questioning by Scott Kreamer, she seemed to say she had dropped it on the seventeenth. She also affirmed that three or four weeks before Chris's disappearance she and her mother and Jimmy had discussed buying her brother a car.

In his last examination of Suzanne Moore asked, "Did you talk to Ed about the problems that you had with Chris regarding Skateland?"

"Yes."

"Did Ed tell you to do anything about that?"

"Ed said he'd talk to Chris, but evidently it didn't work."

"So then Jimmy was supposed to talk to him after that?"

"Right. And it worked," she said.

"Yes, it worked," Moore said sadly as the spectators gasped.

15

Suzanne's testimony had taken most of the morning. When she was allowed to stand down, the jury was led from the room and the sparring over whether to admit into evidence the tape of her interview began. John Douglass was called to the stand to describe how the tape was taken, but he was soon ignored and the lawyers stood before the judge's bench arguing about its admissibility. It was afternoon now and Judge Jones decided to recess for lunch.

Hugh and Scott Kreamer ate on the south side of the courthouse square in a long darkened tavern with linoleum on the floor. They sat in a brown, dirty booth with Hugh's beautiful, blond sister-in-law and her friend. Both lawyers were despondent. If the tape were admitted, they said, the case would be over; they might as well not even call their witnesses, might as well rest the case.

John Douglass had a quick lunch in the small cafeteria in the basement of the courtroom and made his way up through the crowded hallways back to one of the two witness rooms to set up Suzanne's tape on the cassette player. The courtroom was cleared and the spectators had to line up again in the hallway for the afternoon session. The witness room was empty and Douglass left the door ajar as he reviewed sections of the tape to make sure that nothing had happened to it in the two years since the interview. Apparently Suzanne's voice carried back through to the other witness room. Douglass said, "I was back getting the tape ready to be played and Ed Hobson charged in the door in a rage and yelled, 'What do you think you're doing?' I said, 'Ed, I'm going to play this tape in about five minutes.' He goes, 'Oh, well, yeah! yeah!' and kind of calmed back down, and then he said, 'It was so loud, everybody could hear it outside.' I said, 'Well, I'm sorry, I don't know what gave you that idea. If it's too loud, we'll make sure it's turned down.' That was all he said, and he went back in the other witness room." That was the only time Hobson ever said anything harsh or threatening directly to Douglass or to any other detective.

When the trial resumed, Scott Kreamer and Dennis Moore began arguing again out of the hearing of the jury over admitting the tape as evidence before the judge. When they returned to open court, Judge Jones said, "The court notes that the witness testified and she was frightened; she denies portions of the statement and didn't recall others. The court notes that the witness indicated that what she was to say was suggested to her." Then he paused for a moment and declared, "The court is going to allow the tape recording for the jury to consider, for whatever benefit it might be for the jury, in determining what did transpire." The jury was brought into the courtroom and Douglass played the tape for them. A written transcript of the tape was flashed on a large screen near the jury box so that the jurors could read it as well as listen. After the tape was played Scott decided not to cross-examine Suzanne.

16

It was midafternoon now and the prosecution called Margie Hunt-Fugate to the stand. Margie entered quietly. She was a striking woman of thirty-five, with blond hair dyed a little too light for her skin. She wore a tight skirt over her broad hips and her garters showed softly through her skirt as she approached the witness stand. The young women reporters whispered together, smiling, "I wonder what she does for a living? What do you think?" She seemed when she came in to bring something with her, something not quite visible.

Tatum questioned her first and she looked directly at him. He asked her where she worked in March and April of 1980. She said, "Brookridge Country Club. I was a bartender and a banquet waiter." During that period Margie said she saw Sueanne several times a week at the condominium.

Before Tatum could go any further, Hugh Kreamer objected

and argued that Sueanne would have to testify before Margie could be questioned about conversations with his client. Otherwise it would be hearsay. Out of the hearing of the jury Tatum declared, "The proffer of what she will say is this: Sueanne asked her if she knew anyone in the Mafia who could take care of somebody and then she further was asked if she knew whether or not the name Sorrentino was the name of a Mafia family. I'm not quoting exactly, but words to that effect certainly would qualify as an admission against interest. In fact I have several quotes that would show the state of mind of Sueanne Hobson regarding Christen Hobson." The Kreamers objected vigorously.

Tatum narrated another incident in which Jimmy, Sueanne, and Margie were riding in a car together. Tatum said Margie, after Chris's murder, confronted Sueanne. "You probably asked Jimmy to take Chris out in the woods and waste him or something, to do away with him," Margie said. According to Margie, Sueanne and Jimmy, who were in the car, did not respond at all. "There is clear law on that," Tatum said. "Silence in the face of accusation is admissible evidence."

Even Scott Kreamer qualified his objection to the last statement. "I'll agree, that's a closer question," Scott said.

After a half-hour debate Judge Jones ruled for the defense. "The court will find that those prior statements would be hearsay excluded under the hearsay rule at this time," he declared.

Again Tatum began to question Margie, but after two or three exchanges Hugh Kreamer objected again. Exasperated and confused by the judge's rulings, Tatum gave up and said he'd recall Margie later and he would now call another witness. It was nearing five and Judge Jones adjourned the court for the day.

17

On Friday morning, the thirtieth of April, the fourth day of the trial, Tatum again argued out of the hearing of the jury that the statements Sueanne told Margie about Chris "would not constitute hearsay and that they're not being offered to show the truth of the matter asserted; they're offered to show her state of mind at that time. Since these are intent crimes and require an intent, it is a most essential part of the state's case to show there is a motive involved as to why she would intentionally want to do something to Christen Hobson." Overnight Judge Jones had completely reversed his position and he now permitted Margie to testify, ruling that her testimony about Sueanne's intent was an exception under the hearsay rule. Tatum, despite repeated objections by Hugh Kreamer, was able to proceed fairly quickly now.

Margie said, "Chris had been causing a lot of problems between her and Ed and she couldn't put up with that any more. Sueanne said she hated him and she wished that he was gone; she wanted him out. She said he had been determined to be an extremely violent primate schizoid. She said that he wasn't mentally right, that it had been determined that he should be put away, that he shouldn't be left in the home atmosphere, that for his own good he needed to be put in an institution."

Margie also told the court about Sueanne's plans to redecorate Chris's room, "to completely redo the room as a study." She also told Tatum about celebrating Chris's disappearance with Suzanne and Sueanne in Belton, Missouri, the day after his murder, and about Chris's clothes that Sueanne had given to her.

Tatum asked if Margie was ever with Sueanne and Jimmy during the weeks before the body was discovered and, if so, did Sueanne appear to be frightened of her son. Margie said she was with Sueanne and Jimmy "quite a bit," that Sueanne did not appear to be frightened of him, and that after the murder she and Sueanne visited his apartment "a couple of times. I remember one afternoon we went over and brought him an iron and different household things that a young man would need starting up his first apartment."

When Tatum was finished, the damage Margie had done to Sueanne was perceptible. There were passion and confidence in her answers. Immediately the Kreamers sought to bring up the charge that Margie had stolen Sueanne's jewelry. Standing before the bench, out of hearing of the jury, Scott said, "You can tell by the tone in her voice that she's vindictive against our client. It's obvious she is because of what's happened. She's been sued; a judgment's been rendered against her; my client filed a criminal complaint against her." The argument continued for more than a half hour while Margie sat quietly on the witness stand staring down at her lap and the spectators whispered together in boredom and frustration. Finally Judge Jones said, "This is a collateral matter. The court is not going to get sidetracked into a squabble as to whose property it is." The defense was permitted to ask about the jewelry, but not to mention the legal steps courts had taken inquiring into the matter.

The jury was brought in again and Hugh Kreamer began to question Margie about the jewelry. Hugh established that Margie had not answered the suit the Hobsons had filed and a default judgment of forty thousand dollars was issued against her while she was residing in Connecticut. Hugh was not allowed to state that because of this default judgment, there was a Kansas warrant out for her arrest.

After another series of objections by Tatum, Hugh Kreamer returned again to question Margie. Drawing out his words, his voice dripping with contempt, he asked, "Is it Mrs. Fugate, is that what your name is now? Or Hunt?"

"Hunt is my maiden name," she said curtly. "Fugate was my married name, but since there is a new Mrs. Fugate I go by my maiden name."

Everyone perceived Hugh was mocking her. "I just wanted to know how to address you," he drawled out.

"Margie," she answered curtly, and looked directly at him. When she said it, the spectators almost jumped. It was as if she had slit his throat by that word, as if she had defined honesty for that moment.

Kreamer never recovered; in the rest of his cross-examination of her she was in charge and said what she liked. "She knew she was being fooled with and she just laid him out," Detective Douglass said later. If at times she seemed too angry, too certain, too passionate, she had a courage in the face of threats against her that many admired and all felt.

"Now, I believe you testified that Sueanne described Chris as an 'extremely violent primate schizoid,' is that right?" Hugh asked.

"Yes."

"Where did she get that language, do you know?"

"She said she got it from Bob Craft on some testing that he had been doing on Chris."

"So when Bob Craft shows us his records, that will be in there?"

"I don't know," she said reasonably.

"Okay. She said he was not mentally right?"

"That's right."

"You said she said he needed to be put in an institution, is that right?"

"Yes."

"Did she mention any attempt to do that?"

"She said that she had tried, but Ed wouldn't have anything to do with it; he refused to let Chris leave the home."

"Where did she try to put him?"

"She didn't name a specific institution."

"And as far as Chris's room, you say she was fixing it up as a study, is that what you told us?"

"Yes."

"Are you telling us that Ed knew that she was trying to put Chris in an institution?"

"She told me that she had discussed it with Ed."

"Okay. Was Chris ever around there when you were around there?"

"Yes."

"Did he act like an extremely violent primate schizoid?"

"No, he didn't."

"Did he seem mentally all right to you?"

"He did to me."

"I believe it was yesterday you said something about Sueanne wanting you to find some Mafia type to do a job for her, right? Is that what you said?"

"She asked me if I knew anybody in the Mafia, if I had any idea what it would cost to have somebody taken care of, or if I had ever heard the name Sorrentino connected with the Mafia."

"Okay. When was that?"

"It was around the first of April, maybe the end of March."

"Did you call the police and tell them that?"

"No."

"Why not?"

"Why should I?" She was clearly his equal and he tried to answer her questions.

"I don't know. It sounds threatening, doesn't it?"

"It sounded a little strange."

"And that's all? That's all, it just sounded strange?"

"Sure, it sounded strange."

"And did you tell some police officer about it at all?"

"No."

"When you say that our client here, Sueanne, told you that she wanted to get rid of Chris, when was that?"

"Several times."

"Well, like when?"

"Through the whole course that he lived with them."

"Well, would you have any idea why she'd go out and spend the money to adopt him as her own child, then? Does that make any sense to you?"

"No." Margie's simple answer turned the question back to an indictment of Sueanne and a statement about her character.

"Did it seem strange to you that this child, that she supposedly hated, she was taking down to Dr. Craft for family counseling and trying to put the family together as a unit? Did you know that?"

"Yes."

"And it seemed, I guess, strange to you, or something, that Chris's bedroom was the one in the house that had not been redone, right? Did it strike you as funny?"

"Yes."

"Did they remodel and redecorate the rest of the house?"

"Yes."

"And they were doing it room by room, weren't they?"

"But something was done in every room."

"Aren't you the one that they gave some furniture to so they could get new furniture and make his room into what you call a study?"

"After he was gone," Margie said, dramatizing Sueanne's behavior between the murder and the discovery of the body.

Margie was clearly in control of the interrogation.

"They called it a den?"

"After he was gone."

"What?" Hugh Kreamer appeared confused.

"She gave the things after Chris was gone," Margie emphasized.

Irritated, Hugh foolishly persisted. "Well, I know it was after he was gone, but it was before anybody knew what was wrong with him, wasn't it?"

"What?" She feigned confusion, emphasizing the absurdity of the question.

"It was before his death was known, wasn't it?"

"Was known to who?"

"Those things were given to you?"

"Was known to who?" she repeated.

Surprisingly Tatum failed to perceive the effect on the jury of the devastating question Margie repeated. He stood to object to Hugh's question on the grounds of clarity and let him escape for a moment.

"What all did they give you out of that house?" Hugh asked.

"Some of his clothes, some of his sheets, a bedspread, his desk and chair."

"How long had she been giving you some of Chris's outgrown clothes for your own kids?"

"That was the first time she ever had."

"And is that your testimony?"

"Yes."

"Under oath?" Sueanne said sarcastically. For the first time in the trial the court reporter noted Sueanne's angry exclamation. Presumably the judge heard Sueanne also, but he did not admonish her.

"Did she give you some shelves from the garage?" Hugh asked.

"Yes."

"And they gave you a dresser from the basement, do you remember that?"

"I thought it was out of his room."

"Well, I know what you thought. That isn't where it was," Hugh said.

"Shit!" Sueanne exclaimed. Again Judge Jones did not admonish her.

"Did they give you a dresser?"

"Yes."

"And you say that during your long acquaintance she never gave you any of Chris's outgrown clothes before?"

"No."

"Do you remember making a statement on the fifth of May, 1980, I think it was, while you were on the elevator with Ed Hobson and a couple other people that you knew she was innocent and you'd do everything you could to help her? Do you remember making that statement?"

"I was never in the elevator with Ed Hobson."

After Hugh Kreamer finished, Tatum carried up to Margie the box of Chris's clothes that she had been given by Sueanne and briefly questioned her about them.

When Tatum sat down, Hugh stood and asked one last question, apparently not quite realizing what had happened in the last hour. "One more thing, did you try any of these clothes on your children?"

18

In the past two years Suzanne had missed Margie. It was as if Margie disappeared off the face of the earth the day of Chris's funeral. After Margie's testimony and the publicity it engendered, Suzanne sought to see her, despite her mother's disapproval. "All mother would talk about was how Margie stole her rings," Suzanne said. "She couldn't get it out of her head that her best friend had walked away with her diamond rings. I didn't care about that. She was somebody I liked and trusted and had known since I was little."

Suzanne phoned Detective Moore, but Moore would only say he'd contact Margie and have her attempt to reach Suzanne. She herself called Margie's sister and brother-in-law in Oak Grove, Missouri, in the hope that she would be there, but Margie's brother-in-law insisted that he knew nothing about where she was and he wouldn't even take Suzanne's number or her message.

19

Jimmy Crumm was called next by the prosecution. He looked like someone who knew he was in for an ordeal and wasn't prepared for it; he first slumped and soon slipped down in the witness chair after he was sworn in.

In a series of questions Dennis Moore elicited from Jimmy a narrative of his life up until the day he accepted the Hobsons' invitation to join their household. The rest of Moore's questions focused on the period from May 1979 to May 1980.

Moore asked Jimmy what Sueanne told him in the early fall of 1979 about Chris's relationship to Ed. "She said that Chris tried to control Ed," Jimmy answered. "It seemed to bother her." At that time Jimmy did not recall any serious problem. "The only problems that I can remember would have been family problems, where one of us would act out or goof up or something."

By late fall of 1979, Jimmy said, "The conversations started turning more serious; she was saying that something had to be done about Chris and that she was thinking about military school or something, but something to get rid of him. I usually didn't say too much because at first she was just talking about going to military school or a mental hospital or something. When they started taking a more serious tone, I usually just hurried to get the conversation over with so I could leave. She was making implications that she wanted him dead. She wanted to know if I knew of anybody that could get rid of him for her."

In February Sueanne was talking to Jimmy two or three times a week. "She was insistent that something be done about Chris in a hurry, that he was causing unrest around the house. She said that she couldn't understand why I couldn't do this one little thing for her. I was just getting desperate to, you know—so I would be left alone, and so I just approached Paul Sorrentino."

"Jimmy, when we started today you told me you didn't dislike Chris. Now you're thinking about finding somebody to get rid of or kill Chris, is that right?" Moore asked.

"Yes, sir."

"Why?"

"So my mother would leave me alone."

"Were you afraid of your mother?"

"I don't know." For Jimmy, now twenty, to admit before a crowded courtroom that he was afraid of his mother was a humiliation. Though he didn't quite admit his fear, he felt humiliated.

"Did you usually try to do what she said?"

"Yes, sir."

"Why?"

"That's what was expected, you know, to do what she said."

"Well, you didn't always do what she said, obviously, did you?"

"No, sir."

Jimmy testified that his mother had asked him in February of 1980 "to make it look like a drug overdose or a suicide or something like that," and that she had scheduled his hunting trip with Chris. Still, she gave no specific instructions about how Paul and Jimmy were to kill Chris once they had abducted him. Moore pressed Jimmy on this, for it appeared to be a weakness in the conspiracy, a lacuna in the story he wanted filled. Omission of detailed plans did not fit Moore's conception of Sueanne's character.

"Was there a discussion about how this killing was to be done? I mean were you to use poison or knives? Did you ever talk to her about that? Did she ever say?"

"No, sir." Yet later Jimmy testified that "she wanted him gotten rid of and then she meant, you know, kill him, and then she asked if there was any way that she could help or if I would teach her how to, like, fire a gun."

Jimmy didn't remember the climactic scene in the plot against Chris, the meeting of the Crumm family in the parking lot the evening of the murder, a scene that both Suzanne and Sueanne recalled in detail. His mother had phoned him at his apartment at five, he remembered. "She wanted to know why Chris was at the house and why we had not picked him up from the racquetball courts like we had said we would. I told her we had decided not to do it."

"So what did that have to do with making you decide to go ahead and do it?"

"She said that it was too late to back out now, that if Chris came home and found the things missing, he would tell Ed when Ed got home and she said that Ed would kill her." Jimmy seemed to forget that Chris, according to his mother's report and his testimony a minute before, was already at home.

Jimmy narrated the murder of Chris for a quarter of an hour. When asked if he told his mother these details, he responded, "No, I didn't want to."

Moore concluded his examination of Jimmy by asking what psychological term his mother used to describe Chris's mental illness. Jimmy replied, "The term was schizoid primate, I believe."

Jimmy came out relatively unscathed from Moore's questioning in the morning. After lunch things were different. Hugh Kreamer had a bad morning with Margie and needed a good afternoon with Jimmy to recover. Hugh said to the judge, out of the hearing of the jury, that Jimmy was "the only real witness they've got; this is the key accuser of the defendant. Only two people in this would know who did it or what happened, this man and our client." Hugh seemed to forget Suzanne momentarily.

The Kreamers pressed hard on Jimmy's insanity defense in Miami County. If Jimmy thought he was insane, then an insane man is the chief accuser of his mother. When asked if he had any "mental defects" or mental "disease," Jimmy repeatedly said he did not know, in part because his murder conviction was still on appeal to the Kansas Supreme Court.

This jury, Scott Kreamer said to Judge Jones, is not bound to find him legally sane as did the one in Miami County. "They may think he's crazy."

Under pressure from Hugh, Jimmy lied on the stand about certain aspects of his crime. To Hugh he insisted, for example, that the car he was to get for killing Chris was never talked about before the murder and provided no motivation for him. And he did agree finally that he "possibly" said he hated Chris and that he was upset and angered by Chris's narking on him. He denied knowing the name of a girl he dated who lived across the street from him and who was soon to testify. He denied telling his cousin David Reffitt that he was going to kill Chris.

Jimmy had some difficulty lying. He looked quite uncomfortable, and when the lawyers would go up to the bench to argue, he would stare down at his lap throughout the hiatus, never raising his eyes to look around the courtroom. In those long intervals he appeared virtually asleep or drugged. If the confidence and righteous passion Margie exuded gave her extraordinary force as a witness, the hesitant manner of Jimmy and his lack of energy diminished the power of his remarkable assertions.

Hugh Kreamer made clear that Jimmy had used every kind of drug one could name–Valium, LSD, speed, marijuana, alcohol. Jimmy sought to exaggerate his use of drugs throughout all the legal proceedings against him. He seemed to think the influence of drugs removed some of the opprobrium from what he had done. When he killed, he was stoned out of his head, he said, and even when he confessed, he was drunk.

Hugh sought to demonstrate that the intention to kill Chris could not have come from Sueanne because no clear intention to kill existed on the highway down to Miami County. He came surprisingly close to demonstrating this. Jimmy didn't like to admit that he was as cold-blooded as the facts of the case made him out to be.

"In your mind at that time as you were going down the highway, where were you going?" Hugh asked.

"To Wichita," Jimmy said. "I was thinking of a way to get out of killing him. I wasn't sure until I saw the sign that said Wichita and then that's when I had an idea. Just take him to Wichita and put him on a bus and leave."

"When you took him from the house and started down the road, you didn't ever intend to kill him, did you?"

"Sir, we've been over this before," Jimmy said, asserting himself for once. "I told you that it was not my idea, not my intention."

Moore objected vigorously to Kreamer's tactics. In the hearing of the jury Hugh said, "Well, let's don't go around the mulberry bush here. He's the one that did it. She didn't. And if he had no intention to kill, and it grew up somewhere out of

Sorrentino's warped mind in another county, she couldn't be guilty if we stayed here the rest of our lives." The judge ordered that Hugh's remarks be stricken from the record.

At the end of Jimmy's testimony Kreamer noted that he had been kicked out of school, that he used drugs, that he stole, then asked, "Are you sure it wasn't you that was causing the problem in the household? Answer that truthfully."

"I couldn't be for sure, sir," Jimmy replied.

When they let him off the stand, Jimmy felt that he had done badly, felt Hugh Kreamer had had his way with him.

Jimmy was the last witness on Friday, the thirtieth of April. Dr. Chester Day, Sueanne's psychiatrist for the last two years, had made arrangements for Sueanne to be admitted to Suburban Hospital. "The court," Judge Jones said, "will allow her to be released solely in the presence of her husband or one of her attorneys for the purpose of going to her attorney's office in trial preparation, but for no other purposes. She will be required to remain there in the hospital room and not receive any visitors and receive only such medication as directed by her physician."

20

On Monday, the third of May, exactly two years after he handcuffed himself and was arrested on the steps of his father's town house, Sorrentino was called to testify. Paul seemed a comic figure, at least to the rows of reporters that day. He was outside the family, outside the family's intense passions, a gratuitous addition, hardly worth interest or attention. While Paul testified Tom Leathers whispered, laughing softly, "Three hundred fifty dollars to kill a boy! We could pass the hat around here and collect that much."

Though Paul's sentence before an opportunity for parole had been cut from fifteen years to seven and a half years by his agreement to testify against Sueanne, the state got very little from him. Still, they got all the evidence he had against Sueanne.

In response to Tatum's question Paul described Jimmy's invitation to kill. "He came to me back in early '80 and he explained to me that he had taken Chris out hunting and tried to shoot him, and that he couldn't, and he wanted somebody with him. And in that same conversation he also stated that his mother had tried to give Chris an overdose of Quaaludes and cocaine."

Paul had had no conversations about the crime with Sueanne herself. Tatum's direct examination lasted no more than ten minutes.

Hugh Kreamer, on the other hand, had plans for Paul and he totally dominated the witness. He would ask Paul a question and Paul would look down as he answered and Hugh would say, "Now look at me! Look at me Paul, when I talk with you, please!"

Like Jimmy, Paul described the murder of Chris, though quite briefly. When he finished, Hugh said, "And you're the one that fired the first shotgun blast into this poor child sitting in this ditch, aren't you? And you're the one that all the authorities let plead to something less than first-degree murder, didn't they? Our client is charged with first-degree murder and she never left home."

Paul, like Jimmy, claimed that, without drugs, "I wouldn't have done what I did." Kreamer asked him what "stoned out of your mind" means. Paul said concisely, "To be aware of your surroundings and yet not really caring what happens." Like the others involved in the case, he appeared to be quite intelligent.

Kreamer did make one mistake in his effort to cut Sueanne off from Paul. "All those things you've heard about any disagreement Sueanne Hobson had with Chris came from Jimmy, did they not?"

"No, sir," Paul said.

"All right. What didn't?"

"Well, when I was over at the house the few times that Chris and Sueanne were home together, I always had the impression that she never really cared for him; she didn't want him around."

"Did you know she'd gone to the trouble and expense of adopting this boy as her own son?"

"No, sir."

"So when all the media for two years has been saying it's her stepson, they're wrong. It's her own loving son." Half the spectators and even some reporters in the crowded courtroom gasped or whispered or laughed out nervously. Judge Jones ordered the crowd to be quiet and threatened to clear the courtroom. Later, after Sorrentino finished testifying, Jones excused the jury and awkwardly admonished the spectators again. "This is not a public hearing in the respect of your going to have a say in something like a town meeting."

Hugh Kreamer then explored Paul's version of the abduction of Chris. He knew what Paul would say and he began ironically. "Jimmy Crumm said you went in the house and sat down at the table and told Chris a big story about you going out on a drug scam or something, right?"

"No, sir."

"And you weren't ever there, were you, to pick up Chris?"

"I was with Jimmy when we picked Chris up."

"But not at the house?"

"As best as I can remember, no. From what I remember, we picked him up around five-thirty at the Fox Hill Racquetball Club." Kreamer sought to make much of this discrepancy. If Paul were correct, then Sueanne was tied much less closely to the abduction. She did not pass Paul and Jimmy on their way in to the condominium to get Chris, as Paul asserted. Further, if Paul were telling the truth, Jimmy demonstrably lied about the events of the murder, another in his series of lies. Certainly the jury would expect Paul to remember where he picked Chris up, and if the place of the pick up did nothing else, it confused the time frame of the murder.

Kreamer wanted as much convincing detail as he could get. "Where did you park at Fox Hill?" he asked.

"The parking lot across from Fox Hill. Jim ran in and got Chris and came back."

"And you never went back to Chris's house; you got right on the road and started down the ol' highway, right?"

"As best I can remember."

Hugh Kreamer had handled Paul superbly; he sensed that Paul was a pleaser, that he wanted to please not just Moore, but him too. That afternoon Kreamer had cast doubt about some of the crucial details of the murder and he had cut off Sueanne from Paul in a convincing way. If Paul was one of the conspirators, one of the two major accusers of Sueanne, he had nothing significant to say about her involvement. Kreamer wanted to leave Paul, the way a bullfighter turns his back and struts away from a puzzled bull.

"Did Sueanne Hobson ever pay you one red cent for this heinous crime?" Hugh said indignantly.

"No, sir."

"Did you ever go to her and say, 'Sueanne, I want my money'?"

"No, sir."

"Because she'd never told you she was going to give you any, did she?"

"She didn't, no."

"That's right. And all the information that you got that led up to this murder, which is what it was, came to you from Jimmy?"

"Yes, sir."

"Thank you for being truthful, Paul," Hugh said gently.

In his midfifties, Hugh Kreamer, who would be dead in five months, still could, at times, summon enough energy and skill to perform the way he had done for years before his illness. Even many of those who had no sympathy for Sueanne were pleased by the skill of his performance, especially the lawyers who stood in the center aisle or leaned against the back wall to watch him.

After Kreamer finished, it was now more clearly a family matter than ever. Paul's testimony had not touched Sueanne; only her two children had damaged her defense.

21

Neither Paul Sorrentino nor his family was convinced of Sueanne's role in the conspiracy. Pat, Paul's father, had said to Jim Hooker that he himself had doubts about Sueanne's involvement and didn't believe they would convict her.

While Paul was in the Johnson County Jail in late April and early May waiting to testify, he told two prisoners with him in Cell Unit 6 that Sueanne was not involved. According to Jeffrey Wood, one of his cellmates, "Paul said that Sueanne Hobson had nothing to do with the killing of Chris Hobson, but that Paul had to say that she was involved in order to take advantage of the prosecutor's offer for an early release from prison. Paul acted as though he was very proud of having murdered Chris Hobson; Paul's killing of Chris Hobson somehow appeared to feed Paul's ego."

Mark Williams, also in Cell Unit 6, spoke of similar statements Paul made. "Late one night—approximately two to four in the morning—I do not know how we got on the subject, but we began talking about the trial of Sueanne Hobson. Paul said, 'I don't think she had anything to do with it; in fact, I know she had nothing to do with it.' Paul Sorrentino said that the reason he knew Sueanne had nothing to do with it was because Jimmy Crumm had originated the idea because he thought Chris Hobson was going to receive a large amount of money and Jimmy figured he could get some of this money if Chris was dead. Paul told me that the reason he was implicating Sueanne was 'to watch out for Paul.' He repeatedly told me, 'She's going to get off! She's going to get off!'"

9

PRIME MOVER

1

After lunch Dennis Moore called Detective John Douglass back to the stand and had Douglass read aloud the last brief taped interview he had done with Sueanne just after dawn on the fourth of May, after he and Detective Moore had talked with her daughter, Suzanne. The prosecution then rested its case.

The defense repeatedly moved for dismissal of all charges on the grounds that there was "no showing of any conspiracy" involving Sueanne. After fifteen minutes of arguments Judge Jones ruled against the motion to dismiss the case. The motion was, of course, more ritual than substantial.

Scott Kreamer made an opening statement reviewing the evidence he would present. In midafternoon on the second anniversary of Sueanne's arrest by Detectives Moore and Douglass, Kreamer called his first witness.

As Sueanne Hobson took the stand the spectators began murmuring as if the star had taken the stage, as if they were all lucky to have come on this, the best of all days. Until that moment no one in the crowd was sure that she would testify. With Scott supporting her on the walk from the defense table, she came hesitantly and shakily to the stand. Throughout Scott's direct examination of her, she appeared anxious and somewhat unsure. Only later, when Moore cross-examined her, did she display intensity and confidence, as if she could only show her power before an antagonist.

From very different perspectives Scott and Dennis Moore questioned Sueanne over virtually the same incidents and statements. Both lawyers briefly reviewed Sueanne's life and the end of her first marriage. Sueanne said it was "Jimmy's choice to live with his father" and spoke of her losing track of Jimmy. Her parents had hired detectives to find Jimmy, she said, but they could not do so. In fact, Jimmy was almost always in contact with her parents over the years.

Moore, on cross-examination, exploited the absurdity of Sueanne's claim. To the spectators her inability to find her son seemed incredible. Her assertion that she had lost touch with her parents at the exact same time she lost touch with Jimmy further undermined her credibility. She did not contact her parents to find out about Jimmy from 1973 until Suzanne phoned her brother in 1978. Inadvertently Scott, as well as Moore, developed a portrait of the disintegration of Sueanne's immediate and extended family. In the context of the trial that cruelty, which was done in the heart nearly a decade before, was now given new power and passion.

Yet Sueanne also presented a portrait of a family. When asked what the family of Ed and Sueanne Hobson did together, she said, "We went to dinner; we went to church; we went to picnics; we went skating; we took the kids skating. We took them boating in the summertime." And when she spoke, no one doubted that she had done such things. She had worked with great energy to create a family.

Sueanne's efforts to draw Chris into the heart of her family seemed convincing. "What kind of boy did Chris appear to be?" Scott asked. His voice was drowned out by a freight train that roared through the heart of Olathe just a half block from the courtroom. After an awkward, roaring silence Scott restated his question, adding, "At the time when you first met Chris."

"He was outgoing and liked to play outside," Sueanne said. "Sometimes he was devoted to television, I think too much. He liked to play baseball—Suzanne's real good in sports and he played baseball and basketball and stuff with her, because I can't hit the broad side of a barn, so I wasn't any good—so he always played with Suzanne."

"And did Ed eventually propose to you?"

"Several times."

"And did you eventually marry Ed Hobson?"

"Yes. Chris thought it was great. He called me Mom long before I even told Ed I would marry him." She spoke convincingly of her sweetness to Chris, of his sweetness to her.

"What kinds of things did you and Chris enjoy doing together?" Scott asked.

"We liked to read. I was trying to teach him how to cook. He wanted me to teach him how to iron, but I wouldn't do that because I was—I wouldn't even teach Suzanne how to iron. It's one of those nerve-racking things for me. Ed went to night school as part of his job and Chris used to come in and get in bed with me and watch television with me on the nights that Ed went to night school."

2

During cross-examination later, Dennis Moore asked, "Do you know what Chris's problems were?"

"Insecurity for one. The loss of his mother, a feeling of rejection. He had a fear of the dark at first. He got over that." Sueanne's answer revealed a touching aspect of their relationship.

"How did you know that he was afraid of the dark?"

"Because he told me so and because one night—we have an all-electric home and the electricity went out in our house—I was in the kitchen and he came running downstairs and sat in my lap and was scared to death."

It seemed that the sweetness she felt for him extended right into the hunting trip she permitted him to take on a school day with Jimmy in February of 1980. In response to a question by Moore Sueanne said, "I gave him permission to get off this day because he wanted to go and because things had gone so much better around our house that I was trying to show him extra love and affection by allowing him to do something that I knew his father would probably hit the ceiling about when he got home—which he did."

"You told Chris not to tell Ed about that, right?"

"Yes, I was going to," she said ambiguously.

"Did you?" Moore demanded clarification.

"Yes, sir."

"When?"

"That night or the next night—that night, I imagine."

"What kind of problems did you have with Chris?" Moore asked. With Moore Sueanne admitted Chris's difficulties.

"Not doing his schoolwork, being lazy as far as school was concerned in the beginning—because I knew Chris was bright and he didn't apply himself. He was sloppy, he disliked soap and water and things that." She broke off abruptly to confront Moore. "You know, he did not go around breaking up furniture and slapping people, if that's what you mean."

"Well, I don't mean anything. I'm asking you a question."

"Well, I'm trying to answer it," she said defiantly.

"Did you have other problems with Chris besides those?"

"He did not like always to do his chores."

"And were there some problems that upset you in that relationship between Chris and Suzanne?"

"Yes."

"And what were those problems, Mrs. Hobson?"

"Well, I disliked him telling my husband and I that Suzanne was an alcoholic. That upset me. And the fact that he was telling people at Skateland that she was taking her clothing off at Skateland, which was later rectified."

"And how was that rectified?"

"My husband took Chris up to Skateland, and Chris apologized, because Chris admitted it was not true."

"And why was it necessary then to have Jimmy talk to Chris later about that incident?"

"Because it didn't stop."

"Tell me when it continued after that."

"It continued directly after that."

"The same rumor?"

"Basically the same rumor, yes."

"Were there variations in that rumor?"

"Yes."

"Tell me about those, please."

"Well, I can't give you word for word, verbatim, what he said. It was basically that she was taking off her clothing and displaying herself at Skateland and doing obscene things in general."

"Did you talk to Ed about that?"

"Yes."

"And that upset you, didn't it?"

"Yes, it did."

"And did Ed talk to Chris again about that?"

"Yes."

"And did that solve the problem, then?"

"Of Chris spreading the rumors, is that what you're talking about?"

"Yes, yes," Moore said.

"To some extent."

"What do you mean by that?"

"It stopped it for a while."

"Did it start again, then?"

"Yes."

"And that upset you, didn't it?"

"Yes."

"What did you do then?"

"I asked Jimmy to talk to Chris."

"Did you tell Ed you were going to ask Jimmy to talk to Chris?"

"No, I did not."

"Why not?"

"Because I chose not to." Again she was openly defiant, as if there were only two people in the room.

"Any particular reason?"

"No, no particular reason. Because Jimmy had talked to Chris before and because it had worked before and I knew it would work again."

"So on April seventeenth—is that the day that you asked Jimmy to talk to Chris about this?"

"That was the night he was supposed to come over and talk to him, yes."

"A couple of times before, what did you ask him to do in the way of talking to him?"

"To come over and ask him to try to explain—he had explained to Chris earlier about the sibling rivalry and the jealousy and the fact that we both loved Chris, that we both loved Suzanne, and that there wasn't—there was—there was no partiality and that he didn't need to do that to gain attention."

"So during this period of time Jimmy was causing problems in the family, is that your testimony?"

"Yes, sir."

"But you were asking him to solve the problems in your family, is that your testimony?"

"I asked him to talk to Chris, yes."

"So Ed couldn't handle the problems?"

"I don't know whether Ed could solve the problem. He did not solve the problem."

"Do you recall the conversation that afternoon?"

"Which afternoon, sir?"

"April seventeenth."

"Between whom?"

"Between Jimmy and yourself—and Suzanne was present."

"When—yes, when I took—you're talking about the time I took the ironing board over to him?"

"Whatever," Moore said sarcastically, frustrated by her questions, which seemed designed to indicate that the seventeenth of April was not a special day.

"Yes."

"Was there anybody else present besides the three of you?"

"No, sir."

"And where were you and Jimmy?"

"We were in the parking lot."

"And where was Suzanne?"

"Suzanne was in the car."

"Now, was Suzanne listening to the conversation?"

"I don't know, sir."

"Did you hear the tape played in court here, the interview between Suzanne and Detective Douglass?"

"Yes. I heard the tape."

"And you heard the comments she made on that tape?"

"Yes, sir."

"And did you say that 'he'"—referring to Jimmy—"'told me that he had a friend named Billy that would scare Chris so he would leave Suzanne alone, he would take care of it'?"

"Yes. And that is verbally scaring. Scaring to me is verbally." It was as if language was ethereal, the act itself the only reality.

"And Jimmy said that he might take him out and scare him, is that right?"

"He said he would come over. I asked him to come to my home."

"And where were you going to be when he came to your home or were you going to be there?"

"My husband was at a union meeting and he had called and asked me out to dinner and I was going to be at dinner with my husband."

"You told Jimmy you'd be gone, is that correct?"

"Couldn't—" She faltered for a moment. "I don't know." She had to account for all the members of her family—both where they were and where they were supposed to be.

"Where was Suzanne going to be?"

"Suzanne was supposed to be upstairs in bed."

"In the shower?"

"That's right. She had fallen down the stairs, was under a doctor's care, was supposed to soak her knee and spend the night in bed." She paused. "And I also knew that if she came downstairs while Jimmy and Chris were talking that, she and her mouth would get right into the middle of it and it would do no good whatsoever." Sueanne spoke the last sentence as if she were complaining to Norma Hooker or Beth Clarkson about some ordinary family problem.

"So you told her to stay upstairs when Jimmy came over to pick up Chris, is that correct?"

"To talk to Chris," she corrected.

"And Jimmy was going to bring somebody with him, is that correct?"

"He said he was going to come over and talk to Chris."

"What was the conversation about Billy? Where did you get that name?"

"I got it from Jimmy."

"Do you know who Billy is?"

"No, I sure don't."

"And did you say to Detective Douglass on May fourth, 1980, that Jimmy and Billy were going to scare Chris so that he would not threaten Suzanne anymore?"

"I could have. If you're reading my statement, then I did." Unlike her responses to Scott Kreamer's questions, she was not at all submissive. She was angry and she let her anger show. There was nothing inside to soften the wrath. It was as if a terrible error had been made, but she had not made it and she acknowledged no role in it.

"I'm asking you if you remember saying that."

"I remember Jimmy telling me that he was going to come over and talk to Chris."

"Did the mention of the word 'get rid of him' ever come up?"

"'Get rid of the problem' came up, yes."

"'Get rid of him'?" Moore repeated. Sueanne did not respond. Moore asked again, "Did that come up?"

"It could have, but I do not recall."

"Do you want to refresh your memory?"

After reading the text Sueanne admitted, "You're right. It could have, but I do not recall." In response to Scott Kreamer's questions an hour earlier, she had answered elaborately and emphatically that she had used the phrase. Sueanne said to Scott, "You're referring to 'get rid of' which is one of my favorite expressions. Yes, I did. 'We have to get rid of it,' and I did not mean the child, I meant get rid of the problem and I say—I use the same expression today that I did then."

"You recalled Detective Douglass asking you, 'So when it boils all down to it, you did know that this boy, Billy, and Jimmy were going to take Chris somewhere that night?'"

"Jimmy said he was going to come over, Mr. Moore," she said as if correcting him in school.

"Did you ever tell anybody, namely Detective Douglass on May fourth, that Jimmy was going to threaten him, that he was going to beat him up, referring to beat Chris up—if he hurt Suzanne again?"

"Did Jimmy ever tell anybody that?"

"No," Moore said, biting off the word. She seemed to be deliberately attempting to confuse him. "Did you ever tell anybody that?"

"I could have."

"Why don't you refresh your recollection again."

"Yes, sir," she admitted after studying the transcript.

"All right. So you knew that Jimmy was going to threaten Chris that night?"

"I knew he was going to talk to him."

"That he was going to beat him up if he hurt Suzanne again?"

"I didn't believe he was going to beat him up."

"Well, were you telling the truth to Detective Douglass when you said that?"

"Did I say that I was—that he was going to beat him up? That's what Jimmy said, yes," she admitted after reading the exchange between her and Douglass again.

"So you knew that when you said that to Detective Douglass, is that right?"

"That that's what Jimmy had told me, yes." She carefully attributed the source of the threat to Jimmy.

"All right. So you knew on May fourth and you knew on April seventeenth that Jimmy was going to take your little son, your thirteen-year-old son, out and threaten him and beat him up if he hurt Suzanne again?"

"No, I knew he was going to come over to the house and talk to him.'"

"But you don't deny telling Detective Douglass that, do you?"

"That Jimmy told me that? No, I don't deny that, sir."

"Did you tell Jimmy that he and whoever were going to take him out to wherever and get rid of him, Chris?"

"No."

"Did you tell Jimmy, regarding Chris, that something had to be done and he said, 'We'll go out and get rid of him'?"

"No."

"You said that he was going to take him out and threaten him and maybe beat him up if he had to, right?"

"I said—yes." Sueanne seemed to yield finally.

"Thank you," Moore said. He abruptly changed direction. "So you drove around with Ed looking for Chris and you didn't find him, of course, did you?"

"In the morning?" she asked, as if she were trying to recall.

"Yes."

"No," she replied.

"Anytime?" Moore asked.

"No."

"You didn't find him of course, he was dead."

"I did not know that that morning," she said.

"Did Suzanne ever say to you, 'Have they killed Chris or did something bad happen to Chris'?"

"No, sir, I don't believe so."

Moore paused, walked within an arm's length of where Sueanne was sitting tensely on the stand, then said quietly, "The billfold, Mrs. Hobson."

3

The history of the billfold was particularly complex. There were at least three versions of how it got to Metcalf South. On the night of the arrest, Sueanne told the detectives that after Chris's disappearance she had dropped the billfold at the shopping center to stimulate the search for Chris. In direct contradiction to her mother's testimony, Suzanne, at her interrogation at the police station, said that her mother had dropped the billfold at the mall the night of the murder. Finally, Sueanne, several months later, said that Jimmy had taken Chris's billfold out of his bedroom the day after the murder and dropped it at Metcalf South.

Sueanne had stunned Moore early in the afternoon in her response to Kreamer's questions about Jimmy's visit to his mother's house on the eighteenth of April. Scott had asked, "Did Jimmy pick up anything out of Chris's room?"

"Yes. He went in and took Chris's billfold," she said.

"Did he tell you what he was going to do with it?"

"He was going to get rid of it."

"Now, you've told the police on May fourth that you took that billfold to Metcalf South?"

"That's right, I did."

"And you told them that, didn't you?" Scott emphasized dramatically.

"Yes, I did."

"Now, I want the truth," he said, displaying a thick, intense authority utterly foreign to him. "How did that billfold get to Metcalf South? I want the truth!"

"Jimmy took it there. He went from—we were talking in my bedroom and he went into Chris's bedroom and I followed him in there and he was—said he was going to put it up there because he didn't want to get caught, he didn't want to be implicated because he had nothing to do with this, nothing."

The Kreamers had talked with Sueanne about the billfold. "Before the trial we broke her down on that," Scott said. "She started crying while we were questioning her and she told us Jimmy took it. We just couldn't live with her taking the billfold. Couldn't live with it."

4

"The billfold, Mrs. Hobson," Moore asked now. "How did the billfold get to Metcalf South?"

"Jimmy put it there."

"And when did Jimmy *supposedly* put it there?"

"He put it there the eighteenth."

"Were you there when Jimmy went and got the billfold?"

"I was there when he was at my home, yes."

"Well, did you see him take the billfold?"

"Yes, sir."

"Have you told other people different versions of that story?"

"Other versions of that story?" she said, temporizing.

"Well, did you put it there?"

"I told the police that one time and I told Mr. Kreamer the truth the week that I was bonded out." Apparently "that one time" referred to her interrogation on the night of her arrest.

"Did you tell Suzanne that you put it up there?"

"Yes, I believe I did."

"When did you tell Suzanne that?"

"I don't know. I'm not even sure I told her that, Mr. Moore. I could have."

"When Suzanne said it was in Chris's room, the billfold, and [she was] talking about you, when did you get it, and she said that night, that you put it at Metcalf South, is that true or not?"

"What, on the seventeenth?"

"Yes."

"That is not true because my husband found it the morning of the eighteenth."

"When Suzanne said that you put it at Metcalf South and that you told her that, is that true or not true?"

"That is not true."

"And you told her that, though?"

"That I put it there the seventeenth? No, sir, I did not."

"That you put it there, period."

"No, sir," she said, directly contradicting her statement of a minute earlier when she responded that she believed she had told her daughter.

The matter of the billfold was so filled with contradictions and confusing dates and times that it was less a factor in the minds of the jurors than other matters. Certainly the reporters and the spectators were confused. Even if Sueanne dropped the billfold at Metcalf South, no sensible motive could be found for her doing so, except, perhaps, that she wanted to be caught. The abrupt change in her testimony emphasized the importance of the billfold to the defense and left in disarray witnesses who had narrated Sueanne's elaborate account of dropping it at the shopping center and her motives for doing so. For days the defense was constantly reminded that Sueanne had lied about the billfold.

5

Both Scott Kreamer and Moore asked Sueanne when she had first spoken with Jimmy after the murder and why she had not turned him in to the police. Jimmy phoned her on the eigh-teenth, she said, in response to a question by Scott. "He called me late that afternoon and said that Chris was dead and that he didn't do it and that he was scared and he was crying and that I had to help him and that Paul had gone berserk. It was Paul, it was Paul, it was always Paul. And I have always believed him." Sueanne was crying now as she spoke.

"Did you have occasion on the eighteenth to actually meet with Jimmy?" Scott asked.

"Yes, he came over; he said that they had taken Chris out and Paul had gone berserk and he swore to me that he had nothing, nothing to do with it, and I had to help him. And I believed him. He pleaded with me and he convinced me that he didn't have anything to do with it."

Later Sueanne told Moore almost exactly the same thing. "Jimmy told me what had happened and that he was terrified and that he was an accessory and had done absolutely nothing and that I had to help him and he had nobody to turn to and he was scared to death."

Scott attempted to give Sueanne a motive for her refusal to tell her husband about the billfold right after she returned to the condominium and again started living with Ed. "Why did you tell the police on May the fourth that you had taken the billfold to Metcalf South?"

"Because I was trying to protect Jimmy because he said he didn't have anything to do with it, that Paul had killed Chris, not Jimmy," Sueanne said.

"And did you tell your husband that Jimmy had told you Paul had gone berserk and that they'd killed Chris? Did you tell your husband after you found out on the eighteenth of April?" Scott asked.

"No."

"Tell this jury why you didn't tell your husband."

"Because my husband has a terrible temper and he would have killed Jimmy. He would have," she said, nodding, "and there would be no husband either, no child, no husband, no nothing. I had also been told not to say anything."

"By who?"

"By Jimmy. Jimmy told me that Paul said that if I didn't help and if I opened my mouth that he'd just make it a package deal and he'd just get rid of all of us."

Suddenly there were perhaps too many motives for her silence rather than too few.

6

Later, Sueanne told Dennis Moore that she didn't tell the detectives about the crime until the body was found, "because I was afraid to. Because I was protecting my son."

"Why were you afraid? Who were you afraid of?" Moore asked.

"My son had told me what had happened. He had also sworn and begged and pleaded with me and said that he had not been involved with this. He had been there but that he didn't do anything and I believed him, Mr. Moore."

"Did you ever tell anybody, namely Ed Hobson, that Jimmy had threatened to hurt you and Suzanne if you had told?"

"Yes, sir." Apparently she had told Ed this a week after her arrest.

"You told him that?" Moore wanted to emphasize Jimmy's purported threat to Sueanne and contrast it with her behavior around Jimmy.

"Yes, sir."

"Did you tell anybody else?"

"Now, Jimmy didn't threaten me. He said that Paul threatened all of us." Sueanne couldn't quite remember who was threatening and who was not.

"Were you afraid of Jimmy Crumm during that time?"

"I was afraid of what he had told me."

"Were you afraid of Jimmy Crumm during that time, Mrs. Hobson?"

"Sometimes."

"Well, when were you afraid of him?"

"After he had told me that Paul had said that he intended to wipe out the whole family if I opened my mouth and didn't say anything."

"But you went over and got him and went out and sold your car with him and —"

"That's right."

"—and went over to see him a few times?" Moore said with feigned astonishment.

"That's right, I believed my son," Sueanne said gravely.

"Did you feel you had an obligation to Chris to tell the police what had happened to him?"

"Yes, sir."

"But you didn't see fit to carry through on that obligation?"

"It's not a matter of not seeing fit to carry through an obligation. I had lost one boy. I did not want to lose another one and I did not want to lose my husband and I would have ended up losing both of them."

"And you went out there with Jimmy knowing that Jimmy had been there when Chris was killed, whether you believed he'd done it or not?"

"Yes, sir."

"And you saw Jimmy several times during that period of time following Chris's death?"

"Maybe once or twice," Sueanne said.

7

Moore sought to show how often Sueanne had lied about her involvement in the murder. In the July 1981 publicity blitz she had made many statements Moore intended to challenge. He focused on an interview that Leathers published.

"And in fact you were on a little television program to talk to Tom Leathers in July of 1981. In response to his question 'What did you think happened to Christen?' You said, 'We did not know'?"

"If it's on there, then I said it." Moore gave her the newspaper. "Yes, I said that," she affirmed.

"You said, 'We didn't know what happened to him' in July of '81. Was that the truth?"

"That I knew?"

"Yes," Moore said.

"The eighteenth," Sueanne said, referring to the day after the murder.

"You knew the eighteenth, and so in July of '81 you lied to Mr. Leathers on television, is that correct?"

"My attorney told me not to tell anybody anything other than what I had already said."

Moore had the court reporters read his question back to him.

"Yes, sir, that is correct," Sueanne replied.

"Thank you, Mrs. Hobson. Did you make a statement to Mr. Leathers, 'Yes, many of the children at school were telling us they had seen Chris at Worlds of Fun and Skateland and Oak Park Mall, all these places,' do you remember saying that?"

"Yes, sir."

Moore read the next question Leathers asked and Sueanne's answer. "'Do you think that was true?' Do you recall saying, 'I don't know'?" She did not respond directly, but Moore persisted. "Is that true?"

"That I didn't know whether he had been to Worlds of Fun?" Sueanne asked.

"During the period of time after April seventeenth," Moore said.

"I knew he was not at Worlds of Fun after April seventeenth." She quickly corrected her error. "After April eighteenth."

"But you told Mr. Leathers in July of 1981 that you didn't know if that was true or not that these kids had seen him out there, is that right?"

"Those are the stories we had heard, yes."

"My question was, when you said that he had been sighted at these places and Mr. Leathers said, 'Do you think that was true?' and you said, 'I don't really know,' was that true or not, that you really didn't know?"

"No."

"You knew where he was, didn't you?"

"After April eighteenth, yes."

"And you knew on April eighteenth that he wasn't out at Worlds of Fun, didn't you?"

"Yes."

"And you knew he was down in a grave in Miami County, didn't you?"

"No, I did not know where he was."

"You knew he was dead?"

"Yes, sir."

"So this was a lie to Mr. Leathers again, is that correct?"

"Yes, sir."

"When did you first start believing that Jimmy really had done it?"

"Well, I didn't believe it at the time of his trial, I didn't believe it at the time of his preliminary, I did not believe it until he himself said it." She did not recall when this was.

Moore had established that Sueanne and Ed had had frequent arguments about Chris, "maybe once a week, once every two weeks," she had said. Moore sought to develop a semblance of a motive for the crime as he came to the end of his cross-examination of her.

"Did you ever tell one of Chris's teachers or counselors that you were very unhappy with your marital situation?" Moore had talked with Lee Shank and he knew that she would not exaggerate.

"That I was very unhappy with my marital—not to my recollection, no."

"Possibly?"

"I would say no."

"Well, there's some hesitation. Is there a question in your mind about that?"

"Well, anything is possible. I can't tell you that that is not something that I did or didn't say for sure, because I don't know, but that doesn't sound probable."

"Ed has told us how great things were in the Hobson household and I wanted to know if you had a different opinion."

"No, I didn't have a different opinion. We had our disagreements, but everybody does."

"You didn't tell anybody that? Did you tell Lee Shank or Delores Louis the whole marriage was a mistake and you wished you hadn't gotten into it?"

"Not that I recall, no, sir."

"Possibly?"

"There again, that's that vague word."

"Did you ever tell those two ladies the kid, meaning Chris, was impossible to live with?"

"Not that I recall."

"Possibly? I mean—you're not saying you didn't say that, is that right?"

"No, sir, I'm not."

8

Moore hadn't made much progress on establishing a reasonable motive for the murder, rather, he had brought out the bewildering confusion of Sueanne's statements about the crime. What he sought to underline at the end of her testimony was the sixteen days of silence she admitted she maintained before her arrest, sixteen days in which she gave away Chris's clothes and redecorated his room.

"What were you going to do if Chris miraculously showed up on the twentieth or twenty-first of April?" Moore asked insidiously. "Where was he going to sleep? Did he have a bed in his room still?"

Sueanne answered him elaborately, almost tenderly, as if caught in her own "charade of ignorance," as Moore called it. "I don't know whether Ed had given the—taken the bed down to work by then or not, I do not remember that. Ed would know the date he took the bed down there. We would have gone out that night and gotten one or he could have slept in our bed or he could have slept on the floor. We have all slept on the floor at times, and we have two sofas."

"Of course, by the twentieth and twenty-first you knew he wasn't coming back?"

"Yes, sir."

"So you could get rid of those things and not worry about it, right?"

"That's a very callous way of putting it."

"Well, we're down to that now, I think."

Judge Jones interrupted. "The court is going to direct counsel not to make comments. The court will direct the witness to answer the question and not make comments."

"Mrs. Hobson, did Ed Hobson love Chris?"

"Yes, sir."

"Did it bother you at all to see Ed Hobson wondering what had happened to Chris during those three weeks that he didn't come back?"

"Yes, sir."

"You knew these police were out searching for Chris?"

"Yes, sir."

"And all those people out looking for Chris and you didn't tell the police and you didn't tell your husband?"

"That's right," she said.

"Thank you, Mrs. Hobson," Moore said as he sat down.

9

Scott Kreamer stood; he walked toward her with energy, his deeply tanned face jutting forward just ahead of his body. "Do you still carry a picture of Chris with you at all times?" he asked. Sueanne said yes. "Would you find that for me, please?" Scott positioned himself so she would have to turn toward the jury in order to speak to him.

"I have had this picture ever since the child was alive," she said as she opened her purse to get it. Scott didn't notice the strange phrasing of her statement, the ambiguity of it, though it struck a few of the spectators. Her sentence would have been more coherent if the last word were replaced by "dead," for how could she have carried the photo since his birth?

Slowly Sueanne took out of her purse her billfold and out of the billfold the school photograph of Chris. She was sobbing now, her shoulders shaking and tears running down her cheeks. As she stepped down from the stand, Scott put his arm around her shoulders as she walked unsteadily back toward the defense table. She involuntarily held herself away from his touch, so that Scott's embracing arm appeared not to rest upon her thin body at all but touched only the white dress she wore.

10

With that, the testimony on the third of May ended. The Kreamers had at least twenty or thirty people in the courtroom behind the defense table, sitting together beyond the railing that separated spectators from participants. Scott's elegant, wealthy aunt, her beautiful, lean, sophisticated face, fitting so poorly among the puffed faces of perfumed young secretaries from the law firms around the courthouse. When the court recessed, Scott leaned over to the railing as if from a cage to speak to several of his relatives and friends, saying that what Sueanne did was just speak vaguely to Jimmy that night in the parking lot and he misunderstood. "Jimmy took it in a way that wasn't intended, took it so as to kill Chris. That's all that happened. That's all the evidence."

Moore had taken a bite toward the end of her testimony. He had again emphasized those two and a half weeks of silence. What the spectators and the jurors saw on the witness stand was a victim, a woman trapped and cornered. Neither could follow the vagaries of the billfold or Sueanne's failure to redecorate Chris's room, or the language used in the parking lot by a convicted liar and murderer. What weighed on all on the drive home was Sueanne's silence, her "charade of ignorance," for that was a crime that had gone on minute after minute, day after day, week after week. If murdering Chris required an understanding of a complex series of motives, that deathly silence was easy to understand, the motive for it simple and clear. The exquisite cruelty of it, if unappreciated by Ed Hobson himself, was fully experienced by others.

11

On Tuesday, the fourth of May, the defense called nearly a dozen witnesses: Jimmy's roommate at the Oak Park Apartments, who testified that Jimmy hated Chris and always referred to him as "the little shit"; Lee Shank, who saw Sueanne's display of anger against Chris at the teachers' conference in January at Indian

Creek Junior High; a girlfriend of Jimmy; a boyfriend of Chris. There were also six character witnesses for Sueanne who spoke convincingly of her honesty, of her warmth, and of her devotion to her family.

12

The last defense witness of the day was Ruth Sallee, Sueanne's mother, a tiny, intense, frail woman, barely five feet tall. She was to testify about her relationship with her grandson and her daughter. Scott Kreamer had been worried about putting her on the stand; he didn't know what she would do when she got up there. When he tried to interview her, she never stopped talking, while Don Sallee wouldn't say a word about his daughter.

"I want to direct your attention to February the twenty-third, 1980," Scott said to Mrs. Sallee. "Did you happen to have a conversation with Jimmy Crumm at that time?"

"I did."

"Did you make notes regarding that conversation?"

"I did, in shorthand and abbreviation." The judge had given her permission to use her notes to testify.

"And do you recall when Jimmy moved out of the Hobson home?"

"Yes, February the nineteenth."

"Regarding this conversation with Jimmy on February twenty-third, where did that conversation take place?"

"At my home, in the den."

Moore interrupted Scott to ask when these notes were taken.

"I said that I took notes, some shorthand, some abbreviated," Mrs. Sallee said. "I sat there at my kitchen table and put down everything Jimmy said. Then I immediately put it into longhand to tell my husband because he was very confused about how Jimmy had been acting." Moore sat down, content for the moment to whisper his astonishment to Tatum.

"Now, please tell the jury about the conversation with Jimmy, February the twenty-third," Kreamer said. With that Mrs. Sallee began a long monologue that Scott scarcely interrupted.

Jimmy Crumm came to my house on Saturday afternoon. He was in a highly emotional state. He came in. He walked up and down. I asked him what was the matter and he told me he had left his mother's house, that he had been involved in a lot of drugs and the theft of a credit card and subsequently he had to leave. He said that Chris had told his mother about this stolen credit card and the merchandise.

He got up. He threatened to kill Chris. I recall he put his hands up to the top of my den door and he said, "I'm going to kill that kid, you wait and see. I am going to kill him." I remonstrated with Jimmy. I said, "I don't want to hear you say anything like that. What is the matter with you?"

And he said, "I'll tell you what's the matter with me." He said, "I brought home some merchandise, a pair of boots and running shoes. Chris came down to my room, I showed them to him. In a little while Chris went up and told my mother, Sueanne Hobson, 'Jimmy has some stolen merchandise down there on a stolen credit card.' Whereupon Sueanne Hobson went downstairs and demanded to see it."

Then Sueanne Hobson came upstairs and called the police. The little boy, Chris, according to Jimmy—everything I'm telling you is what Jimmy told me that February the twenty-third—he ran downstairs, alerted Jimmy Crumm that his mother had called the police. Jimmy said, "Whereupon, I ran upstairs and took to my heels."

I said, "Where did you go?" He said, "I bummed around all afternoon and I went over to a friend's house that night. The next afternoon I called my cousin David Reffitt and asked if I could come over to his house"—because he had stayed at his aunt Dorothy's and uncle Chuck Reffitt's house. And that is where he was.

And then while he was talking, again he said, "You wait and see, Grandma, I'm going to kill him." And as I say, he was in a highly emotional state. I said, "What is the matter with you, Jimmy, have you been drinking?" He said, "No, I haven't been drinking." I said, "Are you on drugs, Jimmy?" And he looked me straight in the eye and he said, "No, I'm not on drugs, but I'm going to get even with him, I am going to kill him."

Then he said, "A few days after I had to leave the house

because of the stolen credit card, I arranged to meet a detective from the Overland Park police station at a restaurant"—Denny's out on 103rd, I think it is, and Metcalf. And during the course of the conversation Jimmy said he told the detective, "I am going to kill that kid for snitching on me and getting me in this trouble."

And he said the detective said, and I quote, "Look, kid, we have come after you for theft. We don't want to come after you for murder, so cool it." When he told Paul Sorrentino about Chris snitching on him about the credit card and telling Sueanne Hobson, Paul said, "Jimmy, you ought to get even with him and beat him up or take him out and do something to him."

"Did Jimmy call you in May 1980?" Scott interrupted.

The first time, yes, from Paola, Kansas. He called me in the afternoon. And during the conversation I asked him how all of this could happen. Naturally, I was Jimmy's grandmother, I was his closest confidante and we were bewildered. He said, "Well, frankly, there's been an awful lot of lying going on." And I said, "Who has been doing the lying, Jimmy?" And he laughed a little and says, "Well, really Paul and I have been doing an awful lot. We haven't exactly told the truth."

And I said, "Well, you certainly talked and lied pretty good at the Overland Park police station whenever they first took you." He replied, "Yeah, well, Paul and I already had our stories together way ahead of time in case we got unlucky and got picked up."

And when he called me the first time, he said his taped confession was a bunch of lies. He said, "I wasn't even there at the murder, Grandma, I was at Papa Joe's, a disco, and my lawyer has signed statements from ten people who saw me there and there are five more besides who are going to give statements." I said I didn't believe him and he kept lying over the phone and said all his taped confession and Paul's was "one big bunch of lies."

13

After Scott Kreamer ended his direct examination, Dennis Moore cross-examined her. He himself had phoned Mrs. Sallee once and he began by asking her about their conversation. "You told me you didn't want to talk to me, isn't that right?"

"I did not say that, Mr. Moore. I said, 'I'm very ill today, I have heart trouble.' And you said, 'Is your husband there?' I said, 'Yes.' You said, 'May I speak to him?' I said, 'Certainly.'"

"At any rate, you had all this vital information at that time and you didn't see fit to try to put that exculpatory information to the police or to the district attorney at that time, is that correct?"

"I didn't know I had information. I make notes all the time on my conversations from people who call me long distance. I didn't realize it was any value. I was in a state of shock."

"You realized your daughter was charged with murder at that time, didn't you?"

"I realized my grandson, who I looked upon as my own son, had killed somebody and I couldn't believe it."

"Did you also realize at that time that your daughter, Sueanne Hobson, was charged with conspiracy to commit murder?"

"I never believed that," she said, avoiding a direct answer.

Moore broke in quickly. He didn't want any monologues. "No, I'm asking you if you knew Sueanne was charged at that time."

"I don't recall that. I just recall that one minute I had an adored grandson, the next minute I had a boy who was charged with murder."

"Ma'am, do you know when I talked to you?"

"Yes, of course."

"When was it?"

"It was around July the ninth or tenth of 1980. The reason I remember that is because it was shortly after the Fourth of July."

"And did you know your daughter had been charged with conspiracy to commit murder?"

"I think I read it in the paper, yes."

"All right. She didn't tell you that?"

"No, I had no conversation with her."

"When did he tell you over the phone that he did kill Chris?"

"On two or three occasions when he called me from Paola. He broke down and cried and he said, 'I'm sorry I did.' I asked him; he said, 'Yes, I did kill him.'"

"Did he ever tell you that Mrs. Hobson hired him to kill him?"

"He said his mother had nothing to do with it, Mr. Moore."

Moore was incredulous; of course he knew what Jimmy had said and what he was going to say. In many ways she was as tough and wily as Sueanne. "You're saying under oath that he never told you Sueanne Hobson was involved in that?"

"That is correct."

"And you never told him that she and he ought to go in and plead guilty?"

"I don't understand the question," Mrs. Sallee said.

"I'm asking a question, did you ever tell Jimmy Crumm or Jimmy Hobson that Jimmy and his mother ought to go in and plead guilty?"

"Why, no," she said calmly.

14

The next day Jimmy was briefly called back to the stand by the prosecuter to refute his grandmother's testimony. Again he couldn't look directly at anyone. The first conversation with grandmother Sallee that Jimmy recalled was in June 1980, not the twelfth of May.

Moore asked, "Did you tell your grandmother Ruth Sallee, at any time, 'There's been a lot of lying going on, we haven't exactly told the truth, Paul and I had our stories ahead of time in case we got caught'? Did you make that statement to her?"

"No, sir, I did not," Jimmy replied.

"Did you at one point tell your grandmother that you were— you weren't there when Chris was killed, that you were, in fact, at Papa Joe's and you had given—your attorney had ten sworn statements to that effect?"

"I think there is a good possibility I might have."

"Why would you do that?"

"Not wanting to admit to the guilt."

15

Ed Byrne was also called to rebut the testimony of Ruth Sallee.

Byrne's voice was tight and irritated and he reddened as he spoke. He knew mother and daughter were liars and he shared Jimmy's anger at Mrs. Sallee's betrayal of her grandson. As in his previous testimony, what Jimmy said gave as much to the defense as the prosecution.

Byrne said, "I have had conversations with Mrs. Sallee on the telephone. I've never met her personally. One of the conversations I know for certain was on September third, 1980, because I have some notes taken. The other conversation that I remember clearly was some time either in March or early April of 1981, last year."

"Did you have any conversations with Mrs. Sallee about any information she might have about James Crumm's case?" Moore asked.

"I can't separate out for you the two conversations that I had, but during each of the conversations that I did have with her I asked her to tell me basically everything she knew about Jimmy, about Mrs. Sueanne Hobson, about Jimmy's family life, about Chris Hobson, about Jimmy's upbringing, his school history—any family problems that he might have had. I asked her naturally to tell me any information she might have about Jimmy's involvement in the murder of Christen Hobson. In short, I asked her to give me any information which she might have which either might be helpful in his defense or might be relevant with respect to his case."

"Do you have a copy of the notes that Mrs. Sallee testified in court yesterday that she prepared as a result of her conversation with Jim Crumm?"

"No, sir, I've never seen such notes."

"Did she ever tell you she'd made such notes?"

"No, sir."

"Did she ever tell you that Jimmy Crumm had allegedly threatened Chris Hobson's life?" Moore inquired.

"No, sir."

"Did you ask her to testify in that case?"

"Yes, sir, I did." Byrne was particularly upset by Mrs. Sallee's assenting, then withdrawing. He knew that he couldn't express that directly. "She originally was willing to come forward and testify and then on the eve of two different court hearings she backed out and refused to come out and testify." Byrne thought she was putting and taking, doing what Sueanne had done with Jimmy. It was, he thought, a family trait.

16

There were several witnesses the defense was not allowed to call to the stand. Dr. Chester Day, Sueanne's psychiatrist after the murder, was not permitted to testify about his client's character and her ability to participate in a conspiracy. Scott Kreamer argued in vain that "the relevancy is her emotional state, and how she talked about Chris and his death, and the progression she gave to him, and his professional opinion as about what kind of mother she was and how she took his death and that Ed was the aggressor in pursuing her for remarriage and matters of that nature that have all been brought up, and which are relevant to show the type of person that the defendant is and her predisposition to commit this kind of heinous crime."

Moore retorted, "I can just imagine in the future, if defendants hear about this and this is allowed and if it works, defendants will go out, once they kill somebody or commit a crime, and they'll immediately, two or three weeks later, go in to a psychiatrist and put on this big act and be grief-stricken and talk to them about all of their guilt feelings, or whatever. They're just starting right then to make a defense for themselves." Judge Jones promptly ruled in Moore's favor.

Six weeks after the trial, Dr. Day wrote a letter to the court:

I have seen Mrs. Sueanne Hobson in individual outpatient psychotherapy from May twenty-third, 1980, until June second, 1982. Mrs. Hobson was seen approximately every week or every two weeks during that period of time. Mrs. Hobson was seen almost exclusively alone. I did have some contact by phone with her husband during that period of time. Mrs. Hobson had been referred to me by her previous clinical psychologist, Dr. Robert Craft, in May of 1980, after the death of Christen Hobson.

The primary emphasis in therapy over the past two years has been simply to try to help Mrs. Hobson emotionally to cope with her situation. She expressed a great deal of grief over the death of Chris Hobson and profound distress at the involvement of her own son, James Crumm. At no time did any indication appear that she had anything to do with planning or ordering the murder of Chris Hobson.

We did discuss at length her profound naivete and complete lack in judgment as to how to handle the knowledge of Jimmy's involvement after the fact. She admits to being very poor in handling "crises" and was extremely intimidated and genuinely feared for the safety of the remainder of her family and herself. Her lack of judgment and poor decision-making is probably the consequence of her early experience; she seemingly was quite over-protected and did not learn to deal with many realities in her early upbringing by her parents.

That timidity and passivity also contributed to what sounds to be an illconceived first marriage which ultimately ended in divorce. She claims that she was physically abused in the first marriage and ultimately mustered the courage to obtain a divorce. However, she never did consistently demand child support payments from her ex-husband alleging that she was threatened by him. She did manage to make her own way for a number of years, establishing a very good work record and was able to well attend to the needs of her daughter. She did not feel, however, that she could adequately care for both of her children and her son was sent to live with her ex-husband.

Her naive outlook toward life, her poor judgment and difficulty in making decisions, her fear, and perhaps some guilt at having had to leave her son some years previously, and a very strong mothering instinct, may all have combined to lead her to the mistakes of protecting her son, Jimmy, after he related what had occurred. She indicated that she had had no idea that Jimmy could or would be violent and had noted a previous positive relationship in many ways between Jimmy and Chris Hobson. She indicated that she had hoped that Jimmy could talk in an adult manner with Chris and help him to modify some of his manipulative behaviors at home.

She appeared genuinely grief-stricken and shocked at Chris's murder and her mistakes thereafter in participating in a coverup had been simply attempts on her part to minimize the losses in the family, fearing losing her own son, fearing losing her husband and daughter, possibly at the hands of Jimmy's accomplice. Having observed and talked with Mrs. Hobson in nearly ninety interviews over a period of two years, I do believe that her explanation of the events is consistent with her personality, her upbringing and her view of the world.

17

Ernestine Bean, earlier called by the defense as one of Sueanne's character witnesses and the woman who had taken her in after Margie kicked her out the day of Chris's burial, was called by the prosecution to refute Sueanne's testimony. In a deposition taken before the trial Bean had said she could tell the district attorney exactly what Sueanne told her that Jimmy had said to his mother over the phone the day after he murdered Chris. "He said, 'Paul and I have taken Chris. We have killed him. If you breathe a word to a living soul, we'll take you all down the tubes with us.'" On the stand Bean recalled that Sueanne said Jimmy as well as Paul threatened the entire family. She unwittingly contradicted the testimony of Sueanne, who denied that Jimmy had threatened her.

As a witness Mrs. Bean was excluded from hearing Sueanne's testimony. Thus she directly undermined Sueanne's new accusation that Jimmy, in fact, had dropped the billfold.

"I said to Sueanne, 'Did you take the billfold and leave it at Metcalf so that they would look harder for Chris?' Sueanne simply said, 'Yes.'"

18

Ed Hobson was the first witness called by the prosecution and the last called by the defense. He was in an angry mood, shaking and red-faced even when he first sat down. His broad shoulders and thick arms pulled taut his short-sleeved shirt and he leaned forward toward his interrogator.

"Jimmy Hobson has testified that he didn't believe he was at your house on the eighteenth of April, 1980," Scott Kreamer said. "Do you remember seeing him there?"

"Yes, I do," he said, his voice almost out of control, accenting and cutting off each word. "Jimmy is a damned liar."

"There's also been testimony that you didn't have any pictures of Chris in the family home at the time of his disappearance. Is that correct?"

"I had a picture of my son—his birth, well, it wasn't his birth picture, he was eighteen months old—hanging in the hallway. I had a picture in the family room, I had a picture in the living room, and I had a picture in his bedroom."

"Some teachers testified that Chris said that nobody cared about him, is that true?"

"Oh no, my wife loved Chris very much and I could see that."

"What were your observations about your wife and Chris?"

"I saw my wife and I saw, I *saw*," he said poking himself hard in the chest with his middle finger, "my wife and my son have a good relationship. He kissed her before he went to school every morning and I saw her put her arms around him every night. And that I *saw*. I didn't ask my wife whether she loved him or not; I could see it. I could see the things that she did for him and the things he did for her."

Scott Kreamer sat down and Moore rose to ask his last series of questions in the trial. "Mr. Hobson, your wife knew that you loved Christen very much, didn't she?"

"Sure."

"She didn't tell you that she knew Chris was dead for a period of two to three weeks after he disappeared, did she?"

"I could understand that," he said defensively.

"My question was, did she tell you?"

"No."

"Thank you," Moore said.

As Moore sat down Scott stood slowly and walked up very close to the witness stand to ask one more question of Ed. "What would you have done to Jimmy if she told you that she knew Jimmy had—"

"I'd have killed him," he snapped.

19

On the morning of Thursday, the sixth of May, the reporters were relaxed, in a festive mood really, asking each other which side would win. Tom Leathers whispered, "You know this must be the last day. Look at Dennis Moore! Look at Scott Kreamer in summer tan to match his skin! Both wore their best suits today. Must be time for closing arguments!"

Leathers had already published a front-page article in his weekly newspaper declaring that Sueanne would be vindicated. A reporter asked Leathers if he thought Sueanne was guilty. He said, "I don't think she's legally guilty. That's as far as I go." He looked at the rows of reporters gathered together, saying, mockingly, in a loud voice, "Why are the reporters all so young? Where are all the old, experienced hands? What's happened to them?"

Ed and Suzanne were sitting together on a bench just inside the balustrade separating spectators and participants. As witnesses they were excluded from the trial until the last day.

Scott Kreamer dragged the heavy lectern from the middle of the courtroom over near the jury box. He did it as if he were a young professor showing his vigor, showing who was in charge. His energy seemed scarcely contained. He spoke without notes, moving out beyond the lectern frequently, yet coming back again, then venturing out from his base.

> Chris Hobson in the last three months before his disappearance was making excellent grades, had outstanding discipline and friendliness, and outstanding behavior. Now, does that sound like the kind of person that a woman with no violent background, no predisposition for crime, no history of antisocial behavior would want to have murdered? It doesn't sound like the kind of kid that you would spank, let alone murder.

Ed Hobson told you that the problems were normal adjustment problems until Jimmy Crumm came to move into that house. When Jimmy Crumm came to move into that house, things went bad because Jimmy brought with him his drugs, Jimmy brought with him his predisposition for thievery. Jimmy didn't go to school, Jimmy dropped out of school. He drops out of school and he drops acid. He does cocaine, it's found in the house. He carries knives, one in his boot and one in his belt.

That's when the problem started and I would imagine Jimmy was in trouble at home all the time. Chris probably was not, because Chris was a good kid. Jimmy probably hated Chris because Chris, he perceived, received preferential treatment in that house. Jimmy never had had anything. He came into a house where Chris had a nice home, a good family, a good relationship. Jimmy had never had that. He felt like his mother was the one who had deprived him of that and here she was giving that, in effect, to a boy who was an adopted son.

We put Sueanne Hobson on the stand, she didn't have to take the stand. We put her on the stand so that you folks could sit ten feet from her and observe her demeanor as she answered the questions. And she answered up. Observe the emotion she showed.

Mr. Moore would say, "Well, that was a strategically timed emotion." Do you believe that for a second as you saw her testify that that was planned emotion, that she "cried on cue," to quote the prosecutor? Jimmy Crumm didn't shed one tear. He didn't show one bit of emotion and neither did Paul Sorrentino, because that's the type of people that they are.

If there's no reasonable doubt in your mind, ladies and gentlemen, consider Ed Hobson. Chris Hobson is not with us. The living victim is right here, ladies and gentlemen. This is the father of that boy, here he sits. He has testified to you that knowing everything about this case—now, you folks have been here for, I think, seven or eight days—knowing everything, he remarried this woman because he was convinced she was innocent. Tell me that you don't have to prove much farther than beyond a reasonable doubt, to the man who's lost his only flesh and blood, the innocence of a person before he would do that!

He says to you folks, "She did not, did not arrange for the

murder of my son." Are you folks going to go back in that jury room and come back out here and say to Ed Hobson, "Ed, you don't know what you're talking about. We've been with this case for seven days, you've been with it for over two years, but we know better than you."

Doesn't that give you some reasonable doubt? Reasonable doubt just in and of itself? Ladies and gentlemen, Suzanne Hobson and Ed Hobson are here seeking the return of their mother to them. Please let them go away together. Thank you.

Hugh Kreamer presented the last part of the closing argument for the defense. Sometimes he lost the flow of a sentence, leaped from topic to topic. He appeared tired, but he had a passion for the case and a conviction of his client's innocence. Hugh's presence seemed to emphasize that Scott was playing a game, thinking only of winning. Hugh began calmly, reflectively.

I'm pretty well schooled in the field of prosecution of criminals and the defense of criminals for the reason that I was a prosecutor in this county for sixteen years and now I'm a defense counsel for some ten years. This case is really one of the strangest I've had the misfortune of being involved in, and I mean misfortune, because it's an unfortunate happening that we're all here. I've seen lots of cases like this when there was a murder, but I've never seen one when the murderer and his mother were involved, I'll tell you that for sure.

So you take the credibility of our client—and I'll admit she's lied and I would venture that if this had happened to me, and I've raised children like all of you have, I don't know what I'd have done under the circumstances. What I might have done might have been very unusual and strange and her things were, her actions.

But she had so much fear of what could happen to her, her little daughter sitting over here, her husband, the whole family circle, that she did what she thought at that time was best and that was to save them and try to help her son.

Now, I can find no reason in my mind that Sueanne Hobson would go to the expense of hiring an attorney and filing a suit to adopt someone who was to be killed—I guess by her, as they say—within a few short months thereafter. She adopted this young boy as her own, and you've seen Ed, and he's a good man, he's worked all his life and has had probably the worst tragedy befall him of anybody in this courtroom, and now another one is being asked to be placed on Ed's poor shoulders by the State of Kansas by having you find his wife guilty of, in fact, killing her own son.

So find a motive for this lady to kill this young man and if you can't find a motive, then you can't find her guilty of anything. It's got to be intentional; all those long words, they seem to mean *motive* to me. They may mean nothing to Mr. Moore. Apparently they don't, but to me, most people who get murdered get murdered for a reason, and if Sueanne Hobson found herself in such a situation that was intolerable—that Chris was so bad that she had to have her own son murder him—she had enough friends and people of intelligence to get her out of that situation.

Instead of going and filing an adoption, she could have walked right upstairs here in the courthouse and filed for divorce. And I'm sure that Chris would then have gone with his father if she had, and Suzanne would have stayed with her and they could start all over again, but it would have been a lot easier and a more expeditious way to handle things than going out, with these fictitious stories with these dopeheads, and killing her son.

So, on the one hand, you've got Paul Sorrentino, who knows nothing about it from her. All he knows is from Jimmy Crumm—and I think that last name fits him, he's a crumb and he had a vendetta against his mother because she apparently, he thought, abandoned him, which isn't the evidence. She tried to find him and couldn't.

But he saw that Chris was getting favorable treatment in the home, and why shouldn't he? His natural father was living there, probably paying most of the bills. Chris probably did get favorable treatment.

Now, the only one making a claim against our client, other than secondhand Sorrentino, is Jimmy Crumm, and if you can find it in your hearts to convict this lady of first-degree murder, or a conspiracy to commit a crime such as that, from the testimony of a person who's been breaking every kind of law—he has broken every kind of law now, I believe, that we practically have on our books: he drinks, he steals, he's a doper, and a murderer.

This killing was done by two young boys, like you read about in the papers over and over and over again. They got loaded up on dope, they're drunk, they're stoned out of their minds, and maybe hallucinating and do all kinds of horrible, gruesome things that we'd like not to hear about, and you don't want to hear about them here either, but unfortunately you have to.

They always talk about the victim of the crime. The victim of the crime is dead, but Ed Hobson isn't dead, and all he has left is the person he's supported through an ordeal—I can't even imagine what it would be like—and he's stood by her side in every respect and told you, from what he could observe in every way, shape, and form for two years, this woman had nothing to do with this killing.

And our client sits here, innocent until all twelve of you agree to the contrary.

20

Unlike the Kreamers, Dennis Moore spoke from elaborate notes. Steve Tatum remained silent, sitting at the witness table. Moore had been criticized by Tom Leathers and others for trying very few cases, for being primarily an administrator and a public-relations man. Politically it was important for Moore to be seen as the prosecutor in this sensational case and to be interviewed several times daily on television.

Moore was nervous, frowning, angry, but superbly prepared and much clearer and more coherent than either of the Kreamers. To the jury and the reporters and the spectators, it was not an easy case to understand. He began with an impression of Sueanne's psychological state.

There are two sides to Sueanne Hobson. You may or may not have seen them both in court. Obviously she has some friends who are willing to come into court and testify as to her character, as to her honesty, and still stand by Sueanne, even when confronted with the fact that she's lied to numerous people on various occasions.

But there's a dark side to Sueanne Hobson. A side that can plan and execute the murder of her thirteen-year-old stepson, the boy who called her Mom. Sueanne Hobson is masterful at deception, at manipulation of others for her own ends.

Sueanne Hobson would have you believe that she's a warm, caring person, a good mother, but does a good mother abandon her son for seven years? Sure, she testified that she tried to find him, but Jimmy testified that he had frequent, very frequent contact with his grandparents, the Sallees—her parents—and she didn't bother for four years to go check with them to see if they knew where Jimmy was, if she even wanted to see him.

Sueanne Hobson would have you believe she's a warm, loving person, but does a warm, loving person abandon her parents, not talk to her parents for four years, no matter what the dispute is? Sueanne Hobson would have you believe she's a warm person, a loving person. But does a friend lie to her own husband, her daughter?

Consider the various stories she told different people about Chris's billfold—all that she put it up at Metcalf South. Sueanne Hobson, by her testimony, is a self-confessed liar. She testified on cross-examination that she lied to Tom Leathers. She testified that she lied to her husband and she lied to the police. Sueanne Hobson is a study in deception.

She feigned ignorance of Chris's whereabouts while he was missing for eighteen days. She kept police officers running in circles looking for a runaway boy. She cruelly kept information about what had happened to Chris from Ed Hobson, her husband, while, as you know, Ed Hobson was deeply concerned, deeply worried, worried sick about where Chris was.

The problem with such tactics, members of the jury—deception and manipulation—the problem with those tactics is you don't know when she's using those tactics on you.

Did Sueanne Hobson really love Chris or did she hate him? Did she want to advise and aid and counsel and assist his murder? Margie Hunt testified she hated Chris: "Sueanne Hobson hated Chris, she wished he was gone, she wanted him out. She said he's a problem and he's causing a lot of trouble, a lot of problems between Sueanne and Ed and she wasn't going to put up with it anymore."

Sueanne called Chris a "primate schizoid" to Margie Hunt. He wasn't mentally right, she said. According to Sueanne Hobson, for his own good he needed to be in a mental institution. Well, how prophetic a statement is that? "He would be better off in a mental institution."

Motive? The state is not required to prove motive. But the motive is here anyway. And the motive is probably the oldest motive in the world for murder. She didn't like Chris. She hated Chris. You heard testimony about the problems in the family, and Sueanne wasn't happy in her marriage and wanted out of her marriage in February of 1980, just a couple of months before this murder, but she didn't have the money. She didn't want to split up and divorce at the time because she didn't have the money to support herself.

Sueanne Hobson aided, she assisted, she advised, and she counseled a vicious, brutal murder. The evidence shows only two people fired shotgun blasts into Christen Hobson as he sat in a shallow grave in a rural part of Miami County on a night more than two years ago, but I can tell you there was a third person there.

Now, in fact, maybe, maybe she didn't stand there by those two boys, but the presence of Sueanne Hobson at that grave site was very real that night and her hands were on their shoulders, the shoulders of her son Jimmy Crumm, and the shoulders of Paul Sorrentino, as she urged them on and as she tried and they tried to get enough courage from each other and from the dope they'd smoked that day to go ahead and kill this thirteen-year-old little boy.

And perhaps Sueanne Hobson didn't actually level a shotgun at Christen and tell him all the reasons that she wanted to kill him and she wanted him dead, but she did it just the same. Sueanne Hobson was the Prime Mover in this murder case and Sueanne Hobson set into motion a terrible chain of events that resulted in the death of thirteen-year-old Christen Hobson.

And the woman touched and twisted a lot of lives as she went about this plan. And plan she did and scheme she did and she manipulated people to, in her own words, "Get rid of a problem"—that problem being little Chris.

She used her son Jimmy, she used his background, his desire for material things, his desire for her love and approval, and she used Jimmy to insulate her from anybody else connected with the crime. She never talked directly to Paul Sorrentino, and I submit to you that was probably by purposeful design on her part. She didn't want any more people contacting her personally than absolutely necessary, and in this case all the conversations with Paul were through Jimmy Hobson.

Sueanne Hobson never, never thought that her curious little thirteen-year-old daughter, Suzanne, would overhear that conversation in the parking lot and know what they were talking about and later report that conversation to the police. But we do have that conversation, as you know, you've heard it before and now at this time I'd like for you to listen to the truth as told by Suzanne Hobson.

For the first time in the trial Moore was eloquent. Before, his anger and his self-consciousness had separated him from the events he spoke about. Suzanne's taped interview was played again with the transcript again thrown on a screen before the jury. Moore concluded his argument quickly.

In any murder case there's always more victims, it seems, than the intended victim. Chris Hobson is dead, but the other victims in this case are Ed Hobson and Suzanne Hobson. You will recall this testimony one more time when Sueanne told her later that evening that Jimmy took care of Chris. Suzanne said, "I didn't know if they just beat him up real—just enough to put him in the hospital or not." And when Chris didn't come back, Suzanne said, "I figured they killed him." Suzanne's lived with her mother longer than Ed has and certainly longer than Jimmy has. She probably knows her mother better than Ed or Jimmy, and when she figured that they'd killed him, she *knew* they'd killed him.

There are two sides to Sueanne Hobson, and Christen Hobson knew the dark side only too well. And when Sueanne tearfully told you in court that she meant for Jimmy to get rid of the problem, not the boy, don't you see, the problem was the boy. The problem was Chris Hobson. The problem and the boy were one and the same and Jimmy got rid of the problem when Jimmy got rid of the boy.

21

The jury began deliberations late that Thursday afternoon and the crowd scarcely had time to leave the courthouse before the jury returned. The jury asked to hear the tape of the police interview of Suzanne for the third time. Tatum, Moore, Sueanne, and Scott Kreamer all were present. The jury promptly retired again to consider the case. They stayed until six o'clock, but didn't reach a verdict.

On Friday morning, the seventh of May, they resumed deliberations. The hall outside the courtroom was filled with bored cameramen and reporters and lawyers. By late Friday there was a sense of camaraderie and of wanting it to be over. Exactly two years had passed since Steve Moore and Darrell Urban and Ed Hobson had buried Chris. When Judge Jones re-called the case that afternoon, the bailiff had already passed the word to the reporters and they half-filled the courtroom. The reporters were tense and in their tension they were noisy, almost boisterous, wagering and joking. It was the end of something many had worked on for two weeks, one or two part-time for two years.

"Mr. Knight," Judge Jones asked, "has the jury arrived at a verdict?"

"Yes, we have, Your Honor." Knight gave the verdict forms to the bailiff.

The bailiff read: "We, the jury impaneled and sworn in the above-entitled case, do upon our oath, find the defendant guilty of the crime of murder in the first degree. We find the defendant guilty of the crime of conspiracy to commit murder in the first degree." After the first of the guilty verdicts was read, Sueanne

Hobson stretched her neck, tipped her head back slightly, and closed her eyes.

Hugh Kreamer rose quickly and requested that the members of the jury be polled. Judge Jones asked each by name. "Is this your verdict?" Each stood and said it was.

Sueanne and Hugh came back through the center aisle, forcing their way past reporters and the spectators who had filled the courtroom and adjacent hallways, many coming from offices in the huge courthouse. Sueanne saw Leathers on the opposite side of the courtroom and called out, "Oh, Tom, it's so awful!" Leathers came across quickly to embrace her before he and Sueanne and Ed and Hugh disappeared into the witness room just outside the courtroom.

22

"This is the most complex murder case I've ever tried," Hugh Kreamer said later in court. "Their witnesses lied! Our witnesses lied! I don't even pretend to understand it."

1 0
FAMILY

1

The night Sueanne Hobson was convicted, Dennis Moore asked the Olathe Police Department to watch his house and Steve Tatum's house. By Sunday Ed was circling Moore's house, as if engaged in some ritual threat. At times he'd park in front of the house and wait for Moore to emerge. When Moore finally would come out, Ed never even looked directly at him, just waited in silent, patient rage.

When he thought Moore was gone, Ed would park in front of Judge Jones's house for hours at a time as if he were in some way advancing Sueanne's cause, mitigating the sentence to come. Hobson thought Moore had gotten something on Judge Jones, that Moore was the leader of a conspiracy against Ed's wife. He seemed filled with impotent rage, but he was feared. By Monday evening Moore and Tatum were carrying guns. Neither had ever done so before.

When Detective Urban heard about it, he laughed right out. "Why are they afraid of him?" he asked. "He ain't never done nothin'. Nothin'! He puts up this big front, puffs himself up like some cock, but he'll never go off. He's a pussy! A pussy! He can't even stand up to his wife."

For a time Ed disappeared. He took a couple of weeks off from Ralston Purina and he and Sueanne and Suzanne stayed at a cottage at a lake twenty miles from the city. "Every friend who was left came out there for a while," Suzanne said. "I swam and we didn't talk much and we pretended nothing was going to happen. We talked about how the appeal would get Mom off. I was afraid because if she were jailed, I wouldn't have anyone outside of prison I cared about."

In July, two months after the trial, Judge Jones held a sentencing hearing. Hugh Kreamer argued that Sueanne should be left free pending appeal, that she presented no danger to the community. Dr. Day, her psychiatrist, testified about her emotional stability and her strong sense of community.

Once the hearing was done, Judge Jones promptly sentenced her to life imprisonment in the Kansas State Penitentiary in Lansing, forty miles north of Kansas City. For a short time she was jailed in the Johnson County Courthouse before she was transported to Lansing. "She was a big help right away," one of the women jailors said. "She'd got a couple of women prisoners to stay with her everywhere she went and she'd talk to the others, help them think about lawyers. She was in charge right off."

2

A week after Sueanne was sentenced Ed appeared unannounced at the district attorney's office in the Johnson County Courthouse. He was wearing a white, short-sleeved shirt drawn tightly over his muscles and his thick, broad shoulders. When Ed came in that afternoon and told the secretary behind the glass cage what he wanted, he insisted on talking with Moore right now. He was so angry that he couldn't sit down. His face was flushed and he paced back and forth across the tiny reception room as if he himself were caged.

Ed, usually garrulous, wouldn't talk to anyone in the lobby. Within a minute or two Moore sent an armed uniformed policeman out. The policeman stood awkwardly in the corner by the magazine rack calmly watching Ed pace.

When Ed was led back through to the prosecutor's office, Moore, Tatum, and three uniformed men were waiting.

Surrounded by the police, he refused to sit down in Moore's large cluttered office. On a table and a couch were several books of transcripts and tapes related to the Hobson case.

"I want two things returned to me—my son's billfold and my wife's freedom!" Ed said coldly.

Moore started to respond calmly. "The billfold's held for evidence, Ed, and —"

Before Moore could finish his sentence, Ed shouted, "You said you'd give back that billfold! That's all that's left of my boy. You promised you'd give me justice. I want my wife back. You got her convicted for politics, for your career. I want justice!"

Moore and Tatum hardly spoke and Ed said little more beyond his expressions of frustration and anger. Still, he didn't hit anybody or break anything or threaten the prosecutors in a way that they could charge him with a criminal act. Within minutes Ed agreed to leave quietly and the police escorted him out a side door and down the backstairs to avoid Hoffman and other reporters who were coming up from the courtroom below and gathering in the reception room.

Tatum and Moore were shaken by the ferocity of Ed's anger and his irrational demands. Tatum went back to his office, where a friend was waiting for him to return after he was called away. He sat down for a moment, then got up and walked to a floor-length window. He looked down toward Kreamer's office several stories below and across the street. He stood silently staring down on the street darkening before a summer storm. In a barely audible voice he said, "I hope nobody else gets killed in this."

3

A few days later Ed sent a conciliatory letter to Dennis Moore. In a large hand on small sheets of wide-lined paper, Ed wrote, among other things, "I have many troubles in my life. My stepdaughter and my son was murdered and his mother died of cancer. I don't want anyone to be hurt more. God understands and will help me." Moore, still angry and shaken by his confrontation with Hobson, threw the letter across the desk to his visitors, laughing contemptuously. "He's virtually illiterate. Can you believe it? He can hardly write at all. What do you think of that?"

In the weeks that followed Sueanne's imprisonment, Ed haunted Scott Kreamer's office. Hugh Kreamer was so ill that he seldom came to work. Hobson now had other plans to avenge the mistreatment of his wife. He focused relentlessly on Margie Hunt-Fugate, as if she, and not his stepdaughter with whom he lived, had provided crucial evidence in the trial.

Scott had little interest in Ed and no fear of him. In fact he had no interest in Sueanne, either, and he couldn't understand why others were afraid or fascinated by her. There was no money in it and his father, who'd gotten him involved, was dying and unable to help. Civil law was what interested Scott. That's where the money was and always would be.

For a time Scott contemplated raising money for a screenplay. He wanted to have the dying lawyer at its center, the passionate lawyer arguing his final case. "Dad's the interesting one here," he'd say. "He's given his last breath to save this woman from the prosecutor."

One Friday morning in August a month after Sueanne was jailed, Ed stopped Scott in the street outside the courthouse and said he was going over to the prosecutor's office and ask them why they hadn't subpoenaed Margie to testify in the civil suit Sueanne filed against her. "I'm going to keep after them over there until they get back my wife's jewelry," Ed said. "Why won't they subpoena Margie and bring her back to Kansas? They let her go right out of the state once she testified during the trial; they hid her away and they're still hiding her."

Ed had been laid off for a few days at Ralston Purina. Yet on that morning he appeared tanned and cheerful, wearing the Kliban cat shirt that he had been photographed in a year before. Scott teased him about the shirt. "What's that thing?"

"I hate cats," Ed said. "Hate them. But she loves them, any kind of cat." Then he seemed to bounce across the street smiling, barely containing his energy, yelling back at Scott, "I'm going to get Moore going on that Margie. They're lying to me. You know they're lying to me."

Dennis Moore claimed to know nothing at all about Margie's

whereabouts since she testified. In fact Detective Steve Moore was in frequent touch with Margie. Only the day before he had spoken to Margie in Connecticut and she had asked Steve about the trial. Margie was especially concerned about Suzanne. She knew that there was no one Suzanne could depend on now.

The Kreamers, of course, had little interest in Margie's case now. Hugh came to work and stared blankly ahead, as if engaged in some bodily function. And Scott knew there was no money in the case and little chance of recovering the jewelry.

4

Within three months of the trial the Kreamers had sued Ed and taken their portion of what was left of his condominium in legal fees. The Kreamers were behind some other creditors and had to fight for their place in line. Ed declared bankruptcy and signed over the house. By August, Scott had an agent working to sell the condominium.

In late August Ed moved to a little white house with green shutters that he rented in Roeland Park. It was a quiet, narrow street of small, well-kept houses a block behind a shopping center with great trees diminishing and protecting the houses. The Model-T truck with the license plate SUEANNE was there in the driveway. Alongside it Reverend Adams' car was jacked up; Ed was repairing it for him.

Ed had taken much of the furniture from the condominium and he had hung the living-room paintings thickly on the walls of the small, meticulously clean, narrow room. The paintings of the great cats seemed to leave scarcely any space on the living-room walls. The porcelain cat Jimmy gave Sueanne was displayed prominently and the house was overrun with Sueanne's cats and images of cats. If Ed had been a careless bachelor before he married Sueanne, then the place now looked as if he feared being caught out by her, as if she would return suddenly to inspect and claim the place.

To visitors who came to inquire about the case, Ed was as accommodating as ever. Few came, for his blustering and threats

made them afraid to come alone. The others, the convicted murderers—Paul, Jimmy, and Sueanne—had been mastered. They
seemed to be under control now and order had been restored. It
was as if the public and the prosecutors had focused all their fears
on Ed, and once he found that out, he cultivated the fear as
much as Hoffman did.

In his dream of high-school football he made himself heroic,
an all-stater from little King City in a remote corner of Missouri.
Apparently Ed had forgotten how he would be hurt in almost
every series of plays, forgotten how his father would, absurdly,
study the playing field with binoculars and how father and mother would dart out from the bleachers to revive him, support him
as he came off the field. Now he made a dream of the powerful,
violent figure he was in the minds of reporters and lawyers and
prosecutors—though women of a certain age and detectives
knew otherwise.

Mostly Ed wanted to please, to give you a drink to make you
comfortable, at ease—the way he had done with the policeman
who watched him the night they found Christen's body. When a
visitor spoke of Christen and the wedding to Sueanne he would
half run from the room to get the wedding album and he would
laughingly point to Margie, "that woman," to himself awkwardly
posing, to the beauty of Sueanne, and lastly, to Christen naively
coming forward into every photo.

Then he would remember his grandfather staring down
toward him from the edge of the bookshelf and speak of the land
he gave to Ed, the land Ed sold in the years since his marriage to
Sueanne.

As he drank he spoke openly about his drinking. He could
not drink the way he used to, he said. The doctors warned him
against it, and besides, when he did drink his liver pained him,
warned him off.

He recalled the happiness he had shared in the year and a
half before Jimmy murdered his son. "It was the best time," he
would say. "The only really good time. She was the best thing
that ever happened in my life. I'd never lived like that before. I
never wanted to come home before." In that mood he spoke with
energy and optimism, laughing frequently, joking about the little

things they had done, joking about the wedding and his anxieties during it, boasting about what things cost.

Yet now, in the late summer after Sueanne's conviction and imprisonment, he also had a darker mood. "I need my wife. I want her back well and healthy. I'm scared now. I'm scared." She was still suffering from her hysterectomy. "If they don't give Sueanne the doctor she wants and the medication she needs, I'll destroy the prison. I'll attack it, by God!

"You don't know what it's like in prison," he said. "She can have visitors only twenty-four hours a month total. That's all I can see her. I'm there every Saturday and Sunday. I get there when they open at nine-thirty. I've got some books together—Agatha Christie and Stephen King—that I'm going to take up to her tomorrow. That's the kind of thing she reads all the time."

District Attorney Moore was still the villain. "Dennis Moore lied to me," Ed said. "He flat out lied to me and he made a deal with my son's murderer, Sorrentino, and another with Jimmy. He's going to get Jimmy off. You know it and I know it. The Kansas Supreme Court will give him a new trial for his testimony against Sueanne. Dennis Moore is a cold, cruel man."

Suzanne was living with him, Ed said. "It's hard on Suzanne, not having a mother. This evening she called and she said she was going to stay overnight at a friend's house. I give her a lot of freedom because of what she went through."

Ed seemed to understand nothing of what had happened to him. He had no regrets about the loss of his money or his house. He remained devoted to Sueanne's service and isolated from others by the intensity of their relationship. He seemed to live alone, attended only by Reverend John Adams and by the reporters and the lawyers and by Suzanne, who avoided her stepfather when she could.

Dennis Moore would question Ed's few visitors if he got the chance. Constantly he wanted to know about any direct threats made against him. Even months after the trial Ed made him edgy. What he hoped was that Ed's loyalty to his wife would wane and he asked if he or she had discussed the evidence presented against Sueanne, if the guest had convinced Ed of his folly. "Has Ed come to his senses yet?" Moore would say hopefully. "I think Ed'll get tired of driving up there to Lansing. He won't last out the year. Don't you think so? All of a sudden Ed is going to see what happened to him, what she did."

5

One night in late September Ed and Suzanne spent the evening drinking together in the living room. Without Sueanne to check him Ed quietly assumed the drinking habits he had before he married her. Suzanne had been drinking a little for several years, as Chris and the Hooker family had known.

Apparently, when they were both good and drunk, Ed attempted to hug and fondle Suzanne, now sixteen, as they sat on the couch. Immediately she stood up and told him to stop. "Your mother is gone now and you're going to have to take her place," he said.

Suzanne pushed Ed away and ran straight back through the dining room to the little bathroom in the hall. She got there just before Ed lumbered out after her. She locked the door and started screaming at him. While Ed hammered on the door, begging her to come out, she climbed through the window, ran to a neighbor's house, and called the police.

Immediately the Roeland Park police came to pick up Ed and take him down to the station for questioning. He was calm and remorseful. He was always very respectful of the police in their presence. In fact, he didn't even deny Suzanne's story. "I'm drunk," he said. "You can see I'm drunk. I can't remember doing that to her, but I might have."

"What do you expect?" one of the officers said the next morning. "He's left alone there for months with this sexy sixteen-year-old stepdaughter. His wife's gone. You can make book on the fact that a man's going to try her. It's not like she's his daughter, is it? Run-of-the-mill stuff. What's she doing sitting there getting drunk with him?"

When Dennis Moore came in that morning, every official in the Johnson County Courthouse knew and they were waiting to tell him. Moore certainly didn't see it as run-of-the-mill. Rather, he saw it as an instance of severe child abuse and he wanted Suzanne out of that house for good. Moore immediately scheduled a closed hearing in juvenile court to remove Suzanne permanently from Ed's control.

A day later Sueanne phoned Scott Kreamer. She denied Ed had touched her daughter.

"He wouldn't do it," Scott said. "She was sure. I think maybe the girl just wanted to get away from a home where everybody's always focusing on a dead kid."

During the closed juvenile-court hearing Moore agreed not to file charges against Ed Hobson as long as he stopped making threatening gestures and statements. Meanwhile Suzanne was taken from Ed and she became a ward of the state. Suzanne's last name was changed from Hobson to Sallee because she was still treated as a pariah by her peers. She was sent to a foster home and she enrolled in Olathe High School.

Tatum and Moore were pleased with the outcome. With an attempted-rape charge hanging over his head, Ed wouldn't be threatening the prosecutors or complaining about their handling of the case to reporters.

Suzanne was humiliated by the juvenile-court proceedings. Her sexuality was at issue in court for the second time in four months. If she were embarrassed by hearing in court again and again Chris's accusation that she was taking off her clothes at Skateland and his saying she was the easiest lay in town, she was certainly ridiculed and victimized by accounts of Ed's rape attempt. "How would you like to be sixteen and everybody talking about you and your stepfather? What I know is that Ed is not to be trusted. He's not to be trusted! That's one thing I know about him."

From prison Sueanne supported Ed, took his side. "Mother had to believe him; she had to support him," Suzanne said. "What did she have left? All she had was Ed."

From prison Sueanne organized her friends to get control of Suzanne's case against Ed, though Sueanne herself didn't address the problem directly with her daughter. "Once they heard about it, all of Mom's friends called me and came over to see me," Suzanne said. "Ernie Bean and Colleen Carter came over and they asked, 'Why are you doing this to your mother? You need to tell the truth. None of this is doing your family any good.' They all thought I was lying. They all took her side. I had nobody to depend on. Dennis Moore, I thought, was trying to do the right thing, but I didn't have anybody to talk to."

She was sixteen, but it seemed to her that since her mother married Ed when she herself was thirteen, she had lost her childhood. Since Chris was murdered in 1980, she had moved from place to place with her mother, then moved in with Ed, then was sent to a foster home. She had wasted two years preparing for her testimony in preliminary hearings and in her mother's trial, and still it seemed to be going on. She seemed almost too old, or too young and uncertain, to be invited to parties of her peers.

Since the trial, she was viewed almost as badly as her mother, in part because she had been so identified with her in the trials and appeals and transcripts. Sometimes she told her friends who she really was and sometimes she was discovered and singled out and humiliated. She was as sensitive as Jimmy and quite as alone. She was cut off absolutely from Jimmy and she was full of guilt over her testimony against him in the trial. And she was afraid Ed and others would learn of her complicity in the crime.

Right before Christmas 1982 Suzanne tried to kill herself by taking a drug overdose. She was found in a coma and placed in the Kansas State Hospital in Topeka.

"They tried to treat me as if I were crazy," she said. "Then they sent me back to Kansas City and put me in a Crittenden Home for disturbed girls. I kept in touch with mother for a time, then I decided I gave enough to my mother. I gave everything to her and her obsessions. She took everything I had and I just had to let her go. I've got to live."

Sueanne had other plans. Ed, responding to Sueanne's directions, sought her out. "Ed and Mother can make people believe anything," Suzanne said. "He charmed those people at Crittenden when he came to inquire about me and they let him in despite my warnings.

"I wouldn't listen to him after what he did," she said angrily. "For weeks he'd wait for me to come out, drive up beside me when I came out, and follow me in his car. He'd get me to stop and talk and he begged me to see my mother, begged me to rejoin what was left of the family.

"Once he gets started, he never gives up," she said. "He doesn't just want me back with my mother—he wants revenge. He won't give up. He won't let me go."

6

Ed Byrne had appealed Jimmy's conviction in August. After his oral arguments before the Kansas Supreme Court, Byrne said quietly to a spectator, "Fifteen years is a long time. I hope he gets off, gets another trial, but he did kill somebody, didn't he?"

On December third, 1982, Jimmy's appeal was denied and his life sentence affirmed.

7

On December ninth, Ed Hobson and Reverend John Adams, now a resident chaplain at St. Luke's Hospital, drove down to the state reformatory at Hutchinson to talk with Jimmy.

Jimmy was very nervous about meeting Ed. Jimmy had killed Ed's boy and he wanted to tell Ed directly that he was sorry about what he had done. Ed, Reverend Adams, and Jimmy sat side by side in plastic chairs in the large green-walled waiting room, the walls a shade darker than the robes doctors wear at operations. They talked quietly together while other visits went on around them.

"I told the truth in court in Mother's trial so Ed would know for once what the truth was," Jimmy said. "He never could accept it. He never will now.

"Ed said, 'What I want is for her to get out. I want you to tell the truth.' Reverend Adams sitting there would say, 'Tell the truth. The truth will set you free!' He'd say it over and over again, 'The truth will set you free!' I was near tears hearing him say that and angry, too, that a minister would do that. I said to both Ed and Adams, 'I told the truth.'

"Then suddenly Ed said, 'If you change your story, I'll get you the best lawyers I can buy, give you money. What I want is my family back again—you and Sueanne and Suzanne. I want my family back.'

"What bothered me was he wasn't interested in what happened to Chris anymore. Ed was so dependent on Mother that that was all he cared about now."

Yet that day when Jimmy spoke of Ed's visit he wore a gold chain that Sueanne and Suzanne had given him on his seventeenth birthday, the only birthday he had in the Hobson house. To the chain he attached a St. Jude medal. He had little interest in religion, but because of prison regulations he must wear the medal in order to wear the chain.

8

After Ed's visit Sueanne began to write to Jimmy from her cell in the women's prison upstate at Lansing. Until then she had not exchanged a word with him for two and a half years—not since they had spoken in the days before Chris's body was found. There was no phone call, no letter, no embrace, no word exchanged in the hearings and the trials. Now in each long letter to her son she wrote repeatedly between evenly spaced lines, like grace notes, "Love ya! Love ya!"

Ed began to send a little money to Jimmy monthly. Jimmy thought Ed "was fixated. He'll stop at nothing to get her out."

That Christmas Jimmy also began to get letters from Henry Floyd Brown, a prisoner at Lansing. Brown had murdered a policeman during a manhunt after a bank robbery twenty years earlier. Now approaching sixty, Brown was easily the most intelligent and influential prisoner in Lansing. Brown wrote that Jimmy should think about his role in the conviction of his mother; he himself respected Sueanne and believed in her innocence.

At the same time Paul Sorrentino also received a Christmas card and a letter from Brown. Paul immediately mailed Brown's letter to his father. Paul later testified, "I understood what he was asking and I decided that what he does is his own business and that I want no party to it. I will not lie for anyone."

The pressure on Jimmy to recant his testimony was more intense. Brown, Jimmy thought, was a genius, the most feared prisoner in the state system. Like Paul, Jimmy well understood what Brown could do, yet he said, "What do I care? What could he do to me? I'm a dead man already." The word that came to Jimmy through the grapevine was that "Brown didn't like little boys who testified against their mamas."

Brown's interest was not just with Sueanne, though the two did exchange photographs and each kept them on the walls of their cells. Brown and Sueanne never met and were kept in adjacent prisons. Brown was due for a parole hearing and Ed Hobson agreed to let Brown live with him; each prisoner had to have a place to live before he could be paroled.

In concert with Hobson, Tom Leathers, the Johnson County publisher, offered Brown a job in his business. The first big story Leathers had covered in his career was Brown's killing of a policeman. Leathers interviewed Brown in the hospital right after he was shot and captured. He saw how Brown refused anesthesia when the doctors removed the bullet and, later, he was impressed by his intelligence and befriended Brown.

Leathers' offer to employ Brown further alienated Dennis Moore and Johnson County law enforcement generally. Whatever happened in his reporting, Leathers always made himself the center of the story. His friendship with Brown had long been an open sore for police.

In fact Leathers' articles on Sueanne's case and his role in suggesting that Brown's correspondence and guidance might help her adjust to prison first brought the Hobsons and Brown together. With Sueanne's encouragement Ed was soon visiting Brown every weekend.

Leathers seemed naive or careless, unaware of the actual danger to Jimmy and Paul that Brown presented in his alliance with Leathers and the Hobsons. There were numerous prisoners in both Hutchinson and Lansing who owed Brown favors.

In many ways Sueanne was already Brown's counterpart. In the world outside she could thoroughly dominate simple men and some women. In prison she sought control and there was a clear system she could promptly master. She understood quickly that raw physical power was nothing, that alliances were what she needed.

Jimmy also understood this, though he didn't seek domination. "Down in Hutchinson I always liked to be number two in the pecking order," Jimmy said. "There were six bunks in each cell, and when somebody wouldn't turn off the light at night, and it got to me, I'd talk to my tough friend and he'd jump right down and say, 'What the fuck is going on down here?' That way I didn't have to do any fighting. They're barbarians! Barbarians!"

9

"Henry Floyd Brown is a very dear friend of mine, and his family also," Ed wrote.

"Henry is such a nice person," Sueanne wrote. "He's been so good to Ed and I. He calls Edward often and Ed sees him every week before he visits me. He's a good man to know, and I know he would help you if you let him. He has friends here and everywhere. He has pictures of our family and I have one of him on my wall. He's a member of our family, honey, just like you."

Sueanne and Brown continued to send Jimmy subtle, gentle letters telling him how all the prisoners are members of a family, how all will surely be there to welcome him when he is transferred upstate to Lansing.

10

In September 1983 Sueanne's appeal of her murder trial was heard by the Kansas Supreme Court. Scott Kreamer spoke to overturn her conviction, Steve Tatum to affirm it. The main issues in dispute concerned the admission into evidence of Suzanne's tape and of Margie Hunt-Fugate's testimony, and the suppression of Dr. Chester Day's account of Sueanne's psychotherapy.

There were several hours of delay before the case was called up. Ed Hobson paced the hallways of the supreme-court building; his optimism and nervousness and great energy seemed scarcely contained. He came forward to be interviewed repeatedly about his loyalty to Sueanne and his belief in her innocence. Though many knew of Ed's improper advances to Suzanne, no one asked about it or about his stepdaughter.

Tatum spoke guardedly about Suzanne. Though everyone involved in law enforcement in Johnson County knew, it had not reached the newspapers. Ed had been much less aggressive since that night. The charges against him could be reinstated at any point, Tatum said, but for now it kept Ed under control.

After the appeal, while the participants were standing together waiting for the elevators, Tatum whispered to another lawyer that he was not getting on Hobson's elevator. Tatum watched Hobson as he stood just inside the elevator door, chatting happily with a lawyer friend; he was half smiling, eager, and hopeful.

11

Strangely, the old relationship when Jimmy first moved into the house with his mother was there again all that year, the fourth year after the murder. Again she wanted something and he was tied to her with a deadly intensity beyond that of mother and son, still held to her as tightly as if she were the cruel, fair one, the beloved.

He wanted to escape that bond. "I lack emotion," Jimmy said. "I've always lacked emotion. They're giving me therapy here, trying to get me to feel things." As he spoke his beautiful face expressed every nuance of his speech, as if he were drowning in emotion. "I hope to God I've got emotion now. They told me that anger is a secondary emotion, that the emotion behind the anger is sadness.

"Paul is more cynical than I am," Jimmy said. "I don't think he feels any remorse yet. When we eat together, I tease him and say, 'You're only sorry you got caught!' Still, what did Paul do to have remorse? He was just a hired gun really.

"Chris's death blew apart the Crumm family and the Hobson family and the Sallees and I'm sorry about that," he said.

Like Paul, Jimmy was sorry about himself, too. "I'm an Andy Gump! An Andy Gump! How did she get me to believe her? How? How did she get me to do it? I'm so gullible."

Unlike Suzanne, Jimmy couldn't let go of his mother. "I accept her as my mother. I love her because she's my mother, despite what she did. The therapists say I should, so it's okay," he said hesitantly, falling back into himself.

In the midst of his affirmation of his love for his mother and her elaborate attempts to get him to recant his testimony, he paused. "We did it together. Why wouldn't she tell me why she did it? She owes me an explanation. If we ever see each other again, do you think she'll tell me why?"

12

On the seventeenth day of October 1983, while a decision on Sueanne's appeal to the Kansas Supreme Court was about to come down, Scott Kreamer received a call from Ed Merrick, a prisoner at Lansing. Apparently Sorrentino had told Merrick that Sueanne had nothing to do with the murder of Chris.

Kreamer immediately drove up to Lansing to take a deposition from Merrick. Merrick's information was completely based on Paul's statements. "Paul told me that the reason Chris was murdered was because Jimmy thought Chris was going to inherit a sizable amount of money. If Chris was dead, Jimmy reasoned that his mom would have access to these funds and would share the money with Jimmy. Paul told me that they implicated Sueanne Hobson only because they thought things would go easier on them if they could convince the police that it was Sueanne's idea to kill Chris."

Merrick concluded, "I am somewhat afraid of making this information known as I am fearful that Dennis Moore might try to block my application for early parole."

Four days later, on the twenty-first of October, Sueanne's conviction was confirmed by the supreme court. The court emphasized that the questioning of Suzanne and Judge Jones's admission of the tape recording of her interview at the police station was permissible. The court appended eight pages of Suzanne's testimony to support its position.

The supreme court also attached the testimony of Margie Hunt-Fugate. The court declared that Sueanne's casual, incriminating remarks to Margie were properly admitted into evidence: "Spontaneous statements made by a defendant prior to the commission of a crime are admissible to show intent, plan, motive, design, malice, or ill will where the defendant's state of mind is an issue in the case or is relevant to prove or explain acts or conduct of the defendant."

If Kreamer had little interest in Sueanne and none of his father's excitement about the case, he did hate to lose and he did like being the center of attention. Now that the supreme court's decision was in, on Saturday, the twenty-second of October, Kreamer, with the deposition of Merrick in hand (a convicted forger and a writer of worthless checks), immediately went to the press with quotes from Sorrentino that apparently contradicted his trial testimony. Kreamer said he intended to file a motion for a retrial based on newly discovered evidence.

On Sunday, the twenty-third of October, Mark Williams, a former client of Kreamer, out on parole from Lansing for passing bad checks, read the newspaper article on Kreamer's discovery of new evidence. Williams called Kreamer the next day. In a deposition taken on the twenty-seventh of October, Williams said that Paul told him "he was 'on the state's side' and that he did not want Mr. Kreamer to 'screw up my deal.' Paul Sorrentino said that the reason he knew Sueanne had nothing to do with it was because Jimmy Crumm had originated the idea because he thought Chris Hobson was going to receive a large amount of money and Jimmy figured he could get some of this money if Chris were dead. Paul Sorrentino told me that the reason he was implicating Sueanne Hobson was 'to watch out for Paul.'"

Merrick's statement and Williams' were essentially similar. Kreamer's principle seemed to be, "If two people say it, it must be true." And for once Jimmy's motives were made quite clear: money.

On the twenty-sixth of October Jeffrey Wood, a man convicted of murdering his wife, phoned Kreamer. Kreamer met him in Lansing on the fifteenth of November. According to Wood, "Paul said that Sueanne Hobson had nothing to do with the killing of Chris Hobson, but that Paul had to say that she was involved in order to take advantage of the prosecutor's offer for an early release from prison."

Kreamer was elated. It was as if these three men coming forward were a marvelous coincidence. "Those two boys killed Chris," Scott said, "and one of the two said Sueanne had nothing to do with it. What could you want better than that? This is new evidence. If we had paraded those three people past the jury last year, the prosecution wouldn't have had a case. One of the two said that one of the three had nothing to do with the murder."

13

The retrial motion was heard on the twenty-first of December. Fortunately the prisoners had been transported to the Johnson County Courthouse the day before. The heaviest snow of the winter, nearly a foot, had drifted across major roads. Most of the highways were impassable without four-wheel-drive vehicles. Except for Sueanne's retrial motion, no offices in the courthouse were open and Judge Jones was answering his own phone.

Even the reporters didn't appear on that cold, snowy morning. Still, sitting quietly in the front row of the courtroom was Dorothy Reffitt, a heavy, round motherly woman in brown. She was whispering to her sister, Joyce Koonce.

Sueanne Hobson was led in first. She had a yellow four-inch-square identification card pinned above her right breast; a woman jailor removed her handcuffs after she sat down at the table beside Kreamer. Sueanne was dressed in a lime-green prison uniform. She had short bangs on her forehead. Her reddish-brown hair hung down past her shoulders and she looked girlish, younger than she had in two years of hearings and trials. Her face was a little heavier, a little fuller, and the weight flattered her. Her hands were set formally in her lap. Her face and hair looked like that of passive waiting women in Pre-Raphaelite paintings by Rossetti.

Judge Jones formally acknowledged the motion for a retrial and asked Kreamer to proceed. Scott immediately called Paul Sorrentino to the stand. Paul's appearance had changed in the year and a half since Sueanne's trial. Dark, subdued, speaking in a soft voice, he had grown a thick, black mustache and his body had thickened, too, had become even more muscular, as if the pads of fat were not reduced at all but had become muscle.

The prosecutors were anxious to keep Jimmy off the stand, concerned about the potential threat posed by Brown. In fact, Tatum lied about Jimmy's whereabouts the day before the trial. He also explored with reporters who had spoken with Jimmy what they knew and would testify to in court about Brown's statements. If Jimmy had to testify, his situation in Hutchinson might become more dangerous. He might be ostracized further or even assaulted. Still, if they had to, they'd call him to keep Sueanne in prison whatever the consequences might be.

Paul claimed he did not recognize two of the three people Kreamer paraded by him. He did not know Williams and Wood; Merrick he acknowledged. Even with Merrick he claimed not to have discussed the crime.

Kreamer asked, "Have you ever told anybody, anyone at all, that Sueanne Hobson had nothing to do with the murder of Christen Hobson?"

"In my opinion, I might have." Paul was still seeking to please everyone—a little for the defense—a little for the prosecution.

"Whom did you tell that to?"

"Some cellees, people who I lived with." Paul could not recall the names of the people he had met in Johnson County or down in Hutchinson with whom he had spoken. This was as far as Kreamer could get Paul to go.

Moore cross-examined Sorrentino. "Paul, do you know if Sueanne Hobson had something to do with the murder?"

"I have absolutely no idea. I have an opinion, but I have no facts."

"And why is that?"

"Because all the information I received came from a third person, Jimmy Crumm."

"Mr. Sorrentino, have you received any contact or any correspondence from any person regarding your testimony about the matter here in court?"

"Yes, Henry Brown."

"Do you recall when you received a letter or correspondence from Henry Floyd Brown?"

"Yes. Around September of '83, August. Last Christmas I received a Christmas card."

"So out of the blue, you get a Christmas card in December of '82 from Henry Floyd Brown?"

"Yes."

"Paul, where is the Christmas card and where is the letter?"

"The Christmas card I no longer have. I threw it away. The letter I mailed home—had several copies made."

"Where are the copies?"

"With my father."

"Were you concerned about the letter and the implications to you?"

"I was concerned with what he was asking me to do. It was my hope that—if I not necessarily forgot about the letter, but not have correspondence with him—he would pursue another avenue."

During the hearing Scott Kreamer was impaled on his dead father's brilliant cross-examination of Sorrentino. Hugh Kreamer had intended to demonstrate that Sorrentino had nothing to do with Sueanne Hobson, that Sorrentino could not be used to convict her because he had never even spoken to her about the conspiracy. Hugh had made Paul irrelevant and the state had given back to him seven and a half years to get his useless testimony. During Sueanne's trial Hugh mockingly called Paul "Secondhand Sorrentino."

Now Scott was trying to show that Sorrentino knew about Sueanne's involvement and that he had provided information used to convict her. What already seemed clear was that Paul had said to several people that Sueanne had nothing to do with the murder. He readily admitted this. What Kreamer needed to establish was logically impossible—to prove that Sueanne was not involved , in fact to prove a negative.

14

Kreamer's next three witnesses were the men he deposed. Ed Merrick was the first called to the stand. He had reddish-blond hair and an untamed beard and mustache. He, too, wore a green prison uniform that matched Sueanne's in color.

Scott Kreamer asked Merrick when they first spoke together about the case. Merrick said, "We were sitting on a bench right outside the electric-shop office. It really seemed like a real, real bad crime, and then Paul went on to say that Sueanne never knew nothing about it and I couldn't understand any of that either, why a woman who supposedly wasn't guilty was in prison doing time. And Paul went on to say the only reason they ever brought Sueanne into the case was because they thought the court would go easier on them, or they were going to get off."

"And what else did Paul say?" Kreamer asked.

"Paul said that supposedly Christen Hobson was going to get an inheritance, and supposedly from Ed Hobson or whoever. If Christen Hobson was out of the way, Sueanne would be in line to get it and that's why they did what they did to Christen Hobson."

"Did Paul say anything about Sueanne's involvement in this crime?"

"He said she had absolutely nothing to do with it."

"Okay. And who did you tell about the conversation you'd had with Paul?"

"Sueanne Hobson and Ed Hobson."

"And why did you tell them?"

"Well, Sueanne and Ed got to know my little boy and my wife fairly well. We would always talk, and Sueanne never really did talk about her crime. All she said was she was innocent, and you know, to me, the more I got to know Sueanne, it didn't seem like she could be the type of woman to have any involvement in this."

"And why had you not come forward before then?"

"Well, usually in prison, you don't, you know, people talk, and you usually don't come off saying, repeating what other people said, because you either end up with a pipe upsides your head or you end up dead."

Merrick knew Sueanne was a friend of Henry Floyd Brown. "The reason I found out is that when Henry Floyd Brown came up for parole, it came out in the Topeka newspaper that he was trying to parole to Ed Hobson, and that he was denied parole. Supposedly, Ed Hobson was going to sponsor him when he got out on parole, at least that's what it said in the Shawnee paper in Topeka."

Merrick said he had written to Brown before he signed the affidavit. "There's rumors going around all the time, you know, it seemed like when you do something, it's everybody's business. It's either a guard there telling another inmate or an inmate talking, or a couple of guys come up to me there and said that I'd be labeled as a snitch if I come forward to help Sueanne.

"Brown wrote her, and he just told her that I wouldn't be labeled as a snitch."

15

Kreamer called Jeff Wood to the stand. Wood was a dark-complexioned, shaggy man who had murdered his wife.

According to Wood, "Sorrentino said that she had nothing to do with the killing of Christen Hobson, that the prosecutor made him an offer for his testimony—he would be released seven and a half years early. I talked to him a couple of different times. He seemed like he was the leader in that cell, more or less."

"Do you know Henry Floyd Brown?" Kreamer asked.

"Yes, I do."

"Henry Floyd Brown ever make any promises to you or threats against you to cause you to give this testimony?"

"No."

Moore stood up to cross-examine Wood. "Anybody suggest to you that you contact Scott Kreamer?"

"Yes, they did."

"Who?"

"Henry Floyd Brown."

"How do you know Henry Floyd Brown?"

"We're incarcerated together at the Kansas State Penitentiary."

"In fact, you know him pretty well, don't you?"

"I know him fairly well," Wood said.

"Has he got a reputation in the prison?"

"He might, to some people."

"What's his reputation to you?"

"To me?"

"Yes."

"I think he's a nice guy," Wood said.

"Been around a long time, hasn't he?"

"Yes, yeah."

"Knows the ropes?"

"Yeah, he does."

"Help people?"

"Some."

"If he wants to?"

"Some, I guess. I don't know. He's never done that for me."

"Do you know Sueanne Hobson?"

"No, I don't."

"Do you know Ed Hobson?"

"No, I don't."

"All right. You know Jeff Wood," Moore asserted. "That's you."

"That's me."

"And you know yesterday you were riding down here with Ed Merrick, is that correct? What did you tell him Henry Floyd Brown was like?"

"I told him he was all right. I don't really know Henry all that well."

"Where is your cell, Mr. Wood, in relationship to Henry Floyd Brown's cell?"

"He lives downstairs. Well, they call them walks. He lives on the flag, and I live on two walk."

"Flag is the bottom floor?"

"That's correct. We're not even really close. He's the laundryman. He brings socks and towels by the cell, and he runs the laundry room there in 'B' cellhouse."

"What does Henry Floyd Brown tell you about Sueanne Hobson?"

"He doesn't talk that much about her."

"What does he say when he talks?"

"He thinks she's a nice girl. Guess he doesn't think she should be in prison. He doesn't agree with her son testifying against her. He said that he thought that was a pretty low thing to do, to testify against his own mom, but other than that, he hasn't said too much."

16

Mark Williams was Kreamer's last witness. Well dressed in a gray suit, he had a sophisticated, complex, handsome face. He was on parole after being in prison for passing twenty-three bad checks. He was now selling Honda cars. The jail record showed that Williams and Paul were in Cell Unit G together with nine or ten other prisoners during Sueanne's trial. Scott Kreamer was the lawyer of record for Williams during this period.

"What did Paul tell you about his involvement?" Scott asked.

"He told me some of the details—that he had, you know, pulled the trigger on the young son." Williams spoke in a facile way.

"Did he ever talk about Sueanne's involvement in this case?"

"Yes, we did. The first time I met Paul was the evening I was transferred into the cell and we talked privately from that time on."

"Do you recall some of the other things that you and he discussed?"

"Yeah. It was idle conversation—like cars, where he'd like to go on dates, people he knew, where he had lived, idle conversation."

"Let's go to the conversation where you talked about Sueanne Hobson's involvement."

"I don't know how we transcended in that conversation, whether I initiated it. I know we were talking about the case, Paul's involvement, Jimmy Crumm's involvement, and

Sueanne's involvement. And Paul made an outstanding statement which sticks in my head. What he said was, 'I don't think
she had anything to do with it. In fact, I know that she didn't.'"
The rhythm of the Williams quote reflected exactly the way
Sorrentino commonly spoke—repetition and a rising note of
certainty.

"Did he tell you why he knew that she had nothing to do
with it?"

Williams answered vaguely. "As I recall, it was planned by
he or Jimmy, or he and Jimmy, for money for the purpose of
acquiring some money coming from some unknown source."

"Did Sorrentino make any statements about why he was
implicating Sueanne?"

"He made some off-the-wall comments and statements, but
he was not specific in his perceivement." Williams occasionally
inserted words like "transcended" or "perceivement" as if to
impress a Honda buyer. "I don't think I tried to corner him or
pin him down or anything. I found it very peculiar that Paul did
not want to talk to Hugh Kreamer."

Dennis Moore began his cross-examination by asking
Williams, "Have you always told the truth?"

"No, sir, I have not."

"Who is Dr. Terry Allen?"

"Dr. Terry Allen *Estes?*" Williams emphasized the last name,
adding it almost proudly, as if it were his own. Everyone present
except Williams, Moore, and the judge smiled. "That's a fictitious
person who I made up to impose a scam."

"So you were Mark Williams, also known as Dr. Terry Allen
Estes?"

"Alias Dr. Terry Allen Estes," Williams interjected. He spoke
solemnly and precisely, as if he were correcting a student.

Moore thought that was enough to besmirch the character of the
witness and he turned to Williams's conversations with Sorrentino.
"What did Paul Sorrentino tell you to make you believe that he was
telling the truth when he told you that he knew Mrs. Hobson didn't
have anything to do with the murder?"

"He was there. He pled guilty to the act. He was a main character in the event. If anybody would know, I would guess it

would be Paul Sorrentino and James Crumm."

"You would guess, right?" Moore said sarcastically.

"I would guess." Williams leaned back in the witness chair, his hands and face looking like he was smelling something bad.

"Please listen carefully. How do you *know* that Paul Sorrentino knew or did not know that Sueanne Hobson was involved in that murder?"

"Mr. Moore, I personally do not know."

"Do you have any motivation for coming here and giving this testimony?"

"Maybe a—I was going to say cleaning my conscience, but I'm not sure if that would be totally true. I have information, I have been told things that may be important to a lot of people, one person in particular," he said, glancing at Sueanne.

17

Ed Hobson was the first witness Moore called and the last before lunch. Moore asked, "Mr. Hobson, do you know Henry Floyd Brown?"

"Yes, I do."

"How do you know Henry Floyd Brown?"

"He mailed me a letter. That's how we met."

"When was that, sir?" Moore asked.

"Oh, I'm trying to think." Hobson didn't want to be precise. "Either prior, during, or right after Sueanne's trial." He hated Moore. Like a child he did whatever he could to aggravate him.

"What happened after that letter came to you?"

"I wrote him back."

"Why did you write him back?"

"Because he knows my wife is innocent, just like I do." Ed's hands were folded in a triangle and held between his legs, reflecting the inverted triangle his body made as if restraining any motion. He wore a dark blue suit, a tie, and a vest.

"Did he say that to you in the letter?"

"Yes, he did."

"Did he say how he'd know that?"

"No."

"He just knew it?"

"Uh-huh." Ed drew out the sound as if he were mocking Moore.

Moore ignored his tone. "All right. And you wrote him back, and struck up a friendship with Henry Floyd Brown. Is that correct?"

"Yes."

"In fact, you visit him regularly."

"Yes, I do."

"And you visit him when you go to see Sueanne Hobson. Is that correct?"

"Yes, I do."

"Have you had contact or written to him frequently?"

"Yeah. I sent him a Christmas card."

"But you see him personally about every week? And have you talked with Henry Floyd Brown about what you and Henry Floyd Brown might do to try and get a new trial for your wife?"

"No, I have not."

"When did you last talk to Ed Merrick?"

"Oh, last—this last summer."

"And how did that come about, Mr. Hobson?"

"Oh, I don't know. Up there in the summertime you can go out and sit on the picnic benches. And his wife and his little boy was up there, and his little boy was sitting on one side of the picnic table, playing with some dominoes that Sueanne and I play on weekends when we're up there, and we got to talking a little bit. Probably a couple weeks later we were talking again and Merrick knew Sueanne was innocent." Innocence seemed quite as tangible as any other commodity.

"Okay. Did he tell you how he knew that?"

"Yes, he did. He said that he was in Hutchinson with Paul Sorrentino, and Paul told him that he knew that Sueanne was innocent."

"Do you know if Henry Floyd Brown has ever talked to anyone about testifying or filing an affidavit?"

"Not that I know of. Wait a minute. I think he knows Jeff Wood."

"Do you know if he talked to him about filing an affidavit in this case?"

"No. I don't know for sure. No. I never asked him that question."

"Have you ever tried to see Jimmy Crumm?"

"Yes, I have."

"Who is Jimmy Crumm?"

"He is my stepson."

"Have you talked to him about coming forward with some new evidence?"

"I asked him to change his story." Unlike Sueanne, he seemed to hide nothing.

"When was that?"

"December ninth, 1982," Ed said.

"What did you ask him to say?"

"I asked him to tell the truth."

"Have you written to Jimmy Crumm?"

"I wrote him a little while—two or three letters around last Christmas."

"Did you send him any money?"

"Yeah. I sent him ten dollars oh, once a month, or something like that, for a little while."

"Do you know if Sueanne Hobson has written to Jimmy Crumm?"

"She wrote him one letter."

Moore asked, as if astonished, "One letter?"

Ed said, "Uh-huh," with a note of sarcasm.

"Could there be more than one?"

"No." He was certain.

"How do you know that?"

"That's what she told me." Sueanne's authority was enough to convince him.

"Do you know if she's ever talked to Jimmy about changing his story?"

"No, she has not."

"You're certain about that?"

"Yes, sir, I am."

"Would it surprise you if I showed you—"

"Yeah," he interrupted, reddening. Perhaps she was deceiving him.

"Do you know if Henry Floyd Brown knows Jimmy Crumm?"

"I don't think he knows him, I don't think he's ever met him."

"Do you know if Brown's ever written to Jimmy?"

"Probably has."

"Why do you say that?"

"Well, I've got a Christmas card."

"What do you mean you've got a Christmas card?"

"Well, the institution searched Henry Floyd Brown's cell and pulled out four Christmas cards, one to Sueanne, one to myself, one to Paul Sorrentino, one to James Crumm. They opened Paul Sorrentino's and James Crumm's, sent a photostatic copy of the one of James Crumm to the Overland Park Police Department."

"How did you know that?"

"I've got a letter from Henry and a letter from the lawyer at the institution stating this."

"Do you know if he's written Jimmy more than Christmas cards?"

"I don't know. I've never asked him. We talk about playing soccer and stuff like that when I go up there."

"Do you know if Henry Floyd Brown has ever written Paul Sorrentino?"

"Possibly has. I don't know."

"Do you consider Henry Floyd Brown a part of your family, Mr. Hobson?"

"In a lot of respects, yes. He's a very nice man."

"What's he in jail for?"

"Bank robbery and murder."

"Nice man," Moore said sarcastically. Judge Jones let it pass.

"Uh-huh." Ed paused for a second or two. "He doesn't lie," Ed said, implying that Moore did.

Hobson admitted to Moore that he had written at least three or four letters to Jimmy and that some of these letters referred to Henry Floyd Brown. "Mr. Hobson, I'm handing you what's been received in evidence now as State Exhibit Number One, and ask, did you say to Jimmy Crumm, 'Henry Floyd

Brown is a very dear friend of mine, and his family also'?"

"Yes. I also believed at that time I was going to have Henry come live with me if he made it out on parole. That was public knowledge."

Kreamer objected strenuously to the admission of the letter in court. Moore summarized the evidence: "Judge, the relevancy to all of this, and the only reason the name Henry Floyd Brown has come up, is time and time again, Henry Floyd Brown has talked to people who do have knowledge or claim to have knowledge about this case. Henry Floyd Brown knows Jeff Wood. He lives in the cell directly below him, and he sees Jeff Wood every day. Henry Floyd Brown is known, at least, to Ed Merrick, and Ed, riding down here with Jeff Wood, asked out of the blue, 'How's Henry Floyd Brown?' You've heard Ed Merrick testify that Henry Floyd Brown wrote him a letter because he was the only inmate he knew at Kansas State Penitentiary, and I think we can show, if we're allowed to go forward with this, that there's an effort by some people to try to get, as Mr. Hobson said, some other people to change their stories or to come forward with certain evidence here. That's the relevancy."

"Whether Henry Floyd Brown and Ed Hobson are friends makes no difference," Kreamer argued. "It doesn't have any relationship to whether or not the three people who have testified are telling the truth or not. It's a smoke screen, Judge. It's a smoke screen. It's all they've got. They keep throwing Henry Floyd Brown's name around here but it's not relevant because the people have already testified they don't know him. I mean, talk about going out on a tangent."

"Judge, the state's position is that Henry Floyd Brown's whole scheme bears directly on the credibility of the persons who filed affidavits in support of Sueanne Hobson's motion for a new trial," Moore said.

Judge Jones overruled Kreamer's objection and allowed Moore to resume his direct examination of Hobson. Moore began, "Did you make the statement to Jimmy Crumm, 'I know Henry would like to be your friend and help you. He's a very lovely man. There are so many ways he has helped us and he will do the same for you if you let him'?"

"Yes, I said that."

"Do you know if Sueanne Hobson's written to Henry Floyd Brown?

"Sure."

"Does she have a picture of him?"

"Yes."

"Where?"

"Well, I say she has a picture of him. I've never seen it. I've been told she has a picture of him."

With that Moore ended his direct examination of Ed Hobson.

Kreamer began his cross-examination focusing again on Henry Floyd Brown. "Ed, in that letter, is there anything in there about Henry Floyd's going to hire people to come in and testify?"

"There's nothing in here at all about Henry doing this or asking Jimmy to change his story or putting pressure on Jimmy to change his story—absolutely nothing."

"Is Jeff Wood's name mentioned?"

"Jeff Wood's, nobody's name, is mentioned except Henry Floyd Brown and my"—Ed falters for a moment—"and my daughter's."

"At one time you went down to talk to Jimmy. I think you've been down once since your wife was convicted, correct?"

"Yes."

"And did you put the pressure on Jimmy down there and threaten him?"

"No, I did not. I went down there for about three reasons. Number one was my own peace of mind, to see if I could face him because he killed my son."

"Had someone suggested to you that you do that?"

"No, but I had to live with myself. That's the reason I started writing Jimmy, to just try to get a line of communications open, to where I could go see him, because I had to keep my own mental stability as well."

"Okay. And what were the other two reasons you went down?"

"I went down there to ask Jimmy to tell the truth."

"What else?"

"Because I know my wife's innocent."

"What else?"

"I went down there to find out the deal Dennis Moore made him to testify."

"Okay," Kreamer said. "That's all I have."

Moore had one more thing he wanted to explore. "You said that Henry Floyd Brown's helped you. Have you helped him?"

"I think I sent him twenty-five dollars last Christmas."

"You obviously promised to take Henry Floyd Brown in if he were placed on parole with you."

"Right."

"That's help, isn't it?" Moore asked.

"Sure. I'd do the same thing for a dog."

18

During the lunch hour Tom Leathers drove across town to observe. Two or three other reporters showed up. Moore and Leathers spoke openly before the reporters and the lawyers who came downstairs to watch the hearing. It was Brown everybody wanted to hear about. Leathers didn't see anything wrong with Brown; he was a good prisoner and Leathers had known him for twenty years. Brown certainly knew the prison system and could work within it—perhaps he was better off there, Leathers said.

Moore was angered by Leathers' casual remarks about his friendship with Brown. Leathers was hard to confront; he seemed to agree and disagree affably, as if there were no principles at stake in any of this. He was playing, he was having fun.

A few other lawyers, including Ed Byrne, Jimmy's lawyer, gathered in the virtually empty courthouse hall. One said quietly, "Why this fear of Brown? What makes everybody so afraid of him?"

"Would you like to get a letter from Brown? In or out of prison, would you like to get a letter from him?" Byrne responded. Without question Brown was feared, whether in prison or out of it.

Before the hearing began again, Judge Jones had to dispose of a series of brief legal motions. He had to provide a legal statement allowing prisoners to be incarcerated subject to further hearings. Twenty prisoners were led in handcuffed and chained to each other. Most were shaggy-haired and wearing green uniforms as loose as pajamas. They seemed anonymous, evil, green-looking creatures, helpless now but waiting for something.

For a span of half an hour Judge Jones listened for a minute or two to those prisoners who had lawyers present and then ruled monotonously to send them back to their cells. When Jones had finished with them and they were led out of the room, he slumped for a moment and said to no one in particular, "My God!" as if he'd barely maintained control through something horrible.

19

Immediately after lunch Moore called Sueanne Hobson to the stand. "You are the mother of James Crumm?" he asked.

"Yes, sir," Sueanne said.

"Stepmother of Christen Hobson?"

"Yes. Adopted mother, yes."

"Mrs. Hobson, do you know Henry Floyd Brown?"

"Through correspondence only. I've never met him."

"How did you start corresponding with Henry Floyd Brown?"

"He sent a letter to Tom Leathers, and Tom forwarded the letter to Ed and I, and I called Tom and asked him if I could write a thank-you letter to Henry because, at that time, I didn't know prisoners were allowed to have mail."

"And you corresponded with Henry Floyd Brown?"

"Yes, sir."

"And you consider Henry Floyd Brown a friend?"

"Well, as much as he can be through the mails. I've never met him."

"Is he an important person to you?"

"Important? I—well, I don't know exactly what you mean. You mean in comparison to my husband, no."

"Well, no. I didn't mean that. But do you have a picture of Henry—"

"In comparison to Scott, no," she said, interrupting Moore.

"Do you have a picture of Henry Floyd Brown on your wall?"

"I sure do."

"Do you have a picture of Scott Kreamer on your wall?"

"No, but I have a picture of another man that I write to in Michigan City State Prison in Indiana."

"Is he important, in the sense that you have a picture of him on your wall?"

"Well, I have lots of pictures on my wall."

"Well, have you talked to Henry Floyd Brown or corresponded with him about this motion for a new trial?"

"No, sir. I have—I write to him, but I'm not allowed to talk to him."

"Have you corresponded with him or has he corresponded with you about how you might go about getting a new trial?"

"No, sir."

"Has he corresponded with you about the correspondence with Jimmy Crumm?"

"No, sir."

"Have you had any correspondence with Jimmy Crumm?"

"I wrote him one letter after he asked my husband to ask me to write him."

"One?"

"Uh-huh," she said. Ed had already spoken of only one letter to Jimmy.

"Could it be two?"

"I don't remember. I remember one clearly."

"Okay."

"I would have to see the other one."

"Do you recall when the one was that you do remember?"

"Beg your pardon?"

"Do you recall when you wrote the one letter that you do remember?"

"Well, it was in '82. I don't remember the exact date, but I'm sure Jimmy still has the letter."

"Did you talk to Jimmy in that letter about Henry Floyd Brown?"

"No, sir."

"You didn't?"

"No, sir." She seemed to be waiting for a confrontation she would not win.

"Did you ever talk to Jimmy, write Jimmy, about Henry Floyd Brown?"

"Not that I recall. No, sir."

"Let me refresh memory."

"All right."

Moore handed Sueanne a letter. After a few moments he asked, "Did you get a chance to look this over, Mrs. Hobson?"

"Yes, I read it. "

"What is that?"

"It's a letter that I wrote to Jimmy, but the date isn't on it." It was as if she intended to distract Moore from the scent by mentioning her failure to date the letter.

"All right. Does it refer to another card that you might have written to Jimmy?"

"Uh-huh."

"That would indicate that maybe you wrote at least twice?"

"It says I decided to rewrite the paragraph I crossed off the card, and I do not remember the card." According to Jimmy and Ed Byrne there were many letters.

"Okay. Do you remember talking to Jimmy in that letter about Henry Floyd Brown?"

"Uh-huh. This—it was written right after I went to Lansing."

"Would that be in January of '83?"

"Could it have been written? I don't know. The date isn't on here."

"All right."

"And Ed went to see Jimmy in December of '82, so it could have been. It would have had to have been after that because that's when he asked Ed to ask me to write him."

"So it could have been in January of '83, this letter?"

"It could have been, yes. Uh-huh."

"All right. And did you tell Jimmy, 'Henry is such a nice person. He's been so good to Ed and I'?"

"Uh-huh. He has helped us a lot."

Moore continued to read the letter slowly. "'He's a good man to know, and I know he would help you if you let him.'"

"Uh-huh."

"'And he has friends here and everywhere.'"

"Uh-huh."

"Where is here and everywhere?" Moore asked.

"In the penitentiary. He helped me to adjust because I'd never been in jail or in the penitentiary before, and Henry's been locked up so long, and he wrote to me about the games that they play in prison, and what to do and what not to do, and not to get involved, and to stay to myself, and to be myself."

"Henry has friends at Kansas State Industrial Reformatory in Hutchinson, doesn't he?"

"That I don't know, sir."

"Is that everywhere, when you say here and everywhere?"

"I don't know."

"'He's a member of our family, honey, just like you,'" Moore continued.

"Uh-huh."

"'He calls Edward often, and Ed sees him every week before he visits me.'"

"Uh-huh." Sueanne made virtually no response.

"'He has pictures of our family and I have one of him on my wall.'"

"We had a picture—Ed and I had a picture taken at Lansing together and sent one to him."

"Mrs. Hobson, do you know if Henry Floyd Brown was writing letters to Jimmy Crumm?"

"No, sir."

"He wasn't or you don't know?"

"I don't know that he was."

"Do you know if he wrote to Paul Sorrentino?"

"No, sir. I don't know," Sueanne said.

Moore turned the witness over to Kreamer. "And you wrote this letter down to Jimmy. Why did you write it?" Scott asked.

"Because when Ed went to see Jimmy, Jimmy asked him to ask me to write him, and I wrote him." In family matters Sueanne seldom was direct.

"And I haven't even looked at that letter, but is there any-

thing in there at all about Henry Floyd Brown's exerting influence on anybody?"

"No, sir. I thought Henry could help Jimmy adjust because
Henry had been in the system for so long. And knew how hard
penitentiaries are, and they are hard, and even the women's penitentiary is hard."

"You have always hoped that Jimmy would someday come forward and tell the truth, haven't you? And you hope so today?"

"Yes, sir."

<h1 style="text-align:center">20</h1>

Kreamer called Reverend John Adams as his last witness. Adams
walked heavily and slowly to the stand. Kreamer asked, "Did you
have an occasion to go with Ed Hobson on his visit down to
Hutchinson to see Jimmy?"

"Yes, I did."

"And I want to ask you, did Ed, in any way, threaten Jimmy?
Did Ed ever suggest that Henry Floyd Brown was going to exert
influence over Jimmy or anyone else?"

"No."

"What was the general tenor and demeanor of the conversation?"

"We met for approximately thirty minutes. This was the first
time I met Jimmy. I had very little to say."

"What was the meeting between Ed and Jimmy?
Confrontational?"

"No."

"Was it cordial?"

"Yes. They sat in chairs next to one another. There was some
talk about—Ed had just seen Sueanne, and shared what they
were doing. She was doing fine. Jimmy was glad to hear that."
There was no mention of Adams' reported shouts that "the truth
will set you free."

Kreamer turned the witness over to Moore's cross-examination. "Do you think Ed Hobson would tell you that if he was
going to threaten somebody?"

"Knowing our relationship, yes."

"Had Ed Hobson suggested to Jimmy Crumm that he should change his story?" Moore inquired.

"He asked him to tell the truth and change his story. He felt that the story should be changed now. Said he wanted his family back."

21

Moore's closing argument was brief and quite specific. Rather than concentrating on the so-called new evidence, he reviewed the entire case against Sueanne. He began quite directly:

I would submit to the court that this new evidence that's been presented through the three affiants who have been called to testify here, is not really new evidence at all. To be newly discovered evidence, it must be evidence that can be received in court, and what these people have testified to is that Paul Sorrentino said words to them to the effect of Sueanne Hobson didn't do it. That's not far, Judge, from what Paul Sorrentino testified in court a year and a half ago when he said, "I don't know whether she did it or not. Everything I know about this case, I heard from Jimmy Crumm. He told me that Sueanne Hobson wanted me and Jimmy Crumm to go out and kill Christen Hobson."

I can't prove that Henry Floyd Brown conspired and seemed to get all this put together. You have seen evidence that Henry Floyd Brown meets weekly with Ed Hobson, corresponds with Sueanne Hobson. They have corresponded with Jimmy Crumm, and Ed's tried to get Jimmy Crumm to, quote, "change his story, to tell the truth." The only reason I brought up Henry Floyd Brown was to say, "This is the information we have. The court should consider it, give it whatever credit and weight it believes it deserves." We have not obviously proven that Henry Floyd Brown has exerted any influence. You heard Jeff Wood testify that Henry lives right above him. Henry's been in there, knows all the ropes, been around for a long time, probably has a while to go, and I would suggest to you that if Henry Floyd Brown is going to make threats or promises to induce somebody to change his story, he's not going to be very blatant about it. I would suggest to the court that when Henry Floyd Brown speaks in that prison, probably people listen to what he has to say, and when Henry Floyd Brown said to Jeff Wood, "Jeff, here's Scott Kreamer's telephone number and his address. Why don't you contact him and submit a statement?" Jeff Wood did it, and when Jeff Wood rode down here yesterday with Ed Merrick, Merrick, out of the blue, says, "What's this Henry Floyd Brown like? What kind of guy is he?" Well, there's more to it than meets the eye, I'd suggest to the court.

Jeff Wood is a convicted murderer, shot his wife with a shotgun, killed her. Ed Merrick is charged with thirteen bad checks or thefts. And Mark Williams, who didn't know Henry Floyd Brown, but whether he's Mark Williams or Dr. Terry Alan Estes, or whatever his name was, he was charged with twenty-three counts of bad checks, theft, fraud, whatever.

They're not beyond reproach. Maybe they're telling the truth, but if they are, so what? The real truth is Paul Sorrentino doesn't know. Even if he told them something that's not true—that he knows "Sueanne Hobson didn't do it"—I suggest to the court, the real truth is he doesn't know.

22

Scott Kreamer began his closing argument aggressively:

They all say, "Paul told me she had nothing to do with it." Can you imagine the effect on a jury if I parade in these three people, put them on the stand, and everyone says, "Paul Sorrentino told me she had absolutely nothing to do with it"? There's no motivation for them to lie. They don't know one another. There's no reason, Judge, for them to come in here and tell you this. One saw an article in the paper and said, "I've got to tell them what I know." The other one, it was eating on him. He saw Sueanne and knew she was nice—and the third one wrote me that letter.

If you had a videotape of Paul Sorrentino, and he's in these various cells, at the electric shop, telling these people, "Hey, she had nothing to do with it," you'd grant a new trial in a second. Paul actually said that on the stand today. He testified—I couldn't believe it—he said, "I told some cellees that in my opinion, she had nothing to do with it."

But we've got three other witnesses that we're offering to make our case, not one, not two, but three, and Mr. Moore says, "Well, there's not much difference between him saying, 'In my opinion, she's innocent,' and saying, 'She had nothing to do with it.'" It's like the difference between lightning and a lightning bug!

Again, Your Honor, I'd just submit that one of the two people that killed this boy says, "Folks, you've got the wrong person. She didn't do it at all." This absolutely, without question, entitles us to a new trial.

The jury worked long and hard on this case. It took them a long time to decide it, and I submit to you, if they come back in here, and you put on three different people, under these circumstances, with nothing to gain by giving this testimony, and everyone of them says, "Paul Sorrentino told me she had nothing to do with it," that's going to change their minds. It corroborates the grandmother's testimony; she testified that Jimmy called her from the Miami County prison and told her that she had nothing to do with it.

To get up and suggest to you it is insignificant evidence, Your Honor, is beyond me. I can't believe the prosecution did it. They knew it was so significant that they tried to defend this by bringing Henry Floyd Brown into the case. It's significant. They've brought all these people up to their office, questioned them, worked on it, because it's significant. It is important. It is devastating.

One of the two killers—I'm not talking about Margie Hunt coming in and saying, "Now, she had nothing to do with it." Margie Hunt doesn't know, but Sorrentino and Jimmy talked about this thing, put it together, carried it out, drove young Christen out to his grave, shot him, and one of them says, "You got the wrong person. She didn't do it." He couldn't say that on the stand because, if he said that, he would be of no value to the state.

Sorrentino would not be able to avail himself of the plea arrangement. He would have gone to jail, just like Jimmy did, for fifteen years instead of seven and a half, but, by golly, thank goodness things always work out right. We always get the truth somehow, some way, and fortunately we got it through these people, right from the mouth of the man who, without question, was one of the two that carried out this crime. I don't know what better evidence you could have on that—right from the mouth of the guy that shot him.

While Kreamer spoke, Judge Jones could scarcely control his anger. Under his thick mustache his mouth slanted up in a sneer. He kept his hands on the bench, then he suddenly realized what he was doing and he covered up his mouth totally with his right hand.

23

For twenty minutes Judge Jones sat at the bench while he pondered the decision. He seemed acutely conscious of the eyes upon him, shifting his position slightly again and again, but he never looked up. At first no one left the defense or prosecution tables. Though it was still only three in the afternoon, the sun was weak, whitened by the snow, and was already descending rapidly through the wall of windows on the west side of the courtroom, the dead cold leaking in.

The few people who were there were quite silent and tense as Judge Jones scribbled notes. Scott sat at the defense table with his thumbs, little fingers and index fingers, in opposition.

Moore sat beside Tatum, but they seldom spoke. Once off the stage of the courtroom, he always treated Tatum as an employee, one he could berate or yell at. Moore turned sideways looking back into the courtroom, trying to catch the eye of the one reporter present, and when he did he smiled knowingly and broadly. He also caught Kreamer's eye. Kreamer answered Moore's confident smile with something that stopped just short of scorn.

Ed Byrne walked over through the snow from his office to hear the verdict. Moore got up to whisper over the railing to Byrne, telling him that he had not used Jimmy for fear of Brown. Jimmy, Moore said, would have been very helpful, but he feared what Brown or other prisoners would do to him if he testified again.

One coming suddenly into the room would find only one victim. Sueanne held her face slightly away from the few spectators and she seemed to be crying. Despite the beauty of her hair and her well-shaped face, the dull, lime-green prison gown gave Sue's face a greenish cast in the last rays of the cold sun.

Again Ed Hobson, excluded from the courtroom, paced outside the eastern double doors. He appeared and reappeared, not quite stopping to look carefully through the small windows in the door. Ed scarcely could contain his fear and his anger.

Reporters were not so shy. Through excluded from the courtroom, they photographed Sueanne through the glass in the door as she waited for the decision.

Finally the judge looked up. "The court is going to overrule the defendant's motion. The court finds that there was not newly discovered evidence as such, that those statements, if true, were statements of opinion and comment by Mr. Sorrentino."

Kreamer asked for clarification. "Are you ruling that there's not newly discovered evidence or that it was not sufficient to change the verdict?"

Jones was irritated. "Understand that counsel. In finding there was no substantive, substantial evidence of newly discovered evidence. It's not substantial."

Sueanne closed her eyes and tipped her head back. When the hearing concluded, Ed came through the eastern doors and past the few spectators and the gate to the bar itself. He half embraced her as she still sat at the defense table. She was in tears as Ed and Reverend Adams led her back to the witness rooms beyond the courtroom itself. Within minutes she was led out in handcuffs and taken back to the jail for transport to Lansing.

24

Ed Byrne walked slowly back to his storefront office through the heavy snow. "Jones isn't a bad judge," he said, "but he's so inarticulate. It's embarrassing! Embarrassing! He can't get out a complete sentence."

As soon as Byrne got back to his office he phoned Jim Crumm in Dallas, Texas. Byrne said to him, "Jimmy didn't testify, so I guess it's okay. He'll meet with trouble if he crosses swords with Brown. Neither Dennis nor I wanted to use him. We feared he'd get hurt at Hutchinson. We can't let Jimmy go upstate to Lansing.

"Sueanne looked as cold and cruel as she ever has. She sat up there when she testified and dabbed her eyes. I'm telling you I never bought that shit that she was terrified of Christen. I saw the Bitch of Buchenwald in person today."

25

More than a year later Sueanne's appeal of her motion for a retrial was denied in a perfunctory ruling by the Kansas Supreme Court. Of Brown the court wrote, "There was also considerable testimony concerning the involvement of one Henry Floyd Brown, an inmate convicted of bank robbery and murder and an acquaintance of the Hobsons', in contacting people and urging them to come forward with their evidence or, where applicable, to change their stories." From a distance of sixty miles and fifteen months, the tensions of the motion for retrial appeared a transparent, routine effort to overturn a verdict in a murder trial and hardly worth the court's attention.

The prisoners seemed to have fallen from any action of public interest. Nonetheless, those free as well as those in prison seemed held by the small explosions in the woods years before, their lives determined by them.

11

PRISONERS

1

During the days immediately before the retrial motion was heard, when Jimmy was kept in the Johnson County Jail awaiting a call to testify, Dennis Moore tried to arrange a meeting between Suzanne and her brother and failed. Soon though, Suzanne was visiting Jimmy in Hutchinson every few months and regularly he would phone her collect.

Despite the fears of the prosecutor and the wardens at Hutchinson that Henry Floyd Brown would avenge Jimmy's betrayal of his mother once he was moved upstate, he sought to be transferred to Lansing. He wanted to be nearer his sister; from Kansas City the drive to Lansing took an hour, the drive to Hutchinson four. Of course he was not granted a transfer. Nonetheless Jimmy and Suzanne assumed an intimacy they had briefly shared in the years before the arrests. They clung together like abused children

"I would do anything for my sister," Jimmy said. "I'd rather sixty thousand bad things were said about me for every one that's said about Suzanne."

Reunited in the green-walled prison room at Hutchinson, Suzanne rediscovered how alike they were. Now, after the murder and the trials, she resembled him even more. Since Suzanne had left him, there was never anything under Jimmy to break his fall. People had always drifted in and out of his life, appearing and disappearing without great pleasure or pain.

To Suzanne this rootlessness came upon her only after the murder. Though both grew up in very different circumstances, they were now treated in a similar way—abandoned by all.

Suzanne had kept with her in these years of separation a photo of her and Jimmy that had been taken right before the murder. Being like Jimmy was important to her.

"Jimmy's eyes are dark," she said, "but not quite as dark as mine. They're kind of light brown eyes. We're not exactly alike, but we look a lot like each other, like the Sallees, like Mother. My father, Jim, didn't look like us at all. And Jimmy and I got our smarts from my mother, not from my father." Trying to be fair, she added, "I got my athletic ability from my father, though, a star fullback, I guess."

Yet in the years since her mother was imprisoned, Suzanne had returned to the Crumms, especially to the families of Jim Crumm's sisters, the Reffitts and the Koonces. There she would see her father briefly three or four times a year, but she had little good to say about him. "He stuck by Jimmy, I guess, after Chris died. Mother married simple men so she could manipulate them as much as possible."

Six years after the arrests, at nineteen, Suzanne seemed unfinished, as if she had unwound the cloth of her sophistication that her mother had wrapped around her. At Sueanne's trial she had seemed to reporters a half-dozen years older than her actual age—she seemed twenty or more, not fifteen.

Now she was fifteen again. Razor thin, poorly clothed in a thick, gray gunmetal coat, mousy, wearing little or no makeup, her teeth yellowed and untended, shy, hesitant, anxious, she bore little relationship to the finished teenager Chris had known.

She still appeared an adolescent really, one who had been suddenly severed from her mother's grip at fifteen. She bore a stone with her, a responsibility that fixed her there on the day of the discovery of the body.

Yet she could transform herself so that when you saw her a month later, her face would be alert, attractive, and she would exude energy. And then she looked much like her mother, Sueanne, with intense dark eyes and a fragile body.

In fall 1985 she had dropped out of school because of an illness; she had, she said, burned herself out. Now, in early 1986, she was again taking two courses at the University of Missouri in Kansas City and working twenty-five hours a week to support herself. She seemed compelled to work, getting up at six in the morning to run in the bleak wintry streets near the huge medical center in the fallen neighborhood.

Suzanne had been awarded a Pell Grant to support her studies. "I'm better organized than most students," she said. "I have to be." Yet even on the best of days there seemed no one to depend on except Jimmy and a therapist.

"Ed and Mother are never going to face what happened," Suzanne said. "She never admitted her guilt to me after the murder. I believe my mother really believed she was innocent. 'It happened somehow.' That was my mother's position." And from that point on she was as isolated as Jimmy in his cell in Miami County or in Hutchinson.

"If Mother didn't say she did it, she didn't do it," Suzanne said. "Jimmy and I alone have faced our responsibility. Chris never had any way to face up to it; he never suspected anything. He was totally without knowledge of what was going on. Mother never told me Chris was dead. She didn't have to. I'm not that stupid."

It was her mother before the marriage that Suzanne admired. "You'd like her," she said, "the way you'd like Beth Clarkson or Margie Hunt-Fugate. Mother was witty and charming and intelligent." Her mother had studied a year at the University of Kansas, she said. In truth, she didn't make it through a semester.

Surprisingly, Suzanne admired the Sallees. She had dropped the name Hobson, calling herself Suzanne Sallee. She had taken their name and she aspired to become like them. She wanted to affirm the upper-middle-class background of her grandparents, Don and Ruth Sallee, and to shed the names Crumm and Hobson. And she was angered that the Sallee grandparents and great-grandparents were brought into this at all. Still, the Sallees continued to ignore Suzanne before, during, and after the trial; they did nothing for her. To her it was almost as if the Sallee veneer of respectability excused their long indifference to their granddaughter and their newly minted fear of her.

Yet Suzanne was contemptuous of Johnson County and of the

places she had lived with her mother and the values the two had assumed. "I never want to go back to Johnson County. It's too snooty, too concerned about money and status, like 'Knot's Landing,' but the people in 'Knot's Landing' are nicer than those in Johnson County."

Suzanne was always ambivalent about her mother's conviction. She was angry at "Norma Hooker, who blew the whistle on Mother." Norma was one of the first of Sueanne's friends to turn on her. Except for Margie Hunt-Fugate, Suzanne criticized all of those who testified against her mother. Through the two years of legal proceedings she desperately wanted her mother to get off, wanted her to refute the indictments filed against her.

And she was angry that she had to testify in the trial. She knew of her mother's guilt and despised what her mother had done, yet she held in equal contempt those whose testimony established such guilt.

Suzanne would regularly blame Ed Hobson for her and her mother's plight. "Ed put up a front of caring about Chris," she said. "Do you know about Ed's life? Everybody he lived with ended up dead. Even Mike, who worked with him at Ralston Purina; Mike was the only friend of Ed at the wedding and he was murdered a year or so later." It was as if she escaped her guilt by accusing Ed, as if it were Ed and not the three members of the Crumm family who conspired to murder Chris.

Suddenly she would contradict herself, asserting that Sueanne organized the whole thing. "Mother was the mastermind behind everybody—Paul, Jimmy, Chris. And when Mother said jump, Ed said how high."

"Mother didn't love Ed," Suzanne said. "She'd say, 'Take care of Ed. You've got to take care of Ed at the funeral.' But Mother didn't love him, that I know for sure."

Though Suzanne saw herself as a victim of the law, she also believed she was a crucial figure in her mother's conviction. "Jimmy and I were the ones who convicted her," she said flatly.

"Ed is a con," she said, again making Ed more ominous and intelligent than the puppet her mother, "the mastermind," seemed to manipulate. "He's able to con everybody, like he did the people at Crittenden when they let him in to see me."

Suzanne was swollen with self-contradictions and ambivalent feelings that she tried constantly to resolve. Yet how seldom she was on her mother's side during the two years before the trial. In fact, Sueanne constantly lobbied her daughter for support and they argued about the distortions and lies that Suzanne had to testify to, that put her at risk for a perjury charge.

A year after the trial she told Dennis Moore of her confusion and he sent to her a transcript of portions of Sueanne's trial. "The complexities were never there in the documents. When the case first started, I thought I wanted to be a lawyer. I'm taking a prelaw course in criminal law now. But the lawyers maligned and mistreated me in court, humiliated me in front of my friends and the Crumms and everybody. And when I read the transcripts and remember what really happened, I know that everybody lied in the case. Everybody who testified lied in some way. Ed lied. Mother lied. The newspaper accounts were false." Certainly Suzanne knew that she had not told the whole truth. And Jimmy, protecting his sister, had not ever mentioned her involvement as a go-between.

Years after the murder and the trial, Suzanne still seemed extremely vulnerable, friable, uncertain of her stability. Grown now, she appeared to be an abused child who dared not recall fully, a child hourly aware of an event long past, yet imprisoned by it.

"I'm just learning to trust again," she said. "I didn't really trust anybody. I couldn't even trust my mother during the trial. I don't date much. I don't have time. I'm living alone now. I have close friends and my best friend is my holistic therapist.

"I'm an only child and I can stand solitude," she said. If she thought herself an only child, Jimmy seemed less than a brother, more than a friend. "It's what I'd like to continue doing—to be my own boss. Sometimes I get afraid at night because of strange phone calls."

She seemed like a child who should be playing freely, but who was held by her brother's punishment in the whitened kitchen. She could bear his punishment only in her imagination, and she had her own punishment, however ill deserved it was.

Suzanne came to Hugh Kreamer's funeral in late 1982. In the open casket Hugh was dressed fully in the red clothes and hat he wore fox hunting. Of all those involved in the prosecution or defense it was Hugh she admired most. "Hugh took me aside after the verdict and told me quietly that I wasn't responsible for Mother's conviction. He said I shouldn't even take that into consideration."

2

After years in prison Jimmy's face had hardened a little and he had gained weight. His body was more muscled than before. On one forearm were more tattoos; above the peacock were a couple of parrots, the last unfinished, its application interrupted by the guards. He had, at one point, worn an earring. He wondered aloud if he had become inside and out like the other prisoners, minted liked them. His beautiful profile, his light brown eyes, and his sharply cut face were now those of a man. He was a serious man and he had a morose sense of humor.

Jimmy no longer seemed as wired as he had been three years before. The intensity he wore was diminished and with it had gone the querulousness and the frightened condescension that used to emerge despite his efforts to conceal them.

He sat on a redwood picnic table under great cottonwoods and Chinese elms. The tree trunks were all painted white to the height of a man. The table was near the edge of a small man-made lagoon inside the high barbed wire enclosure. It was a beautiful sunny day in September and there was a strong southerly wind. The limestone Kansas prison loomed in the background, appearing exactly like a Victorian prison in Dublin or London. When the Sunday visitors came, they had to file past a large, heavy gazebo to be searched. Anyone over twenty-five—whether a prisoner or a visitor—seemed marked for life, condemned to be separated out, not by the spirit, but by the flesh.

The men who came out from the prison across a barren stretch of fifty yards were much less repulsive that their visitors. A great bucktoothed woman in gingham awaited a man in blue denim, a handsome middle-aged man as alert as an accountant. Children ran toward him yelling, "Daddy! Daddy!"

Jimmy seemed no longer quite as puzzled about his mother's motives, less interested in their imagined complexity. "Mom did it because she hated Chris," he said curtly. "People mostly do things because of what they feel and what she felt was hatred. Feelings were everybody's motive in this. You've got to accept that. Ed Byrne tried to find ways Mother was going to get money after Chris died and couldn't. She hated him. You don't need to look any further than that." He stared back toward the gazebo and fell silent for a while.

"In Johnson County," he said, "it's hard to get somebody to realize people do things out of emotion. In Johnson County people are supposed to have interest and feelings only for money. Money, not hatred, is supposed to be a motive to kill somebody. But what do I know about Johnson County? I didn't even last a year there."

Like Ed Hobson, Jimmy was totally unprepared for life in the suburbs. From the age of eight or nine he had lived a life devoid of travel, of art, of space. In moving to Overland Park, he had cut himself off from any friends but those who took drugs or engaged in petty crime.

"Mother was narcissistic," Jimmy said. "In narcissism it's not just how she appears to herself, but how she appears to others, how her image comes back from them. The way things looked to others was more important than the way they were. She was obsessed with what others said about her or her family."

Jimmy withdrew or modified his earlier tales of his being abused by his mother. She did not break his arm at five or six years old, as he told the psychiatrists at Menninger's years ago. Rather, Jimmy said, "I had sneezed without a Kleenex. She was chasing me to the Kleenex box and I fell and broke my arm." Though he said she was always angry about something, it certainly didn't seem to him that Sueanne physically abused him.

The choice Jimmy was forced to make between his mother and his father on the day she left him for good seemed to embody his life and his central psychological drama. People drifted in and out of his life, he said. He was used to that and surprised when they returned. The window he always looked out of was the one in the upper bedroom with Sueanne carrying her bags out to the car and his saying quietly to himself, " 'Bye, Mom. 'Bye, Mom."

Despite Jimmy's remorse for "adding to the hell Ed went through," Ed faded for him. For Suzanne the really bad stuff began with Chris's murder, her mother's imprisonment. For Jimmy the bad stuff started with his birth.

Like Suzanne, Jimmy wanted the truth to come out. He, too, tried to read the transcripts of Sueanne's trial, but he soon quit.

Jimmy had a strong motive for testifying against his mother. "I decided to testify against Mother because of her relationship with my sister—so Suzanne wouldn't end up like me. Mother's trial reminded me of my own. The rules were against telling the truth. It was how you said it rather than what you said." It was as if Jimmy's trial and his mother's trial were two fictionalized accounts.

In prison Jimmy felt increasingly cut off from life, increasingly frustrated. He said he'd stand between two lines of prisoners and dare people to bump into him. He was constantly irritated.

Inside the prison Jimmy had become an organization leader for the Junior Chamber of Commerce. Soon the group had become so large that the prison staff felt threatened. In response the guards severely limited the number of members. "You don't want to call attention to yourself in prison," he said, "either to the authorities or to other prisoners.

"I've got to keep busy so I won't think about the case. I'm studying to be an electrician, and when I get out, I'd like to go to an engineering school. I won't get out right away after I've done my fifteen years because of the complexities of the case. They work against me. The authorities don't quite know what to make of me. 'You're stable before the murder and you're stable afterward. You don't get into trouble in here.' They're puzzled. Parole boards don't really understand sophisticated things. It's a pretty complicated case."

3

On the afternoon of her seventy-fourth birthday more than six years after the murder of Chris, Ruth Sallee stood just outside the entrance to her green-shuttered, saltbox house, the white shades drawn tightly down to the sill. She wore a white shirt setting off her steely gray hair, lavender slacks, and white mules. She closed only the screen door against the July heat. Inside Don Sallee sat in a relaxer chair reading a newspaper by the light of a table lamp. Just beyond the screen door Ruth spoke about her neighborhood and her life.

Only five feet tall, she displayed great energy in the summer heat. She paced constantly, picking up a small stick fallen from a tree, pulling off a dead leaf from another.

"We've been here for thirty-four years," she said. "There were houses just on this street when we moved here from the Country Club Plaza. The rest of the area was fields. We paid for the house seven years after we bought it. My husband's very talented with wood. He does woodworking as a hobby. He's made a lot of our furniture.

"When we moved here, there were children in the neighborhood," she recalled. "We took our little girl up to Somerset School at the end of the block. I'd have parties, invite the mothers, and let the children play in the backyard on the swings we had then. I'd rather have them where I could keep an eye on them. Now there's a little girl and a little boy, about six, who walk around the neighborhood after dark. The parents drink a lot and they don't watch the kids. People shouldn't have kids if they don't want them. I was married eight years before I had a child.

"Years ago you could walk over to the drugstore at night and get ice cream with nuts or something on top," she said. "Somerset was a really nice school. I worked with the Girl Scouts. The neighborhood turns over now; one house sold four times in recent years."

Mrs. Sallee paused, thinking about other changes in her life. "I'll be married fifty-four years in September. We live moderate, tempered lives. I don't care what my neighbors do—it's their business. Our neighbors have parties and go to Las Vegas. They'd be bored if they were in our family. We eat out every night and use valet parking if they have it—eat at the Alameda Plaza or at Steak and Ale. We leave home at four-forty-five to get to the restaurant when it opens at five. That way the salad bars are fresh.

"Don always drives," she said. "I haven't driven in two years. My right eye is gone and my left has stringy vitreous humors—

like spaghetti. When I had trouble with my right, my doctor told my husband; he was afraid to tell me. Don said, 'Tell her. She's not the kind of person who'll fall apart.'"

Ruth recalled that Don said, "'Your face shows your character.' I have wrinkles, no crow's-feet. See?" She smoothed her face with her hand. "I had coal-black hair once. I used to wear my hair really long and pulled up on the head. It's too much trouble now; I can't see well enough.

"My husband's name is Sallee—it's French. When my husband dies, his name dies with him. I've known him since kindergarten. He was in the Boy Scouts with my brother, though they didn't hang around together. Don lived in a fourteen-room house with three colored servants. They always treated the servants well. Once when I was pregnant and fainted, a black janitor in the Plaza Apartments where we lived helped me. Don visited him in the hospital before he died. No one else visited him. Don's father owned a chemical company.

"We were married in Kansas City in September 1933," she said. "Don likes the house calm in the morning. His brothers were rowdy, but he was quiet. He liked my Victorian family—my father was Scottish and my mother grew up on a Louisiana plantation.

"Don was," she said, "so different from the others in his family that they wondered where he came from. His family was very social—parties, dances—the house was always in chaos.

"Don's father gave him a set of the Harvard Classics at fifteen," Ruth recalled. "He gave the set to this boy named Jimmy. Jimmy was having trouble with his folks and moved out to live with other relatives. He left the books in Raytown—we called the family who had them and we went over and picked them up. These kids nowadays are always on drugs and drinking.

"Don doesn't like cards," she said. "Oh, he'd play poker with the Marley company people sometimes just because it was the company, but he never liked cards.

"He traveled two or three weeks at a time, sometimes two or three months." Sometimes Ruth would go with him. "In San Francisco we saw everything, things people who live there have never seen—the Hearst Mansion, museums.

"Grandmother Sallee, Don's mother, died at ninety-six, his father at forty-three," she noted. "She was fat, very demanding. She and her brother were so demanding in the nursing home that they had to lay off three nurses. I didn't believe it, so I had a friend check and it was true!" Ruth said, laughing aloud. "It was true!

"We both read," she emphasized. "Don reads Civil War stuff, I read Scottish history. I take the *National Geographic* and the *Smithsonian*. You know, I can't get anyone else to read them. I try to give the *Smithsonian* to the neighbors and they won't take it. They say, 'I can't understand it.'" Reading set the Sallees apart on that street. "I belong to the Smithsonian Institution. If you can't read, you can't do anything."

"When I was young, it was a different world. I'd be different than I was then. . . ." she said, her voice trailing off. "I'd do a lot of things differently. I'd go to college. I had two years. I could have taken classes and finished my degree. I could have gotten a master's. Nothing stopped me. I didn't have that much work to do here."

Ruth was very conservative. "I had a friend who was upset about her son because he was planning on marrying a deaf girl from a lower-class family. I wouldn't want that, either, of course. Then he married a five-foot-nine, two-hundred-eighty-five-pound woman. I told my friend, 'I just think you don't think anyone's good enough.'

"I talked about intermarriage with this sixteen-year-old we gave the books to," she recalled. "I said, 'Now would you go out with a colored girl?' He said, 'Well, they're just like us.' I said, 'Would you go out with her though?' He said he didn't see why not. I said, 'Well, Jimmy, if you do, don't come ringing this doorbell again.'

"I was twenty when we were married in '33. We were affected by the Depression. The first year we were married we started an annuity. We worked hard and lived within our means. People now don't have the same worries. They spend what they make, live beyond their means.

"These relatives still owe us money," she said, returning to her favorite topic. "They have a big car—a Lincoln. They borrowed five thousand in 1981 and they haven't paid us back. Don said not to do it. They signed a note—this relative wanted us to do it; we didn't want to. Don said he didn't trust him. They were going to sell their condo. They should have had plenty of money—a condo, a big boat. They sold them, but we didn't get the money. In 1984 they came into some money and they gave us a thousand. I should have asked for it all then. I feel guilty for asking, like I'm borrowing. I can't stand to owe money to people. He's forty years old and making twenty-five hundred dollars a month. When I called him here recently to see if he could pay fifty dollars a month—I wanted a hundred—he got mad, like I was doing something to him. I know he was afraid they'd never get anything from us—he wanted to inherit something—he didn't want to make us mad, so he paid the thousand dollars. Don says the family knows I'm the patsy. But I'll say this for Don, he never says anything to me about it.

"When I buy something extravagant, Don says, 'Well, someone will have to be disappointed about not getting that money.' What's the use of leaving money? We ought to be comfortable. Most of our relatives are dead. Our friends are dead. The only people we've got to leave anything to is my brother, and he's rich. My two nieces don't even thank me for their Christmas box. We don't need to leave them anything. Their father has plenty. Now we've just decided to give it to the people who need it. Don said, 'You were always interested in those blind kids. Let's leave it to them. And I also want to leave it to those battered wives. There's no relative we could leave it to who needs it or deserves it.'" She doesn't mention her daughter or son-in-law by name.

"My neighbor Judy had a fight with her mother. I told her to call her mother, told her not to let it get too bad. Things are never the same once you fight like that. Don's family had a feud. They couldn't even remember why it started.

"Why, in our own family, we've had them. It's bad. I told Judy not to rehash the problem. You can't rehash things and make up. You just get mad again.

"People used to say this relative of ours had a beautiful figure, like a model, slender. But she had a hard face—always jealous, always wanting more, so critical. When I asked her how she liked a dress or something I was wearing, she'd say, 'It's nice, I guess. I don't have to wear it.' We call her the 'dog relative.'"

4

In August 1984 Special Agent Phil Sprague of the U.S. Department of Health and Human Services filed a complaint against Ed Hobson. Sprague had discovered that after Chris's murder Ed Hobson continued to receive and cash monthly social security checks intended for Chris's support. Chris had been receiving the checks since his mother's death in March 1976.

These checks ranged from one hundred and fifty to one hundred and ninety dollars a month. After Chris's death, Ed Hobson set up a new account in a Mission, Kansas, bank. The account was jointly controlled by Ed and Sueanne Hobson. He was initially charged with "embezzling and converting to his use, and to cause to be converted to the use of another" more than seven thousand dollars. At first the government wanted to charge Sueanne as well. She was the "another" mentioned, but charges were dropped against her.

Carl Cornwell, a blond, attractive criminal lawyer in his mid-thirties, took on the federal case filed against Ed. Cornwell had followed Sueanne's trial in the newspapers and he was convinced that if he had handled the case, he would have gotten her off.

Sueanne had gotten Cornwell's name from a woman prisoner in Lansing. The woman claimed she had been physically abused by the husband she killed; the lower court refused to permit experts on battered women to testify. Cornwell reversed the woman's conviction in the Kansas Supreme Court.

Cornwell wanted to negotiate an out-of-court settlement for Ed. When this became impossible, he decided to plea-bargain. In October 1985 a trial date was set and the news reached the television stations and newspapers. Ed was arraigned and released after posting a ten-thousand-dollar bond.

"Ed was awfully upset that the news got out. He seemed to me just that far from going off." Cornwell gestured with the thumb and forefinger. "I wouldn't want to cross him. He didn't feel he should be charged. He said to me, 'No one would have charged me if I hadn't been named Ed Hobson. Dennis Moore is behind all this. Moore got something to hold over Judge Jones and Jones did what he wanted.'

"Ed was at my office all the time," Cornwell said. "He was always pushing, pushing. You've got to understand he believes everything is political, everything.

"He definitely wanted to go to trial," Cornwell said. "In November I got him to plead guilty. Right before he was sentenced, he told Judge O'Connor that he felt remorse for what he had done, but he needed the money.'"

U.S. District Court Judge Earl O'Connor wrote: "It is adjudged that the defendant is hereby committed to the custody of the Attorney General or his authorized representative for a term of three years. The execution of said sentence of imprisonment is hereby suspended and the defendant placed on probation for a period of five years with the following special condition of probation: that the defendant make restitution of eight thousand two hundred eighty six dollars and sixty cents to the Social Security Administration during the period of probation at the direction of the U. S. Probation Office."

A special note was added to the file: "You shall not possess firearms or other dangerous weapons."

After his conviction Ed was fired by Ralston Purina. A few weeks later Cornwell got him reinstated with the help of the union.

5

Several years after Sueanne's trial, Ed moved north out of the Roeland Park house to a new neighborhood in Wyandotte County. In Roeland Park streets and small houses were overshadowed by great trees. The neighborhood was quiet despite the proximity of the shopping center a few hundred feet to the east.

Montana Street, several miles to the west, was part of a U-shaped development in Kansas City, Kansas. Mostly there were rectangular, prefabricated duplexes lined up tightly. Though the area seemed worn, there were no trees higher than a man. Montana Street was full of cars, at least four or five clustering around each duplex.

Ed's side of the duplex was white with barn-red trim. There was a dusty-gray cat looking out his window under spider plants hanging in macrame holders. With twilight coming on, Ed stood on his neighbor's lawn wearing boots and a meticulously white T-shirt and pressed blue jeans. His amazingly blond, sun-bleached hair and his strong masculine face and broad body made him a handsome middle-aged man.

Ed was helping his neighbor diagnose a problem in his car, shouting instructions to him above the sound of the engine in his hollow, deep, echo-chamber voice. His energy, his simplicity, his goodwill drew others to him. It was a thoroughly working-class neighborhood—children playing in the deteriorating streets, men inspecting cars as a kind of pretext for interaction.

Ed's garage door was open. Inside was a reddish-and-black old car with running boards. The car was his hobby, a project, some-thing to be restored finally years later, then sold to someone who would drive it in a parade.

The garage itself was superbly equipped with tools—quite clean and orderly, unlike those of his neighbors. The garage was lit by a bright bare light yellowing more and more as night came on.

"We got a battery!" he yelled to another neighbor. He was chatting and laughing, a pleaser. He seemed accepted there, friendly and befriended, content with his lot, though still filled with an animal energy that escaped his neighbors. The energy almost seemed to make him strut like a rooster or Mighty Mouse with his great chest puffed out.

In Johnson County Ed Hobson had been neatly severed from his working-class friends. He always felt uncertain there. Like Jimmy, Ed had middle-class life and its values thrust upon him, or at least Sueanne's version of it. Even after years of imprison-ment Jimmy praised Sueanne for refining him and Ed, for teach-ing both of them manners. The refining process was thin and brittle. To Ed and Jimmy middle-class life was a fantasy where you had alarm systems and answering services and French Provincial furniture and space that kept a howling woman away. In their fantasies it was in every way unlike a uniform, unlike working until death as a millwright.

"Ed wasn't cursed," Detective Moore said. "He'd like you to think he was. I know a half-dozen people like Ed. Shit! A guy whose wife was murdered and then his child was crippled in a bicycle accident and then his sister died of leukemia or some rare disease about the time his wife died. Cursed! Bullshit! In my line of work that's about all you see."

Ed always saw himself as a victim—of his father's sloth and oppression, of his mother's filth, of Shirley's rages, of Tani's phantom killer, of Chris's murderers, of a prosecuting attorney's ambition, of a judge's malevolence. And Sueanne was always sitting on his lap, caressing his face.

6

Cornwell became Sueanne's lawyer soon after he took Ed's case. Since the trial there was a dispute about the length of the sentence Judge Jones gave her. The prosecution argued that she would be eligible for parole in ten years; the defense insisted that she could be paroled in seven and a half years. Cornwell clarified the decision and the court agreed that she could seek parole after she had served seven and a half years.

He didn't want money, of course. When it came to accused murderers, nobody had any money. What Cornwell wanted was obloquy and fame at once. He wasn't interested in taking anyone's condominium and that made him dangerous.

Cornwell also wanted to see whether he could find a way to overturn Sueanne's conviction. He was particularly interested in the admission into evidence of Suzanne's interview recorded on tape on the morning of her mother's arrest. He even considered ways to get her case into the Federal Court system. In the end he gave up. Still, Cornwell remained fascinated with the case. "I've got this ego, I know, but I could have gotten her off," he'd say. At first, given the evidence provided in the transcripts, he seemed to have no illusions about her innocence. He assumed she was guilty.

Yet when he went up to Lansing to visit Sueanne, he promptly changed his mind. "I think she's innocent," he said. "I'm not going to talk about my discussions with my client. These are privileged communications, but she did tell me things she hadn't told anyone else. She told me she was innocent. I heard her story and I believed her. I believe she's innocent. Is that so hard to understand?"

Once she was arrested, Sueanne was as obsessed with proclamations of her innocence as she was with the killing. She importuned Suzanne to support her claim of innocence with the same intensity she had importuned Jimmy to kill the boy. Within a week of the discovery of Chris's body, Ed miraculously returned to her side, but then he began drinking heavily, fell into a depression, and divorced her. Slowly at first, then quickly, she won him back. Ed was her evidence. It was as if any lawyer could prove a negative, prove that she did not do it. With Ed at her side she felt strangely confident that others would perceive her innocence, as if innocence involved not an act, but a perception, as if it were as vague a concept as honor. Convincing others of her innocence made her innocent.

Sueanne's whole life had vacillated between fear and anger. The rhythm of it was her mother excoriating her and then heaping her bed with new clothes. She always seemed to be threatened with control by others. Sitting on the couch with a wrench wrapped in her apron beside her, she embodied that fear, that familiar loss of control. It was an act of transubstantiation that turned Chris into her mother. She needed desperately an absolute order in her life.

Yet she fantasized about threats against her. Was her mother any more obtrusive than Chris, who seemed harmless to Jimmy and Ed? Was Chris, as Norma Hooker said, just "a little boy looking for love and attention"?

Through the murder of Chris, Sueanne transformed herself from an abuser to the abused. She put herself in a position to be abused. In fact, the entire State of Kansas abused her.

Perhaps the texture of her innocence is simple and rough. Perhaps it is like Margie Hunt-Fugate's alleged theft—Sueanne deserved to have her jewels stolen. Margie would punish her for it and that was Margie's innocence. And Chris deserved killing for the threats he made against her and her family.

Certainly her conviction that Chris abused her and threatened her was no more absurd than her conviction of her innocence—and perhaps as strongly held. As Jimmy said, she didn't kill him for money or for love, but because of an emotion—she was afraid of him.

Jimmy described her almost lovingly and protectively. "She

was naive. You've got to understand that. She was naive about violence." She thought herself threatened when she wasn't threatened. Despite her intelligence and her will she seemed to have one way of dealing with problems, one way of analyzing things. She must be in control and others must submit.

Even after years in prison she would not talk to reporters except in Ed's presence. "There are things we can't talk about when Ed is there," she'd say. It was as if she fantasized that Ed, hearing the questions and the story properly told, would move out of her control—a risk she would not take.

Sueanne expressed no remorse during her nightlong interview, no remorse at Jimmy's trial, no remorse at her preliminary hearing, no remorse at the trial. To her, remorse seemed to mean loss of control, submission, and to a degree, an admission of guilt, or responsibility. If she had wanted to go free, she had only to display remorse to a confused jury in a complex case. She seemed unable to feign such an emotion.

7

Sueanne was first eligible for parole in late 1989. She had been imprisoned for almost seven and a half years; the murder was nearly ten years earlier. Most of the Johnson County prosecutors who knew about the case had long before resigned. Dennis Moore had run for attorney general of the State of Kansas and he was defeated by a very narrow margin. Later Steve Tatum also ran in a primary election for attorney general and lost.

Johnson County sent over a prosecutor who attacked Sueanne savagely during the parole hearing. After the hearing Ed came out wearing a gray suit and long sideburns; he spoke with television reporters. "It doesn't matter anymore whether she's innocent or guilty," Ed said. "She was convicted. Now I want my wife back. Neither Chris nor I either would want her incarcerated." Sueanne's application for parole was rejected.

A year later Ed spoke to a group gathering evidence for parole reform. Ed again was dressed in a dark suit and he peered out at his inquisitors through half glasses on a gold chain, as if he were an aging legislator. Ed's testimony was taped and used on the local evening news. "Sueanne's done everything the parole board asked her to do," he said. "She's got a perfectly clear record. What's a longer sentence going to do for her, for me?"

8

Ed would visit Sueanne every Saturday and Sunday. Now she had been moved from Lansing Women's Prison to a minimum-security prison in Topeka. Sueanne was always first at the door of the visiting room. The room looked like a church social hall with a large painting of Jesus above the guard station at one end of the room and a gigantic mountain landscape, a mural covering half of a side wall. In fact, the room also served as a chapel.

"I have a visitor," she'd say to the guard at the door who quickly let her pass into the large empty room. In her busyness and assumption of place she seemed more like a matron from the town, a religious volunteer rather than a prisoner. She went directly to the first small table nearest the guard lectern. She carefully set the table at a forty-five-degree angle from the wall and put two chairs tightly together on one side of the table. As if it were a ritual, she arranged on the tabletop a thick wad of Kleenex she had brought with her, her keys, a stenographic pad, and a pen.

She was wearing a dress entirely covered with tiny white dots on black material. The dress was buttoned to her neck. There were large frills coming from the shoulders down to her waist; the sleeves were loose and gathered at the wrist with a ruffle that matched the frills on the shoulders. She wore black hose and white shoes. On her left hand she wore two large rings and one smaller one. On her wrist was a large gold bracelet.

Sueanne's hair was braided and twisted in a top knot, like her mother's now. Thick bangs swept across her forehead.

Lethargically, the other women prisoners entered, setting up their tables and chairs at right angles to the wall. They began at the farthest point from the guards' station and none came up near Sueanne's table. She was in the first pew, it seemed. Most of the women wore slacks and blouses.

Ed, of course, was already waiting. He was chattering excitedly with another visitor in the hall, unable to stand still. When he was announced, he burst in wearing a white-and-blue striped knit shirt, faded jeans, black socks, and white loafers. The knit shirt emphasized his strong shoulders and broad torso. Hanging from his neck was a large, thick gold cross.

As he came toward her she said loudly, "Hi, sweetie." They hugged each other hard and she gave Ed a small kiss, their lips barely touching. Immediately they sat down on one side of the table with their chairs together, their backs turned to the other couples meeting behind them. Ed put his arm first around the back of her chair, then around her shoulder, and they whispered together. For several minutes he drew Sueanne ever closer toward him, but maintained a ninety-degree angle. The black woman supervising the visitors walked up to the Hobson table; she said that such touching was against the rules and quietly asked Ed to remove the arm that he had draped over Sueanne's back.

"Oh, yes, of course! I'm sorry," Sueanne said sweetly to the guard.

After the guard's intrusion they held hands. They huddled together and she kept subtly moving the chairs to a point where they would touch. Often they would giggle together, but seldom did she smile her thin smile, and when she did, her eyes did not change. Once Sueanne waved coyly at an inmate, a young, blond woman. Later she saw a woman with a baby boy and told Ed that the boy had bright eyes. Sueanne ignored an attractive blond boy of seven wearing a baseball cap, though Ed's eyes followed him to his seat. During the visiting hours she spoke to no other inmates.

Together they played a simple game on the steno pad. Ed would call out a letter and she would write. At times she would tear sheets out of the pad, fold them once, and put them under her keys. Ed seemed like a golden retriever, getting up to get her a Coke and a cookie at the canteen, blatantly enamored of her, more so as the afternoon wore on.

Sueanne had a cold or an allergy and she would take two sheets of kleenex from the wad, flatten them, align the top one precisely with the bottom, and wipe her nose. Her eye was sore and they would whisper about it, Ed looking at it carefully as she pulled down the flesh around it, exposing it. They seemed in their own world.

The other women were younger and they kissed their lovers or husbands with passion when they met. Then they settled back with children circling the small table. The hall where they came together smelled like wax in the hot Kansas summer. All seemed like victims, as if some small, precise natural catastrophe had fallen on them a long time ago and far away.

9

"I don't think Ed's missed a single Saturday or Sunday and he's here until closing hours," a guard said. "I don't think we've ever had anyone quite as regular."

Sueanne spoke openly with Tom Leathers, perhaps the only reporter she trusted. Her faith in God had deepened. Once she even appealed for early parole on the basis of being a born-again Christian. She had learned to pray and that is the most productive thing she'd done. "That's the thing that's let me survive here, that and the support Ed has given me. I want to do something useful and worthwhile. I want to do everything I can to be heard on prison reform once I get out. The lives they've had to lead are the key to the crimes they've committed. If you went through what they did, you could be here, too."

Another prisoner said, "She's a calming influence on a lot of new, frightened inmates."

"These are human beings and I want to help make the public aware of that fact." She spoke as if she were a wealthy matron coming down to provide morale for the prisoners. "Just because they've had a terrible background doesn't mean they can't rise above it. All of us want to be loved and needed, but many of these people have never had a moment of real caring. They feel lost and abandoned. Their lives from the time they were little have been punishment enough. In most cases it wasn't their fault. Why punish them more because they came from an environment over which they had no control?"

When Leathers asked Sueanne, she denied any involvement in the murder of Chris. "But I don't want to talk about it. I have some projects I want to get into when I get out and I don't want them clouded by the talk of my innocence of what happened. And that's final. I won't talk about it."

For most of her time in prison she had on the wall of her cell a photo of Christen Hobson and cards saying, "To my special friends, Sueanne and Ed—May God reunite them soon." And there was a card addressed by Ed to "Little Susie Homemaker."

Sueanne had helped start a parenting committee so that mothers in prison might have more contact with their children. "Many of the mothers here never see their children once they go to prison," Sueanne said. "That may be due to a lack of transportation or money or apathy on the part of one or the other. We want the public to be aware that mothers need to see their children and vice versa. It's healthy for both sides."

Leathers wrote, "As for daughter Susanne [sic], the Hobsons don't want to talk about where she is, or, for that matter, what's happened. They may not even know. Ed and Sueanne will say they miss her very much."

Suzanne read the article in frustration and anger. "Jimmy's made into the guilty one again and I look like some moron in an institution. Why can't they let me alone?"

"I've never had a woman want to take care of me," Ed said. Sueanne ironed Ed's blue jeans and prepared his lunch and the two got along superbly. "Perfect would be the right word. We seldom argued. Sueanne and Chris never argued. And when Chris and his stepsister, Suzanne, would begin to get mad at each other, Sueanne wouldn't stand for it."

Sueanne nodded her assent. She couldn't remember a serious disagreement between members of the family until Jimmy moved in.

Of the time right after the murder Ed said, "In my heart I knew Sueanne didn't do it, but I was confused about how all that happened. I loved her and I knew I'd made a mistake in getting a divorce.

"Our love has grown a lot stronger," Ed said, looking over at Sueanne and smiling.

"He's right," Sueanne said quietly, smiling back.

"She's my whole life—my friend, my girlfriend, my love. Every minute of every day we live for the moment Sueanne will be out. That will be the day my luck has changed."

Thomas J. O'Donnell grew up in north central Illinois and earned his Ph.D. in English at the University of Illinois. He has been teaching at the University of Kansas for the last twenty years, and is the author of *The Confessions of T. E. Lawrence*, as well as numerous essays on nonfictional confessions. O'Donnell lives in Lawrence, Kansas, where he is working on his next book.